The Soviet Economy

The Soviet Economy

AN INTRODUCTION

BY

ALEC NOVE

FREDERICK A. PRAEGER, *Publisher*
New York

BOOKS THAT MATTER

Published in the United States of America in
1961 by Frederick A. Praeger, Inc., Publisher
64 University Place, New York 3, N.Y.

Third printing, 1963

© George Allen & Unwin Ltd., 1961
Library of Congress Catalog Card Number: 61-16579

THE SOVIET ECONOMY is published in two editions:
A paperback edition (U-513)
A clothbound edition

This book is Number 118 in the series of
Praeger Publications in Russian History and World Communism.

Printed in the United States of America

PREFACE

The object of this book is to introduce the non-specialist with an interest in and some knowledge of economics to the study of the Soviet economy. The introductory nature of the volume must be stressed from the beginning. Many matters have had to be treated briefly, others have hardly been discussed at all. Thus there is practically no mention of natural resources, soil, climate, very little on the problems of transportation, or social services, or education. This is not to deny for a moment the importance of any of these things and readers interested in finding out more about them can be referred to the bibliography. Their omission is due to the fact that, within about 300 pages, I have attempted to cover at least in outline those features of the Soviet economy which particularly distinguish it from that of western countries. I have tried to do this by dividing the book into three parts. The first, Structure, is a fairly straightforward description of the institutional arrangements, going back into history in so far as it is necessary to explain how and why the present system developed. I start from the bottom, with the productive enterprise, and then go on to the planning and administrative organs, public finance and the structure of prices and wages. The second part, entitled Problems, seeks to identify those elements in the system which give rise to various difficulties, not in order to prove that the system does not work—obviously it does work—but in order to see which problems are of particular importance and how, in practice, means are devised and the structure modified to cope with them. The third part deals with Ideas and Concepts, and includes some attempt to explain and interpret the very interesting discussions which are engaging the attention of Soviet economists, notably on the theory of value and prices. This should not be beyond the understanding of the non-specialist, but whoever does not wish to immerse himself in controversies conducted in unfamiliar Marxist terminology can always skip that part of chapter 11, though this would be a pity. Finally, in the concluding chapter some (I hope) significant generalizations are attempted and a few very tentative morals drawn.

I am not at all sure that this is an ideal arrangement, for there are some regrettable overlaps between the chapters and the parts. But alternative schemes seemed to me even less promising.

Nothing is further from my intention than to pretend to 'solve' anything or to say the last word on any of the subjects discussed, the more so as detailed studies exist, listed in the bibiliography, on most of the matters here all too briefly touched upon. The object is rather to encourage the interested reader to find out more for himself, and in particular, if he knows Russian, to look up the Soviet sources; to facilitate this task, I have been fairly lavish with footnote references to many Russian books and articles.

All or large parts of the manuscript were read at various stages of preparation by Ely Devons, Michael Kaser, Jacob Miller, Leonard Schapiro, Basil Yamey and Alfred Zauberman, and George Morton read the last two chapters. For their numerous and invaluable comments and criticisms I am very grateful. I must also express appreciation for the help given by other colleagues with whom I was able to discuss various points or ideas, to contributors to the seminar on 'Economic problems of the Soviet World' at the London School of Economics, and to the authors of the many books and articles on which I have drawn extensively, and references to which appear frequently in the pages that follow. I hope these numerous helpers will not take it amiss if I do not list them here. If, despite all this generous assistance, I have obstinately persisted in errors of fact or of opinion, the responsibility is entirely mine.

Finally, I would like to express appreciation for the help, patience and accuracy of Dubravko Matko, of the research division of the London School of Economics. Mrs Sarah Craig and Miss Mary Hutchinson performed miracles in translating my illegible scrawl into typescript. I do not know how they did it.

ALEC NOVE

NOTES:

On January 1, 1961, the Soviet Government revalued the internal rouble, ten old roubles equalling one new rouble. All rouble figures given in this book are in old roubles.

Many references to books and periodicals appear in footnotes in abbreviated form. They can be properly identified in the bibliography. References to articles omit the title of the article, save where this is of especial interest, since they can be identified by details of author and publication, and one is saved from reprinting (usually) very long Russian titles.

A 'milliard' is a thousand million (an American billion).

CONTENTS

PREFACE   7

GLOSSARY   14

Introduction: Why and how   15

PART I: STRUCTURE

1 *Productive enterprises*   27
  Categories of enterprises   27
  The state industrial enterprise   30
  Other state enterprises   39
  Co-operative artisans   43
  The collective farm (*kolkhoz*)   45
  The private sector   57

2 *Administration, planning, policy decision*   61
  Introduction: the nature of the task   61
  VSNKh   62
  The rise of the ministerial system   64
  Planning agencies before 1957   66
  The end of the ministerial system:
    the sovnarkhoz reform   67
  Planning and administration after 1957:
    union level   73
    republican level   77
  The planning process and material supplies   79
  Investment and construction planning   85
  Agricultural planning   87
  The planning of trade   89
  Inspection and control organs   91

3 *Public finance and credit*   97
  The state budget   97
  The financing of investment   108
  Banking and credit   111

4 *Wages and prices*   115
  Principle of wage determination   115
  Peasant incomes   121
  Trade unions   125
  The price system: wholesale prices   128

Retail prices — 134
Agricultural prices — 136
Structure: conclusion — 142

PART II : PROBLEMS

5 *The changing nature of problems* — 145

6 *Micro-economic problems* — 155
  'Success indicators' — 155
  Innovation, risk-taking, initiative — 167
  Transmission of demand to producers — 171
  The party and the correction of distortions — 181
  The special problems of agriculture — 182
  The special case of foreign trade — 189

7 *Planning and investment* — 195
  Complexities — 195
  Sovnarkhozy and 'regionalism' — 196
  Planning and material allocations — 200
  Planning by 'balances' — 206
  Investment criteria — 209

8 *The pricing of factors of production* — 218
  The contradictory objects of price policy — 218
  The search for an 'objective' basis of prices — 220
  Agricultural prices and land rent — 224
  Capital charges, interest and amortization — 228
  Wages: a *de facto* labour market — 231

9 *Trends towards reform* — 236
  Reform is in the air — 236
  What is to be done? — 236
  The Party's attitudes — 241
  The Czech and Polish models — 242
  Yugoslavia — 247

PART III : CONCEPTS AND IDEAS

10 *Some basic concepts of Soviet economics* — 251
  National income — 251
  Gross industrial output — 257
  Gross agricultural production — 259
  Other sectors — 260
  Gross social product — 260
  Producers' goods and consumers' goods — 260
  Accumulation fund and consumption fund — 263

11 *Soviet economics and economic laws*   265
   The 'liquidationist' tradition   265
   The post-Stalin revival of economics   270
   The law of value: does it apply, and why   271
   The real content of the law of value   272
   Utility, scarcity, marginalism and linear programming   276
   Some other economic 'laws'   284

12 *Assessment*   288
   The Soviet economy and the economics of development   288
   Can the system cope with a mature economy?   295
   The efficiency of the system in competition with the West   297
   A model for underdeveloped countries?   303

APPENDIX   307

BIBLIOGRAPHY   314

INDEX OF SUBJECTS   320

INDEX OF NAMES   326

GLOSSARY

Russian words and abbreviations which appear in this book are always explained when first used, but it may still be useful to provide a glossary of some words which recur fairly frequently.

ASSR	Autonomous Soviet Socialist Republic (within a federal republic).
Gosstroi	State committee on construction.
Glavk	Department or division of a ministry.
Gosbank	State Bank.
Gosekonomkommissia	State economic commission (current planning body, 1955–57).
Gosekonomsovet	State economic-science council.
Gosplan	State planning committee (commission).
Khozraschyot	'Economic' (or business) accounting, profit-and-loss accounting.
Kolkhoz	Collective farm (sometimes refers to other kinds of collective economy).
Krai	Large province.
Mestnichestvo	'Regionalism', looking after own locality first.
MTS	Machine Tractor Station(s).
Nomenklatura	Appointments lists controlled by the Party.
Naryad	Allocation certificate, supply order.
Obkom	Oblast' committee of the Communist Party.
Oblast'	Province.
Raikom	Raion committee of the Communist Party.
Raion	District (sub-unit of oblast').
RSFSR	Russian Soviet Federative Socialist Republic, or Russia proper.
Sbyt	Disposals, deliveries organs.
Snab	Supply organs.
Snabsbyt	Supply-and-disposals organs.
Sovnarkhoz	Regional economic council.
Sovkhoz	State farm.
Stroibank	Investment Bank.
Tolkach	'Pusher', 'fixer', unofficial supply agent.
Torg	Trading department of a local authority.
Trudoden (plural: *trudodni*)	Workday units, labour units, or a collective farm.
VSNKh (*Vesenkha*)	Supreme council of national economy.
Zayavka	Application, e.g. for an allocation certificate.

Why and How

Why should we study the Soviet economy? There are a number of cogent reasons for economists and laymen alike to know more about it. Perhaps the most obvious reason is simply that the system developed in the Soviet Union is being applied, with some local variations, to a large part of the globe. Within the countries of the Soviet bloc, if Soviet statisticians are to be believed, there will be produced by 1965 over half of the industrial output of the world. It seems desirable, therefore, to examine how the Soviet economic system works. As citizens, we should acquaint ourselves with its special features, with its strength and weaknesses, with the content and credibility of its statistical claims. As economists, we should surely be aware of the way in which so much of the world's economy is run.

Economists should also be interested in the fate of economic laws and economic theory in a philosophic and institutional setting quite different to the one to which they are accustomed. For example, what happens to resource allocation when there is no interest and no rent? Can market forces be replaced by administrative decision, or do they climb in through the window when driven out of the door? How far is centralized planning in practice consistent with any economic theory at all, Marxist or non-Marxist? What happens in their system to wage determination, consumer choice, and so on? An examination of the Soviet economic scene can help us to see our own economic concepts more clearly, to see how far they depend on western institutions or apply to all systems, albeit in altered or distorted forms.

Then, surely, economists, historians and interested laymen could usefully consider why the Soviet economic system is as it is, in response to what needs has the Soviet institutional structure taken its present shape, how far it is necessarily typical of a planned economy elsewhere, or indeed of the Soviet Union itself at a later date. How far has the system been a response to peculiarly Russian conditions, or to backwardness, or to the special problems of rapid industrialization? What lessons can usefully be drawn from Soviet experience by under-developed countries seeking to industrialize? If Soviet growth has been unusually rapid, what special features of the economy facilitate such growth, and what distortions (viewed from the angle of optimum resource allocation) are explicable by the desire to achieve rapid growth as a primary objective of economic policy? These, and many other questions would seem to merit careful consideration. It is, of course, absurd to expect to find in this book a final 'answer' to them all. The author would be well satisfied if he were to provide some background, introduce some stimulating ideas into the minds of readers and persuade them to seek further information elsewhere.

Since it may seem rather obvious that these matters are important and ought to be studied, it may seem odd that so little has been done by professional economists, especially in Great Britain, to study them. Soviet economics has been the province, as a rule, of Soviet specialists, as if the ordinary economist needs to know nothing outside of the traditional theory and practice of Western Europe and America. Part of the explanation may lie in inertia and/or conservatism, but there are more weighty and more creditable reasons, which could usefully be examined here. One, of course, is the language barrier. Another is the belief that Soviet economics is politics, a belief which is by no means unfounded and which can be documented by citing declarations to this effect by Soviet politicians, and that, therefore, it is a matter for politicians rather than economists. It can be argued that while Soviet planners are indeed concerned with the allocation of scarce resources, they allocate resources to priority objectives determined from outside the economic system, a procedure somewhat analogous to the acts of a military supply organization. The Quartermaster-General to the Forces distributes scarce resources, but he is not an economist and his task is not one to which economic theory has much to contribute.[1] It may be further argued, with many examples, that the behaviour of various units composing the Soviet economy is regulated with great precision by the central administrative agencies; for instance, the ways in which maize or potatoes should be planted or cultivated, the number of shoes of children's sizes to be produced, the wage of fitters or clerks of a given qualification, and much else besides, are determined in Moscow for the remotest provinces. If such micro-economic detail is decided by officials, *a fortiori* this is even more typical of macro-economic matters. The drive to industrialize, launched by Stalin in

---

[1] Though linear programming techniques might enable him to choose optimum solutions to his problems.

1928, is often cited as a particularly striking example of purely political arbitrariness in the economic field. Finally, it is widely believed that the study of the Soviet economy is very seriously impeded by lack of information about its functioning and by lack of statistics. Let us examine the soundness of these objections.

We should, in my view, distinguish carefully between two kinds of political decision in the economic field, which both *look* 'arbitrary' but which in fact are fundamentally different in kind. In the one case, the politician issues an order which, affecting economic life, is essentially explicable by extra-economic considerations and is in no sense a response to economic necessity. For example, repeated measures to restrict the private activities of peasants are of this kind. However, a decree to expand the chemical industry, or to reform the wages system, though juridically and politically it looks just as arbitrary, may frequently turn out to be 'induced', an overdue response to necessity, or even, in the case of wages, a reflection of a *fait accompli*. In such cases, it may be useful to regard the government (or the central committee of the Communist party) as a species of super-board of directors, responding to economic forces which they only partially control, or to the economic-technical consequentials of policies which they themselves decided in their capacity as politicians. Even so 'macro' a decision as industrialization is not quite as arbitrary as it looks. There exist some political analysts who, while emphasizing the arbitrary, political nature of Stalin's decisions, also argue that, even without the revolution, Russia would have become a great industrial power. Indeed, Count Witte was urging the development of heavy industry thirty years before Stalin, for reasons in some respects similar to Stalin's. Of course, the methods used to impose rapid industrialization involved political choice between alternatives and coercion on a vast scale. But the general direction of the policy was not invented by the party leadership. At all stages of Soviet development, the central leadership has had to take into account not only technical but also economic criteria, since their efforts to achieve so much in so little time repeatedly presented choices between alternative uses of scarce means. It is true, as will be shown, that the role of purely *economic* criteria played at first a somewhat subordinate role, but this situation is rapidly changing. There is scope for economic analysis, even though in a number of important instances it will be seen that political considerations proved decisive.

The relevance of economics at the 'micro' level is also much greater than it looks. Centralization of decision is always more effec-

tive on paper than it can possibly be in reality. The proper understanding of the actual functioning of the economy (and not only of
economy) is often impeded by the persistence of what might be
called 'totalitarian myth'. The myth consists in the belief that everyone does what he is told, and that everyone can be told exactly what
to do. In this picture, managers produce precisely the assortment of
goods desired by the planners, peasants grow the crops prescribed
in the decrees, workers receive the wage laid down in the officially-
published schedules, officials only issue instructions consistent with
the desires of the top leadership, and the various inspecting and
checking agencies ensure obedience up and down the hierarchy. This
picture does, indeed, correspond to the version to be found (paradoxically) both in official Soviet textbooks and in the works of en-
thusiastic anti-communists. It does not, as will be shown, correspond
to reality. It is necessary to add that this is not to deny the existence in the USSR of something which can be described as 'totalitarianism'. Perhaps the point is rather that the kind of totalitarianism
sometimes imagined by western critics cannot exist at all, anywhere.

The Soviet economist, Academician Strumilin, in criticizing his
own colleagues' traditional attitudes, put the point as follows. 'At
one time it was fashionable among us to deny the existence of any
objective economic laws in our society, in which, so it was said, the
plan was the basic "law", which meant the will of the lawgiver and
the *conscious* direction of the planned economy.' Emphasizing the
limitations imposed on the planners' will by objective necessity,
Strumilin contrasted the nature of juridical and economic laws. The
former are enforced by state organs. 'Economic laws also do not
lack an enforcement mechanism, even though this is not laid down
in any code . . . Economic sanctions operate independently, without
the help of any kind of coercive apparatus, as a result of the very
fact of a breach of (economic) law. To put it another way, economic
laws take their own revenge on those who break them.'[1] Therefore,
to take this thought a little further, planners ought to act in consciousness of economic principles, and, when they ignore them, the
chickens come home to roost, things go wrong. The fact that they
do so provides us with material for study as economists. It also
shows the limitations of 'totalitarian' power in this field, since the
things that go wrong often do so because of the behaviour of *homo
economicus sovieticus*, a close relation of the species found in the
west.

[1] *Vop. Ekon.*, No. 7/1959, pp. 127, 130.

There will be much more to say about economic laws in the Soviet context later on.

The other commonly-held objection to the academic study of the Soviet economy concerns lack of reliable data. It must be admitted that difficulties exist, but they are certainly not insuperable. While in the last years of Stalin's life hardly any statistics were published, it is wrong to regard this situation as typical of the Soviet period. Up to the years 1936-38, there were vast quantities of statistics regularly available (with, it is true, some omissions), and since 1955 there has again been a much more liberal attitude to publication. Indeed, the flood of figures has been such as literally to overwhelm analysts who were used to the leisurely and selective trickle of the late-Stalin period. There still remain some conspicuous gaps. Thus systematic figures on wages have not been made available up to the time of writing. The figures on output, and especially indices, are of varying degrees of reliability and have to be used with care. Appendix A will be devoted to examining these questions of availability and reliability. However, the beliefs that Soviet statistics are confined to percentages of an unknown base-year, or that the figures are mere propagandist inventions, are now baseless legends.

It is not only figures which are needed, but also a picture of the organization and functioning of institutions. Here, too, there were grave difficulties in the late-Stalin era, because of the marked tendency to describe the desirable state of affairs rather than the one which existed. Thus most books on the collective farms, where the contrast between 'is' and 'ought' was perhaps most marked, were generally so misleading as to be downright useless. To this day, textbooks are apt to present an idealized version of whatever they may be describing. Fortunately, there is no need to rely on such textbooks (and it might be fair to add that the Soviet researcher into British economic organization is unlikely to find some of our textbooks very helpful either). Periodicals—party, economic, technical —supply the missing note of realism. They are concerned with the practical job of getting people to act 'correctly', and so must perforce discuss real problems. Here again, the late-Stalin epoch was least productive of frank fact-facing. Many writers and editors were evidently scared of saying disagreeable things, and too often filled their pages with paeans of praise. There was some criticism, of course, but its authors played it safe, and made the criticisms particular rather than general; thus they would attack a local official or local abuse (if they were out of reach of that official's wrath), but without drawing any conclusions of national application. However, since his death there has been much more frankness. Major outbursts of criticism have, it is true, often followed a speech on the same subject by a party leader, but now it would be correct to say that a very large area of the Soviet economy is open to practical, business-like examination in the Soviet press by Soviet experts. There are certain solutions which they dare not put forward; but they can describe the stresses and strains of reality, and, outside the area of heresy, a range of practical suggestions to correct defects can be, and are, made.

This provides the western scholar with a great deal of evidence. But this evidence is seldom systematized, it is raw, it needs to be understood and assessed. The important must be disentangled from the accidental, 'self-criticisms' must be seen in their proper proportions. For the western literature, unfortunately, includes examples of mere assemblages of such self-criticisms, so arranged as to suggest extremely negative conclusions. Others, relying on the textbooks and shrugging off critical articles of Soviet periodicals merely as detailed and local aberrations, have produced unrealistic and over-favourable accounts. But the risk of error is not a reason for avoiding the study of a subject. On the contrary, this provides a challenge for a lively and inquiring mind. Evidence can be sifted with some confidence, if the analyst makes the realistic assumption that Soviet men (including planners, factory directors and workers) are human, and behave in a manner which, given the institutional forms, could reasonably be expected. This, and a general sense of the *vraisemblable*, should provide us with a sound basis for assessing the very wide range of critical material available to us from Soviet sources and building up from it a picture of the real system which should be near the truth. Here are some not untypical examples of 'critical' material:

(a) Cracks have developed in a new apartment house in Kharkov, and in another in Baku.
(b) Collective-farm chairmen in two places have been at cross purposes with the directors of the Machine Tractor Stations (MTS) serving them.
(c) In order to fulfil his plan in terms of gross output, director A has produced the wrong assortment of textiles, to the annoyance of his customers.
(d) A new railway has wrongly been built across an area which was due to be flooded under a hydro-electric scheme.

Clearly, it would be wrong to deduce from (a) that most Soviet houses have cracks, though we may surmise from other reports that the quality of construction leaves much to be desired. Certainly we cannot judge the normal efficiency of planners from the error cited in example (d), though we may note that this is a failure of inter-departmental co-ordination which is not unknown in other sectors and indeed in other countries. However, (b) and (c) are in quite a different category, because, as will be shown in subsequent chapters, these particular 'deviations' were built in to the system itself; they are as much in the nature of the institutions concerned as, for example, the tendency of businessmen in the west to use every opportunity to avoid paying income tax. Indeed, it should be possible to deduce the general occurrence of (b) and (c) even if not a single published example could be quoted. When the author toured the Soviet Union with the British agricultural delegation in 1955, he heard British farm experts who knew no Russian and had never read a Soviet book in any language immediately seize on the collective-farms-MTS relationship as a major organizational weakness. They were unconvinced by the denials of their Soviet hosts. Two years later, Khrushchev himself confirmed the general nature of just this weakness.

Thus there is ample printed material for study. To this must be added the fruits, actual and potential, of investigation on the spot. The USSR is no longer a closed country, and a number of students of Soviet affairs (notably from America) have paid visits to Russia and have discussed various problems with Soviet colleagues, often with fruitful results. But the limitations of the material should not be overlooked. Thus, to take an example at random, if workers at a building site in Kazakhstan go on strike or stage a riot, this would remain unreported in the Soviet press, and no one researching into Soviet labour relations (for instance) should forget that this is so when assessing the evidence available.

In this book, historical description will be kept to the minimum necessary for understanding the present Soviet system. Good economic histories of the Soviet period exist, and it is not the writer's purpose to invade this particular field. However, some general remarks on the historical setting seem indispensable, even in this introduction. The Soviet Union has been the scene of an industrial and social, as well as of a political, revolution. Great changes have been compressed into a short space of time. They have been carried through under the leadership of the Communist party (or by leaders acting in its name), and they have transformed a backward, peasant country into a giant industrial power. This involved the tearing asunder of established ways of life, and indeed the systematic disregard of the pressure of existing economic forces. Soviet policymakers did not seek to adapt themselves to the demand pattern; the point was to change the demand pattern, the institutions, the structure of the economy. The economy was deliberately so organized as to facilitate this drastic and complex process, and this led to the neglect not only of non-priority sectors of economic life, but also of the finer adjustments required for 'optimal' resource allocation. For this reason, the student of the Soviet economy must bear in mind, in making his assessments, the *purposes* of Soviet economic policy, and the high priority given to rapid industrialization. Professor Oscar Lange has described this stage of Soviet development as *'sui generis* a war economy',[1] in the sense of all-out concentration of effort on a major objective determined by political authority. No one would fail to note, in analysing the effectiveness of the war economy of Great Britain or Germany, that all kinds of desiderata had in practice to be sacrificed to the concentration of resources for waging war (and this without necessarily approving of the military objectives of the governments concerned!). All that is required is that one should bear in mind that Soviet institutions were created to serve certain purposes, that many of the problems are intimately connected with—and are often part of the cost of—the pursuit of rapid industrialization in a backward country, and that it is not always useful to criticize the Soviet economic system as if its aim were to achieve the pure static equilibrium of western textbooks.

It is important to insist on a sense of proportion in the study of the Soviet economy because so many persons allow emotion to enter into their assessment of anything Soviet. Economists are apt to compare Soviet reality not with western reality, but with an imaginary model of the 'capitalist' economy. For instance, when (rightly) criticizing the illogicalities and confusions of Soviet agricultural prices, they implicitly overlook the illogicalities of agricultural prices in virtually every western country. Others seize with glee upon evidence of the very real errors or waste in Soviet investment policy, with a cavalier disregard not only for the inherent complexity of the problem but also for the errors or waste which can occur in their own countries. Needless to say, Soviet economists are apt to do exactly the same in reverse. This procedure might be called 'comparing model with muddle'. It needs to be avoided. Of course, it is true that the Soviet economic system contains within itself certain specific weaknesses, certain kinds of waste which are not found (at least to the same extent) even in the most imperfect world of western reality. Part II of the present book will be largely devoted to analysing the

[1] *The Political Economy of Socialism* (Warsaw, 1957), p. 16.

things which go wrong, or raise difficult problems which, within their system, obstinately resist solution. This emphasis on difficulties is not without its dangers, since the reader may obtain a lop-sided view of reality. If this were the whole story, a critic might legitimately say, the Soviet economy would be far less effective than it appears to be. Although an effort will be made in chapter 12 to assess in general terms the strength and weakness of the economy, such a criticism is not without point. It is, therefore, essential to stress that part II is entitled 'Problems', that it therefore emphasizes aspects of the economic system which involve various kinds of snags, just as a book or chapter entitled 'Problems of British education' would seize upon aspects of the British educational system which do not give entire satisfaction. The difficulties to be discussed are not by any means trivial. They are essential aspects of the system, and as such are causing concern to Soviet economists and planners. None the less, the very nature of this kind of analysis, under such a heading as 'Problems', does carry with it a certain unavoidable over-emphasis on things that go wrong. One does not write there about, say, the speed with which the Trans-Siberian railway has been electrified, or about the regular delivery of steel to this or that industry, but it should not be forgotten that many things are effec-tively and punctually accomplished all the same. Yet at the same time one should certainly not overlook the very considerable evi-dence of conspicuous misdirection of resources, of the sacrifices im-posed or of the means adopted to impose them.

A last word about political bias. It is sometimes thought that it is impossible to write on the Soviet Union in an objective spirit. Some critics even believe that to attempt to do so is wrong, since it shows lack of proper militancy in the face of 'evil'. It is my firm belief that one can only usefully examine the Soviet economy if one is not trying thereby to find proof in support of preconceived notions, as by 'selective' research it is all too easy to 'prove' anything. In any case, the evaluation of economic activities can (indeed should) be politically neutral. A Soviet steelworks is a steelworks. If its products are used to shoot political opponents, its existence is doubtless de-plorable, but no cause is advanced by pretending that its efficiency or its output are other than what they are. Opponents of the Soviet régime should remember that their opposition is not generally based on its alleged or real economic inefficiencies, but on its political-social system. It is pointless self-delusion to deny that it has to its credit, or is capable of, great achievements in the field of production and technique. There was a time when any Soviet writer who discussed the west without 'militant' epithets was denounced for 'objectivism'. Their understanding of the west has suffered, and to a great extent still suffers, in consequence. It is to be hoped that the reader will feel that the author is guilty of the sin of 'objectivism' which indeed it is his aim to commit.

It is certainly true and important that the Soviet economy is controlled at the top by persons who have the declared purpose of achieving a state of affairs which they describe as 'communism', that they wish to change society, and that they have an ideology which affects their choice among possible solutions to practical problems. It should be possible to note this, and also the dominance of the Communist party organization, as part of the basic facts. Whether what they do is morally justified is not a matter on which, in the present context, it is necessary to comment.

A note on political structure

The following is a brief sketch of the political framework.

The USSR is a federation of republics, which at present number fifteen. Sovereignty is nominally exercised by an elected body. Until 1937 this was the all-union Congress of Soviets, indirectly elected by lower territorial soviets. The congress elected an executive committee (known as VTsIK), which elected a praesidium. Since its first meeting in 1938 the sovereign 'parliament' is the Supreme Soviet, which consists of two houses, the Soviet of the Union and the Soviet of Nationalities, both elected directly by adult suffrage. In practice the deputies are nominated by the Communist party machine, and contested elections are unknown. The Supreme Soviet meets infrequently, often for no more than one week in the year, though its committees, including a finance committee, and an economic committee of the Council of Nationalities, now play a more active role. It elects a praesidium which exercises its legislative powers between sessions, subject to subsequent ratification. In principle at least, laws can only be adopted by the Supreme Soviet, and its praesidium can also issue decrees (*ukazy*) which are supposed to conform to existing laws, but in practice often change them. (Before 1938, laws and decrees emerged from a variety of bodies, including VTsIK or its praesidium, the government and even government committees such as the Council of Labour and Defence.)

The government was known before 1946 by the designation of the Council of People's Commissars, and since that date as the Council of Ministers. In this book, to avoid unnecessary brackets and qualifications, the terms Minister, Ministry, Council of Ministers, will generally be used, and *not* Commissar, People's Commissariat, etc. The Council of Ministers is elected by and is responsible to the Supreme Soviet (or its praesidium between sessions). It is empowered to issue binding orders (*postanovleniya*) within the constitution and the laws. In practice, it can issue *de facto* laws on any subject, since the Supreme Soviet has never used (and is most unlikely ever to use) its formal powers to challenge and revoke the actions of the government.

All the above relates to the all-union government, but the same structure was and is almost wholly duplicated in each of the fifteen federal republics. They have Supreme Soviets, praesidia, councils of ministers and so forth. Despite the apparently formidable powers with which they are endowed by the constitution, the republics are in fact subject to orders from the all-union government on any conceivable matter, though the amount of autonomy actually allowed them has fluctuated and has recently shown a tendency to increase. The relationship between centre and republics in particular sectors of governmental activity varies, and has given rise to three different kinds of ministry: there are, first, the *all-union ministries*, which directly run from Moscow the activities of their subordinate units within the various republics. Secondly, there are *'union-republican'* *ministries*, which exist both at the centre and in the republics, in which case the republican ministry is simultaneously subordinate both to its elder brother in Moscow and to the Council of Ministers of the given republic. This is an example of 'dual subordination', which is very commonly encountered in Soviet administration: a local organ is simultaneously an integral part of the local authority and the representative in that area of the appropriate unit of the central government. Finally, there are purely *republican ministries*, which have no direct superior in Moscow, though naturally they have to conform where relevant to central policies and plans. The word 'ministry' does not cover all organizations of ministerial status either at the centre or in the republics: there are a number of state committees, commissions and other bodies, whose heads are members of the Council of Ministers. One such body, Gosplan, has been of key importance in the economy.

The republics are divided into provinces (*oblast'*, plural *oblasti*); there are also large provinces which are called *krai*[1], and finally certain national areas within some of the republics are given the dignity of Autonomous Soviet Socialist Republic (ASSR) and their top officials have the title of ministers; examples include Tartar, Chuvash, Komi and Bashkir ASSR. However, the power of these bodies *vis-à-vis* the authorities above or below them is hardly affected by the differences of designation.[2] In this book, therefore, when the word *oblast'* is used, it may be assumed that the same functions or powers apply also to the ASSR and *krai*.

Local government in towns is run by elected town Soviets. The big towns have a status similar to the English county borough, in the sense of not being subject to the *oblast'* authorities but depending directly on the republican government.

The *oblast'* is sub-divided into urban and rural districts (*raion*, plural

---

[1] Some of these have autonomous sub-units, including even *oblasti*, but these refinements are hardly worth pursuing here.

[2] Except that the ASSR are represented as such in the upper house of the legislature, the Soviet of Nationalities.

raiony) which also have elected soviets. At the very bottom of the scale are village soviets, with only minor powers. When the economic functions of local government are referred to, the village soviet can virtually be ignored.

Underlying all this elaborate governmental structure is the Communist Party of the Soviet Union, the 'directing nucleus' (as the Constitution itself emphasizes) of all state organs and social organizations. In a very real sense, the government at all levels exists to carry out the policies of the Party. Its own structure is as follows: party congresses are nominally supreme; they elect a central committee, which in turn elects other committees, of which by far the most important is the praesidium (known before 1952 as the politbureau). The latter is in effect the supreme organ of government. At the party headquarters there are departments which duplicate the various governmental organs. There are party committees in the fifteen republics, and in lower territorial units (the most important from our point of view are the *oblast'* committee, the town committee and the *raion* committee, known respectively as the *obkom*, *gorkom* and the *raikom*). It is important to note that the party committees are wholly subordinate to the Moscow leadership, in the fifteen republics as well as at *oblast* level and below. Thus, for example, the Ukrainian or Uzbek committees of the party have no greater rights *vis-à-vis* the all-union central committee than are possessed by, say, the Leningrad or Omsk *obkom*. Therefore the degree of independence of any federal or local body in the USSR must always be severely limited, in so far as it is at least partially controlled by a party committee on its own level, and the party itself is highly centralized.

The party's specificially economic functions will be dealt with in greater detail on page 94 below, along with other agencies of inspection and control.

PART I: STRUCTURE

CHAPTER I

Productive Enterprises

Before describing the governmental organs which plan and control the economy, it is desirable to start at the bottom and consider the organization and finance of enterprises and individuals actually engaged in the production of goods and services. These may be conveniently divided into the following categories:

(a) State enterprises.
(b) Non-agricultural co-operative enterprises.
(c) Collective-farms (*Kolkhozy*).
(d) The private sector, subdivided into

    (i) Agricultural holdings of collective farmers and state employees.
    (ii) Private craftsmen, individual peasants, professional services.

Before describing each of these forms, it is necessary to mention the types of economic activity, familiar in the west, which are not to be found in the USSR, or are illegal there. The laws and regulations have changed very little in these respects since the liquidation of NEP[1] at the end of the 'twenties.

It is illegal for any private citizen to employ anyone to produce a commodity for sale. For example, a private shoemaker, whose existence is legitimate under category (d)(ii) above, may not employ an assistant. It is legal to employ a domestic servant, who 'produces'

[1] NEP: New Economic Policy, which succeeded the so-called War Communism period in 1921, and under which a wide range of private economic activity was legalized.

nothing in the Soviet sense of the word, and no doubt many writers employ a typist privately, but in principle the 'exploitation of man by man' is repressed by law. It is also illegal for an individual to sell anything he has not himself produced (unless, of course, he is an employee or member of an organization which has the right to produce goods for sale). For instance, a peasant can sell a cabbage he has grown, any citizen can make coat-hangers in his spare time and sell them in the free market. But if a man buys on his own account a sack of cabbages from peasants and then resells them at a profit in a city where cabbages are dear, or if he buys a scarce commodity in a state store and resells it at a higher price, he is guilty of a criminal offence and, if caught, would probably serve a term of imprisonment. Of course, this does not mean that such activities do not exist. On the contrary, it may readily be observed that ticket touts outside a Soviet football stadium or the Bolshoi theatre are as active as their equivalents in London or New York, and there can hardly be a peasant in all Russia who has not committed the technical 'crime' of selling in the free market not only his own produce but that of some fellow-villager. However, none can doubt that the legal principles mentioned above deeply influence economic organization.

Since even within the sectors in which private or co-operative activities are nominally permitted, the state organs have and frequently use the right to refuse the necessary registration permits, it follows that a wide range of goods and services are either provided by state organs or are not provided at all. To take two small instances, it would not be open to an individual to open an agency to provide addresses for holiday accommodation, or a café, and if the appropriate state organs do not feel that it is necessary or desirable to provide them, then they cannot be brought into existence.

The relative importance of the various categories can be expressed in a number of different ways, according to the sector of the economy and the basis of the comparison. Thus, taking gross industrial production as a measure, the figures are as follows:

Gross industrial output by forms of ownership
(Per cent of total)

	1928	1937	1950	1958
State enterprises	69·4	91·8	92	94
Co-operative enterprises*	13·0	8·2	8	6
Private	17·6	—	—	—

Source: *N.Kh. 1958*, p. 127. For definition of industry, see p. 257, below.

* Includes some industrial production on collective farms.

Building is not included in the above table. The relative importance of the non-state sector there is much larger than in 'industry'. Collective farms erect various farm buildings and other constructions, while private persons built houses in substantial numbers throughout the Soviet period. Thus in 1958, out of a total new housing space of 71·2 million square metres (exclusive of peasant construction), 24·5 million were privately built; in addition, peasants and 'rural intelligentsia' put up about 700,000 dwellings.[1]

Total agricultural output is not subdivided, in published statistics, by forms of ownership, but the following are the relevant figures in respect of land area. These strikingly demonstrate the effect of collectivization, and also of the growing importance of state farms.

Sown area (millions of hectares)
(Soviet territory as of the given date)

	1928	1937	1956	1959
Collective farms	1·4	116·0	152·1	130·2
State farms*	1·7	12·2	35·3	58·8
Private holdings, collective peasants	1·1	6·24	5·65	5·3
Private holdings, state employees	n.a.		1·6	1·9
Private land, individual peasants	108·7	0·86	0·03	0·01

Source: *N.Kh. 1956*, p. 108. *N.Kh. 1959*, p. 312, 1937 figures— N. Jasny: *The Socialised agriculture of the USSR* (Stanford, 1949), pp. 774, 788 and 790).

* Includes other state enterprises (see p. 40).

However, a high proportion of livestock was, and is, privately owned; though this proportion has been falling, even as recently as January, 1959, over half of all cows were private, and this sector also produced over half of the meat and potatoes and nearly all the eggs of the Soviet Union. An American calculation, based on a mixture of official statistics and estimates, gives the total output of the private sectors as about 30 per cent of all agricultural production for the year 1956.[2] This is likely to be close to the mark.

[1] *N.Kh. 1958*, p. 636.
[2] *Comparisons of United States and Soviet Economics* (Economic Committee of us Congress), Part I, p. 206. See also p. 60.

The relative figures for labour were given as follows for 1959:

	(milliards of man years)
State farms	4·5
Collective farms	21·5
MTS and RTS*	0·2
Private holdings (collective peasants and state employees)	6·8
TOTAL	33·0

Source: *Sel. Khoz. 1960*, p. 450.
* Machine Tractor Stations and Repair Technical Stations.

State and 'co-operative' trade—the latter to all intents and purposes being a branch of state trade (see page 41, below)—was responsible for over 94 per cent of all retail trade in 1957 and 1958, the remainder being accounted for by the free market. However, the free-market data include only urban sales, intra-village trade being omitted. The statistics also omit many unrecorded transactions between individuals.

Transport is run by state enterprises, with the significant exception of collective-farm haulage. There are a few privately owned horses, and some private cars run an illegal taxi service.

For other economic sectors, mostly services, no statistics are available for the relative importance of different types of enterprise.

THE STATE INDUSTRIAL ENTERPRISE

A state enterprise belongs to the state. From this apparently tautological statement of the obvious flow a number of consequences which are perhaps less obvious. In essence and in law, the enterprise is a convenient unit for the administration of state property. It is a juridical person, it can sue and be sued, but it *owns* none of its assets. The director and his senior colleagues—the chief engineer, who acts as his deputy, and the chief accountant—are appointed by state organs to manage the state's assets for purposes determined by the state. This is why there is no charge made for the use of the enterprise's capital, since it belongs to the state anyhow. This is also why the state is entitled to transfer the enterprise's profits to the state budget, save for that portion which the state's regulations or *ad hoc* decisions permit the enterprise to retain. That is why it is within the power of state organs to take away any of the enterprise's assets, if they think fit, without financial compensation.

The director is in sole charge, in the sense that he is responsible to those who appoint him and must be obeyed by his subordinates. However, this principle of 'one-man command' is subject in practice to a number of significant limitations. Not only are the director's hierarchical superiors liable to issue detailed orders on almost every conceivable subject, but he must also take into account a number of inspecting and checking agencies. The most important of these, which also exercises a controlling influence over other agencies, is the Communist party; this generally possesses an organized group within the enterprise, of which the director is usually a member but in which he holds no official position. There is also a trade union branch, to which certain questions (such as distribution of premia, overtime work, norm-setting, questions of labour discipline) must be referred. Since 1958, there is also an elected 'permanent production council', which, though without direct executive authority, is entitled to deliberate on many questions directly affecting planning and management. There are also outside agencies of inspection and control: the banks, financial inspectorates and some others; these will be examined in due course (see pages 92 and 111). The successful director requires to possess qualities of diplomacy, to obtain the support or avoid the opposition of these various controlling, checking and inspecting agencies. None the less, he is in command; he is to blame when things go wrong and is rewarded when they go right.

The primary task of the director is to fulfil, and if possible to overfulfil, the output plans, and to utilize the resources placed at his disposal with due regard to economy. The output plan specifies the quantity of the product required in the given month, quarter or year, with some details of type, design, assortment, etc., where this is relevant. The aggregate output plan of industrial enterprises is frequently expressed in physical measure (tons, square metres, etc.), or, where this cannot be done, in terms of value (roubles of gross output). There are usually a number of other plan 'indicators': cost reductions, increase in labour productivity, economy of scarce materials and sometimes other indicators appropriate to the given sector or the result of some campaign of the moment. Fulfilment of plans expressed in terms of these various indicators carries with it moral approbation and material benefits, in the form of substantial premia to the director and his senior staff, and so they could be conveniently designated 'success indicators'. Overfulfilment carries with it increased rewards, material and spiritual. Thus in the oil industry in 1956 the director received a bonus of 40 per cent of his salary for fulfilling the output plan, and 4 per cent for each 1 per cent overfulfilment. Those who overfulfil, or fulfil ahead of time, receive praise, sometimes see their picture in the newspapers and may receive decorations. Of course, not all of these plans are equally important, either from the standpoint of premia or in the weight given them by superior authority in assessing the success of the enterprise, and, since it often happens that directors are unable to fulfil all the various plans, they naturally choose the ones that seem to them the most important. This has generally been the production plan in quantitative terms, reflecting the great emphasis on growth, though recently it is being modified by insistence on cost reductions. The consequences of the 'success indicator' system will be discussed at length in chapter 6.

Soviet enterprises, with very few exceptions, now operate as autonomous financial entities with their own profit and loss accounts, a status known by the Russian words *khozyaistvennyi raschyot* ('economic accounting'), usually abbreviated to *khozraschyot*. It was not always thus. In the period of 'war communism', that is, before 1921, most state enterprises had no funds of their own, wages and other expenses being met out of the state budget. In the years of NEP, before 1929, all except very large state enterprises were still 'not on *khozraschyot*', in the sense that their revenues were paid into, and their expenses were met out of, the accounts of trusts, which grouped together varying numbers of enterprises. It was only in 1929 that a decision was taken to place state enterprises on *khozraschyot*, and since this date there have been few exceptions to this rule. The basis of *khozraschyot* has been defined as follows: 'A method of planned operation of socialist enterprises . . . which requires the carrying out of state-determined tasks with the maximum economy of resources, the covering of money expenditures of enterprises by their own money revenues, the ensuring of profitability of enterprises'.[1] So far as the enterprise is concerned, prices of outputs are fixed, prices of inputs are fixed, and, as we shall see, the choice as to which inputs to use is severely limited by the system of allocation. Within these bounds, it is the director's job not only to fulfil the various plans already referred to, but also to cover his costs and to make a profit. This is encouraged by providing an incentive linked with profits. The

[1] *Ekonomika promyshlennosti SSSR* (Moscow, 1956), p. 393. Sub-units of enterprises are sometimes said to be 'placed on *khozraschyot*', meaning that their profitability is separately calculated, though they have no financial independence.

incentive is related not so much to profits as such as to *overplan* profits, since it is considered that some enterprises earn profits because of 'unearned' advantages of location or equipment, and such advantages find expression in the planned profits; only a very small proportion of *planned* profits may be retained, whereas enterprises are encouraged to make overplan profits, that is, to make special efforts to economize. The incentive to maximize profits takes the form of the so-called *enterprise fund*, known until 1955 as the *director's fund*, which the enterprise retains and uses mainly for purposes which benefit its personnel; these include the financing of investments in addition to plan, primarily in housing and amenities, and also in bonuses to outstanding workers. The trade union branch must be consulted.

The rules governing the enterprise fund have often been changed. From 1956 it is based on the following percentages, subject to the total not exceeding 5 per cent of the wages bill:

Allocation to Enterprise Fund

	Per cent of Plan profit	Overplan profit
Metallurgy, oil, coal, cement, etc.	6	50
Engineering, electricity, timber, etc.	4	40
Textiles	2	30
Food, and local industry	1	20

Source: *Direktivy K.P.S.S.* (Vol. 4), pp. 457–9, (but see p. 35, below).

In addition, under a decree issued in 1957, up to another 30 per cent of overplan profits can be devoted to housing.[1]

By decree published on July 2, 1960, exceptional treatment is accorded to 'machine-building and metal-working'. Enterprises in this sector are entitled to retain 10 per cent of those planned profits which arise from the production of new equipment in the course of the first year of mass-production. The maximum upper limit is raised to between 6 and 7 per cent of the wages bill in those enterprises in which new products form a high proportion of total output.

The same decree altered the rules for other industrial enterprises. The maximum limit is now 5·5 per cent of the wages bill. The use of the enterprise fund is more precisely specified than before: at least

[1] A. Zverev, *Voprosy natsional'novo dokhoda i finansov SSSR* (Moscow, 1958), p. 91.

20 per cent for new technique and modernization, at least 40 per cent on house-building and repairs, and the remainder on premia, places in sanatoria and holiday rest homes, and so on.

Since, as will be shown, selling prices of any given commodity are fixed by the Government at levels based on average, not marginal, cost in the given industry, many enterprises make planned losses. In these cases, payments into the enterprise fund are related to planned or actual reduction in production costs.

The enterprise's financial plans, approved by higher authority, are closely integrated with its output and investment plans, into a consolidated whole known as *tekhpromfinplan* ('technical industrial financial plan') which includes the expected level of profits or losses. The financial standing of the enterprise is related to these expected, or planned, profits or losses. Financial embarrassments, if any, therefore follow not from losses as such, but from a smaller profit (or larger loss) than was envisaged in the plan. For example, if a given enterprise was expected to make a profit of 40 per cent and actually makes one of 'only' 35 per cent, it would be in greater financial difficulties than one which made a planned loss of 10 per cent, since the entire pattern of its financial arrangements would have been geared to the planned level of profits.

Profits (and losses) are expressed as a percentage of *costs*. Thus if costs are 100 and revenues 105, there is said to be a profit of 5 per cent. 'Costs' for this purpose sometimes include so-called 'commercial' expenditures, incurred when enterprises are called upon to bear costs of packing and despatch. Costs in state industry (apparently 'production' costs only) were divided as follows in 1957:

	Per cent
Materials and fuel	72·6
Amortization	3·4
Wages and social insurance contributions	20·9
Other	3·1

Source: *N.Kh. 1958*, p. 171.

Most of these items are self-explanatory. The important point to note is the virtual absence of interest and rent payments; the small sums paid as interest on short-term credits appear on the residual ('other').[1] Amortization (depreciation) is based on the expected life of capital assets. The latter were revalued in 1959, to eliminate many

[1] Part of the cost of housing is included in the costs of the coal and timber industries, along with part of the costs of canteens, etc., in these and some other industries.

anomalies in valuations which had accumulated over time. The 'amortization fund' is divided (since 1938) into two. One part, ear-marked for capital repairs,[1] remains with the enterprise; the other is transferred to the investment bank and is available for new (notionally replacement) investment, subject to decision of superior authority.

In 1958, profits were to be used as follows:

	(milliards of roubles)
TOTAL (all state enterprises)	188·4
of which:	
To state budget	128·6
To increase in 'own' working capital	14·3
To investment	25·1*
Other	20·4†

Source: A. Zverev, *Plan. Khoz.*, No. 12/1957, p. 18.

* On page 20 of the same article, profits used to finance investment were given as 29·1.

† This is stated to include repayments of credits for mechanization and new technique, geological surveying, research, housing losses, etc., as well as the enterprise fund.

Little is published about the utilization of overplan profits, but the following was the result of a sample survey carried out in three *sovnarkhozy* in 1958.

Per cent utilization of overplan profits in enterprises

To enterprise fund	19
To building dwelling houses	25
To 'Socialist competition' premia	10·5
Return of bank credits for new techniques	6
To 'consumer goods fund' (see footnote)	3·5
To sovnarkhoz funds	18
To state budget	18

Source: A. Rumyantsev (ed.): *Ekonomika sotsialisticheskikh pro-myshlennykh predpriyatii* (Moscow, 1959), p.441

Oddly, enough, this is inconsistent with the 'enterprise fund' rules cited on p. 33, above.

The relationship with the budget is a complex one, since often an

---

[1] 'Capital repairs' are supposed to designate major repairs or replacement of worn-out parts, which are neither small enough to be current repairs nor 'qualify' as new investment. The dividing line is vague, but not only in the USSR.

enterprise receives allocations from the budget to cover investments and some other expenditures while at the same time it pays a large part of its profits into the budget.[1] This state of affairs is sometimes explained by the need to maintain tight control over enterprise spending, though some economists criticize the practice.

The enterprise's working capital (*oborotnye sredstva*, 'circulating resources') consists of two parts. The part which is required for normal operation 'belongs' to the enterprise, and increases in such working capital may be financed out of profits, if this is agreed by superior authority, or from the budget if profits are insufficient for the purpose. A new enterprise is endowed with its 'own' working capital from the budget when it begins its life. That part of working capital which is needed to cover seasonal or purely temporary needs —for example, the time-gap between production and payment, or, in retail trade, between buying and selling—is generally financed through short-term credits from the State Bank, at rates of interest of 2 per cent or less.

Investment finance will be separately considered (chapter 3). It is sufficient at this stage to list the sources of finance available to expand the basic capital of an existing enterprise. The major sources are: the state budget, profits and that portion of the amortization fund not earmarked for capital repairs. All the above may only be used for investment projects if these projects and the given method of financing is approved by the appropriate state organ. However, there are also the following resources which are more directly within the area of enterprise decision: firstly, the enterprise fund and some other minor funds;[2] secondly, the so-called 'mobilization of internal resources' (for example, unplanned economies, or carry-over of stocks of building materials), and also (since 1955) short-term credits to cover the introduction of new technique, which can be obtained from the State Bank on a two to three years' term. Though this last item has grown with some rapidity, in 1957 it only provided some five milliard roubles out of total investments in the state sector of 210·6 milliards.[3]

---

[1] All enterprises *must* in all circumstances pay at least 10 per cent of their planned profits into the budget (K. Plotnikov, *Finansy i Kredit SSSR* (Moscow, 1956), p. 81). See also chapter 3.

[2] For instance, the so-called *Fond shirpotryoba*, 'Consumers' goods fund', into which are paid the bulk of profits made from any workshop which, in a factory primarily devoted to something else, makes consumers' goods as by-products.

[3] *Vest. Stat.*, No. 4/1959, p. 94, and *Den'gi i Kredit*, No. 1/1958, p. 7. For details of regulations governing such credits, see *Direktivy KPSS* . . . (vol. 4), p. 454.

Some types of state enterprise, notably state farms and many purely local workshops run by local soviets, retain a larger proportion of their profits, and their use for investment purposes is not so tightly controlled by the planners, subject, however, to various restrictions especially over any projects above a certain size, and over the allocation of materials and equipment.

Not only the bulk of the investment, but also most material inputs are subject to control. A large proportion of the materials and components required by enterprises may only be obtained against an allocation certificate (*naryad*), which commonly specifies not only the quantity but also the supplying enterprise, with whom the director must enter into a contract. Therefore, in most instances the enterprise is tied by the allocation system to particular suppliers or customers. It is true that contracts must be negotiated, containing detailed specifications, precise dates of delivery and so on. However, these contracts are based on the allocation decisions of the supply and/or disposal authorities, generally (since 1957) the so-called *snabsbyt* departments of the Gosplans of the republics or of the Union. There is generally no right, in the case of allocated commodities, for enterprises to enter into free contractual relationships with one another. In particular, no long-term arrangements are possible between enterprises. For each year, or sometimes even a shorter period, enterprises must apply for a *naryad* for the required goods, and the supplying enterprise must await the issue of a *naryad* before the two enterprises negotiate the details of their contract, even though in practice they have been dealing with each other for many years and continue to do so. The contracts provided for in a *naryad* must be negotiated, and it is the task of the state arbitration tribunals not merely to settle disputes arising from alleged non-fulfilment of contracts, but also to compel the parties to agree to sign, in the event of disagreement over terms, using the intentions of the planners as the criterion for judgment.

On the face of it, supply matters are decided very largely above enterprise level, save in the relatively few instances where the commodities are not subject to allocation. However, as so often in the USSR, things are not as strictly centralized as might appear to be the case. Thus the actual application for an allocation, initiated by the enterprise, has some influence upon the process of distributing the commodities in question, even though the planning organs amend or reduce the amounts, guided partly by material utilization 'norms' and partly by the suspicion (usually well-founded) that enterprises tend to overstate their needs. Then the allocation certificates themselves are usually couched in general terms—so many tons of a given metal, for instance. But there are many varieties of this metal, and complicated negotiations are, therefore, set in train to obtain the desired variety. In this process, as well as in deciding what materials to indent for, the management is able to reflect its own initiatives in matters of design, technical changes, adjustments to demand. (For reasons which will be discussed in chapter 6 it may well fail to do so, but that is another question.) The system of materials supply will require separate consideration, in greater detail (see chapter 7, below). At this stage it is necessary to mention only that Soviet directors have had constant worries about their supplies, and that this has affected their behaviour in three principal ways. Firstly, they have often felt compelled to set up small-scale workshops to manufacture components, or castings, or tools, the delivery of which from outside could not be relied on. Secondly, there is a powerful inducement to hoarding. Thirdly, there have developed semi-legal materials procurement arrangements: lobbying for allocation certificates in Moscow, string-pulling through powerful friends or party officials, unofficial arrangements between enterprises ('I have a surplus of X, and will exchange it for Y', or, 'I will send you A if you promise not to let me down next month over B'), and even bribery. Specialists in such dealings as these are known in Russia as *tolkachi* ('pushers'). The personnel establishment of enterprises, which is determined by state authority, does not know such persons, who therefore nominally hold other positions. These semi-legal or illegal operations supplement and correct the official system, and it is often said that a Soviet director can hardly do his job without at least conniving at the breach of some law or regulation.[1] The wages bill, basic wage rates, personnel establishment and the rules governing incentive bonuses to management and men, are also laid down from above (see chapter 4).

The Soviet director appears at first sight to have little power, since he requires the sanction of his superiors for almost any decision of consequence and is subject to their orders in all matters. Such a view would be somewhat misleading. We have already noted that even highly centralized material supply can be influenced by requests from enterprises. The same is, in varying degrees, true also of other matters nominally outside the responsibility of the director. It is also wrong to imagine that he is, or indeed can be, told exactly what he should do. For example, it is often impracticable to specify in the plan the detailed assortment of the product. The various aspects of

[1] For more on *tolkachi*, see chapter 7.

the plan may be inconsistent with one another. Plans for gross output, profit, cost reduction, wages bill, materials allocation and orders received from customers cannot be expected to be fully coherent, giving the director room for choice and for manoeuvre. There will be occasion in chapter 6 to quote many examples of the effects on the operation of the economy of the *de facto* autonomy of the enterprise, of the number of decisions taken, or affected, for better or for worse, at enterprise level. The Soviet system involves a complex interaction between the planner-administrators on the one hand and the productive enterprises on the other; the former are in command, frame the rules and must be obeyed when they issue clear and direct orders on any subject, yet much that happens in Soviet microeconomics is explicable only by the existence of loopholes in the system of rules and orders. In fact, these 'loopholes' are essential, because the planners desire to stimulate initiative at the grass roots, and so 100 per cent centralization would be regarded as undesirable even if it were physically possible.

OTHER STATE ENTERPRISES

The above analysis has been concerned primarily with state industrial enterprises, but these general accounting and operating principles are common to state enterprises in general. However, certain peculiarities of non-industrial sectors call for brief comment.

Construction enterprises are of two types. The first, dominant in the 'thirties but now of less importance, is created *ad hoc* to do a given building job, by the organization for whom the job is being done. The nearest English equivalent would be the building of houses by 'direct labour', i.e. by a municipality directly. This species of building is known rather oddly as being done *khozyaistvennym sposobom*, literally 'by economic means'. The building unit undertaking the work possesses little or no working capital, since it only lives a temporary life. It has other financial peculiarities, into which it is unnecessary to go.

Most common is a building enterprise, carrying out work on contract (*podryadnym sposobom*). This is a true enterprise, with the degree of financial autonomy enjoyed by industrial enterprises in general, with working capital and other attributes of *khozraschyot*. They receive payment from their customers for building work. The customer could be another enterprise, or the building order may be placed by a *sovnarkhoz* or ministry.

In many localities, especially in large cities, there grew up a large number of construction enterprises, great and small, owing allegiance to many different organizations and ministries. To assure a necessary degree of co-ordination, a number of trusts were set up grouping together for operational purposes all the building enterprises located in certain large cities. Examples are Mosstroi (Moscow), Lenstroi (Leningrad), Kievstroi (Kiev).

Some construction enterprises make or procure some of their own materials, and to this extent contribute to industrial production in its Soviet definition. By contrast, many industrial enterprises carry out their own maintenance and repairs to buildings with their own labour, usually with a very primitive technology.

State farms (sovkhozy) for many years received very large subsidies. Thus in 1953 the subsidy of 4·6 milliard roubles amounted to 48·3 per cent of the cost of the product which state farms delivered to the state.[1] However, from 1956 they have generally made a profit, and they are permitted to retain a large portion of this. State farms sell produce to state wholesalers, except that they sometimes sell also to collective-farms (for example, pedigree livestock, tested seeds) and also direct to the retail trade network (notably vegetables). As state-owned enterprises, in which peasants become wage-earners, state farms are considered ideologically superior to collective-farms, and, as can be seen from the table on page 29 above, their numbers and relative importance have been growing. A variant of state agriculture to which the designation *sovkhozy* is not strictly applicable are the 'subordinate enterprises' (*podsobnye khozyaistva*) which are run by industrial and other state organizations, mainly to supply the factory canteen and store. There are many thousands of such agricultural productive units, mostly quite small but of appreciable magnitude in the aggregate.

A unique form of state organization in agriculture were the MTS (Machine Tractor Stations). The past tense is used because they are disappearing. Their role was closely linked with collective-farms and will be discussed with them (page 46, below). Their uniqueness lies in the fact that they were not based on 'economic accounting' but were wholly budget-financed, the only important form of economic enterprise on this financial basis. The reasons for this state of affairs will emerge in the course of the examination of the collective-farm system.

Trade and material supply organizations derive their revenues from authorized trading margins. The larger part of their activities

[1] S. Nedelin, *Finansy SSSR*, No. 10/1957, p. 35.

are predetermined by plans handed down to them from above, but, like other state enterprises, they are expected to use their initiative in making applications to wholesaling and superior supply organizations, reflecting as far as possible the requirements of the purchasers, though this at times conflicts with the fulfilment of plans expressed in aggregate turnover. Trade and supply questions will repeatedly arise in subsequent analysis; at this stage it is sufficient to distinguish between organizational forms in retail trade, which might otherwise confuse the issue. Since the outlawing of private trade at the end of the 'twenties (except for the free or *kolkhoz* market), there have been two principal categories of retail outlets: state and 'consumer-co-operative'. The latter were confined to rural areas in 1935, and their urban network transferred to the state; consumer-co-operative activities in towns have been confined to the sale there of farm surpluses (in 1946-49, and again, on commission, after 1953) at and just below free-market prices. Their primary task has been to operate shops and stalls in villages. They are nominally co-operatives, in the sense that the bulk of rural householders (over 33 million of them) each hold one share and are entitled to 'dividends' which must not exceed 20 per cent of total profits. In 1956 there were 21,000 consumer-co-operative associations, controlling 270,000 small retail outlets.[1] At their head is a central union of consumer-co-operatives, known as *Centrosoyuz*. But here the resemblance to a co-operative ceases. They act in practice as the rural branch of the state retail network. Trade plans are state-determined, managers are in fact state-appointed (though, at the lower levels, owing nominal allegiance to the consumer associations), employees are included in all statistics with state-employed persons. These 'co-operatives' run minor industrial enterprises, notably rural bakeries, and these are treated as state and not co-operative in statistics of labour and of output. Finally, these 'co-operatives' have been used by the state to sell a wide range of producers' goods to collective-farms, and to act on the state's behalf as purchasers of farm produce.

State shops proper, in urban areas, are generally run by the trading departments of local soviets, commonly known by the abbreviation *torg*, and/or by republican or even all-union trading organizations; the repeated and complex changes in subordination of shops cannot be described here.[2] The normal state store is available to all

---

[1] For a useful account of the situation, see *40 let sovetskoi torgovli* (Moscow, 1957).

[2] See E. Lomatovski and G. Gromova, *Upravlenie gosudarstvennoi vnutrennei torgovli SSSR* (Moscow, 1957). See also chapter 2, below.

the public, but there have at various times been 'closed' stores, reserved to particular groups of employees. These survive in the form of so-called 'workers' supply departments' (known by the initials ORS, *Otdel Rabochevo Snabzheniya*), which sell canteen meals and other goods to employees of particular factories. There are also military canteens. Their turnover is included in the statistics with state trade.

Transport enterprises raise few structural problems peculiar to the USSR. The railways are organized in a manner similar to that of West European countries. *Aeroflot* functions in a way very reminiscent of nationalized undertakings which run other countries' airlines. Perhaps the only point of difficulty is road transport, where one encounters the problem of the specialized haulage organizations *versus* the ownership of lorries by the user enterprise. In recent years, the policy has been in favour of developing lorry 'pools' to serve many different enterprises, especially in large cities. Trams, buses and taxis are operated by local authorities. Some transport services in rural areas are provided on hire by collective-farms, and here and there one encounters a lively but illegal ('pirate') taxi service. The charges levied by all state-enterprise providers of transport services are fixed by the state; there is a high degree of centralization of decision, applying even to the tram fares in all the towns of the Soviet Union.

Service undertakings of many kinds (baths, laundries, pawnshops, etc.) are organized by local authorities on a *khozraschyot* basis. State-owned *housing* either 'belongs' to the local soviet, or to other state enterprises or institutions (for example, factories, building organizations, even the Academy of Sciences, erect and administer housing space). Rents are centrally fixed at a low level, far too low to cover running costs and repairs, and substantial housing subsidies are the rule. Housing space is severely rationed, there being a very serious shortage.

Finally, there is one further special category of state enterprise: this is the *foreign trade corporation* (*Vneshtorgovoe ob'yedinenie*). The USSR has, since its earliest years, reserved all foreign trade dealings to state organs. After a period of experiment, there were set up trade corporations specializing in the export and/or import of particular commodities, under the general control of the Ministry of Foreign Trade. For example, *Exportles* sells timber, *Exportkhleb* sells grains and also (despite its name) purchases it. There are roughly two dozen such corporations, some specializing on imports, some on exports, but mostly on both. For any particular commodity, [one corporation always has a monopoly position.[1] No detailed description of their functioning, or of their relations with Soviet commercial-diplomatic representations or foreign businessmen will be attempted here.[2] The corporations are autonomous enterprises, which, acting within the plan, buy abroad and sell to wholesalers and productive enterprises within the USSR, or place orders with Soviet enterprises and wholesalers for goods which they sell abroad. The corporations, in other words, act as intermediaries in all foreign trade matters. No ordinary Soviet enterprise has the right to import or export, save through one of these corporations.

CO-OPERATIVE ARTISANS

Through the 1920's and especially in the early 'thirties, the government sought to discourage the private artisan, by fiscal and other pressures, and to make them join producers' co-operatives, and these remained until 1960, a significant, though diminishing, sector of economic activity. These co-operatives undertook a wide range of production, such as making clothes, furniture, musical instruments and a variety of other consumers' goods. They also ran workshops for repairs, and sometimes also retail outlets for the sale of their own produce to the public. The co-operatives' capital assets are not provided free by the state; they may be expanded out of profits, or credits can be sought from the banking system. Unlike the collective farms (which, as will be seen, have no profit and loss account), the producers' co-operatives base their operations on the payment of what is in effect a wage to their members. Depreciation and current productive expenses are charged against cost. The balance represents the profit, and this is subject to taxation at a steeply rising rate: thus if profits are below 5 per cent of production costs the tax is 20 per cent, and this rises steeply, so that profits exceeding 15 per cent of costs are charged 90 per cent.[3]

The precise rules governing utilization of retained profits were frequently altered, and partly depend on a vote taken at a meeting of members. The following was 'recommended' in 1955: 45 per cent at least should be allocated to the basic fund of the co-operative (i.e.

---

[1] Except that the all-union-consumer co-operative centre (*Centrosoyuz*) makes small-scale barter agreements covering commodities which also fall within the competence of other corporations.

[2] Readers are referred to A. Nove and D. Donnelly, *Trade with Communist Countries* (Hutchinson, 1960).

[3] E. Perikov, *Analiz khozyaistvennoi deyatel'nosti promyslovoi arteli* (Moscow, 1956), p. 136.

available for expanding fixed or working capital), 20 per cent should be transferred to a general co-operative fund for the provision of long-term credits to those co-operatives which require them, and 'up to 20 per cent' may be used to pay out bonuses to members, in proportion to the basic wages they received for their work.[1]

Producers' co-operatives may employ up to 20 per cent of non-members in the capacity of ordinary wage earners. Some have in fact employed more than this. These non-member employees play no part in the running of the co-operative workshop, which is in the hands of the members' meeting and of persons elected at the meeting. One characteristic of many co-operatives is that many members do their work in their own homes.

These co-operatives do not, as a rule, receive any allocation of scarce materials from state sources, but must rely primarily on locally-procured materials, by-products, sub-standard or rejected materials, and so on. Their output plans are each confirmed by the local council of co-operatives (*promsovet*), which is nominated by the co-operatives in the given *oblast'*. This council has also the right to decide selling prices, which are often well above official retail prices for the same commodities. Thus, for instance, 'in the Tatar autonomous republic the price of iron spades made by producers' co-operatives was fixed at 8·50 roubles, whereas better-quality state manufactured spades sell at 3 roubles'.[2]

Until 1956, there was an all-union body, nominally representative of the *oblast'* co-operative councils, known as *Centropromsovet*, which issued general guidance to co-operatives and sought to integrate their production plans with the economy as a whole. In 1956 the all-union council was abolished, and republican councils are now the top bodies, in line with the general tendency to transfer control over industry of local significance to republican bodies. The same decree[3] transferred large co-operative workshops to the status of local industry, that is, they ceased to be co-operatives and became 'nationalized'. This reduced the number of co-operative artisans from 1·8 to 1·2 million.[4] Finally it appears that they were all but wholly 'nationalized' in 1960, and no longer exist to any appreciable extent.[5]

[1] Perikov, op. cit., p. 138.
[2] Quoted from Decree of Council of Ministers of USSR, November 20, 1948.
[3] Decree of Council of Ministers and the Central Committee of the Communist Party of April 14, 1956.
[4] *N.Kh. 1956*, p. 203.
[5] *Pravda*, January 26, 1961, reports that 1·4 million members of producers' co-operatives became state employees during 1960.

It will be seen that the producers' co-operatives have (or had) many more features of autonomy and of genuine co-operation than have the collective-farms, though the latter share the same juridical status.

THE COLLECTIVE-FARM (KOLKHOZ)

The collective-farm is nominally a form of co-operative. The peasants of a given village or group of villages join together to cultivate land in common, under an elected management committee headed by an elected chairman. We shall see that reality is far removed from this definition, but it is legally valid and certain important organizational and financial peculiarities stem from the 'co-operative' nature of these *kolkhozy*.[1]

It is impossible to understand the nature and evolution of collective-farms without considering the political-social background, which has had a much deeper influence on structure than has been the case in industry. Thus the shape of the basic productive unit in industry, a factory, is largely predetermined by sheer technical necessities, and factories in Russia and in the West are in many respects similar. But there has been nothing like a collective-farm outside the Soviet bloc. For this reason, they have to be considered here in somewhat greater detail than other economic organizations.

After the revolution, the bulk of the land remained in the possession of private peasants. A small area was cultivated by state farms, and peasants were also encouraged to engage in joint productive activities of various kinds but the peasants remained obstinately attached to private farming. In 1927, all the various forms of state and co-operative farming covered a mere 2 per cent of the peasants.[2] But in 1928 came the launching of the first five-year plan. To carry it through, Stalin's government needed assured supplies of food for the towns, and exportable surpluses to pay for machinery for industrialization. They needed labour to move from village to town. They needed finance for investment, and, in a market situation favourable to the peasant seller, they were anxious to obtain produce without having to pay the full market price. Experience in the period

---

[1] *Kolkhoz* (plural *kolkhozy*) is the Russian abbreviation of the two words *kolletivnoye khozyaistvo*, literally 'collective economy'. The word *artel'*, a peculiarly Russian term designating a team of men working together in a self-governing group, was and is also used to describe this general organizational form. The term *kolkhoz* is also used to describe a significant group of fishing co-operatives, whose members also cultivate some land.

[2] N. Jasny, *The Socialized Agriculture of the USSR* (Stanford University Press, 1949), p. 779, citing official data.

of war-communism suggested to them that no attempt to squeeze the peasants could succeed so long as land and produce was in peasant hands.[1] For this reason, and also on general ideological-political grounds (that the individual peasant is a 'petty-bourgeois' force hostile to socialism), it was decided to eliminate the individual peasant as quickly as possible as an economic force. This was achieved by coercion (notably by deportations on a mass scale of richer peasants and opponents of collectivization generally) and by fiscal and administrative pressures of many kinds. It is not possible here to go into the history of collectivization, and it seems hardly necessary to stress that by giving reasons for the policy pursued one is not for a moment arguing that the policy was reasonable. The point is that the structure of *kolkhozy* and the relationship between them, the peasants and authority cannot be understood unless one bears in mind the circumstances in which, and the purposes for which *kolkhozy* were created by a 'revolution from above'. After a period of experiment, in which the attempt to collectivize the bulk of private livestock ended in disaster (a large proportion of the animals were slaughtered by the peasants), a species of compromise was arrived at within the collective between interests of the farm and of its members, which became enshrined in the Collective-farm Statute of 1935, which lasted with only little change until 1957.

Under this statute, the collective-farm is a co-operative of peasants of the given village or group of villages, which occupies nationalized land[2] rent-free in perpetuity. Management is in the hands of a meeting of members; such meetings must be called to take important decisions affecting the work rules, membership and income distribution of the farm. The meeting elects a management committee and a chairman, the latter being the operational manager of the farm. He is assisted by a deputy or deputies, and also by an accountant. The peasants are organized for work purposes into 'brigades' each led by a 'brigadier'. A sub-unit of a brigade is known as a *zveno* ('link', or 'nucleus'). Until 1958, the power-driven machinery used by the farm remained in the possession of state Machine Tractor Stations (MTS), which were simultaneously service agencies carrying out work on contract, and supervisory agencies on behalf of the state. Each MTS had a political deputy-director (until 1953), or a party secretary based upon it (in 1953-57), for carryng out its poli-

---

[1] For the background to all this, see the excellent survey by A. Erlich: *The Soviet Industrialization Debate* (Harvard, 1960).

[2] All land was formally 'nationalized' in the USSR in November, 1917, but *de facto* ownership was the peasants' until collectivization.

tical-control functions. The MTS were partly staffed by their own employees, and partly used collective-farm peasants on a seasonal basis. The collective-farm paid for MTS work almost wholly by deliveries in kind, based on a valution of various operations, in terms either of a given quantity of produce or a stated share in the harvest. Exceptionally, payment was also made in money.

Thus collective-farm production involved the joint effort of the farm and a state-owned machinery operator, the MTS.

The average size of collective farms varied, and varies, widely by area; in general, they are bigger in the prairies of the south and east than in the forest-and-bog country of the north and west. It has also varied over time. Thus in 1949 there were over 250,000 collective farms, averaging 80 households and 453 hectares (about 1,150 acres) sown area each. Amalgamation in the following years reduced numbers by 1957 to 76,500, averaging 245 households and 1,696 hectares of sown area, and numbers fell further to 53,436 by the end of 1959.[1] The number of MTS never exceeded 9,000, so that each served many collective-farms.

The influence of the state and party was exerted through the MTS, but was (and is) also to be felt throughout the collective-farm sphere of operations. The 'election' of the chairman was in reality in the hands of the party secretary of the *oblast'* or *raion*, and they could and did repeatedly reprimand or dismiss him. The output plan, sowing plan, livestock plan, even the dates of sowing and harvesting, were decided by state or party authority and 'handed down' (the Russian verb is *spuskat'*) to the farm to be acted upon, though the extent and detail of the orders from above were modified in 1955. The basic duty of the collective-farm was to meet the state's compulsory delivery quota, and to hand over produce in payment for the services of the MTS. The quota was related until 1940 to the sown area under the given crop or to the number of animals owned; then the basis was changed to area of arable land. But, as Khrushchev stated,[2] this was in practice disregarded, because the local party and state authorities were themselves under pressure to meet delivery quotas imposed on their areas from above; in consequence, they often arbitrarily increased the delivery quotas of successful farms, in order to make up for the failures of the unsuccessful.

Subject to carrying out the requirements of higher authority concerning output and deliveries of produce, the collective-farm chair-

[1] Full details may be seen in *N.Kh. 1958*, pp. 494-7, and *Sel. Khoz. 1960*, p. 51.
[2] *Pravda*, September 15, 1953.

man and his colleagues have rather more control over their finances, operations and investments than do directors of state enterprises. This is due partly to the nature of agriculture, where local circumstances vary so very widely, and partly to the fact that the state's primary interest has been to obtain deliveries of produce, and, despite a large number of decrees and orders of many kinds, the planning authorities have not in fact attempted any very tight control over what the farms do, once the required deliveries have been made. This may be seen from the financial and operational structure of collective-farms, to which we will now turn.

Cash revenues of collective-farms arise from a number of activities, not all of them agricultural. Thus, collective-farms have engaged in small-scale industry. This has taken the form of producing cartwheels, minor implements, bricks, or in some cases of processing vegetables (e.g. pickling, canning), as well as miscellaneous handicrafts. Income is also obtained from providing transport services (e.g. loaning out horses and carts, or lorries, to other enterprises). These non-agricultural activities have in some areas been a major source of revenue: thus in the Moscow *oblast'* in 1937, 63 per cent of all revenues were non-agricultural.[1] The authorities from time to time took measures to restrict these activities, because they were deemed to distract the peasants from their primary agricultural tasks.[2] The distraction was doubtless due in large part to the very unattractive prices paid for agricultural produce, of which more in a moment. In more recent years the agricultural sources of income have been dominant, and, as the table shows, total revenues have been rising:

	(milliards of roubles)		
	1940	1950	1957
TOTAL REVENUES	20·7	34·2	95·2
of which:			
Sales of farm produce to state*	9·1	21·5	74·1
Sales of farm produce in market	7·3	9·1	13·6
Other revenues	4·3	3·6	7·5

Source: *N. Kh. 1958*, p. 498.

* Including consumer-co-operatives.

Sales to the state, until 1958, were of two kinds. Firstly, there were *compulsory deliveries* of produce, at a low (sometimes purely

[1] D. Abramov, *Vop. Ekon.*, No. 6/1957, p. 80.
[2] See, for example, the decree of the Council of People's Commissars of October 23, 1938, and the resolution of the 19th party congress (October, 1952).

nominal) price. Then, when this quota had been met, there were *over-quota purchases* by the state (*gosudarstvennye zakupki*) at higher prices. These over-quota sales were partly due to administrative pressure, in the many cases where the higher price was unattractive, and partly to *quid pro quo* inducements, in the form of state deliveries of scarce goods (or of goods at reduced prices) to those farms which made over-quota sales. In the case of industrial crops, this two-price arrangement bore a different designation, but was essentially similar. Thus a collective-farm selling cotton would undertake to sell its entire crop to the state, a given quantity being paid for at a low price, and additional quantities commanding a higher price. This arrangement was known as *kontraktatsia*. The level and principles of agricultural prices will be examined in greater detail on pages 136-141, below.

Mention must be made at this point of sales to consumer co-operatives, which act as *de facto* state agencies. In some years (e.g. 1946-49) they were empowered to purchase farm surpluses at free prices.[1] In others (1949-53, for example) they were limited to paying the prices applicable to over-quota sales. After 1953 they could buy from the farms for resale on free markets on a commission basis, at prices which were not fixed or limited by the state. These purchases by consumer-co-operatives are included in the revenues from sales to state agencies in the above table.

Then there is the *free or kolkhoz market* (*kolkhoznyi rynok*). Markets are maintained by the local authorities in all towns, and anyone may sell their produce there. While citizens may be observed selling non-agricultural commodities in these markets (such as home-made clothes-pegs, pictures and the like), the bulk of business is in foodstuffs. Collective-farms are among the principal sellers in these markets (though, as we will note, the peasants in their private capacity are more important). If there is a surplus of produce, after state needs have been met, then collective-farms can decide, if they wish, to sell them in the free market, at prices which have been generally much higher than any offered by the state. Farms located near big cities have often kept permanent stalls in the market precincts, and derive considerable incomes from these sales. There is scope here for enterprising chairmen; thus a prosperous farm near Alma Ata, visited by the author, sent vegetables and fruit to the free market of Novosibirsk, a distance of 1,000 miles. However, many farms have been unable to develop such trade owing to inadequate communications. The farms also obtain re-

[1] *40 let sovetskoi torgovli* (Moscow, 1957), p. 101.

venues from selling foodstuffs in villages, particularly to their own members, often at specially reduced prices.[1]

It must be emphasized that these free-market sales are within the discretion of the farm. For example, of a total output of 10,000 tons of potatoes, there may be 5,000 tons left after making deliveries to the state and providing seed potatoes for next year. This 5,000 tons can be used for fodder, for paying the peasants in kind (see below), or for free market sales, in proportions which are largely within the competence of the farm to decide. The only ruling on this subject is the frequently repeated injunction that the distribution in kind to the peasants should not be 'too large', in the sense of providing them with a surplus over their needs, which they might themselves take to the free market; but this in fact has often happened. A small amount must also be set aside for purposes of relief of aged and infirm members, since social insurance does not extend to collectivized peasants.

Thus the revenue of the collective-farm can be seen as consisting partly of the proceeds of sales (at different prices), and partly of produce used on the farm. Expenditures, similarly, are partly in money and partly also in kind.

There are no recent systematic statistics of the money expenditure of collective-farms. The following can be used as a basis for description.

Collective farm expenditures
(milliards of roubles)

	1938	1952	1956
TOTAL	16·60	42·8	94·6
of which:			
Taxes and insurance	1·58*	6·9	10·9
Capital fund contribution	2·32	7·4	16·7
Paid to peasants ('workdays')	8·70	12·4	42·2
Production expenses	3·25 ⎤		
Cultural fund	0·50 ⎬	16·1	24·7
Administration	0·25 ⎦		

Sources: A. Arina and T. Basyuk, cited in Jasny, *op. cit.*, p. 687.
N.Kh. 1958, p. 498.
Pravda, January 25, 1958.
Finansy SSSR, No. 10/1957, p. 34.

* Including repayment of past credits.

[1] Proceeds of these sales are included in statistics of revenues from market transactions of collective farms, but statistics of free-market turnover is confined to urban areas, and so excludes these 'village' transactions.

The basis of *taxes* has been several times altered. Until 1958 these were differentiated according to the source of revenue (e.g. they were especially high on proceeds from free-market sales), and also included a tax on the value of produce used on the farm, with some exemptions. From 1958, there is a standard rate, 14 per cent, on all cash and value of produce, excluding money spent on and produce used for certain productive purposes.[1] It is noteworthy that the tax is not levied on net income or on profits, however defined, but on the bulk of *gross* income. It is, therefore, a serious burden, as may be seen by relating it to the total payments to peasants.

Insurance is partly compulsory and partly voluntary. Collective-farms, unlike state enterprises, cannot expect to have their lost assets replaced at the expense of the budget, and are therefore bound to take out insurance against fire, natural disasters, etc.

The *capital fund* is officially entitled 'indivisible fund' (*nedelimyi fond*). Into it were paid the original contributions, in cash and in other assets, of the collectivized peasants. The total capital fund at any given moment covers the capital assets of the farm plus cash in the capital account. The annual contribution to the capital fund is laid down in regulations. It ranged for many years between $12\frac{1}{2}$ and 20 per cent of gross cash revenues (this has been increased in 1958, following the acquisition of MTS machinery). The money is earmarked for expenditures on building materials, tools, lorries and other capital goods, and also the salaries of outside persons employed on capital work. Since 1956[2] the allocation to the capital fund can also be used to pay for the labour of collective-farm peasants engaged on such work. In assessing the burden of the capital fund contribution, it is again necessary to stress that the amount is based on *gross* revenues, and the impact is therefore greater than it looks. Investment by collective-farms may also be financed by *credits* from the banking system. Unlike state enterprises, collective-farms do not receive capital assets free. There is (so far) no amortization or depreciation fund in collective-farms, and the equivalent of 'capital repairs' seems to be financed out of the capital fund.

Production expenses largely speak for themselves; they include fuel, fertilizer, fodder, seeds and the like, and also payments to outsiders hired for operational purposes. It is important to note that most commodities bought by collective-farms are obtainable only at

[1] Full details in A. Nove, 'Rural Taxation in the USSR', *Soviet Studies*, October, 1953, and, for the reformed version, see *Vedomosti Verkhovnovo Soveta*, September 21, 1957.

[2] Decree of March 6, 1956, printed in *Direktivy KPSS . . .*, Vol. 4, pp. 603-5.

retail prices, which are generally higher than those charged to state enterprises for the same items.

The *cultural fund* is used for books, newspapers, the running of a clubhouse and similar objects. Up to 2 per cent of gross revenue may be devoted to it, under the model statute.

Administrative expenses include stamps, stationery, telephone, and also money salaries of administrative personnel. Total expenses under this head are limited to 2 per cent of revenue by the model statute, but this figure has often been exceeded.

When all the above expenditures have been met, the remainder is available for distribution to the peasants, along with produce set aside for the same purpose. This cash and produce is then paid to peasants in proportions determined by their contribution to the work of the farm. The proportions were (and mostly still are) measured in conventional work units (*trudodni*, literally 'workdays'). All work in farms is graded in these *trudodni*, piecework being widely used. This intricate system will be examined in detail later on (p. 121, below). At this stage it is sufficient to emphasize two aspects of this method of payment. Firstly, it involves no definite scale of payment. The amount available (in cash and kind), divided by the total number of *trudodni* earned, determines the earnings per unit of work. It is because the amount available could not be known in advance that the *trudodni* system was invented. Secondly, there was (and in most of the USSR still is) no fixed or minimum scale of payment.[1] The amount distributed was not a wage, it was a residual. It is true that it was within the competence of the farm to vary some items of expenditure to some extent; for instance, it could decide to buy less fertilizer, or feed fewer potatoes to pigs, in order to make more money and potatoes available as payment for *trudodni*. However, this only partially modified the 'residual' essence of peasant rewards for their work. Wage payments are among the first calls on the revenue of any state enterprise in the USSR, or any enterprise in the west. But in collective-farms the peasant share is what remains when other requirements have been met, and, in most farms at least until 1958, the payments to peasants were irregular, often occurring only once or twice a year, as well as varying very widely from year to year and from farm to farm. It is also worth noting, as the above table makes abundantly clear, that the share of the peasants in gross revenues fell in post-war years, and was particularly low in 1952.

---

[1] Except that peasants employed for any period by the MTS were entitled to a minimum scale of payments while working for the MTS on collective-farm fields.

This system of payment has had three consequences. Firstly, an uncertain and generally inadequate reward for collective work necessitated the introduction (formally in 1939) of a *compulsory minimum* number of collective workdays for each able-bodied person. The minimum varied by area, and has tended to increase. Since 1956 each collective-farm is empowered to impose whatever minimum is necessary to carry out the necessary work. Secondly, the normal principles of economic accounting (*khozraschyot*) could not be applied to collective-farms, since, with payment of labour a residual, it was hardly possible to identify either the labour cost or the profit element (see chapter 6, below, for further discussion of this point). Thirdly, the peasants could not, in most of the USSR, obtain a livelihood by working for a collective, and so it was necessary to permit the peasants to possess a *household plot of land* and some livestock, which constitutes the most important private-enterprise sector in the Soviet economy (see page 57, below).

However, from the standpoint of the authorities, the system should be judged by reference to the objects for which it was brought into existence. The compulsory delivery system ensured that the state took its share of the produce and thus supplied the growing towns. The fact that it took this share at well below the equilibrium price provided a vital source of revenue, since this produce could be resold at much higher prices to the population. The residual nature of payment of peasants meant that they shouldered not only much of the burden of industrialization, but also of the year-by-year variations in the harvest. In a state-farm, the wages of the workers are a first charge on the revenue of the enterprise, and must be paid by the state if the enterprise makes a loss; in a collective-farm, the state has no responsibility to pay any given level of income, and any 'loss', which is in any case unidentifiable in the accounts of collective-farms, simply results in smaller distributions to members, i.e. is borne by the peasants. There will be much to say about the weaknesses of the system, but it must not be forgotten that these weaknesses are in part the consequence of organizing agriculture primarily with the object of obtaining at minimum cost the material and financial resources for industrialization. After Stalin's death in 1953, there were in fact a number of changes, designed to make the system work better. Thus prices paid by the state for farm produce were substantially increased, and some effort made to improve the planning and control system. In particular, the powers of the MTS were enhanced and there was a measure of decentralization. However, the basic pattern remained, until 1958.

In March, 1958, a law was adopted providing for the sale of machinery to the collective-farm and the abolition of the MTS over a short period of time. The reasons for this measure were essentially as follows. Firstly, the division of authority and responsibility (between the management of the farm and the machinery it used) caused unnecessary waste and much conflict. Not only were there 'two masters' in the fields, but their material interests were necessarily conflicting. The collective-farm was interested in maximizing the harvest and its net revenues in cash and kind. The MTS was rewarded by the authorities for carrying out its work plan (expressed in standard work units) and for earning produce in payment for its services; this encouraged it to carry out such work as was 'profitable' in respect of the above criteria, even if it was wasteful from all other points of view. The MTS were wholly budget financed, that is were not 'economic accounting' organizations. A decision to make them such was taken in 1953, but could not be implemented. The reason for this failure was, essentially, that the whole system of payments in kind, and indeed of MTS work, had no economic *rationale*. Thus, for instance, the payments in kind not only had no connection with the costs of the given MTS, but in a sense were inversely related to cost; they were higher in the south than in the north, though costs of operation were higher in the small fields of the north than in the southern plains.[1]

The higher level of payments in kind on the better lands of the south may be regarded as a disguised tax, or a species of land rent, but certainly it could have had no meaning as an economic measure of MTS activities. Thus no way was found to place each MTS on an economic basis. There was also no way of assessing the profitability of this or that machine or type of tractor, and no attempt was in fact made to do so. Machinery was centrally allocated to MTS, despite numerous complaints that it was often unsuitable to the requirements of the given area.[2] The inefficiencies of MTS operation had become a serious burden to the state, which had to cover their ex-

[1] This may be demonstrated in the following examples: in 1955 the MTS in the fertile Krasnodar region spent 301 roubles for every ton of grain received in payment in kind; by contrast, in Ryazan the MTS expenditures per ton of payments in kind were 1,149 roubles, and in Belorussia or the north they were higher still. Yet the scale of payment per conventional unit of tractor-work was 150 kilograms of grain in Krasnodar, but only 35 kilograms in Belorussia and 30 in Karelia. See S. Ilyin, *Gosudarstvennye zagotovki zerna* (Moscow, 1957), pp. 62 ff., and L. Kolychev, in *Voprosy sovetskikh finansov* (Moscow, 1956), p. 204.

[2] For a typical instance, *Pravda*, February 25, 1957, printed complaints from north-west Russia, to the effect that machines supplied were ill-adapted to their type of soil. Similar complaints were common in 1960.

penses out of the budget. Produce received as payments in kind, when measured against these expenses, appeared very dear. All these objections to the artificial separation of MTS and collective-farms were known for many years; for example, two economists, Sanina and Venzher, proposed to Stalin in 1951 that the machinery be transferred to the collective-farms.[1] The arguments of economic expediency were rejected; the MTS were still needed as state organs of control, and indeed in 1953 the powers of the MTS *vis-à-vis* the farms were actually increased. However, the anomalies of the relationship became abundantly obvious, while the mechanism of state and especially party control became strong enough to make it apparent that the MTS were unnecessary. There remained the ideological arguments that it was wrong to hand over state-owned assets to non-state ('co-operative') organizations, and that the payment-in-kind system was a higher, more 'socialist' form of exchange than straightforward buying and selling. But these ideological difficulties were overcome.[2]

The law of 1958 provided for the transfer to collective-farm employment of the staffs of the MTS, and for the purchase (usually on instalments) of the machinery by the collective-farms. It should be noted that the principle was maintained that non-state organizations must pay for their capital assets; state farms, like other state enterprises, received the bulk of their machinery free, but collective-farms must pay for theirs. The same law also provided for the setting up of a new species of state enterprise, the *Repair Technical Stations* (RTS), which were at first intended to sell machinery and spares to farms,[3] and at the same time to carry out major repairs and to hire out specialized machinery (e.g. for carrying out drainage work) of types which collective-farms would not find it economical to purchase. The RTS are not supposed to possess the control function which formerly resided in the MTS, and to operate on *khozraschyot*. At the time of writing, their role *vis-à-vis* collective-farms is the subject of debate, since many farms have set up their own workshops and avoid using those of the RTS. It seems that they will be merged with a new material supply organization in 1961.

The abolition of the MTS necessarily involved the state in buying from the farms the produce which was formerly handed over as pay-

[1] The proposal was discussed by Stalin in 1952. See his *Ekonomicheskie problemy sotsializma v SSSR* (Moscow, 1952), pp. 88-94.
[2] The necessary adjustments to theory were carried out by K. Ostrovityanov, in *Pravda*, March 3, 1958.
[3] A decree in 1960 removed this function from the RTS (*Pravda*, May 7, 1960).

ments in kind. Consequently, it was necessary to review prices. This was desirable also on general grounds, discussed in chapter 4, below. The wide 'spread' between the compulsory procurement (or basic *kontraktatsia*) price and the over-quota prices led to a number of undesirable consequences: successful or favourably situated farms were given a disproportionate bonus, since they had most to sell over the quota, while their less fortunate brethren were correspondingly depressed. In addition, the multiple-price system impeded economic calculation within farms. Consequently, in June, 1958, a decree[1] established new purchase prices for all farm products, differentiated by area. Farms henceforth would sell to the state at the one price applicable to the given product in their area. The details of the system of agricultural prices will be examined subsequently (see page 136).

The same decree abolished the compulsory procurement quota as a legal category, but this did not end the element of compulsion in deliveries to the state. Collective-farms continue to receive plans for deliveries, and must so arrange their productive activities as to fulfil these plans.

The organizational basis of collective farming is still in flux, since it remains in important respects economically and administratively unsatisfactory (see chapters 6 and 8). The trend at the time of writing is towards a shift in the status of *kolkhozy* and peasants nearer to that of *sovkhozy* and *sovkhoz* employees, though retaining many of the elements of greater operational autonomy which *kolkhozy* possess. There is talk of linking *kolkhozy* together into local, regional, conceivably even republican, associations to support each other financially, thus reducing or eliminating the very large differences which exist at present between financial resources and rewards for labour in different *kolkhozy*. There is also talk of resettling peasants from outlying hamlets into big, urban-type rural settlements, the *agrogorod* with which Khrushchev's name has for long been associated and which he advocated already in 1951.[2] Kolkhozy are being actively encouraged to use their revenues to rebuild villages, to build schools, clinics, roads. They are also urged to join together with neighbours to form *inter-kolkhoz enterprises,* which make bricks, operate small electric generating stations and so on, employing members of the participating *kolkhozy* and also some outsiders, and there appear to be changes in prospect in their relationship to

[1] Decree of Council of Ministers, *Pravda*, July 1, 1958.
[2] *Pravda*, March 4, 1951, but these ideas were officially disavowed at the time. He had organized some model *agrogorod* settlements in the Ukraine.

local planning organs. Another change in price policy was also foreshadowed, at the central committee plenum of December, 1959, this time in a downward direction. Thus we must be aware that, in analysing *kolkhozy,* we are dealing with a most unstable organizational form which is in process of active change.

THE PRIVATE SECTOR

By far the most important private economic activity in the Soviet Union is in agriculture. Neglecting the individual peasant, who is not now significant (see page 29, above), we must examine the two forms which this private agricultural sector takes: private plots of collectivized peasants, and private holdings of state employees.

The collective peasants' private plots are held by each household (*dvor*), as an entitlement under the 1935 model kolkhoz statute. Their size is normally ¼ hectare, sometimes higher where land is plentiful and/or of poor quality. There is also private livestock, with fixed maxima; usually the peasant household may possess one cow and one sow, with offspring, and some other animals also. The peasants benefit from *de facto* pasture rights in respect of their animals. In the first stages of collectivization (1930-32) an effort was made to collectivize all private livestock, with disastrous results. About half of the livestock was slaughtered. It was then decided to permit private ownership within collective farms of animals (other than horses and bulls, boars, etc., which could be used as a source of income from hire, though a very few horses remain in private hands).

Until 1958, peasants were subject to compulsory delivery quotas, at the low prices applicable to collective-farm deliveries. Before 1953, not only were the quotas exceedingly onerous, but the burden fell on the household regardless of whether or not they in fact produced the commodity in question. For instance, the milk deliveries had to be made even if there was no cow, and so the peasant was compelled to purchase milk, at whatever price it was necessary to pay, in order to deliver it to the state at a very low price. In 1953, the quotas were appreciably reduced. With effect from January 1, 1958, the compulsory delivery quotas on private plots of collective peasants and other private holdings (except for the few surviving individual peasants) were abolished altogether.

The reason for the burdening of private plots with delivery obligations was two-fold. In the first place, in many products the private sector predominated (see page 60, below), and, secondly, it was considered desirable to make the private sector relatively less profitable. This latter reasoning also operated in respect of the tax burdens on private plots. Whereas the receipts of the peasants from the collective-farm were and are untaxed, the private plot was assessed for a curious 'agricultural tax', which was based on the notional income delivered from private activity. The details of this tax were complex,[1] but in essence the basis of it was, until 1953, a valuation of area sown and livestock owned. For instance, a cow would be deemed to be 'worth' 2,400 roubles, a hundredth-hectare under potatoes— fifty roubles, and so on. These valuations were added together to represent the 'income' of the peasant from his private holding. This was then subject to tax on a sliding scale, which, in 1952 ranged from 12 to 48 per cent. The valuations and the tax scale were such as eventually to cause a net fall in production in the private sector, and this must have been the object of the authorities. No doubt it was believed that, by making private activities less attractive, the peasants could be persuaded to work for the collective-farms. However, since the latter paid so poorly at this period, the effect was to discourage all effort. Many households found themselves in a desperate situation: they were unable to live on what they received from the collective-farm, unable to pay the tax on their cow or pig, yet still liable to compulsory deliveries of milk and meat if they disposed of the cow or pig to avoid the tax.

In 1953, as part of the post-Stalin reforms, the 'agricultural tax' was much reduced, and its basis changed to land area actually held by the household, subject to regional variations.

The peasants can sell their surpluses in the free market. This they do on a large scale; for many years, they derived more income from this source than from any other. They also feed their families very largely from their private production, with the important exception of bread grains, which generally form the major part of payments in kind by the collective-farm. (In some areas specializing on industrial crops, as, for instance, in the cotton-fields of Uzbekistan, the bulk of collective-farm payment is in money, and the peasants buy bread or bread grains.)

The peasants generally take their own produce to market, thereby wasting a great deal of time on long journeys with a comparatively small quantity of goods. Millions of peasants waste millions of mandays in this extremely inefficient and primitive system of distribution. It is true that peasants can let the collective-farm arrange to take their produce to market for them, and there also exist sales on

[1] For detailed description, see A. Nove, 'Rural Taxation in USSR', *Soviet Studies*, October, 1953.

commission through the consumer-co-operatives. However, neither has so far replaced the peasant himself as a trader, to any decisive extent. This is due partly to lack of enterprise on the part (especially) of the consumer-co-operative organization, partly because of the peasants' inborn belief that they and no one else can strike a good bargain. The very great importance to peasants' welfare of this source of cash income causes them to exploit its possibilities very vigorously, often to the detriment of their work for the collective-farm. This has been a constant source of friction.

A decree in 1956 gave *kolkhozy* the right to diminish the private holdings of members who do not work when required for the *kolkhoz*.

In 1959, pressure to sell livestock to the collective-farm and to reduce private plots began gradually to be effective; private livestock numbers fell significantly. In 1960 this process continued. Both from the standpoint of ideological principle, and for the purpose of organizing collective-farm labour on a regular and full-time basis, the private sector is a nuisance, which the Soviet leaders hope to subject to a gradual process of erosion.

State-employed persons' plots and allotments are to be found in all rural areas, and also in or near many towns. State-farm workers, railwaymen, even 'rural intelligentsia' (teachers, local officials, etc.) very commonly cultivate a small plot and possess some livestock, if only because the villages are so poorly supplied with shops. Many urban citizens, especially in smaller provincial towns, grow potatoes and vegetables and keep a small number of animals on allotments. These private holdings were also, until 1958, burdened with compulsory delivery quotas, and (with some exemptions) were and are subject to 'agricultural tax'. The government at first encouraged these private productive activities, since they relieved pressure on food supplies. They grew enormously during the war. However, in recent years the attitude has changed, in so far as these holdings distract the state worker, and even more his wife and family, from regular work. There were instances of private 'suburban' livestock being fed with bread, so as to fatten them to take advantage of the relatively higher price of meat. As a result, measures have been taken in 1958-59 to limit livestock ownership in urban areas, and state-farm employees have had to dispose of their cows.[1]

The relative importance of private activities in agricultural production has been particularly great in the livestock sector. The fol-

---

[1] Khrushchev's speech, *Stenograficheski otchyot*, Central committee plenum, December, 1958 (Moscow, 1958), pp. 54-5.

lowing table shows that it was still substantial in 1957, though no longer as dominant as in past years:

Per cent of total output of USSR

	1940	1950	1957
MEAT, total private	72*	67	53
of which:			
Collective-farm peasants	(46)	(50)	(39)
MILK, total private	77*	75	54
of which:			
Collective-farm peasants	(44)	(51)	(37)
EGGS, total private	94*	89	86
of which:			
Collective-farm peasants	(58)	(61)	(57)

Source: *Zhivotnovodstvo SSSR* (Moscow, 1959), pp. 161–9.

* Includes 'abnormal' number of individual peasants in newly-annexed areas. These are not significant in other years.

Clearly, these percentages are destined to continue falling. In terms of actual output, the private sector revived somewhat in the years 1953-58, following the relaxation of Stalin's policy of heavy taxation. However, there was a clear downward turn thereafter. Thus while Soviet agriculture remains based on a species of compromise between state, collective and private sectors, so that a substantial portion of the labour force has private economic interests to pursue, the balance is changing appreciably, and it is official policy to continue the process of change.

Little need be said about *non-agricultural private economic activities*. Artisans, seamstresses, shoe repairers and the like are permitted a precarious existence, subject to discriminatory rates of income tax (see chapter 3, below). There have been many reports of semi-legal gangs (*arteli*) of building labourers hiring themselves out in rural areas. There are also a wide range of other semi-legal or illegal economic activities: unlicensed taxis, 'speculation' of many kinds, and so on. Judging from things seen in Georgia, for instance, there must be a sizeable volume of unrecorded and quite unofficial economic transactions. Another source of private income is rent from letting rooms in privately-owned dwelling houses, which is legal unless the house-owner has acquired housing-space in excess of need in order to derive the major part of his income from rents, in which case action is taken against him.

CHAPTER 2

Administration, Planning, Policy Decision

INTRODUCTION: THE NATURE OF THE TASK

So far we have been considering the nature and organization of economically active enterprises. Now we pass to an examination of the ways by which the political, administrative and planning organs control and direct these enterprises, and thereby the economic life of the Soviet Union. There must be a flow of operational orders to enterprises, plans must be devised for various sectors and co-ordinated with those of other sectors. The orders given to enterprises about what to produce must be backed by the necessary material supplies, and the output plans must, of course, be related to the planned inputs. Every economic decision is interconnected with a great many other decisions, or involves a number of necessary consequential effects. Therefore, the situation appears to call for an all-knowing and all-seeing Planner, whose brain takes decisions in full awareness of all the relevant alternatives and of all the consequences of his acts. However, such a Planner cannot exist, outside the imagination of model-builders or of over-simplifying writers of textbooks. The tasks must be divided, and each possible arrangement of planning and operational powers involves its own set of advantages and disadvantages, solving some difficulties and creating others, a fact familiar to the management of large firms in the west. We should distinguish between several major aspects of organization. The first category lays stress on industrial *sector*; the process of planning and control is then based on the particular industry (e.g. textiles, metallurgy, coal), with general co-ordination between industries at government level. The second is often referred to as *functional*: powers are given to functional bodies, concerned on a national scale with supplies, labour, investment, wholesaling and so on, which give orders within the scope of their responsibility to subordinates in the industrial hierarchy. Finally, there is the *territorial* principle, which would devolve planning and operational powers to regional authorities. It must be emphasized from the beginning that none of these categories are ever present in pure form. Thus planning and control

61

which operate 'functionally' or territorially must involve separate consideration of the problems of each industry in some office in Moscow, headed by an official; the office may have the status of a branch of some larger organization, such as Gosplan, or possess the dignity of a 'ministry', but it is impossible to do away with it altogether. In any conceivable organizational arrangement, co-ordination between functions, industries and regions, between output plans and investment, between production and material supplier, and so forth, will present difficulties; these difficulties find their administrative expression in the creation of offices and departments to deal with them. None the less, the basis of organization chosen does make an appreciable difference to the chain of command, to the levels at which decision-making on various matters takes place, and to the weight given to certain species of problems within the planning machine; this should become apparent in the following pages.

v s n k h (Vesenkha)

Created as early as December, 1917, with the object of controlling economic life in what was still expected to be a largely privately-run economy, was the Supreme Council of National Economy, known by its Russian initial letters as vsnkh or Vesenkha. With the nationalization of the bulk of industry and trade, vsnkh became possessed of operational powers over the economy, subject to guidance by the government,[1] in which the chairman of vsnkh played a prominent role. In the NEP period, and especially in the years 1922-27, a large part of industry and trade was in private hands, and vsnkh was in charge of the state's economic activities, both in the field of industrial production and of wholesale trade. Its internal organization was repeatedly altered, and, as the recital of these changes would occupy much space without adding significantly to understanding, no attempt will be made here to list them. Essentially, vsnkh was sub-divided into two species of departments: functional and industrial-sector. The former dealt with such matters as finance, planning, economic policy, development and research, and the like. The latter, under a 1926 decree,[2] consisted of 'chief departments' (*glavnye upravleniya,* or *glavki*) for separate industries, and in them

---

[1] That is, of the Council of People's Commissars, and of its powerful Council of Labour and Defence (*Soviet Truda i Oborony*, sto). Both were advised on long-term planning questions by Gosplan, founded in 1921, of which more below.
[2] Decree of Council of People's Commissars of August 24, 1926, and Order of vsnkh of September 4, 1926.

must be seen the germs of the future economic ministries. The coverage and number of the *glavki* was several times altered, and for a time they became known as *ob'yedineniya* (associations), and then again as *glavki,* without changing their essence appreciably. The heads of all the various departments formed the actual council of VSNKh, together with representatives of the union republics, in each of which there was a similar body, which was collectively subordinate to the all-union VSNKh. There were also regional economic councils, known by the abbreviation *sovnarkhozy.* In practice, enterprises of all-union significance (i.e. any large-scale industry) were administered by the appropriate *glavk* of the all-union VSNKh, subject only to occasional representations from republican or provincial councils on matters of local interest. However, minor industries, using local sources of materials and supplying local markets, operated under the direct control of the republican VSNKh and/or local *sovnarkhozy.*

Large-scale industry under VSNKh was organized for production, planning and accounting purposes into *Trusts,* which consisted of enterprises producing similar commodities, generally in some limited geographical area. In exceptional cases where enterprises were very large, they were directly subordinated to the appropriate *glavk* of VSNKh, without any intermediate Trust. Wholesaling was the responsibility of so-called 'syndicates' (*sindikaty*).

Under this system, despite the nominal powers of the republics and local authorities, a high degree of centralization was achieved. Co-ordination between the various functional and industrial-sector departments was supposed to be assured by including them all within one super-department, VSNKh. However, not for the first or last time, it was discovered that co-ordination is not necessarily achieved by placing the co-ordinees under one organizational umbrella. Departments A, B and C are not always easier to manage, or to keep in step with one another, if they are labelled A1, A2 and A3. In the end, especially after the launching of the first five-year plan (1928-29), the common problems of industrial sectors became so large and so urgent as to require a separate organization, with its own functional divisions, to cope with them. After some experimental changes in the VSNKh structure in the years 1929-30, VSNKh was finally abolished altogether by the decree of January 5, 1932. Trusts gradually ceased to be significant in most branches of industry, save where they provided a convenient geographical administrative grouping of several enterprises within the same productive complex.

THE RISE OF THE 'MINISTERIAL' SYSTEM

In 1932, three industrial People's Commissariats (Ministries) were created: heavy, light and timber industries. Their numbers grew rapidly. By 1939 there were twenty of them. The all-time maximum was reached in 1946-48, when they (industrial and construction ministries alone) numbered thirty-two. After a drastic reduction immediately after Stalin's death to eleven, there was another expansion in 1954, and at the end of 1956 there were thirty-one industrial (including construction) ministries. Once again, there is no need to trace the very numerous changes in numbers, coverage and designation. It is sufficient to examine the essence of the system, which may be seen from a brief look at the features common to an industrial ministry.

A typical ministry was divided into a number of departments or chief departments (*glavki*), some of which were responsible for functional aspects (finance, supplies, investment, labour, etc.), some for sub-divisions of the given industrial sector (e.g. oilfields of a given area within the Petroleum Industry Ministry, or woollens within the Ministry of Textile industry). Enterprises were, as a rule, subordinate to a *glavk* or 'their' Ministry.[1] They received their plans from the *glavk*, submitted their applications for materials and investment funds to the *glavk*. The ministry had its own supplies and disposals organizations. In some instances these powers were exercised through identically-named ministries (and *glavki*) of the union republics, i.e. through the so-called union-republican ministries (page 25, above), in others—the vast majority in the Stalin period—the republican authorities were totally by-passed, the line of subordination stretching straight from the enterprise to the *glavk* of the appropriate ministry in Moscow, regardless of the republic in which the enterprise was located. However, in the period 1955-56 there was a considerable move to strengthen the republican ministers' functions.

Many of the changes made when the numbers of ministries were increased or decreased consisted in promoting an existing *glavk* to the status of a ministry, or on the contrary 'demoting' it. Thus the Textile Ministry sometimes existed independently, and sometimes formed part of the Ministry of Light Industry, while in 1954-55 some *glavki* which, within existing ministries, were responsible for building operations were 'promoted' to ministerial rank (e.g. Ministry of

---

[1] In some instances, notably in the coal and fisheries industries, there were and are intermediate organizations, e.g. a *kombinat* covering a coalfield and *Trusts* grouping together a number of adjacent coal mines, or a *kombinat* grouping the fisheries of Kamchatka.

Construction of Coal Industry Enterprises and several others). This last reform was due to a growing concern for the special problems of construction, and these 'building' ministries were supervised by a State Committee on Construction, which was (and is) headed by a deputy-premier.

The Minister, his senior deputies and his heads of chief departments (who commonly bear the title of Deputy Ministers), together with a few other high officials, form the *collegium* of the Ministry, which meets regularly to transact business. Both the Minister and the Deputy-Ministers must be seen essentially as senior business executives or civil servants, not as politicians in the western sense; they are often promoted managers, with an engineering or technical background. They are technical executants, not policy-makers. When ministries became numerous, especially in the post-war period, it became customary to appoint senior party leaders as 'overlords', to supervise groups of ministries; these leaders held the rank of deputy-premier. Immediately after Stalin's death, no doubt because of the need to tighten control in the aftermath of that dictator's disappearance, party leaders became Ministers themselves, which explains the sudden reduction in numbers of ministries in 1953. They resumed their supervisory functions in 1954, and so the number of ministries returned to 'normal' levels.

Because of the activities of each ministry in ensuring or manufacturing supplies and components for 'its' enterprises, and also the habit of making consumers' goods out of by-products in many sectors of 'heavy' industry, the product coverage of ministries was often extremely heterogeneous.

Obviously, the existence of a large number of economic ministries, each controlling their own national network of productive enterprises and supply and disposal agencies, placed a heavy burden on the co-ordinating function. The *power* of co-ordinating plans and operational decisions resided in the government itself, and in its economic committee or economic cabinet, which was known until 1937 as the Council of Labour and Defence, and from 1937 to the war as the Economic Council (*Ekonomsovet*). After the war, it appears to have faded out. So unwieldy a body as the whole Council of Ministers was certainly unable to co-ordinate, and some evidence exists that an inner cabinet (or 'praesidium of the Council of Ministers'), composed of the premier and the deputy-premiers (the 'overlords'), took the necessary decisions. The body which carried out the work of co-ordinating, and drafted plans, was Gosplan; it had no powers to *order* any ministry to do anything, but its submissions appear to have been the basis of government decisions, the more so as it was intimately linked with the central committee of the party.

PLANNING AGENCIES BEFORE 1957

Before discussing the ending of the 'ministerial' system in 1957, it is necessary to refer to the development of the planning agencies, and notably of Gosplan. This body was founded in 1921 under the title of 'State general-planning commission' attached to the Council of Labour and Defence. Until the end of the 'twenties, it was essentially a body concerned with the elaboration of long-term plans, often of a somewhat abstract character. The practical planning, such as it was, fell to the planning department of VSNKh. When the first five-year plan was being drawn up in 1928, the Party's crash programme of industrialization was resisted by the moderate (and very able) economists of Gosplan. Several of these were former mensheviks, and their courage in sticking to their point of view led to their being removed.[1] Gosplan was reorganized, and, following the elimination of VSNKh, çame to play an essential role of co-ordination within the government. Its head usually possessed the rank of deputy-premier. During the 1930's, Gosplan absorbed the Central Statistical Office.[2] Gosplan was responsible for drafting short-term and long-term plans, for allocation of materials and also for developing new techniques. In each instance, these functions were limited by the existence of the ministries. Thus the drafting of plans for enterprises in, for example, the Ministry of Ferrous Metallurgy was the job of the planning department of that ministry. Gosplan's job was to calculate the material needs inherent in the general development programme designed by the political leaders, that is, to draw up so-called 'material balances', which form the basis both of long-term investment planning and of general governmental directives to the ministries, and also to plan material supplies and deliveries (see page 79, below).

In 1948-49, Gosplan, headed by the powerful Nikolai Voznesenski, ran into serious trouble. Its precise nature is by no means clear even today. Voznesenski was arrested and executed, for reasons

[1] V. G. Groman was a leading defendant in a show trial of mensheviks in 1931. The world-famous economist Kondratieff vanished at the same time. Neither has been heard of again, though Kondratieff's name appears to this day on the list of Fellows of the Econometric Society.
[2] This was known from 1931 by the clumsy abbreviation TsUNKhU, which stood for Central department of economic accounting, the word 'statistics' being considered temporarily too bourgeois, since statistics suggests measuring random and uncontrolled events; the term Statistics was restored in 1941. See A. Yezhov, *Soviet Statistics* (in English) (Moscow, 1957), pp. 31-3.

which have never been disclosed. The name of Gosplan was changed from State Planning *Commission* to State Planning *Committee*, and it lost its material allocation department (*Gossnab*), its technical department (*Gostekhnika*) and the Central Statistical Office, each of which became separate committees of the Council of Ministers. Clearly, this was intended to demote and weaken Gosplan. This state of affairs lasted until Stalin's death, when the *status quo ante 1948* was restored, temporarily, except that the Central Statistical Office remained a separate body attached to the Council of Ministers. Then, in 1955, came yet another major reorganization. It was alleged that Gosplan's preoccupation with current planning caused neglect of long-term considerations, and so it was split into, firstly, the *State Planning Commission* (still called Gosplan), which was concerned with long-term planning only, and the State Economic Commission (*Gosekonomkommissia*), which was charged with current planning. *Gostekhnika* was also revived as a separate body, responsible for devising and introducing new techniques into the economy. This, then, was the position when the entire system went into the melting-pot at the end of 1956.

THE END OF THE 'MINISTERIAL' SYSTEM: THE
'SOVNARKHOZ' REFORM

The reform of the system of industrial planning and administration was apparently touched off at the end of 1956 by the errors of the sixth five-year plan. This had been adopted by the twentieth party congress in February, 1956, but was found to be over-ambitious and unworkable, notably in its implications for investment in new industrial capacity. This caused a decision to be taken, at the central committee plenum of December, 1956, to revise the plan. Its principal author, Saburov, lost his job as the head of Gosplan. A general reshuffle of personnel and organization took place. *Gosekonomkommissia* (i.e. the body in charge of current planning) was given powers over virtually all the economic ministries. Even the Ministry of Agriculture was at first put within its purview: the minister (like other senior economic ministers) became a deputy-chairman of *Gosekonomkommissia,* under the chairman, Pervukhin. Thus while Gosplan retained separate long-term planning functions, all current economic matters were concentrated under the umbrella of *Gosekonomkommissia,* which thus partially resurrected the situation of vSNKh.

But not for long. Khrushchev had other ideas, and in the spring of 1957 he piloted through a radical reform, which brought *Goseko-*

nomkommissia to an end and abolished the majority of economic ministries altogether. The motivation was partly a political one; the reform was closely followed by the formation and defeat of the so-called 'anti-party group' (Molotov, Malenkov, Kaganovich, Bulganin, and to a lesser extent also Pervukhin and Saburov), who were against it. The political manoeuvrings were complex and it is no part of our purpose to analyse them here. Like many other important changes in economic and political affairs, this was partly a reflection of a genuine need for reform, and partly was devised (and opposed) by politicians to further their own ends. In any event, the Supreme Soviet formally adopted a law embodying the new structure in May, 1957, and it came into operation in July. With minor amendments, this law is still in force.

The economic arguments for a change were these.

Firstly, each industrial ministry showed strong tendencies towards becoming a self-contained economic empire. This was partly the consequence of the chronic uncertainties of supplies, which led to reluctance to rely on other ministries, and so to the setting up of one's own 'ministerial' supply bases, or ministerial factories to make necessary components. But another part of the explanation for ministerial autarky lay in the weakness of the co-ordinating authorities in the face of the growing complexity of the industrial structure. Gosplan, especially after Voznesenski's downfall, was too weak to keep the various ministries working together effectively. Ministerial autarky showed itself in many kinds of avoidable waste. Thus many small factories made components for nation-wide ministerial empires, and then transported them to all parts of the USSR. For instance, there could be a workshop in Sverdlovsk which supplied factories of the Ministry of Heavy Machine Buildings in Minsk and Kiev, while other ministries had identical workshops in Minsk and Kiev, supplying, *inter alia*, these ministries' factories in Sverdlovsk. This produced numerous instances of unnecessary cross-hauls on the already overloaded railways. In other words, both horizontal and vertical integration was stimulated or limited by ministerial boundary lines, rather than by economic forces. The maintenance of sepparate supply offices in all areas by every ministerial system caused much duplication and therefore waste.

Secondly, there was no effective authority responsible for regional planning. Despite some attempts to strengthen the role of republics after Stalin's death, all lines of command still led to Moscow, and no one in any area had authority to examine and act upon any assessment of the potentialities of the given area, from a viewpoint which transcended inter-industrial boundary lines.[1] All this particularly impeded the development of new areas, for instance, in Siberia. Factories next door to one another, but within different ministerial systems, had no means of collaborating, nor could any local body enable them to do so.

Thirdly, there was much avoidable waste in the utilization (or, rather, in failure to arrange for the utilization) of by-products. For instance, petrochemicals could be based on using the by-products of the oil industry, but there was no direct link between the Ministry of Chemicals and the Ministry of Oil industry, and neither had any interest in taking any action in the matter.

Finally, the concentration of authority in Moscow over enterprises scattered over the country made for bureaucratic delays in settling the many everyday questions which unavoidably arise.

These weaknesses were part of the cost of basing planning and control on industrial sectors, and they had existed for many years, so the fact of their existence was not itself a sufficient explanation for the reform. But the burdens of planning and administration from the centre had grown with the growth of the economy itself, and this had led to a kind of elemental devolution of authority to the ministerial industrial systems, because of the inevitable difficulty of co-ordination. Just as a western firm which grows beyond a certain size eventually requires radical reorganization by reason of its size, so growth and complexity did present new and especially difficult problems, and the errors of the sixth five-year plan project showed that these problems were not being solved.

The new system is based on the territorial principle. All the USSR is divided at present (end of 1960) into 103 regional economic councils, or *sovnarkhozy* (note the resurrection of the old term). These are frequently (but not always) co-extensive with existing *oblast'* boundaries, and not with any recognizable geographical or economic region. For example, the Donetz basin (Donbas) was divided among three *sovnarkhozy*. While enterprises of purely local significance are administered by local (*oblast,* city, etc.) soviets, the vast majority of industrial and building enterprises in each of the 103 regions are directly subordinated to 'their' *sovnarkhoz*. It is not, however, responsible for agriculture, transport or retail trade, save when these activities are associated with industry (e.g. auxiliary farms, factory transport, factory canteens).

Each *sovnarkhoz* is nominated by the *republican* government and

---

[1] It is true that *oblast'* party and local-authority organs could do so, but they had no authority over any but the smallest enterprises in their area and probably lacked information also.

is responsible to it. The smaller republics (e.g. Georgia, Latvia, Belorussia, Armenia) are themselves one *sovnarkhoz*. By contrast the RSFSR (Russian federal republic) has sixty-eight, the Ukraine—fourteen, Kazakhstan—nine. The chain of command stretches now from the all-union government in Moscow through the republican government to the *sovnarkhoz*, and thence to the various enterprises within it. It is the *sovnarkhoz* which has the formal power of appointment and dismissal of senior enterprise managers, which previously resided with the ministerial *glavk*.

The internal organization of a *sovnarkhoz* varies greatly from place to place, depending on the nature and extent of the industrial activity of the region. All possess a 'technical-economic council' as an advisory expert body. All have several functional divisions, dealing (for instance) with supplies and disposals, planning, labour, technical development, and also a varying number of industrial-sector departments. Thus the Leningrad *sovnarkhoz* has departments for heavy machine-building, general machine-building, electrical equipment, chemicals, instruments, metallurgy, shipbuilding, radio-technical, timber, wood processing and furniture, pulp and paper, textiles, leather and footwear, clothing, food, fish, meat and dairy produce, printing, building materials (including glass and pottery), construction and fuel and power.[1] The actual detailed control over an enterprise is in the hands of the appropriate department of the *sovnarkhoz*. The powers and functions of the *sovnarkhoz* are laid down in a long decree of 138 paragraphs, issued by the Council of Ministers of the USSR on September 26, 1957.[2]

In its day-to-day operations, its essential task is to supervise the fulfilment of the plan described by superior authority, though it has powers to decide the detailed composition of production where this is not prescribed by the plan. The *sovnarkhoz* has the duty to encourage new technique, and rational specialization within the region, in so far as this enables the plan to be fulfilled at lower cost and more expeditiously. It is guided in all matters by the orders it receives from its superiors, but has a range of choices as to how to carry them out. This range is carefully defined in the decree and in subsequent regulations. Thus it is in control of an 'investment reserve' amounting to 5 per cent of the total investment intended for the region, which it can direct where it considers necessary, provided

---

[1] See A. N. Efimov, *Perestroika u pravleniya promyshlennostyu i stroitelstvom v SSSR* (Moscow, 1957), p. 63. Other examples are also given in this valuable book.

[2] The most accessible source for this is *Direktivy KPSS . . .*, vol. 4, pp. 784-805.

key sectors of investment are not adversely affected thereby (paragraph 56). A portion of the overplan profits of enterprises are paid into *sovnarkhoz* funds (see page 35, above). It may confirm or amend enterprises' investment projects of a value not exceeding 25 million roubles, subject to general planned limits (paragraph 60). It allocates some materials, and may redistribute materials between enterprises,[1] authorize the overspending of the wages fund by enterprises, decide on the establishment structure of new enterprises and do many other things, always subject to defined limits, and sometimes subject also to the approval of higher authority. It may negotiate with other *sovnarkhozy* about matters of joint interest, and make arrangements for mutual co-operation in supplies subject to this being in conformity with the centrally approved plan. It must give priority to the carrying out of contracts with enterprises located outside the region, on pain of punishment. It may confirm temporary prices for new products (on a cost-plus basis). It may decide whether equipment should be disposed of or scrapped. It arbitrates in disputes between enterprises within the region. The *sovnarkhoz* also fulfils an important function in the process of planning: together with 'its' enterprises, it drafts a regional plan and submits it to the republican government. This may, of course, be substantially amended, but it makes the first draft and can argue in its favour. Thus, some of the detailed powers formally exercised by *glavki* of ministries now fall to the *sovnarkhozy*, while others remain, as we shall see, with the centre and the republics.

By decree, published in *Pravda* on July 2, 1960, *sovnarkhozy* administer a 'fund for the introduction of new technique', this fund being built up out of a levy on 'machine-building' factories and devoted to financing the development of new and better machines.

In June/July, 1960, it was reported that operational control over *sovnarkhoz* activities in the larger republics with many *sovnarkhozy* (RSFSR, Ukraine, Kazakhstan) was being vested in republican Councils of National Economy (resurrecting in the case of the Russian republic the abbreviation VSNKh), of which more on page 78, below.

The *sovnarkhoz* has no powers over small-scale local industry controlled by the *oblast* soviets, nor has the *oblast* soviet any power over the *sovnarkhoz*, even though the latter's territory may be identical with that of the *oblast*. However, there is supposed to be consultation and co-operation.

---

[1] About 35 per cent of materials are either allocated or sub-allocated by *sovnarkhozy*. M. Lyashko, *Finansy SSSR*, No. 10/1960, p. 49.

The system of subordination before and since the *sovnarkhoz* reform may be illustrated by the following somewhat simplified diagrams (but see page 96 for changes made in May, 1961).

It must be emphasized that the chain of command shown above is by no means always followed in practice. Instances have been reported of direct instructions being given from the republican level to a factory, without going through the *sovnarkhoz*, and many all-union decisions, especially in matters of investment and supplies,

A. Before

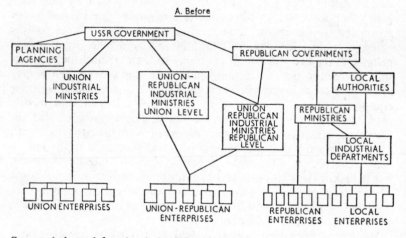

Source (adapted from): A. N. Efimov (op. cit.), p. 15.

(Note several instances of 'dual subordination' (see page 93), and also that the union-republican ministries at union level sometimes by-passed the analogous ministry at republican level.)

inevitably have a direct effect on *sovnarkhoz* or enterprise operations, as will be seen when these activities are discussed. It is very common, too, for enterprises to apply direct to the republic, especially in relation to supplies. It will also be shown that the all-union Gosplan sometimes exercises direct control over important enterprises. Furthermore, the Communist party organizations play a vital role in the whole process (see pages 93-96, below). However, the formal chain of command is an important reality, even though it is sometimes short-circuited and by-passed.

In 1958, *sovnarkhozy* controlled (at least nominally) enterprises responsible for 71 per cent of all state industrial production, most of the remainder being local industry. Six per cent of output was produced in enterprises of 'all-union subordination'.[1] By contrast, in 1953 all-union ministries were responsible for 69 per cent of industrial production.[2]

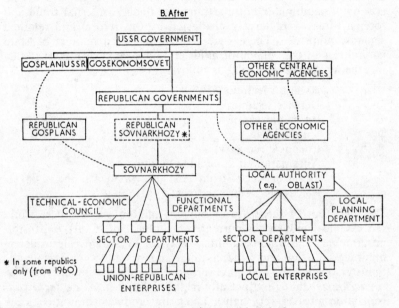

Source: Adapted from Efimov, op. cit., pp. 46 and 52.

The above diagram does not include the 'large regions' into which the big republics are divided, and the smaller republics grouped, and a reform adopted in May, 1961. See p. 96.

PLANNING AND ADMINISTRATION AFTER 1957:
UNION LEVEL

The 1957 reforms eliminated all the specifically industrial ministries at all-union level, with the exception of the Ministry of Electric Power,[3] which administered the interconnected electricity network,

[1] At this date, the most important was the Ministry of Electric Power Stations, since abolished.
[2] *N.Kh. 1958*, p. 127.
[3] And the so-called Ministry of Medium Machine-building, which is believed to be concerned with nuclear matters.

though its power stations were within the area of responsibility of the appropriate *sovnarkhoz*. Construction ministries have also been retained for electric power stations and road and railway building. Then, by decree of December 31, 1958, the all-union Ministry of Electric Power was also abolished. Non-industrial sectors of the economy, notably agriculture, transport, finance, internal trade and foreign trade, were largely unaffected by this reform and retained separate ministries. There were created in 1957 a number of 'state committees of the council of ministers' for certain sectors of industry, the list at present being as follows:

> Aviation technique
> Defence technique
> Radio-electronics
> Shipbuilding
> Chemical industry
> Automation and machine-building
> Grain products (from 1961, Procurements. See p. 88)
> Electronic technique (from 1961)

The first four of these are of obvious military significance, while the chemical industry is currently the object of a vast expansion programme. The state committees play an important role in determining production and research programmes, but do not directly administer enterprises and have no formal right to issue orders to *sovnarkhozy* (though, especially in the military field, *de facto* centralization must be very tight). The grain products committee is the heir to the former Ministry of Procurements, which was responsible for acquiring farm products. It builds and operates elevators and storehouses, and also runs the flour-milling and baking industries.[1]

The government is also advised by a number of other bodies which bear the designation or possess the status of state committees, their chiefs being members of the Council of Ministers. Gosplan (again a 'committee') is one of them, and will be described in greater detail in a moment. Others of economic importance include:

> Scientific and Technical Committee (formerly
> *Gostekhnika*) replaced in 1961 by Research
> co-ordination committee
> Labour and Wages

[1] For details of powers of State committees, see V. Vlasov and S. Studenikin, *Sovetskoe administrativnoe pravo* (Moscow, 1959), pp. 78 ff.

Construction questions
Foreign economic relations
State Bank
Central Statistical Office
Economic-Science Council (*nauchno-ekono-
micheski sovet* or *Gosekonomsovet*)

For example, according to Kostousov, its head, the automation and
machine-building committee 'jointly with the USSR Gosplan elabor-
ates and submits proposals on complex mechanization and automation. It confirms plans for the introduction of radioelectronics in all
branches of the economy. The committee devoted much of its attention to carrying out a unified technical policy and co-ordinating research, design and project-making work' (*Pravda,* July 15, 1960).
The precise division of labour between this committee and the scientific technical committee is by no means clear. The latter seems also
to be responsible for 'the introduction of technical achievements
into production . . . and directing the activity of research, project-
making and design organization in the carrying out of necessary research, working out design, preparation of prototypes', supervising
for these purposes the activities of scientific-technical committees
in the republics and in *sovnarkhozy,* or so it appears from the
speech of its head, Petukhov, at a central committee plenum (*Pravda,*
June 17, 1960). At some point these activities join, or overlap, those
of the Committee on Radio-electronics. All the above have ministerial status, but there are also committees 'attached to' (the Russian
word is *pri*) the Council of Ministers which have lower status and
some of which also seem to overlap the functions of various state
committees. Two such 'junior' bodies are the Committee on Inventions and Discoveries, and the Committee for Standards, Weights
and Measures. There are doubtless others, some of them created *ad
hoc.*

The key position is held by Gosplan, but this has been modified
in 1960 by a strengthening of the Economic-Science Council (*Gosekonomsovet*). Article 16 of the law of May 10, 1957, defined as follows the functions of Gosplan: 'The all-round study of the needs
of the national economy, the devising of long-term and current plans
for the national economy, taking into account the achievements of
science and technology, the carrying through of a tightly centralized
policy relative to the development of the key sectors of the economy
and on this basis ensuring correct location of production and proportionate development of all sectors of the economy, and also the

elaboration of plans for material-technical supplies for the economy and ensuring the full observance of state discipline in deliveries of industrial production'.

After the reforms, therefore, Gosplan acquired many of the general functions formerly exercised at the centre by the defunct ministries, exercised by departments which bear designations similar to the former ministries: ferrous metallurgy, oil and gas, building materials, defence production, heavy machine-building, chemicals, and so on.[1] It also possesses several functional divisions: finance, investment, external relations, prices and costs, labour and wages, long-term planning (until 1960), current planning and, last but not least, supplies. In 1959, it acquired powers over agricultural planning. Finally, there are divisions concerned with regional planning, the USSR being divided into sixteen 'big' regions for this purpose. These departments often inevitably overlap with other state bodies, and close collaboration with them must be established so that planning reflects (for instance) foreign trade agreements, changes in the wages structure, the development of new weapons and the progress of the chemical industry, which are also within the competence of state bodies already referred to. Gosplan's responsibilities are immense. It must co-ordinate and amend the draft output plans submitted to it by the republican Gosplans. It must make them coherent with one another, and with the material supply possibilities, estimated agricultural production, personal incomes, the budget, the expected 'production' of technicians, and the many other questions which must bear directly on planning and for which many government departments and/or republican and regional authorities are responsible. The function of controlling supplies of materials lies at the very heart of the planning process, since it is evident that every decision on output at all levels requires material inputs and simultaneously affects supplies for other enterprises.

Gosplan's *powers* are, formally speaking, small, in the sense that it is not the hierarchical superior of any enterprise, *sovnarkhoz* or republic. It must, again formally speaking, act through the government (and/or the central committee of the Party). However, in practice its powers are very great, not least because of the key role of its supply and disposals (*snabsbyt*) organization, which, through the placing of orders and granting (or not granting) delivery authorizations can take what are in effect production decisions—or veto de-

---

[1] An organizational sketch as at the middle of 1957 appears in Efimov, op. cit., p. 85. The heads of many of these departments have the status of ministers.

cisions taken by others. Although nominally the all-union Gosplan's functions relate to inter-republican supplies and deliveries, in practice it does much more than this. We shall be referring to the supply system separately in a moment.

However, a decree of the central committee and Council of Ministers of April 7, 1960, promulgated a major reform which had the effect of reducing the status and influence of Gosplan. At all-union level, an already existing body—the Economic-Science Council—was reorganized, expanded, given a new chief (Zasyad'ko) and charged with extensive functions of long-term economic planning, and also with drawing up 'long-term material balances, the working out of difficult questions (*problemnykh voprosov*) concerning the development of the economy of the USSR, the preparation of learned reports, forecasts and proposals on these questions'.[1] The research institute of Gosplan, headed by A. Efimov, was transferred to this new council. This measure, therefore, revives the division which existed in 1955-56 between long-term and current planning, but with the confusing difference that in 1955-56 the designation Gosplan related to the body charged with *long*-term planning (the 'current' body was *Gosekonomkommissia*), whereas now Gosplan deals with current planning. However, the 'current' planning period now extends for five years forward; it is Gosplan's job to plan for the next five years as well as for the intermediate years, in all necessary detail. The Economic-Science Council (*Gosekonomsovet*) is senior to Gosplan, in that its name is mentioned first and its chief (Zasyad'ko) is politically senior to Gosplan's chief (Novikov). General political 'overlordship' over the economy appears to belong to a senior member of the party praesidium, Kosygin. Such at any rate, is the position at the moment of writing.

PLANNING AND ECONOMIC ADMINISTRATION: REPUBLICAN LEVEL

Each republic has its own Gosplan, which, on its own level, duplicated the functions of the all-union Gosplan. The scale and complexity of its organization depends on the size and complexity of the given republic's economy. The Russian republic (RSFSR), which covers most of the USSR and raises the most difficult co-ordination problems, has within its Gosplan a small number of regional divisions, which correspond to the major geographic-economic regions which are divided between many *sovnarkhozy* (e.g. West Siberia,

[1] V. Laptev, *Sovetskoe gosudarstvo i bravo*, No. 8, 1960, p. 34.

Urals, Centre, and so on). As will be seen, the republican Gosplans play a vital role in drawing up production plans. Like the all-union Gosplan, they have no executive power. This was a subject of much complaint, especially in the giant RSFSR. Possibly for this reason, or perhaps because of the need to ensure more effective co-ordination between the various economic agencies at republican level, the three biggest republics altered their organizational pattern in June, 1960; the RSFSR, the Ukraine and Kazakhstan each set up a republican Council of the National Economy, which in the RSFSR used the old abbreviation VSNKh (Vesenkha), and was to exercise operational control over the *sovnarkhozy* of the republics concerned so as to ensure that the plans are fulfilled. To them were transferred the vital supply and disposals (*snabsbyt*) functions of the Gosplans of these republics. Gosplans survive, but primarily as planning bodies. The new VSNKh are subordinate to the council of ministers of the appropriate republic.[1] The scope of their powers, and the extent to which they will elbow Gosplan aside and exercise effective control over *sovnarkhozy,* is still far from clear. Republics also possess state committees (for instance, a Scientific-Technical Committee, or a Procurements Committee) and a number of ministries which carry out economic functions outside the industrial field (for example, internal trade, finance, transport, agriculture). In some instances, in the case of the oil industry in Azerbaidjan, timber in Latvia, communal economy as in most republics, industrial ministries have survived at republican level. Most republics also possess a Ministry of Construction. The importance of the republics in the economic field has grown substantially in recent years. It had declined in the last years of Stalin, when, as was already shown, all-union ministries controlled directly the vast majority of enterprises on the territories of the republics. The tendency to extend the rights of republics has been noticeable at least since 1955. This will be observed in relation to the budget (chapter 3, below), as well as in the administration of productive enterprises. The *sovnarkhoz* reform in 1957 speeded up the process. The fact that the republican Gosplan plays an essential role in drafting its own republican plan, that the republic government is the immediate superior of the *sovnarkhozy*, and that the allocation of materials within the republic is most often the responsibility of the republican authorities, all strengthens the position of

[1] For an account of the functions of the RSFSR VSNKh, see *Sovetskaya Rossiya*, June 19, 1960, and also I. Maevski and A. Fomin in *Vop. Ekon.*, No. 10/1960, p. 34 ff. Oddly enough, authority to take these measures was provided only after the event, in a decree of the praesidium of the Supreme Soviet of the USSR on July 5, 1960 (V. Laptev, op. cit.). See also p. 96.

the men in charge at that level. They also control, through their power over 'their' *oblasti*, the operations of local industry, and have a wide range of powers over retail trade, including that of fixing retail prices for a range of commodities which amounted to 45 per cent of total turnover.[1]

The republican governments and Gosplans remain subordinate to the all-union authorities in all important economic questions. Output plans, many basic material allocations, the pattern of investments and so on are still primarily a central responsibility. However, the influence of the republics in the process of taking central decisions, as well as their rights in detailed application of policy, have certainly increased. The premiers of each of the republics are, since 1957, *ex-officio* members of the all-union government.

THE PLANNING PROCESS, AND MATERIAL SUPPLIES

The real importance of any territorial and administrative unit depends on the way in which the planning system operates in practice. The key to the entire system is in the material supplies organization, and this for two reasons: not only does the functioning of any enterprise in industry depend decisively on the provision of the necessary material inputs, but the basic planning procedures are themselves directly concerned with the 'material' consequences of economic policy decisions and react on these decisions. Let us take a simplified example. Let us suppose that the highest policy-makers in the land decide that the USSR should (let us say) become self-sufficient in steel and machine-tools and also develop oil as a major source of fuel. (In practice, these decisions too are not taken *in abstracto*, and bear some relationship to the expected utilization of steel, machine-tools and oil, but one must start somewhere.) These decisions call for certain inputs, which are calculated through technical co-efficients derived from past experience. Thus a given expansion in steel production requires X tons of iron ore, Y tons of coking coal, the construction of new smelting or rolling capacity, and so on. These call in turn for new mining machinery, constructional steel, cement, a new railway line to carry the iron ore, more locomotives (and still more steel, oil, etc., etc.) and all this has certain consequences which have other consequences. The process is repeated for each key element in the plan. Of course, amendments have constantly to be made, as when it is discovered that the requirements for a certain commodity cannot be met within the period

[1] L. Skvortsov, *Vop. Ekon.*, No. 4/1957, p. 117.

in question, and/or if likely export earnings would be insufficient to enable imports to bridge the gap. Input and output calculations are necessarily connected and, in the process of planning, react on one another. Bottlenecks are discovered, and, if the sector is a priority one, become the subject-matter for an urgent investment programme and perhaps a 'campaign', with special inducements provided for those engaged in the enlargement of the bottleneck.

This is a continuous process, which must proceed on various time-scales. In the long term, the expansion of the economy must be expressed as far as possible in an integrated and consistent series of output targets, and the investment programme emerges as part of the process of ensuring that the capacity necessary for the achievement of future plans can be brought into operation when required; this in turn reacts upon these future plans themselves, since these must then include the investments in question. It is also necessary to take into account policy decisions—for instance, concerning the relative importance of consumers' goods, or agriculture, or housing. The central planners endeavour to combine all these data and projects and to calculate the material requirements, modifying the projects or the investment plan, or the foreign trade plan, in the light of discovered disproportions or inconsistencies. They must also take into account the submissions of the industrial-sector ministries (before 1957) and from territorial planning agencies (since 1957), and from trade organs. In the process, the planners draw up a series of product 'balances', which are subject to modification in the light of representations from various economic and political agencies concerned. The process is never completed. The various bodies engaged in the process are constantly influencing each other in a multitude of ways, and one should not see things as happening merely by way of hierarchical and/or political subordination, although, of course, there is both a hierarchy and subordination. Major decisions are taken by the top Party organs, but many of them are 'induced', or based on advice of experts. Thus the Party decisions to triple the size of the chemical industry, taken in 1957, were doubtless based on submissions made to the Central Committee by planning experts charged with calculating input requirements. Plans prepared by the republics and *sovnarkhozy* are influenced by their knowledge of the priorities of the centre, which are in turn related to political decisions and to input requirements, bottlenecks, etc., which are partly reflected in these priorities.

This whole process is often labelled in Soviet literature as 'planning by material balances'. It involves a form of simplified 'input-output' procedure, carried out very largely in quantitative (physical) terms,[1] though there is some evidence of a rather rudimentary cost comparison in making choices between interchangeable alternatives. The considerable shortcomings of this system are referred to in detail in chapter 7.

The long-term (five-year, seven-year) plans which emerge from this highly complex process are not yet 'operational'. They do not directly order any enterprise to do anything. While they should in principle provide (for instance) enough iron ore to fulfil the steel plan, nothing is said about the supplies of ore to any one steelworks, or by any mining enterprise. Indeed, owing to the miscalculations unavoidable in planning far ahead, which frequently call for changes, it is clear that operational orders must relate to shorter periods and must take errors and delays fully into account. All kinds of things could go wrong with a long-term plan. Thus factories may not be finished in time, harvests may not come up to expectations, a big new discovery of minerals may be made, a new trade or aid agreement negotiated, or there may simply have been an under or overestimate of material requirements, or of stocks, or labour proves unexpectedly scarce in a given area, or optimistic prognostications concerning a rise in productivity are not fulfilled, or the Party itself may—as it often does—decree a policy change in the middle of a plan period. Stalin is often quoted as saying that, contrary to so-called western planning, Soviet plans are directives which have the force of law, but to take this to apply to long-term plans would be erroneous, except perhaps in the formal legal sense.[2]

Annual, quarterly, monthly plans, by contrast, are of direct operational importance. They are related to the long-term plan in the sense of being the practical expression of the same economic policy (as amended from time to time), and clearly the investment plans are of their nature a much more long-term affair, but, so far as any given industrial enterprise is concerned, its production and supply arrangements are geared only to short periods of time, and the rewards for success and penalties for failure are similarly concerned with a year, a quarter or a month, although, especially since 1957, the enterprise itself should have a long-term plan and should relate

[1] See W. Leontief, 'The Fall and Rise of Soviet Economics', *Foreign Affairs*, January, 1960, for a critical but essentially true account.
[2] In fact, several five-year plans were not decreed until long after the beginning of the relevant five-year period. Thus the fifth five-year plan, which covered the period from January 1, 1951, was 'adopted' by the Party congress in October, 1952.

to it its initial submission to the *sovnarkhoz* concerning its plan for the coming year.

The annual plan is the basis of the supply arrangements and of the contracts which express them. It is, since 1957, built up from submissions of *sovnarkhozy* to republics and from republican Gosplans to the all-union Gosplan. The latter is responsible for ensuring consistency and the satisfaction of all-union needs (e.g. for state reserves, export), as well as for seeing that 'localist' tendencies do not cause economically irrational output decisions. The immense complexity of the task of integrating output, supplies, deliveries and user-demand often led to delays in approving plans, and to complaints that enterprises did not know either their production plans or the material to which they would be entitled until well into the year to which the plan was supposed to relate.[1] Vigorous measures are being taken to avert this, by insisting that the plan submissions from the republics reach Moscow not later than August, and that the process of amendment and argument be completed and the annual plan drafted and approved already in October.[2] In 1959 it was in fact found possible to submit the plan, with the annual budget, to the Supreme Soviet by the end of that month. But this could not prevent plans from being altered during the year, in the light of errors of calculation or changes of policy, as often happened in the past; and in 1960 the Supreme Soviet did not meet until the second half of December.

Bearing in mind, as one must, that all material supplies involve other enterprises in production and/or deliveries, and that the output of almost any commodity requires the supply of a number of different materials and components, let us now see how the plan provides for the material inputs required for its implementation.

Before 1957, the ministries were responsible for supplying 'their' enterprises, and each possessed a chief supply department (known as *glavsnab*). They were generally also responsible for disposing of the products of 'their' enterprises, and so they had a chief disposals department (*glavsbyt*). Each of these had local offices, as required. Almost all major materials and components were subject to central allocation and were divided into two categories: 'funded' (*fond-iruemaya*) and 'planned' (*planiruemaya*) products. 'Funded' materials

---

[1] See, for instance, article by B. Naimanov in *Pravda*, February 6, 1958, and also p. 202, below.

[2] A valuable description of this process is to be found in Herbert Levine's contribution to *Comparisons Between the U.S. and Soviet Economies* (Washington, 1959).

were the responsibility of the government, which meant in practice the *snab* department of Gosplan,[1] which allocated to user ministries, who in turn allocated to enterprises via the appropriate *glavk* of the ministry. This meant that the producing ministry was told what sector of the economy they should supply, and in what quantities. 'Planned' materials, generally of lesser importance, were allocated by the disposals department of the producing ministries (i.e. by the *glavsbyt*). In addition there was a range of materials and components which were not centrally planned, but were either allocated by local authorities or based on contract between the parties concerned. Some of these were minor, others (like sand, gravel, clay) were of their nature a matter of local arrangement and were often procured by the user ministries.

After the 1957 reform, with the disappearance of nearly all the ministries, the distinction between 'funded' and 'planned' materials became obsolete, and it was formally abolished in 1958.[2] What happens now is this. For a long list of commodities of any importance, the all-union Gosplan is responsible for allocating supplies to republics, and therefore also for ensuring that the supplies produced in one republic are available when needed to other republics. To do this, Gosplan possesses a 'supply-and-disposals (*snabsbyt*) department for inter-republican deliveries', which possesses numerous divisions for particular commodities. It is also concerned with ensuring that the requirements of the centre are met, and that the priorities decided by the centre are observed, especially if unplanned shortages develop. The bulk of the detailed work of allocation fell in 1957 to the *snabsbyt* department of the republican Gosplans, which, despite the existence of *sovnarkhozy*, are constantly concerned with deliveries to particular enterprises. In 1960, as we have seen, this function was transferred to the new republican *sovnarkhozy* in the three largest republics. Finally, for some commodities, the *sovnarkhozy* themselves allocate and distribute to enterprises, or maintain stores from which enterprises may freely buy what they need. The precise list of goods subject to allocation in these various ways has changed from time to time. The present tendency is gradually to reduce the scope and detail of central allocation, but it remains the dominant form of supply, because of the close link between decisions on supply and decisions on what should be pro-

---

[1] Except that, as noted on p. 67, above, in 1948-53 this was a department (*Gossnab*) outside Gosplan. For a short period there was also a food supply organ (*Gosprodsnab*).

[2] For a useful account, see Y. Koldomasov, in *Plan. Khoz.*, No. 4/1959, pp. 54-65.

duced, and because the practice of planning for maximum growth tends to lead to chronic shortage of most supplies.

The actual content of the supply plan is influenced by the original applications (*zayavki*) from the user enterprises and by technical norms of utilization laid down by the authorities to ensure economy, as modified by guidance from above concerning likely availability in the next year. Thus a republican Gosplan may be informed that it cannot expect more than a certain total tonnage of copper or sheet steel, and 'tailors' its plans accordingly. In due course, the enterprises are issued with allocation certificates, and negotiate contracts with supplying enterprises, which are commonly specified on the certificates.

It is hardly possible, without actually working within the system, adequately to describe how the supply organization works in practice. It is known that some key projects or factories are in fact supplied by priority *naryady* issued at all-union level. In the case of construction, a decree of April 7, 1960, envisaged the drawing up of a list of projects of particular importance; these the all-union Gosplan is to supervise, ensuring deliveries of necessary building materials and of equipment for installation in new factories.[1] It is also clear that the republican *snabsbyty* and *sovnarkhozy* to some extent merely administer the sub-allocation of materials earmarked for particular purposes. Indeed, the Ukraine party secretary complained that even the disposal of the products of the purely local (i.e. non-*sovnarkhozy*) industry was at times very tightly controlled by the all-union Gosplan.[2] There appears to be great divergencies in the way particular materials are dealt with at various administrative levels, and the resulting difficulties are discussed in chapter 7. Odd as it may seem, there is no provision in this system for long-term contracts between enterprises, even where these in fact supply each other for years on end. In each instance, for each plan period, the negotiation of contracts must await the receipt of the allocation certificate from the appropriate *snabsbyt,* based on the usual *zayavka*; until recently, inter-enterprise initiative has been regarded with some suspicion by the authorities.[3] Of course, in the case of specialized equipment which takes a long time to produce, a long-term agreement is implied by the production and supply plans, but this does not apply, for example, to regular deliveries of steel ingots or dyestuffs from one factory to another.

---

[1] See I. Maevski and A. Fomin, *Vop. Ekon.*, No. 10/1960, pp. 38-9.
[2] N. Podgorny, *Pravda*, January 12, 1961.
[3] See critical account of this by N. Razumov, *Vop. Ekon.*, No. 10/1960, p. 18.

The process remains extremely complex, and the implementation of supply planning often involves improvisation and short cuts. Thus fully detailed allocations cannot in fact be integrated with production and with stocks throughout the economy, and non-priority sectors anu minor users often have to make do with what remains when the big and important consumers have taken their share. Hence the frequent complaints of breakdown of supplies and also the scope for the 'pushers' (*tolkachi*). When, as often happens, it is recognized that total supplies of any commodity are plainly insufficient to meet requirements (this should emerge from a short-term analysis of 'material balances', of supply in relation to need), efforts will be made to increase supplies, which might well call for changes in the annual, or the five- or seven-year plan, then current, or to the foreign-trade plan.

INVESTMENT AND CONSTRUCTION PLANNING

The general lines of the investment plans emerge from the interaction, within the planning organs, between 'material balances' analysis, requests from below and the guiding lines of Party policy. This is a highly complex task, which involves not only many divisions of Gosplan and *Gosekonomsovet* at the centre, but also many other state committees and ministries directly and indirectly concerned in formulating investment plans, or plans which call for investments for their implementation. Each year's investment plan is submitted to the all-union government, with the largest projects specified by name. At many points investment decisions call forth production and supply decisions : building materials must be made available, machinery for new factories provided, new houses need furniture and water pipes, and so forth. These needs may themselves call forth other investment decisions, required to expand the production of such items. All this is part of the continuous process of planning, and constitutes an essential and continuous link between short and long-term planning, a link which has often been subject to severe strain, which is hardly surprising having regard to the difficulties of the task. Investments must be paid for, and so the Ministry of Finance is intimately concerned, since, as will be shown, most of these funds are provided by the state budget. Control by the financial organs, or 'limits' laid down in money terms, play an important role in restricting the opportunities of the various authorities and enterprises to indulge in investments additional to the central plan; these controls will be described in chapter 3.

Once the given investment decision has been taken, involving, let us say, the construction of a new cement factory, there remain two essential tasks of a planning-administrative nature: one is to choose which of a number of possible species of cement factory should actually be built, the other to organize the actual work of construction.

The task of comparing between alternative projects, estimating costs, preparing blue prints, submitting possible variants to higher authority for decisions if necessary, is the task of specialized 'project-making organizations' (*proektnye organizatsii*), which exist at all-union, republican, *sovnarkhoz* and local levels, specializing in projects for particular types of construction. These organizations were at one time financed by a percentage addition to the value of the given project, but it was found that this encouraged them in extravagance, and from 1950 they have been largely budget-financed, at least so far as work on centrally-planned investments is concerned, though more recently many have been put on *khozraschyot*.[1] These organizations play an important role in the practical implementation of investment programmes, and, when we subsequently discuss the problems of choice between investment alternatives, it should be remembered it is in these offices that alternatives are weighed up, and technical recommendations are made. While the officials who work there (*proektnye rabotniki*) are not endowed with much formal power, their *de facto* position in the planning process is a key one.

Finally, there is the organization of building. As we have seen, before the 1957 reorganization there grew up a number of construction ministries, as well as construction *glavki* within industrial ministries. The building enterprises under this control worked not only within the sector suggested by their name; thus building organizations of the Ministry of Construction of the Coal Industry also worked on contract for others, and erected, for instance, hospitals for the Ministry of Health. Nonetheless, there was a tendency towards an excessive number of building enterprises to be set up in any one place, owing allegiance to many different ministries, many quite small but each with its own office staff, lorries, supply organization; the state committee on construction (*Gosstroi*) had only the most general functions of supervision, though it did endeavour to lay down, not always successfully, standards of construction. In 1957, the separate construction ministries and *glavki* at all-union level had practically disappeared, except for ministries responsible for tran-

[1] See A. Zverev, *Pravda*, December 23, 1958.

sport construction (railway building, etc.) and for building electric power stations. In principle, building enterprises now come under the *sovnarkhozy*, and, as has already been mentioned in chapter 1, are frequently grouped together in big centres into a construction trust, thus achieving much-needed economies. However, in addition there appear still to be some major construction trusts set up *ad hoc* by higher authority to carry out big projects of all-union significance, and some republics have set up specialized construction organizations especially for work in rural areas. Nearly all republics possess ministries of construction, to supervise building within their jurisdiction.

AGRICULTURAL PLANNING

There were and are a number of features peculiar to agricultural planning. There are several reasons for this. One is the division of agriculture between different forms of ownership. This led to the creation of two different ministries, of which one, the Ministry of Agriculture, dealt with *kolkhozy* and MTS, while the Ministry of State Farms controlled and planned the activities of *sovkhozy*.[1] Another reason has been the importance attached to the political aspects of agriculture, including the need to 'defend' *kolkhozy* against the private-enterprise activities of their own members. In the 'thirties, and again in the years following 1946, this led to the creation of a governmental Council on Kolkhoz Affairs (this faded out in the early 'fifties), and at all times to the very active role in all *kolkhoz* matters of the Communist party and its local committees. Still another relevant factor is the large proportion of agricultural output consumed on the farm, which led to the concentration of state organs less on total output than on the level of deliveries to the state. Though it is true that, until 1955, it was the practice of the Ministry of Agriculture and its local organs to specify in great detail the production plans of all *kolkhozy*, these were seldom fulfilled, and the planning organs were in fact more concerned with deliveries. In 1955, it was officially recognized that detailed planning of output was futile, and, so far as *kolkhozy* were concerned, only deliveries to the state were henceforth to be specified in the plans handed down to farms. However, there have been repeated instances since this date of the imposition by local agricultural officials and (especially) by local party secretaries of output targets on farms.[2]

[1] The Ministry of Sovkhozy was abolished in 1959, but such a ministry was re-formed in Kazakhstan (with headquarters in Akmolinsk) to deal with 'virgin-lands' difficulties.   [2] See chapter 10.

Procurements were, until 1956, the responsibility of a Ministry of Procurements, and then, until 1959, of the Ministry of Agriculture. The planning of deliveries was drastically overhauled in 1958, and was considerably decentralized. While a general procurement plan for major products was approved by the all-union government, in consultation with the republican governments, the latter (and also the local soviets) became largely responsible for supplying their own populations from resources within their own areas, with the centre responsible for acquiring produce for central reserves, export, and certain major deficit areas, as well as raw materials for industries which are centrally planned or which, like the cotton industry, draw supplies from other republics. As a result, centrally-planned state procurements tended to be confined to low-cost areas; thus many *oblasti* of central and northern Russia, and the Baltic states, were wholly or partly exempted from grain deliveries. The object was to encourage specialization on livestock, on the growing of fodder grain to feed them, but it did not work out that way. Figures cited by Khrushchev showed that grain harvests in the exempted areas declined, although consumption of grain (and therefore its 'import' from other areas) increased.[1] Consequently, procurement quotas will now again become the rule, since apparently local officialdom will not give due attention to products which are not on the list of state exactions.

At the same time, there was announced yet another reorganization of procurements. In 1959, 'the planning of production and procurements of agricultural products' became the responsibility of Gosplan instead of the Ministry of Agriculture, but others were also involved, including the Committee on grain products, and the meat and dairy industry of *sovnarkhozy*, as well as local authorities. This entire task is now (1961) to be transferred to a new State procurement committee, whose local organs are to make contracts with *kolkhozy* and *sovkhozy* for deliveries of predetermined quantities of produce, under arrangements not yet worked out in detail. Gosplan will, however, retain general responsibility for determining total needs. A further reorganization concerns the supply of tractors, machinery, fertilizer, and other producers' goods to farms. In 1959, Gosplan acquired from the Ministry of Agriculture the task of distributing most of these goods.[2] In January, 1961, however, a decision was taken to create a new all-union supply organization for

---

[1] *Pravda*, January 21, 1961.
[2] Vlasov and Studenikin, op. cit., pp. 352-7, give details of the reforms up to 1959.

agriculture, which is to act as intermediary between the farms, who will place their orders with its local branches, and the industries manufacturing the required items. The new organization is to forward these requests to Gosplan, and to sell to *kolkhozy* and *sovkhozy* as far as possible on a commercial 'purchase-and-sale' basis, rather than by way of administrative allocation. Representatives of the farms are expected to sit on the local boards of the new supply organization.[1]

The Ministry of Agriculture's functions are being reduced to that of providing advisory research and technical services and spreading information on new methods.

While industrial, transport and trade plans are often fulfilled and must always be taken seriously as evidence of serious intention, the same is not true of agricultural planning. Indeed, it is an exceptional occurrence, in Soviet economic history, for an agricultural plan to be fulfilled. This is due in part to the unavoidable dependence of agriculture upon a fickle climate, which makes all precise plans go awry, while tempting the authorities to set plans which assume good weather. In addition, under the special conditions of *kolkhoz* agriculture, ambitious plans (and, for many years, exaggerated harvest reporting) helped in the hard task of procuring produce from a reluctant peasantry. Another important reason for failures was the reluctance of the government, especially before 1953, to provide the necessary inputs and material incentives, reflecting the low priority of agriculture. There were also many instances of unwise policy decisions involving the misuse of resources; farming lends itself least of all to central direction, by reason of its infinite variety. The top leaders were industry-orientated, generally ignorant of farming, unsympathetic to peasants, and people with knowledge had insufficient political influence to correct this.

THE PLANNING OF TRADE

Until 1957, the Ministry of Internal Trade at all-union level controlled the distribution of major consumer commodities between republics, and key products within republics as well. It had taken over wholesaling responsibilities from industrial ministries. However, increases in the powers of republican ministries culminated, at the end of 1957, in the abolition of the all-union Ministry of In-

[1] Khrushchev, *Pravda*, January 21, 1961, and the detailed regulations in *Pravda*, February 21, 1961.

ternal Trade. Its function in centralized distribution of key commodities passed to the all-union Gosplan, which, in 1960, was allocating between republics a short list of staple foods, textiles, footwear, also taking a special responsibility for supplying Moscow and Leningrad.[1] There exists in Gosplan an all-union trade department (*Soyuzglavtorg*). This also takes an active interest in the distribution of a wide range of consumers' goods, judging from the existence within it of a section concerned with bicycles.[2] This department also analyses *zayavki* from the republics, and serves as a link with the industrial production planning divisions of Gosplan in respect of consumers' goods. Its powers have increased in scope during 1960, as experience demonstrated that local arrangements do not ensure sufficient supplies. Republics retain their ministries of internal trade within which there are divisions responsible for allocating various commodities to the localities, and passing on requests to the producers. There are also wholesaling departments within the system of consumer co-operatives (i.e. of shops in rural areas, see page 41, above). Some specialized shops are maintained by other organizations; for example, medicines are sold in shops run by the Ministry of Health, books—by the Ministry of Culture. Many goods are procured and sold under local arrangements by the *oblast'* or city authorities which organize retail trade and (in most cases) actually control the shops in their areas: for instance, local industry, or producers' co-operatives, can and do sell direct to the retail chain. These local trade authorities are representatives of the ministry, as well as being part of the local soviet.

A wide range of consumers' goods must be allocated from central or republican levels, since only thus can the necessary administrative link be assured between retail shops' requirements and the output and material supply plans of productive enterprises. Consequently, there are usually a large number of administrative stages between the retail store and its ultimate supplier. As elsewhere in the economy, planning involves reconciling the requests from below with the production and distribution plans at the higher levels. Thus the requests of the shops of (say) Kharkov for wool cloth are consolidated by the city soviets wholesale department (*torg*) and communicated to the republican Ministry of Trade. In this ministry other requests (*zayavki*) from other Ukrainian localities are consolidated and eventually reach Gosplan in Moscow. This is clearly a

---

[1] Also the armed forces. For a useful critical account of the system see Y. Sapel'nikov, in *Sovetskaya torgovlya*, No. 6/1960, p. 16 ff.
[2] Mentioned in an article in *Ogonyok*, No. 34/1960.

matter of inter-republican deliveries, as little cloth is produced in the Ukraine. In due course, the Ukrainians learn the size of their allocations (*fondy*) for the coming year, and these are sub-allocated to, among others, Kharkov. The actual task of distributing the cloth belongs to *Glavtextil'torg*, the wholesaling division which exists at both the all-union (Gosplan) and republican (Ministry of Trade) level, and has local offices. It is now for the Kharkov shops to turn the allocation into deliveries of the precise types of cloth they require; the *fondy* do not, as a rule, give detailed specifications. Once the allocations have been made, negotiations can be entered into with the *sovnarkhoz* in whose area the supplying enterprise is situated, but to ensure a desired change in specifications it is often necessary to make application to the republican or even all-union level.

Finally, a contract for delivery is signed between the trading organization and the textile factory. Ultimately, the requests of the various trading organizations at all levels affect the behaviour of *Gosplan* and *sovnarkhozy*, but, as will be shown in chapter 6, the system remains clumsy and unresponsive.

INSPECTION AND CONTROL

In the preceding pages, we have been concerned with various administrative and planning agencies which decide what should be done. It is also necessary to see that it is in fact done. For this purpose there are a number of agencies of inspection, checking and control. Some are essentially non-economic in character, though at times they can and do intervene actively in alleged malfeasances in the economic sphere: such are, for instance, the so-called secret police (known at various dates as Cheka, OGPU, NKVD, MVD, MGB, State Security Committee) and the *prokuror* (procurator, sometimes miscalled public prosecutor). Nothing needs to be said about them in the present context, despite their importance in Soviet life.[1] Separate mention is necessary of the activities of the *Committee of Soviet Control,* formerly the Ministry of State Control; the word 'control' must be read in its German-French-Russian sense of checking or inspection (e.g. the French *contrôle des billets*). The Control

---

[1] Large Soviet enterprises possessed, and probably still possess, a 'secret department' staffed by secret police, which organized a network of informers. However, they were more likely to be roused by a disrespectful remark about Stalin than by, say, the overspending of the wages fund. For a rare reference to these secret departments, see Evtikhiev and V. Vlasov, *Administrativnoe pravo SSSR* (Moscow, 1946).

Committee is an all-union body reporting to the Council of Ministers, with republican branches; it has local teams of inspectors with the right of access to documents and accounts, and powers to interrogate. Its task is to seek out and report breaches of rules and instructions of all kinds, drawing in for the purpose anyone who is willing to help. Its functions are not confined to the economic sphere, but it is frequently engaged in checking on the carrying out of economic regulations, notably where it is in the self-interest of officials or managers to evade them. For instance, the Belorussian *sovnarkhoz* was alleged to have distributed premia, which should have been largely used to encourage those engaged on production, to its own officials, and this brought on it the wrath of the Control Committee.[1]

The Ministry of Finance, through its inspectors and regional offices, is another important 'cross-checking' agency. Thus it is the duty of its local officials to audit the accounts of enterprises, noting particularly any failures to earn the expected profits or, where applicable, to pay the planned amount of turnover tax. They must seek out causes, and report inefficiencies or breaches of rules. This Ministry is also responsible, through its Establishments Commission (*Shtatnaya kommissia*), for laying down the permitted establishment of managerial personnel and economic (as well as other) officials at all levels.[2]

The inspecting and checking role of the *State Bank vis-à-vis* enterprises arises from the fact that all the funds of the enterprises must be kept in the bank, and that it is the only source of short-term credits. The local branch of the bank has the duty of scrutinizing all payments and cheques to see that they conform to the plan and to the various regulations (e.g. relating to prices, wages, etc.). Under a decree of August, 1954, the bank assumes a more detailed tutelage over enterprises which find themselves in financial difficulties.[3] The State Bank is a centralized all-union institution, of whose control functions more will be said in chapter 3. Investment expenditure is controlled closely by the specialized *investment banks,* which are under the Ministry of Finance (see chapter 3).

Arbitration tribunals settle the many conflicts between state enterprises, concerning the negotiation of contracts which they are compelled to conclude under the planned supply allocations, or the

---

[1] *Pravda*, November 22, 1958.

[2] This has led to bitter complaints from *sovnarkhozy* about the ministry's interference with staff establishments (see, for instance, G. Lopovok in *Ekonomischeskaya Gazeta*, June 12, 1960).

[3] This includes provision for a species of socialist bankruptcy (see p. 112, below).

alleged failures to carry out the terms of contracts. Within an economic ministry or *sovnarkhoz*, there is an internal arbitration tribunal to adjudge disputes between enterprises or other economic bodies within its own jurisdiction. For other cases the state provides a hierarchy of arbitration bodies, with, at the top, the State Arbitration Committee (*Gosarbitrazh*). Of course, none of these bodies have the right to arbitrate on disputes between a superior and an inferior in the same hierarchy, which are settled by the issue of appropriate instructions.

Other central and republican ministries and committees maintain local offices or send plenipotentiaries, inspectors and auditors. Some of these local offices also form part of organs of local government, under the system of 'dual subordination'. Thus the Kharkov city trading department is directly under not only the Kharkov city soviet but also the Ukrainian ministry of internal trade, and an *oblast'* soviet agricultural department is the representative in the *oblast'* of the Ministry of Agriculture. Naturally, the many bodies of this type can and do act as 'watchdogs' for the central or republican authorities.

Finally, and most important of all, is the *Communist Party*. It plays a vital role, at all levels, in the economic life of the USSR. At the top policy-making level, it is the Party leadership which takes all basic decisions. 'No important decision is taken by the state organs of our country without previous instructions and advice from the Party'.[1] One often finds branches of the government (for instance, Gosplan) reporting to the Central Committee.[2] In republics and in other units of local government there is a parallel Party committee which generally possesses more influence and power than the analogous government body (for example, the secretary of the party's *raion* committee—the *raikom*—is unquestionably the boss over the relatively insignificant chairman of the *raion* soviet executive committee—the *rai-ispolkom*). The party secretary of the *oblast'* plays a key role in the *sovnarkhoz*. In the republics and below, as at the centre, the party headquarters possesses economic departments. For instance, it seems probable that the real 'minister' of agriculture of the Ukraine is not the nominal holder of that post, but the party's agricultural secretary, N. Bubnovski. Of course, the precise extent of party domination at any given level varies, and may in part depend on personalities, on the degree of support the various

---

[1] A. Denisov, *Sovetskoe gosudarstvennoe pravo* (Moscow, 1947), pp. 191-2.
[2] See, for instance, I. Kuzmin's speech to the Party congress, *Pravda*, February 5, 1959.

individuals can muster in Moscow and on the technical nature of the job. It must not be forgotten that senior government officials are also party members of some importance, and that there is some interchange in jobs between the governmental, economic and party hierarchies.

The party organs may be given powers of extremely strict control (in the English sense of the word 'control') of particular sectors of economic life. A recent example is a decision, taken in 1959, that all building projects 'are examined, in accordance with their importance, in *raikoms, gorkoms, obkoms, kraikoms* and central committees of the parties of the union republics, and only then can they be submitted for confirmation to the appropriate [governmental] organs'.[1] The greatest degree of party power over everyday economic life is, without doubt, in agriculture. As abundant evidence shows, *obkom* and *raikom* officials and plenipotentiaries are constantly interfering even in the routine activities of *kolkhozy*.

At the level of the enterprise, there is a party branch, with a secretary (who is a full-time official in the larger branches). This branch has no right to order the director to do anything, but it is in a strong position, since it can appeal to more senior party organizations in the event of any major clash. The party's task in enterprises is the twin one of mobilizing the employees to fulfil the plan and of checking on the director to ensure that he is acting 'correctly'. The party secretary in the factory, through the local party secretary, can also help to pull strings to secure necessary supplies or other requirements from the authorities. The party's tasks of supervision in enterprises were strongly re-emphasized in 1959, when the already-existing party groups were enjoined to keep a thorough and continuous watch on all aspects of the enterprises' activities and reorganized to do this more effectively.[2] The party exercises some of this power through the local trade union branch, which it firmly controls, and through mass bodies such as the 'production council' (page 31, above), of *kolkhoz* meetings (page 46), the trade unions and so on.

Among the most important ways of exercising party leadership is in what is often called 'selection, training and distribution of cadres'. This operates by means of the so-called *nomenklatura* system. *Nomenklatura* is two things: a list of appointments (e.g. in the state hierarchy, trade unions, enterprises, army, etc. etc.) for which

[1] I. Bocharov, *Plan. Khoz.*, No. 12/1960, p. 60.
[2] Party 'control' commissions were established in enterprises, with orders to report irregularities of any kind to the central committee and governmental organs (*Pravda*, July 13, 1959, and also August 3, 1959).

given party committees are responsible, and a list of persons deemed to be qualified to hold such posts. The latter are often known as *nomenklaturnye rabotniki,* that is, as persons on this list, who can be appointed to jobs listed. For instance, it is known that *kolkhoz* chairmen are on the *nomenklatura* list of republican and *oblast'* party committees, and deputy-chairmen and 'brigadiers' on the *raikom* list.[1]

No significant economic appointment, whoever is nominally responsible for making it, can in fact be made without at the very least the approval of a party committee. In all important instances this involves the Central Committee cadres department, which controls the employment of party members above the lowest levels.[2] Knowledge that this is so inevitably affects the behaviour patterns of all state or economic officials. For example, a *sovnarkhoz* deputy-chairman, nominally appointed by the republican government, is in fact appointed (or at least confirmed in his appointment) by the republican party organization, subject to the veto of (or on the suggestion of) the Central Committee cadres department. The high degree of centralization of the party is another essential political and economic fact; decentralization of authority to, for instance, the Ukraine or Uzbekistan must always be affected by the extent to which the party secretary in the republic is allowed some scope for decision. Of course, the converse is also true: the extent to which the party secretary in any republic or locality has power of decision partly depends on the number of matters which, in the governmental hierarchy, are to be settled within his territory. In any event, party control over policy and over its execution is an essential, if not always visible, fact of Soviet life, and affects not only basic planning decisions or the appointment and behaviour of a minister, but also the choices between alternatives which a factory director or a *kolkhoz* chairman may wish to make. This is why, although party organization as such is not a question to be dealt with here, it is necessary to emphasize that it affects all aspects of economic life. It is, so to speak, the board of directors (at the top) and the institutional substitute for the motivating force of free competition, the driving force which tries (with some success) to overcome natural inertia. It is, of course, much else besides, but that is another story.

[1] *Pravda,* March 6, 1954. For an interesting and well-documented discussion of *nomenklatura,* see M. Fainsod, *Smolensk under Soviet Rule* (Harvard University Press, 1958).
[2] For an example of how central committee officials in effect appoint the director of a major building project on the Volga, see F. Panfyorov's novel *Vo imya molodovo* (*Oktyabr,* No. 7/1960).

ADDENDUM

A change in regional planning arrangements was reported in *Ekonomicheskaya Gazeta*, May 28, 1961. Superimposed on the existing *sovnarkhozy* there are now to be seventeen 'big economic regions', of which ten in the RSFSR and three in the Ukraine; Kazakhstan is to be one 'big' region; while the three Transcaucasian republics, the Baltic states and the Central Asian republics (Uzbekistan, Turkmenistan, Kirghizia and Tadzhikistan) will be grouped to form three such regions, making a total of seventeen. For some reason, Moldavia and Belorussia will remain outside the new 'big-region' system. In each of these new regions there are to be 'councils for co-ordinating and planning the work of *sovnarkhozy*' (in Kazakhstan this will be done by Gosplan of the republic). These councils are to make proposals to the all-union planning organs as well as to republics; the authority of the latter in the economic field is thus adversely affected by the newly announced measure. The reasons for the change are discussed, and indeed the change anticipated, on pp. 199-200, below.

CHAPTER 3

Public Finance and Credit

THE STATE BUDGET

The role of the budget is (in all countries) to transfer resources, in accordance with government decision, from one part of the national economy to another. The USSR is no different in this respect. However, the relative importance of the budget is very great there, because of the direct responsibility of the state for the bulk of economic life. Thus in 1960 the Soviet national income (in its Soviet definition) amounted to 1,440 milliard (old) roubles, while the revenues of the budgets of all public authorities totalled 752 milliard in the same year.[1]

However, Soviet finance has an essential feature which distinguishes it from the West: its intimate inter-relationship with the process of economic planning. Expenditures on investment and on other aspects of the economy are the financial reflection of decisions about economic growth and priorities. Revenues predominantly originate in the operation of the state sector of the economy, and, as we shall see, a large portion of expenditure also derives from the economic plan itself. Similarly, financial institutions operate with a copy of the plan before them. Their resources, and their allocation of moneys for credits and other purposes, are intimately related to the output and investment plan and are intended also to serve as a check on observance of regulations issued by higher authority in the course of organizing plan fulfilment. Thus financial plans and economic plans are elaborated simultaneously, and it has become the practice to submit the annual economic plan and the budget to the same session of the Supreme Soviet.

One feature of the state budget is that it includes the expenditure of all republics, and local authorities. Thus the expenditure of, say, the Akmolinsk town soviet on repairing the drains will appear under the appropriate head in the budget voted by the all-union Supreme Soviet. This does not mean, of course, that the repair of the Akmolinsk drains is specifically authorized by the Supreme Soviet. Re-

[1] *Pravda*, December 23, 1960, and January 26, 1961.

publics and local authorities have their own budgets, and only the principal headings of expenditure require approval of the centre, though some detailed items are the consequences of plans decided at the centre, which also decides how much of the total revenue is made available to the republics (more of this in a moment).

The following table shows the principal items of *revenue* in some selected years:

Table 1. Revenue

	1940	1950	1958
	(thousand million roubles)		
Turnover Tax	105·9	236·1	304·5
Deduction for profits	21·7	40·4	135·4
MTS revenues*	2·0	3·6	9·7
Co-operative tax, kolkhoz tax, non-commodity operations tax	3·2	5·5	16·6
State loans	11·4	31·0	10·6
of which:			
(Mass subscription loans)	(9·0)	(26·4)	(3·2)
(Saving bank loan purchases)	(0·2)	(3·1)	(6·5)
Direct taxes	9·4	35·8	51·9
Social insurance revenue	8·6	19·6	33·1
Other revenues	18·0	50·8	110·5
TOTAL	180·2	422·8	672·3
Of which from 'socialist economy'	160·1	354·0	604·0

Source: *N.Kh. 1958*, p. 899.

* Including other specialized agricultural organizations.

Turnover tax remains by far the largest item of revenue, though its relative importance has been falling slightly in recent years. The nature of this tax is often misunderstood, and it plays an important role in the controversy about Soviet price policy (see chapters 4 and 8), therefore it must be examined in some detail.

'Turnover tax' (*nalog s oborota*) was first levied in 1931, when it replaced a variety of excise duties. It covers three kinds of tax, which are in significant respects distinct from one another. The first is an excise duty in all but name, levied at a fixed rate: the taxes on vodka, matches and salt are examples of this. The second may be described as 'tax by difference', and, beginning in 1939, has been commonly applied to industrial consumers' goods where there is very large assortment of product (for instance, textiles). Here the tax emerges as the difference between the retail price (less trade margin) and the wholesale price. In principle, the retail price is fixed in relation to supply and demand, and the wholesale price is based on average cost plus a small profit margin, and the tax emerges as equal to the gap between them.[1] The third species of turnover tax is in some respects similar to the second, but, so to speak, is a 'difference with a difference': it arises from the acquisition by the state of farm produce at low prices. Thus in 1936 the compulsory procurement price for wheat, plus handling costs, was fifteen roubles per ton. This wheat was sold to the state milling enterprises at 107 roubles per ton, the tax amounting to 92 roubles, or to almost nine-tenths of the wholesale price inclusive of tax.[2] The distinction between this and the tax on textiles is that, whereas the latter bears on the consumer of the textiles, the bulk of the tax on the grain clearly falls on the peasants who were compelled to deliver the grain so cheaply. It also implies that it is not very meaningful to calculate the percentage tax on bread grains and use the enormous percentage so obtained to prove that 'bread is heavily taxed in Russia', since the percentage would reflect the extent of under-payment of the peasants. If the grain were delivered free in the guise of a tax in kind, the tax percentage would become infinity! Revenue from this source has fallen relatively in recent years, owing to upward amendment in state buying prices.

Turnover tax falls on consumers' goods or on materials predominantly intended for consumption, except that tax is levied on all uses of electricity, natural gas and oil. Actual rates are generally unpublished since the war.[3] Until 1949, there was a nominal tax of $\frac{1}{2}$ to 1 per cent on practically all products of heavy industry.

It is the Soviet habit, when reporting tax rates, to express the percentage in relation to the wholesale price inclusive of the tax. To illustrate this point, let us imagine cloth worth 100 roubles without tax and 150 with tax. In Great Britain we would call this a purchase tax of 50 per cent, but in the USSR the tax would be described as being $33\frac{1}{3}$ per cent.

The actual method of collection of the tax varies: it is increas-

---

[1] This has consequences to the role of prices as 'transmitters' of demand (see page 135, below).

[2] The figures really were as given here! See S. Azarkh, *Oblozhenie khlebo-produktov* (Moscow, 1936), p. 20 ff. Example relates to the central-Russian zone, soft wheats; an additional tax was then levied on grain or flour sold retail.

[3] However, some rates are published. Thus electricity enterprises pay turnover tax on revenues, which, in 1956, varied from 0 in the Donetz basin to 45-50 per cent in Armenia, with an all-union average of 15·8 per cent (Sh. Turetski, *Ocherki planovovo tseno-obrazovaniya v SSSR* (Moscow, 1959), p. 135).

ingly paid by the producing enterprise, sometimes by the wholesaling organization, which is now generally within the network of the Ministry of Trade, or, in the case of many farm products, by the procurement organization.[1] Producers' co-operatives pay tax on some articles. Sales of farm produce in the free market are exempt. Produce used for stockpiling, or for export, is also exempt.[2]

This tax causes some philosophical confusion. It has become customary for Soviet theoreticians to claim that this is not an indirect tax, but rather a 'profit of the socialist economy'. The state owns industry, and the difference between costs and the final selling price is the state's profit, so it is argued. The division of this surplus between the enterprise's profit and the budget's share is a mere matter of administrative convenience. The economics textbook avoids using the word 'tax', preferring to give the name 'the state's centralized net income' to all its revenues from the economy.[3] It is then claimed that, unlike capitalist countries, the USSR raises nearly all its state revenues without recourse to taxation! It is perhaps not so easy to explain how the vodka tax differs in principle from the whisky duty, or how the revenue arising from the procurement of farm products at low prices is part of the 'profits of the socialist economy', especially as many Soviet economists admit that this tax falls on peasants, either as a form of 'differential rent' or as 'the peasants' share in general state expenditure', or both.[4]

'Deduction from profits' (*otchislenie ot pribylei*) is the state's residual share in enterprise profits, and requires no further explanation (see page 98, above). There is, however, a significant point which relates to this item and also to turnover tax: these revenues should not be regarded as 'net'. Enterprises often receive from the budget sums to cover some of their expenditures, even though the budget takes part of their profits. Turnover tax is sometimes paid by organizations which then have to receive a compensating subsidy; for example, for several years the food industry paid turnover tax and calculated profits on the assumption that all its milk and meat had been obtained at the low compulsory-procurement price, and the extra amounts which had to be paid out for over-quota purchases

---

[1] In 1958, 60 per cent of turnover tax was paid by industrial enterprises, 40 per cent by wholesaling organizations of the Ministry of Trade (Turetski, op. cit., p. 56). There is a tendency towards direct payments by enterprises since that date.

[2] F. Uryupin, *Finansy SSSR*, No. 5/1957, p. 22.

[3] *Politicheskaya ekonomiya*, 3rd revised edition (Moscow, 1958), p. 596.

[4] See the interesting arguments on this whole matter by D. Allakhverdyan, *Vop. Ekon.*, No. 2/1954, pp. 50 ff., and M. Bor, *Vop. Ekon.*, No. 10/1954, pp. 79 ff.

were covered by way of subsidy.[1] The object seems to have been to avoid having to recalculate industrial costs.

This same point arises again in considering the item MTS *revenues*, which is now disappearing with the disappearance of the MTS. These 'revenues' consisted principally of produce received in payment for their services, valued until 1958 at the low compulsory-procurement prices. The resultant sum appeared on the revenue side of the budget, and, when it was resold to processing enterprises or to consumers, the big difference was included in turnover tax revenue. Yet the consequence of so low a valuation was that MTS expenditures (until 1958) greatly exceeded income, though the 'loss' was 'bookkeeping' rather than real.

Co-operative and *collective-farm* taxes have been already dealt with (pages 43 and 51, above). The '*tax on non-commodity operations*', abolished in 1958, was levied on turnover of service enterprises, such as municipal laundries, baths and the like.

Revenues from *state loans* were of three kinds. The first, and for a long time the biggest, was the *mass-subscription loan*, which was to all intents and purposes a compulsory deduction from wages to buy premium bonds, the lottery-prize drawing representing at first 4 per cent, then 3 per cent and finally 2 per cent of the total sum subscribed.[2] In 1958, it was decided to abandon the practice, while simultaneously suspending lottery-prize drawings and repayments on already existing bonds. This is why the sum under this head shows so large a drop in 1958. The second kind of loan revenue arises from the fact that state *savings banks*, in which citizens are encouraged (by a 3 per cent rate of interest) to keep their savings, buy interest-bearing state bonds, their purchases in each year being roughly equal to the increase in deposits during that year. Finally, there are other bond sales, notably to individual citizens on a genuinely voluntary basis (these were not defaulted upon or suspended in 1958). All these loan revenues are included in the ordinary budget.

Direct taxes play a very limited role in the budget. They are of several kinds. There is, firstly, income tax,[3] levied on all revenues other than those of kolkhoz peasants. The rate of tax depends partly on the level of income and partly on its source. Thus in 1958 the rates were as follows:

---

[1] See also p. 141, below.
[2] The reductions were in 1953 (*Finansy i kredit SSSR*, Moscow, 1953, p. 210) and in 1955.
[3] Before the war income tax as such was quite small, there being also a local tax entitled 'cultural and housing levy' (*Kul'tzhilsbor*). This was merged with income tax in 1943.

Table 2.   Tax rates

Annual income (roubles)	Workers and employees*	Writers and artists	Co-operative artisans	Lawyers doctors etc.†	Individual artisans
		(Per cent of income)			
2,000	Exempt	1·5	Exempt	3	4·6
4,000	Exempt	4·0	Exempt	6·65	9·8
6,000	5·2	5·2	5·72	10·1	14·2
12,000	8·2	8·2	9·02	18·5	24·5
24,000	10·6	10·6	11·66	27·6	35·7
36,000	11·4	11·4	12·54	34·9	43·6

Source: G. Maryakhin, *Finansy SSSR*, No. 1/1958, p. 87.

* On income from employment by state enterprises and organizations.

† In respect of private practise.

Kolkhoz peasants pay '*agricultural tax*' on their private holdings (see page 57, above), and nothing on their incomes from collective farms. Then there exists a *bachelor and small-families tax*, which was introduced during the war. Until 1958, it was paid by all single and married persons of child-bearing age at the rate of 6 per cent of income (a fixed sum in the case of kolkhoz peasants), and smaller rates were paid if there were less than three children. In 1958, however, all persons with children, and also unmarried women, were freed from tax, and persons with low incomes were exempted. This tax, and also income-tax, levied on 'workers and employees', will be gradually abolished in the period 1960-65, with some compensating diminution in upper-bracket wages and salaries.

Social insurance revenues arise from the contribution paid by enterprises (see page 34, above).

There is also a large number of *miscellaneous taxes and other revenues,* of which the following is an incompete list: net revenues of the state insurance trust (*Gosstrakh*), timber-cutting levy, stamp duty, automobile registration fees, repayment of credits granted to foreign countries,[1] passport fees, entertainments tax, customs duty, revenue from foreign trade (arising from the overvaluation of the rouble, until the 1961 reform), and also the carry-over from the previous year within the budgets of local authorities. There was also a 'buildings tax' and 'ground rent' levied on property occupied by

[1] This is mentioned by N. Kisman and I. Slavnyi, in the pamphlet, *Sovetskie finansy v pyatoi pyatiletke* (Moscow, 1956). Logically the credits themselves should be included somewhere under expenditure, but where?

state enterprises as well as other organizations. This was abolished, so far as the former were concerned, in 1959.

The bulk of these miscellaneous items, as of total revenues, arise from economic activities of enterprises and not from taxation of individuals, as can be seen from the last line of Table 1. In essence, all these revenues have as their source the gap between costs of production and the final selling price. It is sometimes argued by western propagandists that this is 'regressive taxation', contrasting it with the very much higher rates and steeper progression of taxes on personal incomes in western countries. To a considerable extent this argument is unsound. In so far as incomes from state employment are determined by the state, there is no reason why the fiscal system should be invoked to correct excessive inequalities, when the obvious way out would be to alter the relative incomes themselves. Indeed, there is no particularly compelling reason to charge tax at all on incomes derived from state sources, and this is doubtless why the decision was taken to 'abolish income tax', though nothing is being done to abolish the tax on incomes from private enterprise which, as can be seen from Table 2 above, are taxed at much higher rates.

Given the government's decisions about resource allocation, the budget must find means to cover state expenditures on non-consumption (e.g. investment, defence) or on social consumption (education, health and so on). Direct taxes are of minor importance. Voluntary savings can play only a minor role in the process. There remains the raising of revenue through the gap between costs and final selling prices of goods, and this, in various forms, is the largest source of income for the state budget. In western countries, such expenditures are financed by direct and indirect taxation, or out of the profits of private companies and individuals. In the USSR, the amount which requires financing is relatively larger than in the west, partly because of the higher proportion of the national income devoted to accumulation, and partly because social services play a bigger role relatively to distributed personal incomes. But in all countries these expenditures must be financed somehow. To put it at its simplest, men engaged in industries which do not make consumers' goods, or in the army, or teaching, or medicine, have to be paid and will demand consumers' goods with their money, and, unless heavy direct taxation sufficiently reduces personal cash income, the retail prices of consumers' goods must, therefore, exceed the wage cost of producing them by a considerable margin. This margin in the USSR consists principally of turnover tax plus profits. The magnitude of this margin reflects the proportion of total resources devoted other than to personal consumption. It is futile to 'blame' turnover tax for high prices in general, as if state could simply lower the price level by reducing tax, though naturally the burden could be redistributed between commodities and sectors (e.g. by charging more on vodka and less on textiles).[1] The present price level of consumers' goods is not due to the fact that they bear most of the turnover tax; essentially the price level is determined by the relationship between personal disposable incomes and the goods and services available. Thus, if turnover tax were charged on all producers' goods, the cost structure would certainly be much altered, costs of production of consumers' goods would rise, turnover tax on consumers' goods would fall, but *of itself* such a rearrangement would not cause any fall in retail prices, whatever other advantages it may have. The way towards increased purchasing power of the consumer lies, of course, through increased supplies of consumers' goods. If these outrun the rise in money incomes, prices—and turnover tax rates per unit—naturally fall, as they did in the years following 1947. The reason for making these apparently self-evident assertions is that propagandists have often 'accused' turnover tax of causing high prices, when the problem is one of resource allocation, which can indeed be made the subject of legitimate criticism.

The main headings of budgetary *expenditure* are given in the following table:

Table 3. Expenditures

	1940	1950	1958
	(thousand million roubles)		
Allocations to the national economy	58·4	157·9	290·3
Social-cultural expenditures	40·9	116·7	214·2
Defence	56·8	82·8	93·6
Administration	6·8	13·9	12·0
Loan service	2·8	5·1	3·7
Other expenditure	8·6	38·8	28·9
TOTAL	174·3	413·2	642·7
Surplus	5·9	9·6	29·6

[1] It is often alleged that turnover taxes are highest on 'necessities'. This view is partly based on the rather misleadingly high tax rates which were levied on the low procurement price of bread grains, and partly correctly reflects the fact that, to be effectively collected, the tax (or price mark-up) needs to be largely concentrated on goods with a low elasticity of demand; in any event, the range of luxuries has been comparatively small.

Allocations to the national economy represent non-returnable budgetary grants to enterprises and organizations, of which the largest portion is devoted to fixed investment, the financing of which will be examined separately. However, a large sum, rather over a third of the total, is spent on other things, and Soviet statistics are generally very vague about the actual amounts involved. Figures for two of these items only have been fairly regularly published: firstly, the costs of the MTS, which, it will be recalled, fell wholly on the budget and greatly exceeded the revenue of the MTS valued at procurement prices (this item is now disappearing, with the gradual abolition of the MTS); and, secondly, the budget's share in increases of enterprises' 'own' working capital. Other items which come under this head include subsidies; these are sometimes paid out openly as such, under the name of *dotatsii*, and in some years these were substantial;[1] but many other payments resemble subsidies in all but name. These include so-called 'starting expenses' (*puskovye raskhody*), and also the quite substantial sums paid out to cover losses on housing, which are due to the fact that rents are far from covering the running costs and repairs of houses owned by local soviets and enterprises. In 1958-59, a payment seems to have been made from the budget to compensate enterprises for losses due to the changes in wages and hours, and this was not called a subsidy. Here are also to be found the offsetting payments compensating for overpayment of turnover tax, referred to under that head (page 101, above). There are also subsidies of a special kind, paid to trade corporations by reason of the over-valuation of the rouble in terms of foreign exchange, which caused a loss on export deals (before 1961). Also financed out of these allocations are expenditures on stockpiling, and probably a number of other items on which information is lacking. Thus it can be seen that these 'Allocations to the national economy' are something of a ragbag, including as they do investments, subsidies and certain types of operational expenditures. Statistics on these allocations by sector (e.g. agriculture, transport, heavy industry and so on) are generally published annually, though with gaps. A point to bear in mind in studying the published material is that budget *estimates* include a contingency reserve (for instance, 21·8 milliard for 1958), of which the bulk is used to finance unforeseen expenditures on the national economy.

---

[1] In 1948, subsidies (*dotatsii*) reached 41·2 milliard roubles, of which 35·3 went to industry (A. Zverev, *Voprosy natsional'novo dokhoda i finansov SSSR* (Moscow, 1958), p. 212). (A big price increase in 1949 eliminated most of these subsidies.)

Social-cultural expenditures include education, health, maternity assistance, social insurance and social security. The 'social insurance budget', which until 1938 was an independent entity, is now merged with the state budget, being used principally to cover expenditures on sick pay and pensions. Unlike the allocations to the national economy, the social-cultural budget is published in great detail.[1] It has been growing rapidly. This is not the place for an examination of Soviet educational and welfare policies, and so no further comment is necessary, except to note that the education vote includes an item for *'Science'* (*nauka*, more properly translated Knowledge), under which it is thought that nuclear research is financed, as well as scientific and cultural activities of less dramatic kinds.

Defence is self-explanatory, but, since no information about the content of the defence vote is ever given, it is possible that some defence items appear elsewhere. Thus some military nuclear research may be financed under 'Science', and the stockpiling expenditures under 'Allocations to the national economy' could include stockpiling of weapons. Investment in arms factories quite logically belongs in 'Allocations to the national economy', and para-military security troops are financed out of the police vote (see below). However, investment in American or British arms factories is usually financed by private investment and not from the budget at all, while internal security troops in countries which possess them (France and Spain, for instance) also fall to the Ministry of the Interior budget. Nuclear research is separately financed in many countries. Thus there are no positive grounds for thinking that the coverage of the Soviet defence budget is very different from western practice, though the high degree of secrecy justifies a degree of caution or scepticism. In particular, we do not know the prices at which weapons are acquired by the armed forces.

Loan service includes interest payments on bonds held by institutions (e.g. savings banks), and lottery prizes and repayments of bonds held by individuals. The total expenditure under this head rose to 16·3 milliards in 1956, and fell to only 3·7 milliards in 1958, consequent upon the suspension of payments and prize-drawings on the compulsorily placed mass loans.

The *Administration* vote covers, of course, local and republican governments, as well as the centre. It includes also the administration of justice, but not the police. By long tradition, the Ministry of Interior and the Security organization (OGPU, NKVD, MVD, KGB,

---

[1] See especially a separate volume of figures, *Sotsial'no-kulturnye raskhody byudzheta SSSR* (Moscow, 1959).

etc.) come under a separate vote. No figures are available for recent years, but in 1948 it could be calculated that the interior and security services vote rose to the fantastic total of over 25 milliard roubles, or about double all other administrative and judicial expenses.[1] The police vote is concealed among 'other expenditures'. Since Stalin's death the size of the police and expenditure upon it have fallen considerably, and this is reflected in the fact that in Table 3, above, the item 'other expenditures' was considerably smaller in 1958 than it was in 1950. No doubt some other kinds of expenditure are also financed under this miscellaneous group, but details are unavailable.

Before leaving budgetary statistics, it is desirable to mention a peculiarity which was of importance in 1953 and 1954. In these years, for reasons which have never been explained, both sides of the budget were inflated by the inclusion of 'expenditures on price reductions'. As far as can be ascertained, what happened was this: prices were reduced by aggregate equivalent of a given sum, which represented revenue foregone. This sum then appeared in the budget total, both in 'other revenue' and in 'other expenditure'. Therefore in these years these residuals were abnormally high. This had not happened before, and seems not to have happened since. These were the only two budgets presented during Malenkov's tenure of office as prime minister, though this could be coincidence. This was pure 'padding', in that the sums in question appear not to have ever been paid in and out of the budget, unlike the real in-and-out items which still exist and which do represent real payments.

The detailed powers of republics and local authorities over their budgets has varied, and has been increased in recent years. For example, while in 1953 nearly four-fifths of the state budget was administered directly by the all-union authorities, reflecting the high degree of centralization of the Stalin period, in 1958 over half of total expenditure was within the separate budgets of the union republics (which include those of local authorities in their territories). To a great extent, however, the republics spend in accordance with central instructions. This applies particularly to allocations to the national

[1] Zverev, in the stenographic report of the 1948 (budget) session of the Supreme Soviet, p. 323, gave total expenditure on administration, plus MVD and the MGB (Security Ministry) as 33·1 milliards for *union and republics only,* excluding local government. According to N. Rovinski, *Gosudarstvennyi Byudzet SSSR* (1949 edition), p. 47, local administrative expenses were 5·6 milliard roubles, and these would not include the highly centralized MVD/MGB. Total expenditures on administration and justice, excluding MVD/MGB, was given by Zverev as 13·5 milliards. 33·1 + 5·6 − 13·5 = 25·2. Q.E.D.

economy, since allocations disbursed through *sovnarkhozy* pass normally through the republican budgets, even though the expenditure may be due wholly to the instructions of the central government. However, by a reform promulgated in 1959, republics retain certain revenues raised on their territories: all revenue from kolkhoz and co-operative taxes, all agricultural tax, 50 per cent of income tax, the bulk of the budget's share in profits of enterprises, and some other items;[1] in addition they may or may not receive a portion of the turnover tax revenues, according to the union government's estimate of their needs. In general, as is only to be expected, republics or areas which are being developed (for instance, Kazakhstan) receive more from the centre than they pay in.

THE FINANCING OF INVESTMENT

Owing to its key importance in the planning process, and also the many sources from which it is financed, investment requires separate consideration.

The major part of investment in the state sector is financed by non-returnable budgetary grants. However, a sizeable and increasing share is financed from enterprises' own resources, primarily from a portion of profits, and the amortization fund. With minor exceptions, these sums are transferred to specialized investment banks (see page 113, below), which issue them when and if the expenditure is justified by the investment plan, or, in the case of extra-plan investment expenditures, falls within the regulations governing these.

The central investment plan is submitted to the government of the USSR by Gosplan, and is a vital part of the general long-term planning process, for obvious reasons. The extent to which the process is centralized has varied considerably in Soviet history. From this standpoint, investments in the state sector can be divided into several categories. There is, first of all, the distinction between 'above-limit' and 'below-limit' (*sverkhlimitnye* and *nizhelimitnye*) investments. Investment projects of a value exceeding a certain sum[2] must each be approved by the centre, while those below these value limits do not require approval separately, but form part of aggregate sums allocated for investment purposes to the given sector. There is also a somewhat different distinction between *centralized* and *decentralized* investments, the latter sometimes being confusingly designated *vnelimitnyi* ('beyond limit'). Centralized invest-

[1] *Pravda*, October 31, 1959. Before then they received much less as of right.
[2] This has varied between economic sectors and at different dates.

ments are those covered by the central investment plan, and include 'below-limit' investments if expenditure on these is provided for in the plan. Decentralized investments are financed from sources not covered by the plan at all, such as, for instance, the enterprise fund, profits of local industry or 'mechanization' credits from the State Bank. The extent of decentralized investments was severely restricted during the last years of Stalin's life, and indeed the category as such was formally abolished in 1951.[1] In recent years, however, their importance has again increased. Thus in 1953 the difference between planned and total investment was only 6 milliard roubles against 35 milliards in 1958 and 40·4 in 1959.[2] Of course, these 'unplanned' investments are by no means uncontrolled. There are restrictions on the types of permitted investments; for example, a decree in 1958 forbade local investment in certain types of construction (offices, sports stadiums, etc.) without the special authorization of the republican government.[3] Then control over allocations of materials and equipment provides a further means of preventing diversion of resources into forms of investment not desired by the authorities. The reform of 1957, by expanding the economic functions of republics and through the creation of *sovnarkhozy,* has increased the range of initiative from below, in the process of determining the investment plan and in approving or disallowing unplanned or minor investments at local authority or enterprise level. However, the basic responsibility remains central, and, in an economy of the Soviet type, it is hard to see how it can be otherwise.

The cost of investment projects is carefully controlled. Based on prices of materials, machinery and labour, on centrally-approved norms (e.g. of depth of foundations or thickness of walls), and when possible on approved architectural patterns, costs estimates (*smety*) are approved, and form the basis of the issues of money by investment banks. The laying down of rules and designs for building is the task of the State Committee for Construction (*Gosstroi*), and, in detail, by 'project-making organizations'.[4]

---

[1] D. Ailakhverdyan, *Nekotorye voprosy teorii sovetskikh finansov* (Moscow, 1951), p. 168.
[2] *Vest. Stat.*, No. 4/1959, Statistical supplement, and *N.Kh.* 1958, pp. 618, 628.
[3] *Pravda*, October 5, 1958.
[4] 'Project-making expenditures', i.e. quantity-surveying, designs, blue prints and other necessary investigations, were financed with investments until 1951. At this date it was decided to finance them separately, as a means of maintaining tighter control over projects. From January, 1959, they are again financed with investments. In 1958 the amount involved was 6½ milliard roubles. See also p. 85, above.

Outside the state sector, investments are financed from profits (producers' co-operatives), the capital fund (*kolkhozy*), private savings (notably for private house-building), and from bank credits to *kolkhozy*, co-operatives and individuals. Co-operatives may borrow for periods of up to fifteen years. If the proposed investment is large enough to be 'above-limit', it requires approval by the government. Interest rates are generally 2 per cent, but *kolkhozy* were allowed to borrow for approved purposes at the unusually low rate of 1·75 per cent under a decision made in 1954.[1]

The setting out on a comparable basis of all these various investments, and analysing them by source, presents some rather tiresome difficulties, owing to the incompleteness of the official statistics, and in particular the fact that figures relating to *planned* investments are much more complete (with regard to the sources of financing) than those giving the actual sums expended. The table below endeavours to reconstruct the picture for 1958.

Table 4.　Fixed investments, 1958

		(*Milliard roubles*)
(a)	As originally planned (state sector)	203·8
	of which:	
	Financed from budget	(142·7)
	Financed from enterprise profits	(29·1)
	Financed from amortization funds	(27·7)
(b)	Actually spent: state 'planned' investments	199·1
(c)	Actually spent: 'unplanned' investments	40·4
(d)	Kolkhoz investments, actual	28·2
	of which:	
	Financed by credits	(4·3)
(e)	Individual investments	Not known
	of which:	
	Financed by housing credits	(3·5)

Sources: (a) Zverev, *Plan. Khoz.* No. 12/1957, p. 21.

　　　　(b) *N.Kh. 1958*, p. 628.

　　　　(c) *N.Kh. 1958*, p. 629. Includes producers' co-operative investments, which are unlikely to exceed 2–3 milliards.

　　　　(d) *N.Kh. 1958*, p. 619. *Vest. Stat.* No. 2/1960, pp. 86–88.

　　　　(e) 2·8 was planned in 1957 (*Finansy SSSR*, No. 4/1957, p. 17) and trend has been sharply upwards.

[1] K. Plotnikov (ed.), *Organizatsia finansirovania i kreditovania kapital'nykh vlozhenii* (Moscow, 1954), p. 298.

There is a degree of statistical imperfection involved in any attempt to add together state and non-state investments, because in many instances these occur at different prices; thus individuals have and *kolkhozy* had generally paid retail prices, inclusive of tax, on building materials and other capital goods which are available to state enterprises tax free and therefore much cheaper (see examples on page 133, below).

The total is equal to something midway between gross and net fixed investment. It is more than net because it is financed partly out of the depreciation (amortization) fund. It is less than gross because a large portion of the depreciation fund—that earmarked for so-called 'capital repairs'—is not included in the figures. However, the concepts in question are by no means clearly defined anywhere, and differ widely as between western countries, so perfection should be neither sought nor expected.[1]

BANKING AND CREDIT

Banks were nationalized in one of the first acts of the Soviet government after the revolution, but it was not until the end of the Civil War that the State Bank (usually known by the abbreviation *Gosbank*) was founded, within the People's Commissariat of Finance. In the period of NEP, apart from the normal functions of a central bank, it also provided credits to the state and the private sectors of the economy, on both short and long terms. However, credits were also provided by enterprises to one another, until the credit reform of 1930-32. This did two things. Firstly, it gave Gosbank monopoly in granting short-term credits; secondly, it took away from Gosbank the tasks of financing investments, transferring this to specialized investment banks (see below), and basing investment financing of the state sector on non-returnable grants rather than credits. Its essential functions have remained broadly unaltered since, but its status was enhanced in 1954 by its separation from the Ministry of Finance and the promotion of the director to ministerial status.

Gosbank continues to carry out the functions of a central bank (issue of banknotes, keeping the gold reserve, making international payments),[2] as well as administering tax receipts and the paying out of the state's current expenditures. It also acts as an essential part

[1] For example, compare the treatment of repairs (e.g. to ships) in the capital accounts of Great Britain and Norway. Depreciation in the west is, in any event, more a fiscal than an economic category: it is what the tax inspector can be persuaded to accept.

[2] A specialized branch of Gosbank, *Vneshtorgbank*, deals with foreign trade payments.

of the economic control mechanism, carrying out so-called *kontrol' rublyom*—'control' by the rouble. All state enterprises must keep their accounts in Gosbank, must pay all but the smallest bills through Gosbank, which is thus able to check that cash resources are used only in accordance with the regulations, to pay wage rates and prices prescribed by the regulations, and in conformity with the plan. The Bank provides short-term credits, and this too provides an essential control mechanism. An eminent Soviet expert wrote: 'The Bank issues credits for the purposes and the amounts provided for by the plan. If the plan is overfulfilled, the enterprise can claim and the Bank must issue credits for the needs associated with plan overfulfilment; if the plan is underfulfilled, credits must be reduced. In this process, the Bank supervises not only the amount of the credit, but also its use for the particular purpose which the plan intends, not permitting unplanned redistribution of material and monetary resources in the socialist economy between and within enterprises'.[1] If enterprises are in financial difficulties and consequently do not keep bank credits at planned levels, or fail to repay them at due dates, a series of 'credit sanctions' may be applied; credits may be refused without the guarantee of a superior organ (e.g. the sector division of the *sovnarkhoz*) and, in the last resort, the Bank can declare the enterprise insolvent, publish the fact in its journal and virtually take command over its assets (before such a desperate situation is reached, superior authority generally steps in to dismiss the management and reorganize the enterprise). On the contrary, if the enterprise is financially successful, it is given favourable treatment in obtaining credits.[2]

The role of credits is to facilitate the process of payment and to overcome the time-gap which must arise between payments and receipts. Gosbank credits provide about 40 per cent of all working capital in the economy.[3] However, the division between 'own' and borrowed working capital varies greatly in different sectors of the economy. Thus the role of credits is much greater in trade and in light industry than it is in heavy industry, apparently because the latter has been favoured with more lavish provision of own resources, another instance of the priority which it enjoys. Short-term credits to state enterprises carry an interest rate of 2 per cent, some-

[1] K. Plotnikov, *Finansy i kredit v SSSR* (Moscow, 1959), p. 167.
[2] For a valuable and detailed account of this and other aspects of the Bank's credit system, see I. Kirillov, *Finansy sotsialisticheskoy promyshlennosti* (Moscow, 1959), especially pp. 144-73.
[3] Excluding building and *kolkhozy*. M. Atlas, *Razvitie gosudarstvennovo banka SSSR* (Moscow, 1958), p. 349.

times less, or 3 per cent if return of credits is overdue. (For the role of credits in enterprise finance, and the distinction between 'own' and borrowed working capital, see page 36, above.) Quarterly credit plans must be submitted by Gosbank to Gosplan and the government, since these must be carefully geared in with the general economic plans for which these bodies are responsible. The importance of Gosbank as an organ capable of enforcing centrally determined financial and credit policies, has increased since the 1957 reform gave wider functions to republics and *sovnarkhozy*, for Gosbank is essentially a centralized, all-union institution. Its monetary resources come partly from deposits of enterprises partly from the transfer to it of the bulk of budget surpluses, partly from budgetary grants. The Bank also retains a portion of the profits which it makes.

Though, in principle, Gosbank is not concerned with investment, it is found convenient to use it, rather than the investment banks, for the provision of 'mechanization' credits (see page 36, above) and for credits to local, communal and producers' co-operative enterprises which are used for investment purposes.

Individuals are encouraged (by a 3 per cent rate of interest) to use the network of *savings banks* which are under the control of the Ministry of Finance.

In 1932 there were created four investment banks: *Prombank* (industrial bank), *Sel'khozbank* (agricultural bank), *Torgbank* (trade and co-operatives), and *Tsekombank* (communal and housing bank, which controlled numerous local 'communal' banks), under the Ministry of Finance. Their primary function was to administer investment funds, which reached them from two principal sources: from the state budget and from enterprises (the latter transferred to the investment banks the portion of the amortization fund and profits earmarked for new investment). In the case of investments in the state sector, the banks financed the necessary building or acquisition of equipment. In addition, because of the special position of building enterprises as executants of the investment plan, the investment banks provided credits for these enterprises. The importance of these banks as a checking and controlling agency has already been emphasized. The appropriate banks also provided long-term credits to *kolkhozy* and co-operatives, and for industrial housing.

In 1959, however, the system was altered, and all these four banks disappeared. In their place was created a construction bank (Stroibank), which took over the major functions of the defunct investment banks, shedding some minor ones to Gosbank.[1]

[1] For details, see leading article in *Finansy SSSR*, No. 6/1959.

Soviet currency, the rouble, is nominally on a gold standard. This has no practical signifiance, save that it determines official exchange rates. In theory Soviet currency should be, as is sometimes claimed, 'the most stable in the world'. Planning enables the authorities to limit effective demand to the quantities of goods and services available at established prices, by control over personal incomes and by controlling enterprises' claims on resources by physical allocation and various other forms of regulation. However, things have seldom been so simple, and there have been instances of acute inflation, sometimes open, sometimes concealed. Thus, in the hard years of the first five-year plan (1928-32) and in the period of the war, a sharp diminution of supplies of consumer goods stimulated an upward trend in money wages, which, as will be shown in detail, cannot be very effectively controlled even in more normal times. Despite efforts to keep down costs and to control wages funds, the banks in fact pay out rather more than planned, thereby increasing the volume of money in circulation. The credit reform of 1931, giving Gosbank a credit monopoly, had the effect of greatly stimulating inflation; credits granted by enterprises to each other were limited by their financial resources, but, in the context of the priority given to the achievement of rapid growth of output, Gosbank could and did issue whatever sums were deemed necessary, since financial soundness was repeatedly sacrificed to production achievements. If the level of money wages outruns gains in productivity, increases in prices of producers' goods are the only alternative to subsidies; if the level of money wages increases faster than the volume of goods and services available for sale to the citizens, a price increase is the only alternative to rationing. In the producers' goods field, it is true, rationing (i.e. administrative allocation) is the rule rather than the exception, and so inflationary pressures can show themselves by the severity of such rationing and by frequent breakdowns in material supplies—which happen often enough and are signs of overstrain. A disguised inflation in the consumers' goods sector is possible without any rationing, and indeed has shown itself by lengthening queues at various dates in Soviet history. After the war there was a very sharp rise in the price level, but this was followed by an all-round decline when supplies flowed from a reconstructed economy. In the period 1954-60 retail prices have remained steady, while costs (and producers' goods prices, based on costs) have been declining. But inflationary pressures persist, and prevailing prices tend in various degrees to be below the level at which supply would equal demand.

CHAPTER 4

Wages and Prices

PRINCIPLES OF WAGE DETERMINATION

In most areas of Soviet planning of economic life, as indeed in the west also, it is important to distinguish between formal principles and actuality. Nowhere is this more important than in the field of wages and salaries. The system appears to be far more centralized and far more tightly controlled than it really is. It would appear at first sight that wages can be systematically adjusted to conform to some set of desiderata, that the total level of disposable money incomes can deliberately be made to conform to the value of goods and services available, and that the government's authority over wage payments, in a totalitarian state in which independent trade unions do not exist, can readily eliminate anomalies and illogicalities. It will be seen that the truth is very different. However, it is first necessary to describe the formal structure.

The general level of wages, the 'spread' between grades and areas, and the rates payable in different industries have been the responsibility of the central government. Until its abolition in 1934, the People's Commissariat for Labour was responsible for these tasks. The All-Union Central Council of Trade Unions (AUCCTU) absorbed some (notably the social-insurance) of the functions of this commissariat; it also had, and still has, a central wages department. However, the AUCCTU is not part of the government, nor is it the task of trade unions to negotiate wage agreements, though they are directly involved in the definition of grading (of which more in a moment) and are also brought into discussions on incentive schemes; they doubtless also make representations about wage anomalies, but decisions on wage rates as such are clearly regarded as a governmental task. While the Economic Council[1] existed, wage questions were referred to it, but from the war until 1956 there was no body below the Council of Ministers which could decide these questions, or indeed even consider them systematically, in the absence of anything coresponding to a Ministry of Labour. Indeed, there was no *system-*

[1] See p. 65, above.

atic revision of Soviet wage-rates from 1931 to 1956. Obviously, wages were altered repeatedly between these dates; there were generally-decreed increases by given amounts, as for instance in 1937 and 1946, and many orders relating to particular groups or occupations, such as coal-miners, school-teachers, civil servants and the like. However, these piecemeal reforms were, as a rule, due either to a necessary and indeed delayed adjustment to an inflationary situation, or represented yielding to the pressure of an economic ministry anxious to improve its chance of recruiting good workers. The government's response to these requests reflected its own judgment of priorities, as modified by its efforts to combat inflation. The ministries adopted different geographical zoning arrangements, and wages or bonus arrangements for similar work in different industries became inconsistent with one another, leading to numerous complaints. Under the circumstances, anomalies multiplied. In 1956, a State Committee on Labour and Wages came into existence, charged with the task of revising the wages structure from its foundations.

These anomalies were due in part to the fact that some wage-rates are, of their nature, far easier to control than others. Thus, at one extreme, pay of administrative, managerial and other specialized personnel (engineers, economists, accountants, or teachers, doctors, etc.) can be prescribed in detail in the regulations which lay down the establishments, promulgated by and enforced through the Ministry of Finance.[1] If it is laid down that the headmaster of a school or the chief engineer of a factory of a certain size are respectively entitled to a basic salary of 1,500 and 2,500 roubles a month, this bears the character of a clear instruction, hard to evade. But at the other extreme are the majority of factory workers, state-farmers, shop-assistants and so on, whose pay depends on individual or group piece-work, and therefore the amount they actually receive depends on the degree to which they fulfil the output norms. Here, too, the principles governing wage determination are clear. All workers are divided into grades, the government settles the wage of grade one (the lowest), each step upwards is calculated by co-efficients which are also laid down by the government,[2] and the qualifications required for each grade are published for each industry in a 'tariff-qualification manual' (*tarifno-kvalifikatsionnyi spravochnik*) which also bears the signature of the secretary of the industrial trade unions

---

[1] The Establishments commission of this ministry (see p. 92, above).

[2] For example, in 1958 the typical scale of differentials, from bottom to top of the scale, was in the ratio of $1:2\cdot8$, in a progression of eight grades of skill (Rumyantsev, op. cit., p. 316).

concerned. It was intended that the piece-worker should earn the rate laid down for his grade by just fulfilling the norm. Thus if the day rate for a grade four piece-worker in the textile industry were fixed at 20 roubles, and if in a day's work the average worker should perform 100 operations, then the piece rate should be 20 kopecks. If by good work he overfulfilled the norm by, say, 10 per cent, then, under 'straight' piecework, he would be entitled to 22 roubles. However, in priority sectors of the economy there was often to be found a system known as 'progressive piecework', which entitled the worker to double or even treble rates for output over the norm.[1] At regular intervals enterprises were supposed to revise the norms upwards, to offset and encourage increases in productivity. Timeworkers of the same degree of skill were to be paid less than pieceworkers.

The total wages bill for a given year is calculated centrally, Gosplan and the Ministry of Finance being most directly involved, with, since 1956, the Committee of Labour and Wages. Under the ministerial system, each ministry was informed of the size of its wages fund for the coming year, the magnitude being determined partly by what happened in the previous year and partly by the expected changes in the size and qualifications of its labour force. These, in turn, were related to the output and labour productivity plans for the given industry, in the light of general wages policy, which reflected the expected changes in availability of consumers' goods and services, and decisions on retail prices. The end-result was that a given economic ministry would know that its wages fund had been increased from, say, 20·5 to 21·5 milliard roubles. Since the 1957 reform, the republics and *sovnarkhozy* have replaced the ministries in the industrial sectors, and they are informed of the permitted wages fund for the area for which they are responsible.

They then subdivide the wages fund, until finally an enterprise which paid out a given sum in wages in the last year or quarter, is told that it may spend (say) $5\frac{1}{2}$ per cent more in the coming year, or quarter. This plan is supposed to be in harmony with the expected numbers and qualifications of the employees, and their pay entitlements under existing rates. The State Bank has a copy of the relevant figures, and must not permit the paying out of wages in excess of these figures unless the enterprise overfulfils its plan. Such

[1] In the coal industry in 1956, double rates were paid when the worker exceeded 80 per cent of his norm, treble rates for over 100 per cent, for coal face workers. See V. Nikol'ski, *Poóshchritel'nye sistemy oplaty truda* (Moscow, 1952).

overfulfilment gives rise to legitimate additional expenditures on wages of piece-workers, and on bonuses to time-workers and to managerial and clerical staff, which are all defined in the regulations. These extra payments are not, in theory, supposed to add to production costs, even if progressive piecework is payable, since the extra labour cost per unit is supposed to be offset by economies on overheads.[1]

Thus there are two kinds of controls: over the rate for the job, and over the total amounts which can be paid out in wages and salaries. It would be wrong to assert that these controls are inoperative. At times they were more or less effective. Thus in the period 1947 to 1956, money wages rose by only 27 per cent on average,[2] which compares 'favourably' with the record of most western countries. Yet neither in aggregate nor in terms of wage relativities has practice conformed at all closely to theory; indeed, no general wage increase at all was decreed during the period 1947-56!

One difficulty has been the vagueness of the theory. Labour is not a 'commodity', it is paid in accordance with the quantity and quality of the work. But what is the objective measure of quantity and quality of labour? And, given that A is higher quality work compared to B, by how much should A be paid more? How is it to be related to the supply and demand position, bearing in mind that labour is more or less free to move and is only partially subject to direction? What if the rates laid down in the regulation fail to attract the necessary labour? The state's powers to 'allocate' labour are now confined to the following circumstances. Firstly, graduates of any higher or technical institute must go to work where they are sent, for three to four years; there used also to be a call-up of youths to the so-called 'factory and workshop schools' (*Fabrichno-zavodskie Uchilishcha*, FZU), but these are based on voluntary recruitment since 1955. There is provision, too, for so-called 'organized recruiting' (*Orgnabor*) in villages for industrial and building labour, with preference given to important sectors short of labour, but this too is now a voluntary process. Last but far from least, Communist party members and (to a lesser extent) Komsomols—young-communists— may in effect be compelled to go wherever they are sent, on pain of expulsion. Since there are now eight million members of the party,

---

[1] This has certainly not been so in the coal industry, where the extra pay arising from plan overfulfilment led to heavy financial losses (thus A. Zvorykin and D. Kirzhner, in *Sotsialisticheski trud*, No. 2/1956, p. 70, state that a 5 per cent overfulfilment of plan could lead to an increase of 53·8 per cent in the wages bill, by reason of 'progressive' piecework and bonus payments).

[2] S. Figurnov, in *Sotsialisticheski trud*, No. 5/1959, p. 51.

and many more million Komsomols, this represents an appreciable portion of the labour force, and, as so many of the Communists occupy leading positions, it means that a sizeable proportion of technical and managerial personnel are more or less liable to transfer if the cadres department of the party wishes it. None the less, the door is wide open for the operation of market forces in wage determination, since the major part of the labour force, and particularly of workers and clerical staffs, have the right and the real possibility of leaving their employment.

This was not always so. Decrees adopted in October, 1940, forbade all employees of state enterprises and institutions to leave their work without permission, save in a few narrowly-defined instances (e.g. qualifying for old-age pension, being the wife of a person sent to work in another town, etc.). Disobedience to this decree, as well as absenteeism or even lateness (by more than twenty minutes), were treated as criminal offences, punishable in the last resort by imprisonment, or by a mild form of forced labour ('at place of employment') and financial penalty. The unpopularity of these measures was such that judges and managers were threatened with punishment for failing to apply them. After the war, it was apparently found increasingly difficult to enforce these decrees, and they dropped from active use by 1953, before being finally repealed in 1956. At present, anyone may leave their work, with no penalty if they take another job within a month.[1]

The 'labour-market' in the USSR is highly imperfect, by reason of the lack of adequate information, or of labour exchanges. One encounters a great deal of sporadic and unco-ordinated advertising of vacancies, e.g. on telegraph poles or public notice-boards, or even in local radio programmes, and information does percolate to many of those who think of changing their employment.

Where a factor of production is not—or is only partially—subject to administrative allocation, its price is bound to be influenced by market forces. Labour has the 'advantage' over inanimate factors of production of being able to move of its own volition, even in defiance of rules and regulations. There is therefore bound to be tension between the wages structure, as laid down by authority, and market forces. In some years the net result was a very large overspending of the wages fund, this being part-cause and part-conse-

---

[1] Until 1960, those who changed jobs of their own volition lost their sick pay entitlements for six months and suffered other penalties under social insurance rules. This provision appears to have been repealed, presumably to encourage voluntary moves to the new factories in the east.

quence of uncontrollable inflation. This was particularly so in the chaotic period of the first five-year plan (1928-32), but even in the relatively stable second five-year plan years the wages fund was planned to increase by 55 per cent and in fact rose two-and-a-half-fold.[1] There was a large over-fulfilment of the wages plan also in the fourth plan period (1946-50). These deviations were due partly to unintended increases in average money wages and retail prices, partly to the fact that a much larger number of persons had to be given urban jobs than had been originally foreseen.[2]

In recent years the tendency to excess wage payments has been checked but not eliminated. Thus actual wage overpayments in industry, transport and trade were as follows, in percentage terms: 4·3 per cent in 1953, 3·1 per cent in 1956, 2·1 per cent in 1957.[3] This is by no means negligible, cumulatively, and probably accounts for the major part of the actual rise in average wages in these years.

Statistics of average wages were available in great detail for most pre-war years, but no systematic data have been published since. The following represent average wages and salaries of all state-employed persons, from top directors to unskilled workers inclusive (or at least the nearest we can get to reliable estimates):

(*Roubles per annum*)

1928	1937	1940	1947	1954	1956	1958
703	3,047	4,068	6,997	{ 8,542 8,380	8,909	9,475

Sources: Pre-war years: K. Plotnikov, op. cit., pp. 72, 198. Some
    other sources gave 4,054 for 1940.

1947, 1954 (top figure) and 1956. Calculated from indices
    given by S. Figurnov, *Sotsialisticheski Trud*, No.
    5/1959, p. 51.

1954 (bottom figure). Different index given by *Politi-
    cheskaya Ekonomia, uchebnik* (second edition)
    (Moscow, 1955) p. 483.

1958. Moscow radio, in English, gave the 1965 planned
    wage rate as 995 roubles per month (on Novem-
    ber 14, 1958). This, according to the seven-year
    plan, represented an increase of 26% over 1958.

Needless to say, real wages presented a very different picture. Thus beyond doubt the purchasing power of money wages in 1937,

[1] K. Plotnikov, *Byudzhet sovetskovo gosudarstva* (Moscow, 1948), p. 143.
[2] For instance, for fourth five-year plan envisaged 33½ million workers and employees in 1950. The actual numbers were 38·9 million.
[3] V. Popov, *Gosudarstvennyi bank SSSR*, 1917-57 (Moscow, 1957), p. 170.

1940 and (particularly) 1947 was below 1928, though this needs to be calculated from indirect data, since no Soviet cost-of-living index is published with a 1928 base.[1]

The above are averages, and tell us nothing of differentials. Especially after Stalin's famous attack, in 1931, on 'petty-bourgeois egalitarianism', differentials were greatly increased, with the most skilled workers having roughly three-and-a-half times as much as the least skilled. The officially-sponsored Stakhanovite campaign, launched in 1935, caused very large rewards to be given to outstanding workers, increasing differentials still further. After the war, the wage adjustments of 1946 favoured the lowest-paid workers and this somewhat diminished differentials, although insistence on maximizing them continued to form part of official statements. As late as 1958, plans were based on differentials within the category 'worker' of 2·8 : 1. However, the seven-year plan adopted in 1959 envisaged a sharp rise in minimum wages and a reduction of differentials to 2 : 1. Of course, the gap between managerial personnel and unskilled workers has been very much greater than this, though this too is being reduced.

It is important to note that the contradiction between formal regulations and market forces has led not only to unplanned money wage increases, but to other major departures from the regulations at enterprise level. Thus piecework norms are generally substantially overfulfilled, orders to revise the norms upwards have in various degrees been evaded, unskilled workers have been promoted to skilled grades, thereby upsetting the intended scale of differentials, the link between plan fulfilment and norm fulfilment barely exists in practice. These and other difficulties faced by planners in dealing with wages and labour will be discussed in greater detail in chapter 8.

PEASANT INCOMES

The reader was briefly introduced (on page 52, above) to the *trudoden*, or conventional workday unit. Since, unlike wages, this is an unfamiliar method of rewarding labour, it is necessary to examine it in a little more detail.

The *trudoden* in its present form dates from 1931, and is supposed to relate the quantity and quality of work done to the amount avail-

[1] See a very careful survey by Janet Chapman, in *Review of Economics and Statistics*, May, 1954, which confirms similar calculations by N. Jasny, *The Soviet Economy during the Plan Era* (Stanford University, 1951) and by S. N. Prokopowicz and others.

able in each *kolkhoz* for distribution to the peasants, in cash and kind. Because this amount varies greatly, it was found impossible to value the work directly in terms of either cash or produce. Differential payments for skill and effort are ensured by a system of grading prescribed by the central authorities. Average work of average quality was graded at 1 *trudoden* per day-norm. Unskilled occupations (e.g. night watchman, cleaner) were graded at 0·5 *trudodni*, the most skilled at 2·5 *trudodni*, for a day-norm,[1] with others in intermediate categories. Work on tractors carried out on *kolkhoz* fields, which was also remunerated in *trudodni*, was rated higher still, with 8 *trudodni* and more per day-norm for some tractormen and combine-harvester operators, for instance. Detailed norms were 'recommended' by the authorities in a number of decrees, but in practice they had to be left largely to local initiative, because conditions differed so widely. In principle, a person carrying out a task which was rated at 2 *trudodni* should be given a defined job to do which should take him a day to perform, and this job would then be valued at 2 *trudodni*. If he overfulfilled the task (for example, by weeding or cultivating more than the prescribed amount), the *trudodni* credited to him would rise proportionately. An important contrast with wage-earners lies in the fact that the job is rated, not the man. In industry, or in state agriculture, the man's grade of skill determines his wage scale, even if he is temporarily engaged on relatively unskilled work, whereas in *kolkhozy* it is the nature of the work which determines how many *trudodni* a particular individual earns. Another difference is that a wage-earner is entitled to be paid when his enterprise cannot provide him with work (e.g. in the event of a supply or power breakdown) whereas the *kolkhoz* peasant is only paid for the work he does. This is of importance because there are slack periods, especially in winter, in Soviet agriculture. As in industry, there has been a tendency to fix norms which can be overfulfilled, or to overgrade work done, so that an average *trudoden* is earned in less than one actual day.[2]

The *trudodni* earned by particular individuals do not depend only on the number of graded day-norms of work they perform. There is also a very complex system of bonuses, related either to plan fulfilment (e.g. of the harvest plan in a field cultivated by a particular brigade or team), or to obtaining results above the average in that

[1] Up to 1948, the maximum 'spread' was from 0·5 to 2·0. See full details in H. Wronski, *Le troudoden* (Paris, 1956).
[2] According to E. Karnaukhova, in *Voprosy sotsialisticheskoi ekonomiki* (Moscow, 1956), p. 225, 1·4 *trudodni* were earned in each day's work, on average in the USSR in 1953-5, but there were substantial regional variations.

particular *kolkhoz* (e.g. if one team or brigade has a bigger harvest of a given crop than another). Additional *trudodni* were allocated to the successful, while up to 25 per cent of *trudodni* were deducted from those below plan or below average. To make matters even less simple, there arose in the post-war period the practice of earmarking a priority share in disposable income of the *kolkhoz* to those cultivating some particular crop. The system's many complications were and are frequently the subject of criticism, partly because of this complexity and partly because of its unfairness; thus below-average harvests are often due to natural conditions, so it is unreasonable to penalize peasants who may have worked hard to save what could be saved. Criticism has also been made of the fact that the norms fixed in different *kolkhozy* have differed so widely that it is quite impossible to use the *trudoden* as a comparative measure of work performed.[1]

Trudodni are also allocated to the *kolkhoz* chairmen, who also receive a fixed sum in money, as do other officials (deputy-chairmen, accountants, etc.). Payments are varied by reference to the fulfilment of various plans (output, deliveries to the state, expansion of livestock holdings etc.).

At the end of the year, all the *trudodni* recorded by *kolkhoz* members, officials, tractormen, etc.) are adjusted upwards or downwards under the various bonus regulations, added together, and then divided into the amount available for distribution, in money and in kind. The resultant sum determines the value of each *trudoden*. Thus this might be 2 roubles in cash, 1 kilogram of grain and 1 kilogram of potatoes (or some very different amounts, depending on the *kolkhoz* and the results of the given year). A peasant who had recorded 250 *trudodni* in the given year would then receive 500 roubles in cash, and 250 kilograms of grain and of potatoes. In most *kolkhozy* until recent years, distribution took place at the end of the year, so that, while they were working, the peasants had no idea of the value of the *trudodni* they were earning. However, since 1953 there has been an increasing trend towards more or less regular 'advances' (payments on account) throughout the year, with a final adjustment when the year's accounts are made up. The difficulty has been that some farms are too poor, and in particular have no cash in hand until after the harvest.

[1] K. Okhapkin, *Novoe v oplate truda kolkhoznikov* (Moscow, 1958), pp. 7-8, gives some startling examples, relating to *kolkhozy* in similar natural conditions. For valuable details of recent *trudodni* regulations, see G. Kuparadze, *Spravochnik ekonomista* (Tiflis, 1960), and also *Spravochnik predsedatelya kolkhoza* of various dates.

The actual amounts paid out in *trudodni* have varied greatly not only between *kolkhozy* but also by geographical areas, due partly to the effects of price policy. Even after the reforms of 1953, these disparities continued. For example, in the three years 1954-56, if the USSR average is taken as 100, payments for a day's work to *kolkhoz* peasants were 148 in Kazakhstan, 143 in West Siberia, 138 in Uzbekistan, but only 60 in the 'central non-black-earth region', of which Moscow is the centre.[1] This must be borne in mind when assessing the signifiance of all-union averages which will be cited below, since in no other sector of the Soviet economy are there such enormous differences in payment for the same amount of work.

The cash element in *trudodni* pay may be seen from the following table:

Roubles per trudoden		Millions of trudodni recorded, USSR	
1952	*1956*	*1952*	*1956*
1·40	3·80	8,847	11,103

Sources: M. Osad'ko: *Vop. Ekon.*, No. 2/1959, p. 83.
N.Kh. *1956*, p. 141.

The in-kind element has been more important than cash during most of the above period. As late as in 1956, distributions in kind were half of the total.[2]

It is noteworthy that the state has so far no *direct* means of determining the amounts which *kolkhozy* pay to peasants. Nor can it decide the amount which peasants earn by *sales in the free market*, which for many years was by far their most important source of cash.[3] Of course, the state can exercise an indirect influence on these sources of peasant income by altering the prices at which it buys produce, or by taxation, or by setting up state-farms to sell vegetables in cities in competition with the *kolkhozy* and the free market, or by changing the proportion of *kolkhoz* revenues which must be allocated to the capital fund, and so on. But this is a very different thing from actually laying down scales of payment. The organs of the state do, of course, estimate the likely level of rural incomes, but they do not have direct power to determine what they should be.

Trudodni distributions and free-market sales are the largest sources of cash revenue of the *kolkhoz* peasants, and a large portion

[1] A. Teryaeva, in *Vop. Ekon.*, No. 1/1959, p. 110. See also examples cited on p. 184, below.
[2] T. Zaslavskaya, in *Vop. Ekon.*, No. 2/1959, p. 113.
[3] For example, in 1952 total cash distributions of *trudodni* amounted to 12·4 milliard roubles, while free market turnover in urban areas alone was worth 53·7 milliards, of which 35-40 must have consisted of peasant sales.

of the family's consumption still comes from the produce of the family's own animals and plot of land. However, there are also other incomes coming into the *kolkhoz* household. Among them are payments made by the *kolkhoz* in addition to the *trudodni*, such as, for instance, bonuses in kind representing a stated proportion of over-plan production (e.g. milkmaids retain a percentage of over-plan milk). Many kolkhoz peasants work for part of the year for state enterprises, and many households contain one or more state-employed person, whose income is pooled with the rest of the family's.

This system of remuneration is at present in the melting-pot. The better-off farms have been encouraged to abandon *trudodni* and to go over to a fixed cash payment for work done (plus a bonus at the end of a successful year), and up to the moment of writing several thousand *kolkhozy* have done so.[1] The large majority have retained the *trudoden*, sometimes with a guaranteed minimum value announced to the peasants beforehand. The central committee plenum of December, 1959, criticized the practice of prosperous farms of distributing more than *sovkhoz* employees receive for the same work, and much is being written concerning possible ways of so redistributing *kolkhoz* revenues as to enable all of them to pay wage rates for the job. How and when this will be done remains to be seen.

TRADE UNIONS

Soviet trade unions are organized on an 'industrial' basis, covering all grades, including managers, in the given branch of the economy. The structure of the unions is nominally democratic, with elections of officials and the all-union central council (AUCCTU) elected at national conferences. However, the Communist Party is in full control at all levels, and indeed there was only one national conference to elect the AUCCTU between 1932 and 1954. This central body must be regarded as a quasi-governmental labour agency, which is charged with administering the social insurance fund, and with taking such action as will mobilize the workers in the struggle to fulfil output plans and other policies of the party and the government. At local level, trade union officials are supposed to reconcile these essentially official functions with the task of protecting workers from abuses on the part of the management. Collective agreements between the management and the union branch generally specify a number of measures concerned with welfare and amenities, as well as including

[1] 3,854, about a fifteenth of the total, in 1959, according to V. Rozhin in *Izvestia,* August 21, 1960.

undertakings on behalf of the workers to work harder and better, but they do not determine wage rates.[1] With the object of stimulating output, the unions endeavour to organize various forms of 'socialist competition' between workshops, groups and individuals. Subject to the over-riding general aim of increasing production and fulfilling the plan, union officials on the spot are concerned with planned piece-rates and thereby have a hand in deciding how much is in fact earned by the workers, even though they have no power to negotiate about basic rates. The local branch plays an important role in the settlement of disputes between individual workers and the management (e.g. over grading, demotion, bonus entitlements, allegedly illegal dismissals, etc.), participating on equal terms in the 'conflicts commissions' which, in enterprises, settle such disputes. If the trade union and the management fail to agree in the conflicts commission, the matter is referred to a higher *trade union* body for final decision.[2] However, as travellers have noted, intermediate officials (for example, in city and *oblast* headquarters of trade unions) are not infrequently former directors or party bureaucrats, and there is no particular reason to expect them to be unduly biased in favour of the employees in taking their decisions.

During the Stalin era, the task of mobilizing the workers was heavily emphasized at all levels, and the representational and protective tasks of trade unions took very much a second place. This was justified by arguments such as there being no need to protect the workers against the workers' state. The highly unpopular decrees of 1940, which forbade change of employment without permission and introduced severe penalties for lateness and absenteeism, were stated in the preamble to have been promulgated at the request of the AUCCTU. The trade union branch was directly concerned with the unpopular task of compelling everyone to subscribe to the virtually compulsory but nominally voluntary state bonds. Eventually, things reached a stage which proved intolerable to the government itself. There were too many instances of failure on the part of local trade unions to defend their members against local abuses, breaches of protective legislation were all too common, the so-called 'socialist competitions' organized by the unions frequently remained on paper; the unions, in other words, were failing to mobilize because, *inter*

[1] Collective agreements were revived in 1954, after a prolonged period of disuse.
[2] By decree of the praesidium of the Supreme Soviet, January 31, 1957. For details, see I. Dvornikov and V. Nikitinski, *Novyi poryadok rassmotreniya trudovykh sporov* (Moscow, 1957). If worker or management considers the decisions contrary to law, they can appeal to the courts.

alia, they were not protecting the members and were not felt by their members to represent them. A sizeable crop of articles, expressing dissatisfaction with the trade unions, appeared in the years following Stalin's death, and these culminated in the decisions of the December, 1957, plenum of the central committee, which sought to stimulate the local unions to take their protective tasks more seriously, while re-emphasizing their role as 'mobilizers' of the workers and increasing their functions within enterprises, both directly and through the 'permanent production councils' in which they play a major role.

The argument that Soviet trade unions are not trade unions at all is often heard in discussions in the west. It is clear enough that they are not independent of state or Party, and that their purpose is to organize the workers for the carrying out of state and party policy. Against this, it is sometimes argued that, under Soviet conditions, it is unreasonable to expect conflicts between the managers and the labour force, because the managers are also employees of the state (and, indeed, members of the same union), and/or that the unions do in fact have powers to protect members against arbitrary acts or neglect on the part of the management. Indeed, the powers are there and are impressive. The difficulty, however, is that the unions' task as a 'transmission belt' of party economic policies is often hard to reconcile with their 'protective' duties *vis-à-vis* their members, and, owing to the strong element of party control, in any conflict of loyalties the officials respond first and foremost to those above them, who in fact appoint them or arrange their 'elections', rather than to the membership. Thus if compulsory overtime or rest-day working is resorted to as a means of hastening plan fulfilment, it is in the highest degree unlikely that the union branch would fail to back the management, whatever the feelings of the members. In other words, in assessing the economic forces at work in the Soviet Union, it would be misleading to view the unions as any kind of independent pressure group, even though action is commonly taken by the local branch to ensure that, for example, an expectant mother receives the paid vacation to which the laws entitle her, or a grade IV carpenter is not unjustifiably demoted, though even here the union often neglects its duties.[1]

The trade unions administer the social insurance funds, and bene-

---

[1] Often the failures of the unions are corrected by the courts, especially in cases of unjustified dismissal in which the union branch supported the management. For two of many examples, see *Byulleten Verkhovnovo Suda SSSR,* No. 2/1960, pp. 1, 3.

fits to members are much higher than to non-members, which helps to explain why the vast majority of those eligible are members of their unions. *Kolkhoz* peasants and co-operative artisans have no trade unions and receive no social insurance benefits from state sources; the *kolkhozy* and the co-operatives have to make their own arrangements to succour their members in distress. (Temporary arrangements apply to former employees of the MTS recently transferred to the *kolkhozy*.) Social services as such are outside the scope of this book, but the reader will hardly need reminding of their great importance in peoples' lives and of the need to take them into account in any comparison of living standards.

THE PRICE SYSTEM: WHOLESALE PRICES

It is necessary to distinguish between the following principal categories of prices for industrial products:

(a) *Factory wholesale prices* (*optovaya tsena predpriyatiya*), being the transfer prices at which enterprises dispose of their products to wholesalers, exclusive of any turnover tax payable.

(b) *Industry wholesale prices* (*optovaya tsena promyshlennosti*), these are prices to which goods are transferred to users outside the given industry, and include turnover tax when this is payable. This category is sometimes known as *otpusknaya tsena*, or 'release price'.

Agricultural prices, including those applicable to agricultural raw materials used in industry, and also some prices charged for industrial products to agricultural producers, have had a very different history and will require separate treatment.

Factory wholesale prices

Until 1957, decisions on prices were highly centralized. Virtually no price could be altered without the sanction of the all-union government; the industrial ministry, Gosplan and the Ministry of Finance were those principally concerned, together with the Ministry of Internal Trade if the commodity in question was a consumers' good. Prices for new products had also to receive the sanction of the centre, and, with many administrative organs involved, there was often excessive delay.

After the 1957 reforms, there was a tendency towards a somewhat lesser degree of centralization, culminating in a decision of the Council of Ministers on May 30, 1958. The new procedures are as follows.

The Council of Ministers is responsible for general decisions on price policy. Actual prices for a list of key products ('the most important varieties of industrial production') are fixed or confirmed by the all-union Gosplan, acting as the executant of government price policy. Most other prices are decided by the republican governments, except that *oblast'* soviets confirm wholesale prices for small-scale local industry which is under their control. *Sovnarkhozy* have few powers in this field. They may determine the prices at which 'their' enterprises deliver materials or semi-manufactures to one another, but only if 'for these products there are no prices which have been confirmed through the usual channels'. They also determine, within narrow limits, temporary prices of new products, these prices being based either on the existing price of analogous products, or on cost plus 5 per cent. However, even temporary prices for 'major products' are the responsibility of the all-union Gosplan. The directors of enterprises have, and had, no freedom in deciding the selling price of their products, save for goods and services provided by the enterprise for its own internal needs, and also for components or instruments made to special order for which no prices exist, though this latter case is again subject to a limit of cost plus 5 per cent.[1] However, enterprises doubtless play some role in suggesting new or changed prices to the authorities above them.

General principles underlying price policy appear to be considered also by a 'committee of the praesidium of the council of ministers on prices', the existence of which has been mentioned in some Soviet publications.[2] It is also probable that such questions fall within the purview of *Gosekonomsovet*.

Neglecting the exceptions for the present, let us examine the principles on which the government has fixed or approved the prices at which enterprises dispose of their products. These are supposed to be based on the *average cost of production* of all enterprises producing the commodity in question, plus a small profit margin, often defined in Soviet textbooks as 3-5 per cent, but which is higher than this on average. At intervals, as and when costs are reduced, prices are supposed to be reduced also. The theoretical basis of the average cost principle will be discussed elsewhere (chapter 11). It will be recalled that the term 'costs' excludes charges on basic capital or land rent, and profits are expressed as a percentage of costs, not

[1] This account is taken from Rumyantsev, op. cit., pp. 367-70.
[2] A. Volin, *Kommunist*, No. 3/1959, p. 56, and also Turetski, op. cit., p. 157. The latter refers to a committee 'with legal, organizational and inspecting functions', but it is not clear from his wording whether it actually has these functions or whether he is advocating that it be given them.

of capital. To calculate profits, costs are compared to *sales* (*tovarnaya produktsiya*), not to gross output. This is one reason why the fulfilment of a (gross) output plan, which includes unfinished production, is not necessarily directly connected with the profits plan. However, there may be no profit at all. It follows from the use of average costs that many enterprises make losses. For example, in 1956 the enterprises under the ministry of ferrous metallurgy made an average profit of 7 per cent, but one-third of them were making 'planned losses', i.e. were not expected to cover their costs, as defined above, by revenues from sales.[1] After the 1957 reforms some *sovnarkhozy* found themselves saddled with many enterprises which made heavy losses, since prices had been determined by reference to national average costs under the old ministerial system, and in that particular locality there may have been many loss-making enterprises which were formerly 'netted' against profits made elsewhere, or there may be abnormal local profits, or both. For instance, in 1958 in the Sverdlovsk *sovnarkhoz* there were the following variations among enterprises: in ferrous metallurgy enterprises from 15 per cent profit to 25 per cent loss, in ore mining from 27 per cent profit to 40 per cent loss, in non-ferrous metallurgy from 20 per cent profit to 24 per cent loss, paper and pulp enterprises from 25 per cent profit to 45 per cent loss, building materials enterprises from 33 per cent profit to 55 per cent loss. After giving these examples, the Soviet author remarked: 'The Sverdlovsk *sovnarkhoz* is not exceptional'.[2] The enterprises making losses have to receive subsidies, either from the state budget or by way of redistribution of profits and losses within a *glavk* (under the ministerial system) or sometimes within a *sovnarkhoz*. This enormous variation in profits and losses has been the subject of much criticism in the USSR. It should be noted also that a profit or loss on the part of an enterprise may conceal losses (or profits) in the production of individual items, which are netted against one another in the accounts (many large factories have separate 'economic accounting' arrangements for products or for workshops within the enterprise).

In some instances, where there are very large disparities in natural conditions, a single selling price to users is combined with differential prices to producers. In the USSR, this system was applied for many years in the oil industry, though in recent years the differentials have been applied to oilfields and not individual oil enterprises.[3] These are known as 'accounting prices' (*rashchyotnye tseny*).

[1] Turetski, op. cit., p. 79. [2] Turetski, op. cit., p. 80.
[3] Turetski, op. cit., pp. 125 ff.

After 1939, and especially in post-war years, most Soviet whole-sale prices were fixed 'delivered to station of destination'. They, therefore, include an allowance for average cost of transport. De-livery prices are generally, but not always, differentiated by zones, and this differentiation does to some extent take transport costs into account;[1] thus, for instance, the wholesale price of cloth or sulphuric acid delivered in north-east Siberia is higher than in the Ukraine. However, *any* supplier to north-east Siberia, be he located in central Siberia or in Leningrad, is entitled to charge only the one price laid down for the zone to which the goods are being delivered. This is logical under Soviet conditions, in that the recipient enterprise gener-ally has its supplier designated in the supply plan, and its costs ought not to be adversely affected by the remoteness or otherwise of the supplier so designated. The supplying enterprise, or *sbyt* organiza-tion, in those cases in which it can influence the supply plan or the negotiation of contracts, is naturally interested in minimizing its transport costs, but the system does not adequately penalize the re-cipient enterprise (or *sovnarkhoz*) for any initiatives which result in unnecessarily long hauls, and this system of prices ('delivered at station of destination') is being criticized by some Soviet econ-omists.

However, the above picture of price determination is far from the realities of Soviet economic history. Thus in 1929-35 there was a sharp (and quite unplanned) increase in costs, but the government sought to maintain prices of basic materials and capital goods at unchanged levels, so that very large subsidies became necessary, with prices far below average costs. A sharp price rise in 1936 re-estab-lished a more logical relationship between costs and prices. Shortly before the war, both rose again. Then there was again an effort to keep prices of basic materials steady, in the face of a very large rise in costs due to the war and its aftermath. The result was that very large subsidies were again paid, and the price increase, when it came in 1949, was substantial. Thus a ton of Donetz coal of type 'T' was 'worth' 34·43 roubles from 1939 to 1949, and was then increased at one bound to 91·83 roubles.[2] Since 1949, there have been several general price reductions: in 1950, 1952 and 1955. It remains state policy to price basic materials relatively low, even—in the case of coal and timber in some recent years—slightly below average cost.

[1] This is described in *Economic Survey of Europe, 1959* (E. C. E., Geneva), chapter 4.
[2] Ibid., p. 123. Many other examples may be found in this and other Soviet sources. See also N. Jasny, *The Soviet Price System* (Stanford, 1950).

In general, profit rates have tended to be above average in the light and food industries, but are also high in many branches of the metal-working and machinery industries. There are thus wide variations in profit levels between branches of industry, for reasons sometimes difficult to fathom, but which certainly bear no relationship to the accumulation requirements of the given branch; thus the light and food industries were planned to make profits of more than 30 milliard roubles in 1958, but investment and increases of working capital in these industries were to be only 8·4 milliards; the coal industry was to make a loss of 5·6 milliards, the oil and gas industry to make a profit of 3·3 milliards, but investment expenditure alone for these was to amount to over 30 milliards. Incomplete returns for 1957 showed the coal industry in deficit, the oil and gas industry made a profit of 20·5 per cent, while building materials industries made a profit of only 2·8 per cent. Total profits in industry for 1958 were planned at 98·0 milliards, an average rate of profit of roughly 9 per cent, but obviously these averages conceal very large variations in both directions.[1] In 1955, according to a good Soviet source, profits in different branches of heavy industry varied from − 15 per cent to + 31·7 per cent. Detailed examples given by this source included zinc ore (− 19·5 per cent), steel castings (+ 24 per cent), pig-iron castings (− 2 per cent).[2] These are national averages, and not examples for enterprises which happen to be located in a particular *sovnarkhoz*, as were the figures cited on page 130, above. No wonder some economists are pressing for a total revision of the price system.

It seems clear, therefore, that the practice of price determination is not easily reducible to any set of principles at all, and that this must affect the working of 'economic accounting' at enterprise level. To make things even less logical, there have been spasmodic efforts to relate prices of some interchangeable products to one another, and of some scarce products to their scarcity. An example of the latter is copper and some other non-ferrous metals,[3] while turnover tax on gas, electricity and oil is justified by the need to bring their prices into some undefined relationship with coal and with one another.

Before leaving the question of prices at enterprise level, it is necessary to mention the vexed problem of 'unchanged prices', used for

[1] A. Zverev, *Voprosy natsional'novo dokhoda i finansov SSSR* (Moscow, 1958), pp. 94, 98.
[2] A. Bachurin, *Finansy SSSR*, No. 1/1960, p. 78.
[3] Referred to by V. Novozhilov in *Primeneniye matematiki v ekonomicheskikh issledovaniyakh* (Nemchinov, ed., Moscow, 1959), p. 43.

comparisons over time. For many years—for some purposes until 1949—these were so-called 1926-27 prices, either those actually existing in that year or (for new products or models) nominal prices deemed to be those of 1926-27. Enterprises' plans were expressed in these 1926-27 prices, and, since the real prices were very different, a large disparity developed between planning prices and those in which the current financial accounts of the enterprise were conducted. The 1926-27 basis was finally abandoned in 1950, though certain statistical consequences (growth indices, for instance) are still with us, as will be shown in the Appendix. At present, prices of 1955 are used for the purpose of time-comparisons and new products are more or less effectively converted into the same basis.

Building work has been valued on a different basis. The cost-schedules (*smety*) were expressed in 1936 prices, 1946 prices, then in 1950 prices, and, finally, in 1955 prices. Since actual costs reflected whatever were the current prices of the given year, there was generally some disparity between 'cost-schedule costs' (*smetnaya stoimost'*), in which investment statistics were frequently given, and actual cost. During the fifth five-year plan (1951-55), when prices were falling, actual costs were below the *smety*, and so the investment statistics of the period showed large 'economies', which somewhat illogically were included in the enterprise-financed portion of investment in the figures published at the time.

Wholesale prices of industry

These may be identical with factory wholesale prices, unless, firstly, there is a separate wholesaling organization through which sales to other enterprises are made, and which is entitled to add a wholesalers' margin to the factory wholesale price; and, secondly, because turnover tax may be payable. The latter is charged on a wide range of consumers' goods, and also on oil, gas and electricity.

In the case of many kinds of commodities which are used both by citizens and by state enterprises, one frequently finds partial or complete exemption from turnover tax for state enterprises, and therefore there emerge two wholesale prices of industry, which depend on the use to which the given consignment is to be put. Some examples are salt, many kinds of building materials, automobiles, oil products. *Kolkhozy* had (and frequently still have) to pay retail prices for many goods, inclusive of a sizeable element of tax. To take a particularly striking example, early in 1958 *sovkhozy* and other state enterprises paid 13,769 roubles for a ZIL-150 lorry; a *kolkhoz* was charged 37,000 roubles.[1] The level of turnover tax on consumers' goods is inextricably mixed up with the retail price system; thus, in the many cases in which turnover tax is calculated by 'difference' (page 98, above), the wholesale price of industry is equal to the state-fixed retail price less the retail margin, and is not actually listed anywhere as such.

THE PRICE SYSTEM: RETAIL PRICES

Except in periods of rationing (1929-34, 1941-47), retail prices are fixed so as to clear the market of available supplies to save where there is some social reason for goods to be sold dear (e.g. vodka) or cheap (e.g. children's clothes). The total value of goods and services available should match the level of disposable personal incomes, and price increases or price cuts should follow if calculation shows them to be necessary. This general policy has not been consistently followed, the 'deviation' being usually in the direction of selling too cheaply, relatively to personal incomes (which tend to exceed plan), as may be seen from the prevalence of queues. Indeed, Stalin gave queues a certain *rationale* by suggesting that demand should exceed supply, so as to provide a spur for increasing production. There is a reluctance to make frequent changes in retail prices, and such changes are treated as a political matter, for the top leadership to decide. In the last years of Stalin's life and the period of Malenkov's premiership, it was considered politically expendient to announce price cuts every spring. In the period 1947-50 this had a logical basis; 1947 prices were extremely high, reflecting acute post-war shortages, and the big increase in goods available for sale certainly outpaced the rise in expendable incomes. However, in the next few years, i.e. the last two springs of Stalin's life and the only two springs of Malenkov's premiership, prices were reduced without adequate reason, with the result that shortages and queues developed. The surest indicator of unjustified cuts in food prices was a growing disparity between official and free-market prices, which can be illustrated by the following figures; since in the base year (1950) market

	1950	1952	1953	1955
State food prices (1950 = 100) ..	100	87	78·5	74
Free market prices (1950 = 100)	100	100	93	107

Source: *Sovetskaya torgovlya* (Moscow, 1957), pp. 131 and 182.

[1] Turetski, op. cit., p. 239. After 1958, *all* farms were charged the same price for lorries, tractors and fuel, intermediate between those previously existing.

prices were already above state prices, the disparity may well have been greater still.

The difference between the retail price, orientated at least in principle towards supply-and-demand equilibrium, and the costs of production and handling plus profit margin, is equal to turnover tax. This tax has been considered in chapter 3, where it was shown that in large measure the tax is a consequence rather than a cause of the retail price level. However, its impact on particular commodities does reflect state and price policy. Thus it was the practice for many years to levy a low tax on many kinds of consumer durables, even though they were very scarce. Motor cars, television sets, sewing machines, were systematically underpriced, despite long waiting lists and queues, while textiles and many kinds of foodstuffs bore substantial tax burdens.[1] Perhaps there is an element of irrational traditionalism in tax and price policy in the USSR; certainly no student of British purchase tax would be surprised.

Because differential rates of turnover tax in the USSR 'absorb' the differences between costs and retail prices, and because the retail margin is also a fixed magnitude, the producing and trading enterprises derive no benefit from providing more commodities with relatively very high scarcity prices; though these could act as a signal to the planning organs to direct investment resources into these branches, but so far this has not been the case, in practice or even in theory. Much more will be said of this in chapter 6.

Retail prices for key commodities are the responsibility of the central government and must be confirmed by Gosplan. Until 1957 detailed price lists on a very wide range of commodities, comprising nearly all retail trade, were issued centrally by the Ministry of Internal Trade. However, many commodities, amounting in aggregate to 45 per cent of total turnover, are now priced by republican governments, though complaints about excessive disparities have led to some effort to maintain coherence in policy in respect of this 45 per cent,[2] the more so as in some instances the retail price indirectly determines the factory wholesale price (e.g. for furniture, on which no turnover tax is charged). Key commodities, including those with a

[1] Some other kinds of consumer durables, such as, in recent years, cameras and radios, pay little tax, but here the reason is simply that these goods are hard to sell even at present prices, and hire purchase was introduced in 1959 to keep stocks of these and some other goods moving. Retail prices of motor cars were greatly increased in 1959.
[2] This may well have been one of the reasons for the creation of the committee on prices, referred to on page 129, above.

large element of turnover tax in the price, remain in the province of the central government.

Prices vary by geographical zones, and are on average about 5 per cent higher in villages than in towns by reason of a 'rural addition' (*sel'skaya nadbavka*) which is justified by reason of the higher costs of rural distribution (for some commodities the difference is larger, for others it does not exist).[1]

Prices of goods supplied by producers' co-operatives are fixed either by state organs (central or local), or by the regional co-operative unions. In 1955, only 15-16 per cent of these products were outside the control of the state; however, in the same year co-operative-produced goods were selling '40-70 per cent above' analogous goods produced by state enterprises.[2]

THE PRICE SYSTEM: AGRICULTURAL PRICES

It is important to note that agricultural prices affect income distribution in ways in which other prices do not. For example, the trebling of the price of coal in 1949 did not change the income of anyone engaged in the production of coal, since wages and salaries were, when necessary, met out of a state subsidy. However, the incomes of collective farms and of peasants depended, and still depend on the prices at which their produce is sold. Thus the question of agricultural prices is a matter affecting the distribution of income between town and country, and thus has been one of the very highest political importance, especially as it has a direct bearing on policy questions towards peasants as a class, and also on the problems of accumulation (see page 53, above).

In the NEP period, after a very few years of genuinely free sales at free prices, the state intervened as early as 1924-25 in an effort to stabilize a grain price below the equilibrium level, though prices of many other farm products remained more or less free from control. This contributed to a grain collection crisis in 1927-28, when the government resorted to punitive measures against alleged grain hoarders, which was a foretaste of the even more drastic measures of the following years, which established collective farms.

Once these had been established, the state was able to insist on compulsory deliveries at prices approximating to those which it had fixed in the 'twenties, despite a very large increase in all other prices.

[1] Turetski, op. cit., p. 469. The average 'addition' is 7 per cent for those goods for which an addition is made. Its existence is much criticized.
[2] Turetski, op. cit., p. 60, p. 480.

Compulsory delivery prices for grain and almost all staple food products changed little until 1953.[1] Since the *kolkhozy* and peasants had to transport the produce to the state collecting point, and since in many cases the transport costs alone exceeded the 'price' paid, the element of sale was in reality absent: these were confiscatory prices, or a species of hardly-disguised tax in kind. Khrushchev gave an example to the central committee plenum of December, 1958: before 1953, potatoes delivered compulsorily by *kolkhozy* were 'paid' for at a price of 3 kopecks per kilo or less, which meant, allowing for transport costs, that the *kolkhozy* received less than nothing. An example concerning grain has been cited earlier (page 99), but here is another: in 1948, the wholesale price of 100 kilograms of rye was 335 roubles,[2] yet the *kolkhozy* received for compulsory deliveries a price of around 7 or 8 roubles, or a few per cent more than in 1928; however, rye bread cost 8 kopecks in 1928, 2·70 roubles in 1948.

By contrast, prices for certain industrial crops were much more favourable. Thus in 1935 raw cotton prices were increased three-and-a-half to four fold.[3]

For sales over and above the compulsory delivery quota (or, in the case of industrial crops, above the contracted amount), higher prices were paid. State policy with regard to these prices showed frequent variations, resulting in a bewildering multiplicity of prices. For example, sometimes these prices were maxima, sometimes they were definitive. Sometimes they were so little above the compulsory procurement prices as to provide no inducement to sell; this was true of grain, so that 'whereas between 1937 and 1945 [over quota] sales were insignificant, between 1947 and 1953 they did not in practice take place at all'.[4]

A full account of the entire system of agricultural prices and its many changes down to 1958 would fill a book. The actual prices were greatly increased in the period 1953-55, but the principles remained unaltered: that a quota of produce was to be delivered at relatively low prices, and amounts in addition to the quota were sold at higher, often very much higher, prices, subject to some regional variations. The following will illustrate the pattern; all the examples relate to the period 1956-58.

[1] See in particular an article by M. Moiseyev, *Vop. Ekon.*, No. 7/1958.
[2] A. Suchkov, *Dokhody gosudarstvennovo byudzheta SSSR* (Moscow, 1949). The figures relate to zone II, which includes central Russia.
[3] Turetski, op. cit., p. 225.
[4] Ibid., p. 226.

(Roubles per centner = 100 kilograms)

	Quota price	Over quota price
Rye, central zone	30	85
Soft wheat, south-centre	28	92
Beef, all areas	150	380–410
Flax fibre (USSR average)	556	1,451

Source: Turetski, op. cit., pp. 229, 263, 265.

There were also still higher prices paid by consumer-co-operatives for sales on commission (page 49, above), and, finally, free-market prices.

To make things more complicated still, a confused and illogical series of measures provided for sales of some commodities to *kolkhozy* at advantageous prices, conditional upon their delivering certain farm products to the state. For instance, bread grain, fodder, vegetable oil and sugar were made available, on a *quid pro quo* basis, to *kolkhozy* specializing on certain crops (e.g. on cotton, flax, vegetables), at well below retail prices. The object was to encourage specialization. In some instances, especially in years of acute shortage, *kolkhozy* which made over-quota deliveries were favoured by being given priority in acquiring a list of scarce commodities at the official price. Such transactions were known as *vstrechnaya prodazha,* or counterpart sales.

This whole system came under review in 1958. Its weaknesses were as follows.

Firstly, the existence of multiple prices confused all calculations. The success or failure of a farm in increasing its total production, or the rationality of its choice as to what to produce, depended decisively on the price basis chosen for the calculation (and what allowance could or should be made for the counterpart sales described above?).

Secondly, the prices were not rationally related to one another or to costs. The compulsory-procurement prices retained an element of taxation, while the over-quota prices were historic accidents which often encouraged the wrong disposal of resources. Thus, for instance, it was calculated that farms were reluctant to feed potatoes to pigs, because the relative prices of pork and potatoes made it far more profitable to sell the potatoes. Fodder was dear relatively to bread at retail prices, and it paid peasants to buy bread in the shops to feed to their private livestock. A long list of anomalies could be, and was, drawn up.[1]

[1] Many examples were given in an article by M. Terentiev, in *Vop. Ekon.*, No. 3/1958.

Thirdly, the principle of two or more prices, with a large gap between them, produced economically absurd results. It meant that a farm with a poor crop and low productivity, for whatever reason, was paid less per unit of product than a high-yielding farm was paid. This can readily be illustrated using the prices cited above. Imagine two farms, A and B, both with a delivery quota of 1,000 tons of rye. A had a saleable surplus of 2,000 tons, B of only 1,200 tons. The total receipts would be:

Farm A: 1,000 tons @ 300+1,000 tons @ 850 = 1,150,000 roubles.
Farm B: 1,000 tons @ 300+ 200 tons @ 850 = 470,000 roubles.

The average price in farm A would therefore be 575 roubles per ton (57·50 roubles per centner), and in farm B it would be only 392 roubles (39·20 roubles per centner). Similar results could be obtained for all major varieties of farm produce, whether food or industrial crops. This provided disproportionate encouragement to the already successful farm, and depressed the unsuccessful. Undoubtedly these price arrangements contributed to the very wide disparity of income as between *kolkhozy,* especially if one bears in mind that surpluses could also be sold at still higher prices in the free market by those farms which had surpluses to sell. The situation was illogical not merely as between farms, but also on a national scale, since this multiple price system ensured that average prices for the USSR as a whole would be higher in a good harvest year than in a poor year, i.e. that prices would be lower in the event of scarcity. For example, although prices were unchanged, the *average* price at which the state bought grain from *kolkhozy* was about 3 per cent lower in 1957 than in 1956, although the harvest was almost 18 per cent lower (*Sel. Khoz.* 1960, pp. 27, 117), which was indeed topsy-turvy economics, explicable only by the long-ingrained habit of burdening *kolkhozy* and peasants with a semi-disguised tax through deliveries at low prices.

This habit, curiously, was allowed to affect the prices paid to state farms. Until 1940, they received only the low 'quota' prices paid to *kolkhozy* and peasants, and therefore received large subsidies. In 1940 there was an increase of 40 per cent, but this still left income far below costs, so subsidies continued. An upward price revision in 1954,[1] and again in 1956, finally eliminated subsidies. State

---

[1] I. Novikov, in *Vop. Ekon.*, No. 9/1954, pp. 31-4, gives full particulars. Until 1954, he says, the subsidy was the 'basic source of revenue' of state-farms.

farm delivery prices were varied by zones, but there was no multiple price system for them.[1]

In 1958, the multiple price system for *kolkhozy* and peasants was scrapped, and price relativities were reviewed. The state now buys at a single price for every product, with regional variations. For grain, this price was fixed a little below the former over quota price, but above the average actually paid in past years: the average for all grains was to be 74 roubles per centner, against a national average 'compulsory' price of 25 and an over-quota price of 80-85 roubles. However, in any assessment of the impact of this new price, one must bear in mind the large amount of grain formerly handed over in payments in kind for the services of MTS, and now sold at this price following the absorption of the MTS by the *kolkhozy* (see page 55, above). Prices of meat were very sharply raised above even the over-quota prices of the past, while potatoes and some industrial crops were treated much less favourably. It was announced that the new prices would be long-term averages, and that they would be raised in poor harvest years and lowered when there is abundance.[2] The results of the new price structure will be considered in some detail in chapter 6, below. However, it is becoming clear that these prices will not in fact be long term. Already in December, 1959, at the central committee plenum, numerous powerful voices were raised in favour of cutting them. It was pointed out that state farm prices were lower, and that this was wrong. These voices did not point out that the burdens on *kolkhozy* were much the heavier (see page 183, below). Some prices have apparently been revised in a downward direction, though it is not known at the time of writing just how far.

The wholesale prices of agricultural materials supplied to industry have also had an odd history. Before 1953, the wholesale prices included a very large element of turnover tax, as has already been noted, and the farm price increases of 1953 and subsequent years did not, with minor exceptions, lead to any increase in retail prices, but were 'absorbed' in turnover tax reductions. The multiple price system greatly complicated the accounts of the procurement organizations, which found themselves paying a variety of prices for the same products, while selling to processing factories at one price, and also sometimes to retail stores at another price, and to some users (e.g. specialized *kolkhozy* under the above-mentioned counterpart arrangements) at yet another price. For purposes of assessing

[1] See V. Semyonov, *Finansy SSSR*, No. 1/1956, p. 35.
[2] For details of the prices fixed in 1958, see *Pravda*, July 1, 1958.

turnover tax payments, and for keeping the costs of user enterprises on an even keel, it became customary to assume that all produce had been procured at the 'quota' price, to pay turnover tax on this basis, and then to receive a compensatory payment from the budget in respect of higher prices actually paid. This is the item of budgetary expenditure mentioned on page 105, above. The result was to inflate turnover tax revenues, and also artificially to reduce the costs of the food-processing industry by providing 'subsidized' materials, though the subsidy at this period was not real. In 1955, there was some readjustment of wholesale prices which partially eliminated this purely accounting subsidy, with the result that costs in the food industry showed an upward jump.[1]

The 1958 price reform led to a complete overhaul of this price structure. In the case of a number of products (e.g. most vegetables and dairy produce) turnover tax is no longer significant, because there is little or no difference between the price paid to the farms and the retail price, after allowance is made for handling costs. For meat, there is even evidence of a genuine net subsidy.[2] There remains, however, a considerable element of tax in the wholesale price of grain, flour and sugar.

[1] *Promyshlennost' SSSR* (Moscow, 1957), p. 30.
[2] Compensatory payments from the budget exceed the small turnover tax revenue raised from meat, according to G. Serebryanyi, *Finansy SSSR*, No. 5/1959, p. 39.

Structure—Conclusion

Thus the structure of the Soviet economy consists at its base of quasi-autonomous enterprises, whose task it is to fulfil plans prescribed by the economic administration, supervised at all levels by the Communist party and by a number of inspecting agencies. Side by side with the hierarchy of administration and controllers, there exists a price and wage system, partly to provide the planners with guidance as to relative costs, and to the performance of their subordinates, and partly to encourage desirable initiative in the area of on-the-ground autonomy. Since the central authorities cannot in fact prescribe the behaviour pattern of all local officials and enterprises, even in the many instances in which they have the formal right to do so, the importance of the men on the spot and of their decisions should in no wise be overlooked. The formula 'democratic centralism', much favoured by Communist ideologists, is supposed to describe the proper balance between central control in essentials and local autonomy in execution, but the precise balance between the two is by no means easy to determine, especially because an essential element in the process—the Communist party machine—generally operates behind closed doors, and so many acts apparently taken by a republic or a *sovnarkhoz* may in fact be the expression of a decision taken in Moscow at the central committee offices. But whoever actually decides, it may be surmised that a large proportion of the decisions are not the expressions of free choice, but are the consequences of policies, and often of a marginal character, especially so far as the enterprise is concerned, since almost always it will be doing the same as it did last year, only rather more so, and its material allocations will similarly change little. Central decisions play their biggest role in deciding basic investment programmes, for which the centre alone can provide the resources, but even these are partly shaped by the logical necessities of programmes adopted earlier. It is in adopting these programmes that the central authorities (i.e. the top party leadership plus the government) exercise to the greatest extent the freedom of choice which popular opinion supposes them to possess in all matters of economic planning. This is a point of some importance, since, as we shall see, it has led some Soviet economists to propose the application of mathematical techniques to work out the full consequences, in terms of investment and production, of the basic programmes and policies decided at the top.

The Soviet economy remains in essentials a 'command economy', because, despite all *de facto* operational autonomy, its functioning is based on instructions, and frequently the behaviour of men on the spot in their area of autonomy consists in manœuvring to obtain the biggest advantage within the rules and instructions promulgated by the authorities. This is why a price system which would create an intolerable muddle if enterprises were free to react to the profit motive has not prevented the economy from functioning. It is to combat natural centrifugal tendencies that decisions on materials allocation, investment, credits, wage rates, depend in the last resort on the all-union authorities. Yet there must always be a search for a proper balance between centre and localities, between obedience to orders and initiative, between administrative decision and responses to economic incentives, just as there must be constant efforts to find an administrative and planning structure which gives the best results with minimum bureaucratic deformation. The primary policy object has been, and is, growth, and this permeates its structure and the leaders' attitudes to problems. Nor can we overlook the effect on policies of the régime's ideology. In the 'twenties, this was very much to the fore; the struggle against private enterprise and alleged *kulaks* took priority over economic assessment of costs or even of short-term growth. Nor is it possible to understand either *kolkhoz* organization or the history of agricultural prices without taking into account the party's attitudes to the peasants as such. However, these extra-economic influences on policy have become less marked, with the elimination of most of their causes. They remain significant in relation to *kolkhoz* agriculture, notably with regard to the surviving private sector, and to the minor pockets of private activity (craftsmen, etc.) in towns. Otherwise it could be said that the economic system is firmly established on the basis of state enterprises, and that it is seeking, on this basis, to overcome the many problems which complicate the achievement of a greater degree of efficiency. To consider these problems is the task of the next part of the present work.

PART II: PROBLEMS

CHAPTER 5

The Changing Nature of Problems

The economy which we are considering has developed rapidly over a comparatively short historical period, and one which has seen much violence and hardship. The structure and the problems which have arisen are intimately related to the process of change, and the development of the economy itself sets up new strains and throws up new problems. It is therefore most important to look at the questions discussed in the following chapters with some sense of historical perspective, not in order to argue that the solutions actually adopted were morally 'right', but to see why they were adopted, or why solutions apposite at one period are rejected or questioned at another.

The system of Soviet planning inherited by Stalin's successors was born as a direct consequence of the industrialization-collectivization drive, which began in 1928-29. Essential features of the system were: firstly, the use of extra-economic coercion to force social and economic relations into a new pattern; secondly, a high level of investment channelled into 'heavy industry', i.e. sectors which provided the sinews of future growth and also the basic defence potential; thirdly, the entire economy, as also other sectors of Soviet life, was under the strict control of a highly centralized Party machine, which, with the help of the police, could enforce the economic priorities decided upon by the authorities, despite the very substantial pent-up demand for a wide range of non-priority goods and services.

Of such a period of social and industrial revolution, Oscar Lange, in his lectures delivered in Belgrade in November, 1957, said the following: [1]

'Socialist industrialization and particularly very rapid industrializa-

[1] Op. cit., pp. 15-16.

tion, which was necessary in the first socialist countries, particularly in the Soviet Union, as a political requirement of national defence and of the solution of all kinds of political and social problems, due to backwardness, requires centralized disposal of resources. Thus the very process of transformation of the social system and in addition, in underdeveloped countries, the need of rapid industrialization, impose the necessity of high centralization of planning and management.

'The process of rapid industrialization requires such centralized disposal of resources for two reasons. First, it is necessary to concentrate all resources on certain objectives and avoid dissipation of resources on other objectives which would divert resources from the purpose of rapid industrialization. This is one of the reasons which leads to highly centralized planning and management and also to the allocation of resources by means of administrative establishment of priorities. The second reason why rapid industrialization demands centralized planning and management is the lack and weakness of industrial cadres. With the rapid growth of industry the cadres are new and inexperienced. Such old cadres which had some experience in management of industry and other economic activities are frequently politically alien to the socialist objectives. In consequence high centralization of managerial decisions becomes necessary.

'Thus the first period of planning and management in a socialist economy, at least according to our present experience, has always been characterized by administrative management and administrative allocation of resources on the basis of priorities centrally established. Economic incentives are in this period replaced by moral and political appeals to the workers, by appeals to their patriotism and socialist consciousness. This is, so to speak, a highly politicalized economy, both with regard to the means of planning and management and the incentives it utilizes.

'I think that, essentially, it can be described as a *sui generis* war economy.'

It was a 'war economy' because of the element of all-out concentration on politically-determined objectives, a situation full of campaigning and of emergency, of acute shortages and arbitrariness, which involved neglect of many economic desiderata. In such circumstances, just as in war economies in western countries, central decisions about resource allocation came to be decisive throughout the system. Theoretically, of course, it could all have been done through using traditional economic levers, just as the British economy in 1939-45 could (theoretically) have been geared to war purposes by proper manipulation of a free price mechanism, without either rationing or allocation of materials. The government could have competed for the steel it needed for munitions or warships against the manufacturers of washing machines and private cars, and let retail prices reflect the real scarcities of the moment. No government did this in wartime. All were driven to give some administrative expression to war priorities, and in consequence the price mechanism largely lost its traditional functions. The Soviet economy in peacetime was engaged, in effect, in a politico-military operation. Far from being willing to give expression to the socio-economic forces in existence, it was seeking to alter or to repress these forces. The sheer pace of advance and of change was such that a large part of demand was itself a consequence of the process of change. Thus in the early 'thirties the construction of some giant industrial complex set up such acute and immediate difficulties that emergency programmes were constantly necessary: to overcome material bottlenecks, to train technicians, to build a new railway, to export enough grain to pay for foreign machines, and so on. The planners were constantly struggling with priority problems, which occupied most of their time and demanded unremitting attention. 'Minor' requirements had to make do with what was left, and non-priority sectors (agriculture, housing, textiles, drains, roads, and so on) seldom were enabled to fulfil their plans, even though these plans were not nearly as ambitious as those of the favoured heavy industry. 'Campaign planning', central priorities centrally enforced, and particularly in times of shortage of many necessities, meant the relegation of rational economic calculation to a comparatively minor place in the thought-processes of the leadership. The price mechanism was hardly used for resource allocation at all, except to distribute to the citizens in an orderly way whatever happened to be available for them. As in Britain in wartime, all this by no means excludes some quite considerable attention to need, but it is officialdom, not the citizen through the price mechanism, which decides which needs can be and should be satisfied. Differences between the choices made by officials and the demand-preferences of the citizens are sometimes ironed out in the USSR by rationing (e.g. of housing space), but most often by varying the retail price so that the goods actually produced are bought. This can be done by varying (or, where necessary, abolishing) turnover tax rates, as we have seen.

Another feature of the situation in the USSR was the relative abundance of labour. Of course, labour of particular skills or in particular areas was often short. However, there was substantial underemployment in agriculture, and extra supplies of unskilled labour could generally be made available to fulfil planned tasks or to offset unplanned shortcomings in productivity or mechanization. As has been argued with some force by David Granick,[1] for purposes of decision-making it was largely possible to ignore labour cost. The point was, while enlarging the capital stock as fast as possible, to use existing equipment to the full. As might be expected, this was most easy to observe in *kolkhoz* agriculture, in which, since total remuneration of labour was independent of the amount of labour expended, the marginal cost of using extra labour appeared, from the standpoint of the management, to be *nil* (the more so as the additional labour would be at the expense of working on the private plot). Only thus can one explain the deployment of 70 peasants in two shifts (total: 140) on one grain-thresher, and this form of using machinery and peasants actually won a Stalin prize.[2] Of course, in state enterprises the use of extra labour did make a difference to costs, but the priority given to growth and to plan fulfilment led, where necessary, to the overspending of the wages fund, and the controls designed to prevent this could be, and were, circumvented. The abundance of labour partially explains the institutional arrangements which permitted (or even encouraged) its wasteful use. It is also true that the existence of a large underemployed peasant population presents economists and politicians alike with problems which are not always to be judged by criteria of economic rationality which western economists regard as 'normal'.[3] In addition, if a deliberate programme of modernization is being carried through, there often occurs a long period of extremely uneven development, in which operations which are highly mechanized coexist with others (sometimes to be found within the same industry or in the same plant) in which the still relatively abundant unskilled labour force is working by antediluvian methods and in great numbers. In a sense, it would seem obvious that, with so much labour available—and at low wages—much of the mechanization is economically unprofitable. This may, however, be another way of saying that the industrialization drive itself would not have been launched if criteria of

[1] 'An organizational model of Soviet industrial planning', *Journal of Political Economy*, April, 1959.
[2] For a full description of how these peasants were used, see A. Nove and R. D. Laird, in *Soviet Studies*, April, 1953, pp. 434 ff.
[3] For some interesting ideas on this question in a non-Soviet context, see W. Arthur Lewis, 'Economic development with unlimited supplies of labour', *The Manchester School*, May, 1954.

'normal' economic rationality were used. The Soviet authorities took as given the political decision that rapid industrialization is the overriding aim of public policy. Of course, it does not follow that they proceeded by the most rational route towards the aim they set themselves. There are (at least) two senses of the word 'rational' which should be carefully distinguished. The first relates to some kind of optimum behaviour designed to fulfil the requirements of the *existing* social-economic pattern. This would adapt economic policies to what the Germans (and the Russians) call *Konjunktur*, or the totality of market-determined trends. The second species of rationality takes the aims as determined from outside the economy, and then seeks the most efficient way to achieve these results. This may well require very different institutional arrangements. For example, Holland Hunter has argued that what he calls 'hortatory planning' (targets, strains, campaigns, etc.) may actually be the most rational way, in some circumstances, to achieve rapid 'development' results if certain costs can be disregarded.[1] There are in fact other aspects of this question, and we shall have much more to say on this theme in chapter 12.

But to return to the main line of argument. Revolutionary changes were in progress, imposed by a government disinclined to count the cost, in conditions of ample labour reserves in agriculture (and, we should add, also in forced labour camps). There were hardly any periods of normality in which the system could settle down. A few years after the 'crash programmes' of the first five-year plan, war preparations and the convulsions of the purges disrupted the advance.[2] Then came the war, then a period of recovery, then another arms programme, which takes one up to Stalin's death and even beyond. Therefore, given the nature of the régime, of the economic tasks with which it was endeavouring to cope, the disturbed history of the period, and also the hostility of the ideology to any talk of economic rationality (see chapter 11, below), the net effect was to keep in being forms of economic organization designed to achieve rapid results in priority sectors by quantitative direction. As was also seen in the west during the period of wartime planning, such an approach renders impossible any systematic attempt to achieve rationality in its restricted sense, i.e. the most efficient use of resources to achieve politically-determined ends. This is because the institutional

[1] In a yet unpublished memorandum, 'On planning to catch up', which he kindly let me see.
[2] On the importance of these factors, see a valuable article by A. Khavin, in *Istoriya SSSR*, No. 1/1959.

and price structures are geared to the primary task of mobilizing resources for the achievement of targets set in the process of quantitative 'priority' planning, and for this reason they become unsuitable instruments on which to base economic criteria in choosing between alternative means. We shall be concerned in the pages that follow with many examples of this.

However, this system tends to outgrow itself, to the very extent to which it succeeds in establishing a modern industrialized economy and emerges into a period of relative normality. There are a number of reasons for this, which are to some extent interconnected.

One is the ever-growing complexity of the economy. The innumerable interconnections between sectors and areas, the ever-widening consequences of any planning decision, are such as to overburden the authorities responsible. A comparatively unsophisticated system of 'material balances', with errors corrected by a series of campaigns to enlarge bottlenecks, becomes inadequate for the job.[1]

The second could be defined as 'the multiplication of priorities'. The centralized system of allocation can work only if priorities are few and well defined, and, conversely, if a large part of the economy can be treated as non-priority, its needs as 'expendable'. Only then can the planning authorities cope more or less effectively with their complex tasks; materials are then allocated to priority sectors, and the rest can take their chance. For many years consumers' goods industries, agriculture and housing were relatively neglected, and some quite important branches of heavy industry (for instance, chemicals) also remained underdeveloped, while big advances were made in branches considered to be of key importance. There are both economic-technical and social-political reasons why this can no longer be tolerated. Backward branches of the economy (e.g. chemicals, agriculture) became themselves bottlenecks, holding up the advance of the rest of the economy. The contrast between spectacular technological achievements and low living standards contributed to a political climate in which major improvements in food, housing, retail trade, quality of textiles, and so on, were becoming increasingly a species of political necessity, and were seen to be such by Stalin's successors. This is not the place for a discussion of the political situation; we must simply note that the former 'cinderella' sectors now have enhanced priority, and that this makes the old style of planning correspondingly more difficult.

---

[1] This point has been well made by, among others, W. Leontief, in 'The Fall and Rise of Soviet Economics', in *Foreign Affairs*, January, 1960. See also chapter 12, below.

Thirdly, the period of labour abundance is drawing to a close. This, like all generalizations, is not altogether accurate. Thus the supply of skilled labour has much improved, and there is still a large and inefficiently-utilized agricultural labour force. However, the release of more farm labour requires a marked change in organization, which is still geared to the period of abundance, and the natural increase in the working population is being adversely affected, in the period 1959-65, by the abnormal years 1942-48, when war and its aftermath had a drastic effect on birth and survival rates.[1] It is, in any case, easy to demonstrate that the change in the relative scarcities of labour and capital has added a new dimension to the problems of resource utilization as Soviet economists see them. For example, Academician Strumilin attributed the new interest of his colleagues in obsolescence, a concept whose very applicability to the USSR was denied before 1955, precisely to this factor. 'While the availability of labour permits it, one can utilize all equipment, old and new, and retain old equipment until it wears out . . . In the past, in the early stages of Soviet economic development, in conditions of abundance of labour, there was a tendency towards maximum quantitative increase in production; subsequently, as this abundance came to an end, the trend shifted towards maximum qualitative indicators in the use of labour, above all labour productivity. Hence the growing importance of obsolescence at present.[2] This is an aspect of what the German economist Boettcher rightly calls 'intensification'.[3]

Fourthly, we must recall that Oscar Lange attributed part of the need for centralization of decision to the lack of capable and trustworthy personnel. Now, over forty years after the revolution, with a new and well-trained generation of managers at all levels, this argument gradually loses strength.

Finally, in the USSR at least, we can note the virtual end of revolutionary change, of social upheavals, the carrying out of which so often led to the subordination of purely economic rationality to the achievement of social-political objectives. The one major area in which economically irrelevant arguments still deeply influence economic policy is in agriculture, in anything to do with the private sector and peasants as such. It is also important to note the import-

[1] According to the 1959 census, the numbers of 10 to 15-year-olds in January, 1959, was 17·1 million. In 1939, it was 28·4 million (*Pravda*, February 4, 1960).

[2] *Vop. Ekon.*, No. 8/1956, p. 46.

[3] *Die Sowjetische Wirtschaftpolitik am Scheidewege* (Tübingen, 1959), a most thought-provoking book.

ance of bureaucratic and party vested interest as factors highly relevant to the choice between possible chains of command and organizational forms. None the less, there are many signs of greater normality, of a more calm search for the best way and less slogan-mongering. Undeniably, political control or interference occur in all kinds of ways, but it remains true to say that the general atmosphere is much more business-like, much more congenial for discussions concerning rationality, optima, maximizing the return on investment, minimizing costs and other questions familiar to economists the world over.

As a result of all this, Soviet economists and planners have been anxiously re-examining their theory and their practice, probing for weaknesses, suggesting remedies, and in doing so have provided the scholar with valuable evidence about the way things work. It is true that many, if not all, the criticisms which will be quoted here could have been, often were, made many years ago. The weaknesses now being discussed are not new. However, past criticisms were apt to be sporadic in character, and were particularly muted in the postwar period. They are now much louder and more systematic, partly because of the end of Stalin's terror, but perhaps principally because the defects and strains which are the subject of discussion appear to be less tolerable today, their correction more urgent. It does not mean that the weaknesses as such have become more glaring, or that the economy is about to fall to pieces. Indeed, time and experience have doubtless led to improvement in planning techniques, and the grosser errors of the early 'thirties are things of the past. Yet there is a widespread feeling that a qualitatively new situation now exists, to which the institutional structure devised in and for the Stalin epoch is increasingly unsuitable. It is hardly possible to read the many discussions of Soviet economists, especially after 1955, without coming to the conclusion that they know this very well.

In a sense, the analysis of problems which follows in the next chapters should be replaced by an all-inclusive picture of 'how it really works'. This, unfortunately, is an unattainable aim. No institutions in any country can be fully explained in terms of their formal structure, all are modified by a variety of conventions and informal links which play an essential role in their functioning. Similarly, the de facto exercise of authority is often quite different from the pattern suggested by the hierarchy of power as this appears in a law or a diagram. However, it is often extremely difficult to discover what the real pattern is, unless one has actually worked in the organization in question. As far as the Soviet Union is concerned, there is information on the formal structure, but accounts of what actually happens appear, if they appear at all, primarily in the context of problems, of frictions, of things that go wrong. In the course of examining these various frictions in the pages that follow, we will become acquainted with various aspects of the real life of the economy, as well as with those problems which cause perplexity to its economic administrators and planners. This will not, unfortunately, provide the fully balanced picture of reality which we ought to have, but such a picture is necessarily elusive, and will remain so until there is opportunity for a great deal of 'field work' on Soviet institutions. One should add that many economists and political scientists are very conscious of the fact that our information about how things 'really work' in western countries is often sadly defective.[1]

The plan for this part of the book is as follows. Firstly, we will consider, in chapter 6, entitled 'Micro-economic Problems', the frictions and difficulties that arise at the level of a productive enterprise, so to speak *within* the plan handed down by higher authority. Here will be discussed the consequences of the enterprise's efforts to fulfil the plans, the effect of these efforts and of the various inducements and controls on efficiency, innovation and so on, both in state enterprises and in *kolkhozy*. Chapter 7 will then deal with the planning process, including material allocation, material balances, investment choice, the behaviour of planning organs. In chapter 8 there will be covered questions concerned with prices of materials and of factors of production in general, including wage problems and agricultural rent. The division of the subject-matter in this way is no more than an analytic convenience, since the various micro and macro-economic problems are intimately inter-connected. In fact one could argue that the inter-connections are in fact *the* problem, of which the chapters that follow provide the detailed illustrations. In a sense this is certainly true: the difficulties arise in large part out of the effort to 'translate' the authorities' macro-policy of rapid growth and priorities into effective action at working levels. The inter-connections are by no means one way. Clearly, the resource allocation and planning decisions which formally belong to the central government can be affected by the applications and requests from below, which are in turn influenced by the pressures of incentives and penalties to which directors and local officials are exposed. Thus prices influence both

---

[1] For instance, the Radcliffe committee spent years on inquiring into essential aspects of the British financial system, and many experts still dispute about whether their picture of the facts is correct.

micro and macro behaviour, affect both the enterprise management and the central planners. The absence of agricultural rent affects the pay of peasants and the financial structure of *kolkhozy*, and these in turn react upon agricultural prices and planning, the marketing of food, and so on. All the various aspects constantly interact and affect one another. Yet they cannot be dealt with simultaneously, for obvious physical reasons. One can only urge the reader to keep the inter-connections constantly in mind.

CHAPTER 6

Micro-economic Problems

'SUCCESS INDICATORS'

In the west, firms take decisions by reference to the profit-motive; in the USSR, all decisions must be based on and conform to the plan. This generalization, while not wholly accurate,[1] does underline an essential difference between the systems, despite the fact that considerations other than direct profit expectations do influence actions of managers in the west, and profits do affect to some extent the behaviour of managers in the USSR. The primary task of a Soviet manager, as we have already noted, is to fulfil the plan, or more strictly plans, since he is judged and rewarded under a number of plan indicators. We shall now consider the effect of this on Soviet managerial behaviour and on the output of goods and services, beginning with the influence of these 'success indicators' on the quantity and assortment of output.

This influence is related to the range of choice open to managers at enterprise level, and this in turn depends on two factors: the nature of the product and the degree of detail in which the plan is elaborated by higher authority. Thus, for example, an enterprise producing electricity, or a factory making large specialized machines (e.g. turbines), or arms factories producing to the precise specifications decided centrally by military experts, whatever their other differences, have in common the fact that the product mix depends hardly at all on decisions taken by enterprise managers. In most cases, however, the problem of the product mix is a real one: textiles, shoes, a wide range of metal goods and a long list of other commodities can be made in many shapes, sizes, styles, qualities, colours. It is generally impossible for the planning organs to specify the desired assortment in full detail, or, as we shall see, to enforce its specifications on the enterprise even if they made the attempt to subdivide the product mix. It is also important to note that the actual or potential production of any factory must always depend to some ex-

---

[1] It does not apply, for instance, to most nationalized industries in the west.

155

tent on the management on the spot, since the plan itself can hardly fail to be influenced by what the management declares itself able and willing to do in the next planning period.

If the fulfilment or overfulfilment of plans is to be rewarded, it is clearly necessary first to define what the plans are. To take three of the most common success indicators as examples: in each period there must be specified a quantity of output, a percentage reduction in costs, and a percentage increase in labour productivity. Managerial behaviour must naturally be influenced in the direction of endeavouring to fulfil the plans so defined, with results which may not be obvious at first sight.

Take the quantity of output first. The plan is generally based on the achievements of the previous period, to which is added a percentage increase. The quantity to be produced is usually intended to encourage effort, to induce the management to seek out 'reserves' of underused factors of production. In the process of plan determination, it pays the management of the enterprise to conceal its full potential and in other ways to manœuvre to obtain an 'easy' plan; nor would it pay a wise manager to overfulfil it by too wide a margin, for, if he did so, he might be suspected of having concealed his potential, and plans for the subsequent period might be increased by an embarrassingly large percentage.[1] Of course, all this is known to the planning organs, and in the resultant manœuvring the authorities try to utilize the various supervisory agencies, including the party group and the various 'activist' employees grouped around the elected 'permanent production council', to check up on managerial behaviour. Plans may be deliberately 'tightened', on the not unreasonable assumption that the manager is not being quite honest about his production possibilities or his stocks of materials (as we shall see, it pays to hoard). These circumstances also help to explain the urge to 'overfulfil' output plans, which perfectionist critics of planning often regard as proof of inefficiency, but which springs in part from a knowledge that there are hidden reserves. On the other hand, the 'supervisors' are often themselves interested in being able to report plan fulfilment. Thus, before the reform, glavk officials tolerated understatements of production possibilities, while a sovnarkhoz was said to have reduced a plan in mid-year so as not to have to report that one of its major enterprises had failed to fulfil it.[2]

[1] These defects are discussed by G. Nikolaeva, in Novyi Mir, No. 7/1957, p. 74, comments on readers' letters in Kommunist, No. 1/1957, p. 49, and many others.

[2] M. Sidorov, Vop. Ekon., No. 4/1957, p. 128, and Pravda, April 27, 1959.

However, let us now assume that an output target for the next plan period has been decided. One must now consider how the target figure is expressed in quantitative terms. The ways in which this can be done depend in part on the nature of the product: for example, shoe output could be expressed in number of pairs or in roubles, production of clothing or of furniture is too varied for the plans to be expressed in anything but roubles, sheet metal plans could be in tons or in square metres, cloth in square metres or linear metres or roubles, and so on through a variety of other possibilities. The effect of each of these is to encourage its own species of distortion. In the context of an economic situation in which virtually all goods free of major technical defects can be disposed of, the temptation always exists to adapt the assortment of the product to the method of measuring the quantitative fulfilment of the plan.

Examples can be cited in very large numbers, drawing on material published not only in the USSR but also Hungary, Poland and Czechoslovakia, where a similar institutional structure involved similar problems.[1] A plan expressed in tons encourages the production of heavy commodities; in any choice involving weight, the 'weightier' variant is bound to be favoured, since this facilitates the fulfilment of the plan. Thus, for example, a metal works was reported to have increased its output of roofing iron by 20 per cent over five years in tons, but in terms of area the increase was only 10 per cent; the plan, of course, was in tons.[2] Clearly, an output plan expressed in terms of tons encourages the choice of a variant in which a given weight is achieved with the least expenditure of those resources unrelated to weight. For instance, factories making prefabricated cement blocks, prefer to make large blocks, which is the easiest means of fulfilling a plan in terms of tons, though, as it happens, the result is a shortage of small blocks necessary for completing portions of the buildings under construction.[3] Khrushchev himself gave a particularly absurd example: the chandelier plan was expressed in tons, so chandeliers were unnecessarily heavy.[4] The humorous journal *Krokodil* once pictured, in a cartoon, a factory which fulfilled its entire month's output programme for nails by the manufacture of

---

[1] Particularly valuable in all matters pertaining to the present chapter is the book by the Hungarian economist Janos Kornai, translated into English under the title of *Overcentralization in Hungarian Light Industry* (Oxford, 1959). For a discussion of Soviet experience, see A. Nove, 'Some Problems of "Success Indicators" in Soviet Industry', in *Economica*, January, 1958, pp. 1 ff.

[2] V. Kontorovich, *Sotsialisticheskii trud*, No. 1/1957, p. 50.

[3] But if the cement blocks are calculated in roubles, they avoid making cheap cement blocks (*Pravda*, August 3, 1956).

[4] *Pravda*, July 2, 1959.

one gigantic nail, hanging from an overhead crane the whole length of the workshop.

Output targets in roubles evade such difficulties as these, but at the cost of creating others. In nearly all instances, the money measure is applied to gross value of output—*valovaya produktsiya*—which includes unfinished production, or, strictly speaking, the increase (if any) of unfinished or partly-processed goods over the previous plan period. This encourages a number of distortions. In the first place, an advantage is derived from using dear materials. Obviously, to take a published example, an enterprise making tools, with a plan expressed in roubles of gross output, finds that it 'pays' (in terms of plan fulfilment) to use unnecessarily expensive quality steel, and for many years the production of inexpensive clothes was inhibited by the reluctance of manufacturers to utilize the cheaper cloths.[1] There is even involved in this method of measuring plan fulfilment a quite unintended discouragement of the production of spare parts. This is because, for example, a carburettor is 'worth' more in a completed motor-cycle or tractor, where it is combined with other goods and services many of which were bought from outside the enterprise, than if this same carburettor were produced and sold as a spare part.[2] Spare parts are notoriously short in the USSR, and it is noteworthy that a plan expressed in physical units also leads to neglect of spares. Thus *Pravda* (June 8, 1960) published a bitter attack on those who fail to provide spares for motor-cycles, in the course of which an imaginery person, deemed to be 'the director of an enterprise, head of a *sovnarkhoz* or official of a planning organ', undertakes to increase production of motor-cycles, and, when the question of spares is raised, answers as follows: 'I am not interested in your calculations. All that matters is what is included in the statistical returns and counted in the plàn, i.e. new complete machines. They interest me. As for piston rings, plugs and so on, these are just fiddling little things which don't appear in fulfilment indicators.' Spares, therefore, are unobtainable, for reasons connected with the success indicator system. At the same time, the failure of British car manufacturers to provide adequate spares and service in the first postwar boom years should remind us that these things are apt to suffer in a seller's market, even in a quite different institutional setting.

There is also a tendency to start work on production or on build-

---

[1] See Kontorovich, op. cit., and N. Lyubimov and A. Petrov in *Plan. Khoz.*, No. 1/1957, pp. 38-9.
[2] This point is made by N. Antonov, *Plan. Khoz.*, No. 5/1957, p. 83, and V. Kontorovich, in *Plan. Khoz.*, No. 3/1957.

ing which cannot be completed, which locks up resources unnecessarily, but counts in statistics of gross output (or of the volume of construction). It may appear simple to overcome some of these weaknesses, for instance by measuring plan fulfilment in terms of goods actually completed and sold ('commodity production', *tovarnaya produktsia*), or to measure value-added only. Both these methods have been discussed and sometimes tried. However, they have defects of their own. Thus it is clearly unfair not to include genuinely unfinished production in assessing the work of a factory over a given period of time. As for value-added, this method is now applied in the Soviet clothing industry,[1] and it has indeed increased the range of cheaper garments produced. But it has the opposite weakness of encouraging any activity which adds to the value of work done within the enterprise, while useful forms of sub-contracting may well be avoided lest the value of work done within that enterprise should be lowered. Therefore, despite much discussion and criticism, the 'gross output' measure remains predominant among monetary plan indicators. It is particularly common, unavoidably, in assessing the results of a group of enterprises, within a *glavk*, a ministry, a *sovnarkhoz* or a republic. The anxiety of these administrative bodies to report plan fulfilment, arrived at by adding together the gross outputs of all the enterprises subordinate to them, results in constant pressure on managers to fulfil or overfulfil gross output plans, to the exclusion of many other relevant considerations, a state of affairs a Soviet economist has described as a veritable 'cult of the gross' (*kul't vala*).[2]

Other measures of output plan fulfilment suffer from defects of their own. Cloth was 'measured' in linear metres for many years, with the result that it was made narrower than was desirable from other points of view.[3] Consequently from 1959 the basis was changed to square metres. But this is by no means always satisfactory, since other desiderata tend to be sacrificed to maximize square metres, at the expense, for instance, of quality or workmanship. Roofing metal which was too heavy when the plan was in tons becomes too thin when the plan is in square metres. If a plan for nails were expressed in quantity (e.g. thousands of nails) they would tend to be small, if in tons they would tend to be large. Highly original plan-measurement criteria were devised in some industries; for example, central-heating boilers were assessed for this purpose in terms of the area of

---

[1] M. Zaurov, *Vest. Stat.*, No. 3/1957, pp. 74-5.
[2] D. Kondrashev, *Tseno-obrazovanie v promyshlennosti* (Moscow, 1956), p. 32.   [3] Kontorovich, op. cit., p. 50.

heating surface (of the boiler); consequently, when a new model was devised which heated more efficiently with a smaller heating surface, no one would touch it, as it would worsen their success indicators'.[1] The Soviet economist Aboltin reported that the Stalingrad construction trust wasted metal because, for one of its projects, the plan was expressed in terms of metal used, and he (and others) also mentioned 'plan-fulfilment' simulation in garages, which sometimes took the form of unnecessary waste of fuel (to conform to the reported kilometres covered), sometimes unreasonable economy of fuel.[2] Some restaurants avoid cheap dishes, as the plan is in terms of gross turnover. Other examples, often even more grotesque, could easily fill several pages. One such recent example concerns fish. A great battle was reported, between the fisheries trust of the Far East, the Kamchatka fish *kombinat*, the State Fisheries Inspectorate, fisheries research institutes in Kamchatka and in Moscow, the RSFSR Gosplan, etc. The subject of the battle: is a certain fish a perch or a ruff? Why? Because if it is a perch it must be gutted, whereas no such rule applies to the ruff. 'To gut is not advantageous. It uses time and money, and, most important, the guts and head . . . are almost 15 per cent of the total weight of the fish. And, among other things, there is a gross output plan, which it is desirable to overfulfil (in tons, of course). It is particularly desirable for the managers of Far East fisheries trust. It is they who have discovered a gap in the fisheries standards, through which have penetrated countless ungutted ruff.'[3]

Repeatedly, it has been stated that rewards for the fulfilment of output plans must be made conditional upon the fulfilment of the assortment plan, that it is inadmissible that the product mix be distorted in order to claim fulfilment in aggregate terms. These statements do not appear to have eliminated the trouble, which arises partly because of the very great emphasis given by the authorities to aggregate plan fulfilment, and partly because the product mix cannot be specified in all its detail in the plan.

Rewards for plan fulfilment require not only a clearly defined measure of results, but also a time-period to which the results must be related. Hence the great importance of the calendar, and the phenomenon of 'storming' (*shturmovshchina*), of a mad rush to fulfil the plan in the last few days of the month, quarter or year, followed by a slack and disorganized period in which production falls sharply

---

[1] *Pravda*, September 5, 1958.
[2] *Voprosy stroitel'stva kommunizma v SSSR* (Moscow, 1959, pp. 351-2).
[3] *Krokodil*, June 10, 1960.

until the next mad rush. Denunciations of *shturmovshchina* were, and are, extremely common, and the prevalence of the disease is a sign that it is, in a sense, built in to the structure of the economy. It is worth recalling that this particular form of distortion, as well as many of the other 'success indicator' problems referred to here, occurred also in British planning during the war.[1]

One weakness involved in 'calendar' planning is a certain short-sightedness; one has insufficient incentive to look to subsequent planning periods, the more so because, with a high turnover of directors, someone else might then be in charge. There is little or no incentive for looking far ahead. This affects attitudes to resource conservation, as may be illustrated by a large number of articles pleading, apparently in vain, for preserving forests.

The effect of other 'success indicators' on the behaviour of managements may be partly to correct some of the deviations engendered by pursuit of quantitative plan fulfilment, but often they encourage similar distortions, or cause new ones. Thus an effort to fulfil a plan to increase labour productivity by 4 per cent would, clearly, discourage the taking on of large numbers of additional workers. On the other hand, the calculation of productivity necessarily requires comparing the labour force to total output, and this reinforces the tendency to try to simulate overfulfilment of the output plan in tons, roubles, or whatever the measure may be. Until 1958, the measurement of labour productivity involved only 'productive workers', i.e. excluded clerks, technical personnel and auxiliaries. The effect, not suprisingly, was that the management either neglected to mechanize the auxiliary work or endeavoured to classify as many of their employees as possible in non-productive categories. This particular deviation has been checked; from 1959, labour productivity statistics are based on the entire labour force.[2]

In 1959, after a period of experiment, a change was decreed in the 'success indicator' system, reflecting the realization that a system encouraging maximum quantitative results at any cost is no longer reasonable in present circumstances. Outside of a few particularly scarce commodities, the size of premia now no longer depends on the degree of fulfilment of the output plan, though fulfilment remains a precondition of receiving premia at all. The actual magnitude of the reward is now primarily dependent on the fulfilment (and overfulfilment) of the cost reduction plan, subject also to fulfilling the

[1] See, in particular, E. Devons, *Planning in Practice* (Cambridge University Press, 1950).

[2] Rumyantsev, op. cit., p. 271.

plans for labour productivity, the introduction of new technique and the delivery plans (in particular deliveries to places outside the area of those given *sovnarkhoz*).[1] Costs are commonly calculated as 'per rouble of commodity production', i.e. of output sold. In addition, the decree of July 2, 1960, described in greater detail on p. 170, below, introduced additional premia for innovations. Finally, as will be shown, there now exists a list of products which it is *forbidden* to produce in excess of plan.

All this undoubtedly shows an important qualitative change in the economy, indeed in the economic history of the USSR. Of course, quantitative plans will still have to be fulfilled, and a strong 'traditional' attachment to this indicator can still be observed in reports of economic achievements in the press. Cost reduction now plays a much bigger role, yet there is some ground for scepticism as to the rationality of some of the measures which premia based on costs will stimulate. Admittedly, emphasis on this 'indicator' would discourage plan fulfilment involving a shift in the product mix towards using high-cost materials, but it would encourage lower-quality or lower-cost variants, which, in any multi-product enterprise, can be so selected as to make costs per unit appear to fall. The desire to achieve a 'statistical' cut in costs also influences the adoption or non-adoption of new models, according to whether or not they are considered to be 'comparable' for purposes of calculating costs. The influence of this on innovation and adaptation to consumer demand will be dealt with under these heads (pp. 167-81, below). Here again, there is a much better chance of ensuring that a downward change in costs is genuine if the given enterprise's product is homogeneous and unchanging, such as electric power, or coal of the only quality which the particular enterprise can mine. It is almost impossible to avoid simulation or distortion if the enterprise is able to vary the product mix.

There are a multitude of other 'success indicators', which cause distortions in varying degrees, or correct each other to varying extents. Incredible as it may seem, geological surveying units received plans in linear metres of drilling, 'and the planning departments want to know nothing else. If you have not fulfilled this plan indicator, you are classified as backward', even though the surveyors may have successfully discovered mineral reserves, so that the surveyors 'undertake work they know to be useless'.[2] There are reports, too,

[1] For two useful articles on these changes, see M. Mikhailov, *Plan. Khoz.*, No. 12/1959, and V. Markov, *Plan. Khoz.*, No. 6/1960, pp. 29 ff.
[2] *Pravda*, August 3, 1956.

that taxi-drivers find it 'pays' them to waste petrol by driving an empty cab so as to fulfil the plan, provided their bonus for plan fulfilment exceeds the amount by which the taxi-meter is 'short' of the plan. There are many bonuses calculated in relation to economy of this or that material, or fuel. All are complex, all must of their nature stimulate forms of behaviour not intended by those who originally framed the rules.,

It is essential to appreciate the cause of these and similar difficulties. They all spring from the fact that the activity of enterprises is essentially based on *instructions*, and the incentives provided to the management are rewards for acting in accordance with instructions, with the plan.[1] The authorities are unable to issue unambiguous, all-inclusive instructions, and various aspects of the plan may be inconsistent with one another, as when overfulfilment of output plans may require some increase in costs, or when some other plan indicator or instruction (e.g. relating to saving fuel, or economizing in the use of some scarce material) contradicts the aim of increasing labour productivity, or involves the overspending of the wages fund. These ambiguities are further complicated by the inevitable imperfections and imprecision of the statistics which express the achievements of the enterprise by reference to the various indicators. There is thus an area of choice, of manœuvre. The director, unless prevented by direct orders or *force majeure*, must be expected to act in such a way as to maximize his financial rewards and his standing with his superiors, and minimize the risk of loss of reputation, demotion, reprimand. Not only his own reputation, but that of his staff, of his superiors, of the enterprise itself, depends on plan fulfilment. The permitted wages fund is related to plan fulfilment. For these and many other reasons 'the director . . . must, is bound, is compelled and certainly wishes to struggle to fulfil the plan and its quantitative and qualitative indicators'.[2] Obviously, his choices are complicated by his own assessment of the often uncertain prospects of risk and material and moral reward. He may shrink from exploiting too ruthlessly the possibilities of a situation, because this might well bring trouble. For instance, even if no details of sizes were specified in the plan, and it would be simplest from the angle of various 'indicators' to make all men's ready-made suits of one size only, no director of a clothing factory is likely to act accordingly. However, it is repeatedly a matter of complaint that plans for the production of children's

[1] This thought is developed at some length, with impeccable logic, in the excellent book by Kornai, already cited.
[2] O. Antonov, *Znamya*, No. 2/1957, p. 151.

sizes of both clothes and shoes are underfulfilled, because they are unpopular with directors as fitting badly into their 'success indicators'.

The instructions must leave much to be settled on the spot, or by negotiations between the parties directly concerned (e.g. the wholesaler and the factory), but the one thing which is not rewarded in any way is *use value*, or the satisfaction of demand. As Kornai well put it, 'if the article happens not to be faulty (i.e. is free of defects of workmanship) and is nevertheless not wanted by anybody, then this has no consequences. It does not affect the fact that it will be counted as part of the production value credited to the enterprise concerned'.[1] The system of instructions lacks an all-embracing criterion, which, at least in theory, is provided by profits in a market economy. Of course, the Soviet system does not produce vast quantities of useless rubbish. The system of plans and controls ensures that the bulk of what is produced serves some purpose. However, there is every reason to suppose that the system of incentives which guides the director of the enterprise to choose between alternatives frequently acts in a misleading way, thereby causing some misdirection of resources. The problem is thus one of reconciling a system designed to ensure obedience to instructions (and a maximum growth rate) with what might be called 'micro-rational behaviour' on the part of enterprises within the area of their responsibility.

Indeed, this is part of a wider question. In an economy based on instructions, where the primary object of activity is to fulfil a plan decided by superior authority, all economic units below the centre suffer from absence of objective criteria for taking autonomous decisions, other than the plan indicators determined from above. In the area which is left to their independent judgment, the local authorities and enterprises are frequently left either with no compass to guide them, or the compass is likely to mislead them. Either the plan specifies the requirements with such precision that the men on the spot have no choice at all—such as in the example of the electric power station which generates a homogeneous product when ordered to do so—or they would probably be disorientated by the available incentives. This is so at enterprise level, but it is also an acute problem in any territorial unit, such as a *sovnarkhoz*. It is not for nothing that, in the quotation from *Pravda* about spares on p. 158, the imag-

---

[1] Op. cit., p. 38. On all these questions, see also the valuable books by J. Berliner, *Factory and Manager in the USSR* (Harvard, 1957), and D. Granick, *Management of the Industrial Firm in the USSR* (Columbia University, 1954).

inary obstructionist could have been a *sovnarkhoz* official. To illustrate this thesis one has only to consider the criteria by which *sovnarkhozy* can expect their activities to be judged. Like enterprises, they must fulfil the plan, claim successes in terms of aggregate 'indicators', and this stimulates the issue of orders which facilitate the achievement of the required statistical results in aggregate terms; which is by no means the same thing as producing what is needed. Since the *sovnarkhoz* is a body whose field of vision ends at its own boundaries, it is generally incapable of observing the consequences of its acts, save where these affect enterprises under its own control, and these interest the *sovnarkhoz* most of all when fulfilment of aggregate plans is affected. One can well understand, therefore, why the *sovnarkhozy* are liable to the sin of 'regionalism' (*mestnichestvo*), which will be discussed in chapter 7. It is essential to add that, in practice, the nature of central orders and the operation of various checks and controls keeps the system in fair order most of the time, and that chaos is generally avoided. It would be quite wrong to give the impression of chronic and utter confusion. The point is rather that, in so far as decisions can be taken locally, there is a lack of objective criteria which are effective and are not misleading.

In the above discussion of incentives to management, no mention has yet been made of *profits*, and some readers may be asking themselves the reason for the omission. There certainly does appear to be some interest for an enterprise to make profits, especially overplan profits. However, under present conditions there is ample evidence that this incentive operates irrationally, and also that it does not greatly influence managerial behaviour, except in so far as increased profits may be incidental to fulfilling the cost reduction plan.

The irrationality of the profit motive under Soviet conditions is the logical consequence of the illogicalities of the price system, described in some detail in chapter 4, above. Repeatedly, enterprises find themselves manufacturing, say, ten models, which yield widely different profit margins, or, in some cases, cause losses. Similarly, a *sovnarkhoz* generally finds that some commodities which its enterprises produce, and many enterprises within its administrative sphere, make losses. If they were to allow this fact to determine the production programme, this would be contrary to the intention of the planners and to the needs of the economy. When there is a genuine interest in making a profit, this leads to refusal to accept certain 'unremunerative' orders, or underfulfilment of that part of the plan which involves financial loss. However, profit-making as such is not an important element in judging the success of an enterprise, other criteria are regarded by officialdom as much more weighty, and, in addition, the managerial personnel of an enterprise receive comparatively little direct rewards as a consequence of making profits. The 'enterprise fund' is supposed to be used for general amenities, housing, new techniques, etc., and not to pay bonuses to directors, who, by contrast, benefit greatly from other kinds of plan fulfilment. There are also numerous complaints from Soviet economists that the enterprise fund is much too small, and that it is therefore of no sufficient interest to anyone.[1] It is also criticized as wrongly based, since it is related to a profit rate calculated on 'gross' costs; consequently the same rate of profit (and of any percentage deductions from profit) is much higher in relation to wages in industries in which labour costs form a relatively small part of total costs. For this reason textiles, in which 90 per cent of the costs consist of raw materials, do 'better' than many basic industries under these rules.[2] Another critic showed that the enterprise fund is greatly and illogically affected by the somewhat arbitrarily determined profits plans, while the many enterprises which make planned losses have their fund made up, with anomalous results, on the quite different basis of cost reductions. He cited examples, all from Azerbaidjan, showing *planned* enterprise funds which, per worker, varied from 53 kopecks to 315 roubles.[3] Clearly, it would be going altogether too far to assert that profit and loss questions have no significance in the operations of enterprises or of *sovnarkhozy*. Thus the former wish to avoid large unplanned loss, which would bring down upon them the inspectors of the State Bank, while the *sovnarkhozy* can take the profit and loss situation into account when deciding which of a number of similar workshops in their area could be closed down when it is possible to concentrate production of some component in a few factories. None the less, it would be wrong to see in profits, under Soviet conditions, any kind of all-inclusive criterion on which either planning or operations can be effectively based.

Yet clearly there is need for such a criterion. Soviet economists have been discussing the inadequacies of the existing 'success indicators', and have urged important reforms. Some of these concern the price system and will be discussed in chapter 8. though it should be noted at this stage that all critics agree that greater logic in pricing is an essential feature in any reform, even though the objective basis of

---

[1] Thus E. Manevich, *Vop. Ekon.*, No. 1/1959, p. 46, pointed out that the entire fund in 1955 amounted to only 0·5 per cent of total wage payments.

[2] A. Bachurin, *Voprosy sovetskikh finansov* (Moscow, 1956), p. 38, makes this argument.

[3] R. Karagedov, *Finansy SSSR*, No. 6/1957, pp. 36-7.

price-fixing remains a matter on which there is disagreement. However, a range of possible reforms of the success indicators themselves have been debated, and not only in the USSR. Some very interesting new ideas were tried out in Czechoslovakia, when the earlier copy of the Soviet model was replaced, in April, 1958, by a new pattern. Since the reform is on lines similar to those put forward by some of the Soviet critics, it is worth briefly examining what the Czechs have done, since it is possibly along this path that Soviet development will proceed. For more details of these and also Polish ideas on this subject, the reader is referred to chapter 9.

INNOVATION, RISK-TAKING, INITIATIVE

The situation of the Soviet enterprise is somewhat paradoxical. On the one hand, great publicity is given in the USSR to inventors and inventions, and there are impressive statistics published from time to time about the number of new ideas put forward by employees. In addition, commercial secrecy does not exist, so that new methods or new models devised in one enterprise are available for the use of all enterprises, and effective new ideas are widely publicized on a nation-wide scale. But on the other hand the Soviet specialized press, and indeed also literature and drama, abound in criticisms of stick-in-the-mud directors who refuse to adopt new methods and continue to produce to obsolete designs. In some respects and in some industries, the Soviet economy shows striking progress in technique. In others, one sees a very different picture.

In the case of such 'naturally centralized' production processes as sputniks and jet aircraft, the 'micro' problems we are discussing scarcely arise. Development is essentially a matter of gifted designers and well-endowed research institutes, rather than of enterprise initiative. Nor does the presence or absence of such initiative make any decisive difference to the equipment or the product of large modern plant, erected in accordance with the latest technical know-how on the instructions of central project-making bodies. This applies, *inter alia*, to the wholesale adoption of the latest foreign techniques, and also to steelworks, hydro-electric power stations and the like; the problems here relate more to choices between investment variants, which are discussed in the next chapter. At the moment we are concerned with innovation on the scale of an enterprise, involving the rearrangement of a production line or a new design of a product.

The first snag is a consequence of the concentration on fulfilling the current output plan. Many new ideas involve a halt for retooling or for making other relevant changes, and it is hard to imagine doing this without adversely affecting the production figures of the current quarter. But it is an essential fact of Soviet life that everyone is under pressure to report on the quarter's plan, and this includes the hierarchical superiors of the enterprise, who therefore show understandable impatience with any initiative which affects the current plan-fulfilment statistics.

The second difficulty relates to the financing of such investments as may be needed to change either the model produced or the methods by which it is produced. Retooling costs money. Until the last few years, there was virtually no source for financing such expenditure, without the specific authorization of the ministry concerned. In other words, the project had to be submitted up the hierarchy, which severely limited initiative. If the superior authorities supported the project, on the grounds that the output or costs would benefit by the proposed change, they were apt to amend the plans accordingly, so that there would be little or no gain to the initiators in the event of success, to balance possible loss of bonuses and reputation. It is now possible for enterprises to borrow sums not exceeding one million roubles, and repayable in two to three years, to finance retooling and mechanization; these are the credits mentioned on p. 36, above. They are granted by the local branch of the State Bank, and do not require specific permission from any higher administrative level. The branch of the bank can decide whether or not to give credit, within general limits set by its headquarters. However, not only is the maximum sum modest, but the repayment period is exceedingly short, points which have been made by Soviet critics anxious to enlarge the investment initiative open to enterprises.[1]

The third, and probably most important, snag concerns the impact of innovation on the 'success indicators' of the enterprise, and, linked with it, the failure to reward, or indeed even to recognize, risk-taking. Does the proposed innovation 'fit' into output and/or cost reduction indicators? Then it would be favourably considered. But what if it does not? One example has already been cited: that of the new central-heating boiler. There are other examples. Thus more durable kinds of electronic valves were not introduced, apparently because the existing ones satisfied the producing enterprise, whose 'success indicators' were in no way affected by whether the valves

---

[1] V. Markov, *Vop. Ekon.*, No. 9/1959, pp. 41 ff., and several others. A part of the enterprise fund is available for this purpose, but the amounts are very modest.

lasted three months or three years.[1] 'In order to provide effective checks on cost reduction,' wrote another critic, 'the greatest number of products are considered to be comparable,' even though the design may have been appreciably altered. Consequently, because the management seeks a cost-reduction bonus, 'the question of comparability is often in conflict with the improvement of the quality and range of the products of the enterprise, and sometimes acts as a direct obstacle in the path of introducing new and better products', because of the tendency to avoid 'those products which will be deemed "comparable" if the change in design involves increased costs per unit'.[2]

Innovation may, therefore, lead to difficulties. It is always simpler, in the circumstances, for managers to go on doing what they were doing before, unless some good reason (or order) to the contrary exists. Why take unrewarded risks? A Soviet literary periodical contained the following comment on this subject. 'The system of innovation is unfortunate. Innovation involves risk, and, as in all gambling, capital. If you risk, it is easy to lose. Isn't that so? But even if the director is given the capital, let him just risk and not win! . . . No, it does not behove a director to take risks . . . Suppose your director desires to bring into production a new (plastic) powder . . ., he would have to wait endlessly in ministerial reception rooms. There is a risk here. The risk is not that millions might be lost. He might take up these powders and, God forbid, the quarterly plan will be messed up, and the ministry will show up badly in the statistical report.'[3]

Finally, one must consider the effect on grass-roots innovation of the fact that virtually all prices are determined by superior authority. Since prices remain unaltered, wrote a Soviet critic, 'enterprises have no economic interest in the improvement of design'. It is true, he added, that in 1955 enterprises were allowed to charge extra sums to cover the costs of improvements to machinery, 'but this is seldom done in practice and is limited to certain kinds of equipment only'.[4]

A decree of the Central Committee and the council of ministers, published on July 2, 1960, somewhat improved the situation. Not only are premia received by directors and chief engineers made conditional upon the fulfilment of plans for the introduction of new

[1] O. Antonov, op. cit., pp. 155-6. His article is significantly called, 'Why does the introduction of new techniques have to be fought for?'
[2] G. Vainshenker, *Vest. Stat.*, No. 3/1957, pp. 20-1.
[3] N. Lebedev, *Zvezda*, No. 5/1957, p. 155.
[4] V. Ganshtak, *Finansy SSSR*, No. 6/1957, p. 19.

technique, but some new incentives are provided for initiative at local level. Thus a new premium fund to encourage new technique will be formed by a levy on all industrial, building and transport enterprises, which will form part of production costs and which will vary from 1 per cent (for machinery) to 0·2 per cent (transport) of the wages fund. Most of the resulting sum will be held by *sovnarkhozy* and other bodies, but a quarter will remain at the disposal of the director for use to issue bonuses for innovation at enterprise level. In calculating premia to directors, special attention is to be paid to the economic gain accruing from each innovation adopted. *Sovnarkhozy* will also have more funds at their disposal to support new technical developments, including the production of prototypes and experimental work by enterprises. Prices of new machines will if necessary be kept below their initial costs by temporary subsidy from this fund. The rules governing the enterprise fund have been changed to encourage those who undertake technical developments, and at least 20 per cent of this fund now *must* be used for new technique and modernization of equipment.[1]

Obviously, this decree will do something to improve matters, if only by introducing and emphasizing new technique as a major success indicator. However, one can also envisage endless possibilities of simulation, owing to the unavoidably imprecise definition of 'new technique', and also unnecessary innovation, 'for the record'. Many thousands of measures in this field are prescribed in central and republican plans; for example, in 1960, 'the plan for the introduction of new technique in the Ukraine envisages 2,900 measures', and, owing to fear of not being able to report fulfilment, 'already at the beginning of the year the *sovnarkhozy* of the Ukraine ask for 700 measures to be dropped from the plan'.[2] Despite a small increase in funds and incentives locally available, there is still not much rational basis for the introduction of new ideas and above all of new products, except perhaps in some sectors of engineering, which are favoured by the decree of July 2, 1960.

The stimulation of innovation by administrative order becomes, in the circumstances, an important substitute for grass-roots incentives. Several bodies are charged with these duties at the centre. There are the State Scientific-technical Committee, the State Committee on Automation and Engineering, the Committee on Inventions and Dis-

---

[1] See text of decree in *Pravda*, July 2, 1960, and a good article by V. Markov, *Plan. Khoz.*, No. 6/1960.
[2] K. Petukhov (chairman of Technical-scientific committee), *Pravda*, July 17, 1960.

coveries, the various other committees attached to or integral parts of the all-union government (see p. 75, above). The Gosplan at union and republican level, the *sovnarkhozy* and their various committees, Party committees at all levels,[1] the trade unions, the factory 'activists' now organized in the permanent production council and a large number of research institutes, are also involved in the struggle. Indeed, one eminent critic urged a reorganization of 'innovation organizations' and a reduction of their numbers, suggesting that overlaps and confusion between them are not unknown.[2] The results, to repeat, appear to be patchy, with admirable achievement in some sectors and serious shortcomings in others. These contrasts may partly be attributed to the relative importance of initiative from below in the development of new models or techniques, but are also connected with the priorities imposed by planners. Thus, for example, all concerned may be aware of the advantages of some new sewing machine, but those in charge of the economy may be devoting attention and resources to matters which they consider to be of much greater importance. In these priority sectors, there has generally been much more active encouragement of new ideas, and much more money has been available to reward and develop them.

Here again we should not implicitly overlook the imperfections of the western system. Commercial secrecy, the buying up of inventions in order not to use them, trade-union resistance to new methods, sheer conservatism supported by a price ring and high import duties, these things may be found in various 'capitalist' countries. None the less, it remains true that the structure of the Soviet economy does little effectively to encourage the search for the new at local level, and not a little to discourage it.

TRANSMISSION OF DEMAND TO PRODUCERS

Still on the micro-economic level, we must now consider the influence of demand on production decisions which can be taken at enterprise, local-soviet or *sovnarkhoz* levels. We are not here considering the various ways in which a change in centrally-estimated requirements could lead to a corresponding change in the central plan. Obviously, if the top planning organs decided that the country needs

---

[1] E. Spiridonov, the secretary of the Leningrad party committee, reported the existence of 'technical groups' (*tekhnicheskie kabinety*) attached to local party committees (*Pravda*, June 23, 1960).

[2] A. Kostousov, *Pravda*, August 28, 1959, Kostousov is the chairman of the State Committee on Automation and Machine-building. (A new co-ordinating body was in fact set up in April, 1961. See page 74, above.)

more turret lathes, more soap and less vodka, the mechanism exists through which to issue the appropriate operational instructions and to make necessary investments. The problem here is one of adjustments within the general plan, rather than a change in the plan itself. We have repeatedly had occasion to note that detailed specifications and subdivision of assortment can only very partially be embodied in planning instructions.

Let us first examine the case of producers' goods, other than homogeneous products where questions of assortment do not arise. Suppose that a given enterprise desires to receive lathes, or yarn, or whatever it may be, of some particular type. How can its desire affect the producer enterprise?

It is certainly possible for orders to be placed for the required type. If it is defined as a separate variety of product in the commodity allocation lists, the user enterprise applies for an allocation certificate for the given variety. Alternatively, if it is not so defined, then, having obtained an allocation certificate for lathes or yarn, or whatever it may be, the customer approaches the producing enterprise or the wholesaling organization (or the *sovnarkhoz*, or before 1957 the *glavk*, in charge of it) and requests that the required types be delivered. However, this request may be refused, and, unless backed by administrative instructions from superior authority, there is no particular reason why it should be granted, provided the customer can be compelled to accept the inferior substitute, which, in conditions of chronic shortage and a seller's market, he generally can be.

The reasons for this state of affairs are implicit in the preceding analysis of success indicators. The producing enterprise and also the *sovnarkhoz* which controls it, has no incentive to satisfy user requirements, and every incentive to fulfil output, cost-reduction and other plans which are irrelevant to the use-value of the product. If lathe A and lathe B are 'worth' the same from the standpoint of plan fulfilment, the fact that lathe A happens to be more efficient and more 'wanted' is a matter of indifference (economically) to the producing enterprise or *sovnarkhoz*. If, for any of a large number of reasons, lathe B happens to be more convenient to manufacture, then, unless orders to the contrary are received from superior authority, lathe B will be produced.

A very good example of success indicators stimulating the production of a model undesirable from the user's standpoint was given by a Soviet engineer, and is worth quoting in full. He referred to several indicators peculiar to an aircraft factory, which serves as a reminder that ministries and *sovnarkhozy* frequently devised and devise large numbers of such indicators involving almost any conceivable aspect of the enterprise's activity.

'Suppose that the factory insists on a change in design which ensures an economy of 10,000 roubles a year but increases the weight of an empty aircraft "only" by 3 kilograms. What effect can this have?

'Suppose that the change consists in the elimination of a drilling operation after stamping, reducing the labour input by two hours. The labour input indicator is improved, and sure enough the annual plan of the factory prescribes a reduction in labour time. There is a reduction in machine-tool use—another indicator! There is less waste of metal—yet another indicator! A new "rationalizing" proposal has been adopted—that's an indicator too! There is additional annual economy as a result of adopting a new proposal—another indicator! And what an important one, too! The factory personnel has undertaken the obligation, under socialist competition, to economize 100,000 roubles over and above the (cost reduction) plan confirmed by the *glavk*. In a word, the factory is materially interested in the proposal.'

But, says the engineer, the effect of adding 3 kilograms to the weight of the aircraft is to reduce the carrying capacity of the aircraft by 2 kilograms, and, in the given example, assuming a freight rate of 2 roubles per ton-kilometre, the net effect could well be a loss to Aeroflot of 400,000 roubles, which hardly balances an economy of 10,000 roubles which the enterprise was so anxious to obtain.[1]

In the west, a product which is better from the user's point of view will, in general, command a better price, yield a higher profit, because the users can offer more if they think it worth their while. It is a weakness of the Soviet system that there is generally no means of doing this. Of course, there are efforts to impose minimum technical standards, but this can hardly cure this built-in defect. The system of allocation is itself a further impediment to flexible adjustment. Allocation certificates specify the supplying enterprise, and so the dissatisfied customer cannot threaten to buy elsewhere. In the many cases where specifications are closely defined by the central authorities, they cannot be changed at all at enterprise level, and the effort to secure permission to change them takes time and runs into bureaucratic delays involved in getting several departments to agree,

[1] Antonov, op. cit., pp. 152-3.

a process known in Russian as *soglasovanie*. Where the proposed change can be made at enterprise level but requires delivery of some different material, nothing effective can be done until the allocation certificate is amended.

In a number of instances, failure to meet user demand is a direct consequence of 'allocation' decisions which neglect local require-ments. One of many satirical articles in *Krokodil* (June 10, 1960) de-scribes the repeated delivery of agricultural machines to *sovkhozy* in Kazakhstan which cannot be used there. 'The *Oktyabr'ski* sovkhoz of Pavlodar *oblast'* needs a flax thresher about as much as a fish needs an umbrella. Flax has never been sown in these regions and is not now sown there. Or why does the "Chekhov" grain *sovkhoz* receive all at once 136 tractor-operated reapers? Yet the *sovkhoz* was com-pelled not only to accept the reapers but also to pay 644,000 roubles for them. In vain it begged: "Take away these reapers, pass them on to someone who needs them." ' The very large number of similar complaints from other parts of the country suggest that the alloca-tion of unsuitable machines to agriculture is a widespread phe-nomenon. No one in the allocation, wholesaling or, apparently, manufacturing organizations has sufficient interest in the suit-ability of the machines for use in any given area, and numerous criticisms have yet to cure the weakness, though it is hoped that, following the creation of a new supply structure, the farms will exercise their rights as buyers and refuse unsuitable machinery.

Once again, the effect of these species of difficulty is very unequal in different sectors of the economy. The defects are most noticeable where there is a multiplicity of possible products, and a changing pattern of demand of a kind which no central planning agency can or should reflect in its detailed system of instructions. This is most clearly to be seen in the field of consumers' goods, to which we shall turn.

There is, first, the question of inducing manufacturers to meet the orders of the retail trade network. The latter can judge, by the length of queues, the views expressed by dissatisfied customers and the level of unsold stocks, that certain items should be ordered in greater quantity, and that others are unpopular with the public. But the retail shop, or local *torg* grouping the shops of the given town, has only very limited possibilities of action. It can place orders direct with local and co-operative industry, but the large majority of supplies have to be obtained through wholesalers which operate at republican and all-union levels (see p. 89, above). As a Soviet critic put it, 'between the supplier and the user stands the disposals organization (*sbyt*), which, so to speak, depersonalizes the product'.[1] The wholesaling organs depend for their profits on fixed margins, their plans are expressed in gross turnover, they are remote from the customers and have no significant inducement to be responsive to their needs. They are not adequately penalized for holding unsaleable stocks, because stockholding is automatically covered by credits from the State Bank.[2] The wholesalers also operate, in the case of many major species of goods, within allocation quotas decided by the planners; thus Azerbaidjan or the Ukraine receives a given quantity of wool cloth or leather shoes, which are subdivided by the Ukrainian ministry of trade and Gosplan between *oblasti*, cities, etc., and the request of (say) the Odessa shops for more of a particular kind of leather shoes must be fitted in to these various allocation quotas.[3]

However, let us now assume that, despite all possible obstacles, the order reaches the manufacturing enterprise or the appropriate *sovnarkhoz*. A plentiful literature shows that industry often fails to respond. It 'corrects' the trade orders, to take into account its materials allocation; it has hardly any choice in this, since if the right leather or a red dyestuff is not allocated to the producers, it cannot produce the required shoes or red cloth. Indeed, this problem of linking the ever-changing requirements of retail trade with the industry's material allocations is a peculiarly difficult one to solve. But, as one critic rightly put it, industry sometimes turns down requests from the trade network also because a 'change in the product mix would lead to an underfulfilment of the gross output plan'.[4] It is unnecessary to repeat here that efforts to achieve bonuses under various success indicators are often inconsistent with the satisfaction of the requirements of the consumer. A Soviet writer has commented as follows. '. . . The big rise in stocks in the trade network, together with the existence of unsatisfied demand for many commodities, is the result of discrepancies between the assortment and quality of goods produced and the pattern of people's demand. One reason lies . . . in the "aggregate" (*valovoi*) approach to the determination of commodities required to meet demand.'[5] Indeed, variants (usually

[1] I. Kulyov, *Kommunist*, No. 9/1959, p. 27.
[2] Of course, the credits should not be automatic, but in practice are virtually so (see p. 112).
[3] According to R. Shniper (*Vop. Ekon.*, No. 11/1960, p. 157), the Ministry of Trade of the RSFSR maintains an office through which local trading organs can dispose of the 'wrong' goods to other local trading organs, and acquire others.
[4] R. Lokshin, *Vop. Ekon.*, No. 5/1957, p. 132.
[5] R. Lokshin in *Zakon stoimosti* (Kronrod), p. 458.

less extreme!) of the stories about sending skis to Uzbekistan and textbooks on cotton-growing to north Siberia appear all too frequently in the press.

In fact the retail chain itself is very backward in studying consumer demand, as very numerous articles in the Soviet press make clear. Nor is this surprising. The trade margins are fixed, so there is no extra profit in providing a commodity in short supply. It is, or until recently has been, easy to sell anything. As in all countries under similar circumstances, employees in the retail chain develop a 'take it or leave it' mentality.

Retail prices are, with few exceptions, fixed by the central or republican governments, and at levels which should (and sometimes do) more or less equate demand with supply. This means that, in relation to costs of production, some retail prices are much higher than others. However, this does not encourage the production of commodities or models which sell at relatively high prices, because the bulk of the difference consists of turnover tax and does not benefit the producers. By way of illustration, let us take two commodities, A and B; costs are assumed to be 100 roubles in both cases. The following situation may frequently be encountered:

	A	A
Costs at factory	100	100
Profit margin	5	5
Factory wholesale price	105	105
Turnover tax	50	15
Wholesalers' margin	5	5
Retail margin	10	10
Retail price	170	135

Clearly, no one would find it worth while to switch to A rather than B on their own initiative. In the given example, they would be indifferent as between A and B, but in practice, such are the imperfections of pricing, it is not seldom found that the more desired goods work out to be less profitable. Thus this method of levying turnover tax eliminates a potential means of 'transmitting' the demand pattern to the manufacturers, because, as was shown above (p. 135), turnover tax is often deliberately calculated to cover the variable gap between the wholesale and retail price. Of course, it is arguable that the planning organs ought to use the size of this gap as a species of signal; if it is big, more should be produced of the particular good. However, there is little or no sign that they see it that way.

A further relevant factor has been the unresponsiveness of local authorities, who have many responsibilities in organizing trade, opening shops, restaurants, etc., to the needs of the citizens. This in turn was (and still is) due to the fact that elections are unreal, and that members of local soviets are primarily responsible to party and state officials above them. Only this can explain the remarkable degree of neglect so often encountered in Soviet cities, for example in opening enough shops. Efforts to put these defects right are being made,[1] and an extensive literature shows acute awareness of the problems of satisfying consumer needs in a more rational and more flexible way. This is an inevitable consequence of greater abundance and wider assortment, compared with the acute 'goods famine' which prevailed for so many years. Unsold stocks of unsaleable goods are causing some worry to the authorities. The public is becoming more choosy, as supplies and living standards increase.

Progress is, however, also blocked by a clumsy system of planning consumers' goods production. A particularly notorious recent example—there are all too many of them—concerned electric irons and electric kettles. In 1955 they were in ample supply, so much so that it was decided to reduce production. But in the USSR nothing seems to be done by halves. The output figures developed as follows:

	1955	1958
	(thousands)	
Electric irons	5,290	2,130
Electric kettles	485	80

Source: *N.Kh. 1958*, p. 299.

Consequently, these goods disappeared from the shops, and *Pravda* denounced the acute shortages and published a decree increasing production again.[2] An example of another kind concerns lampshades. As all visitors to the USSR were able to observe, nearly all Soviet homes had old-fashioned, dark red or dark orange lampshades, with tassels. Why? Because, according to a *Pravda* article, no other kinds were made for retail sale; modern lampshades were made for hotels and public buildings, but, since no retail price had

---

[1] Notably in the decrees issued in 1959 on shops, and on restaurants and cafés, and in 1960 on wholesale and retail trade. See *Pravda*, February 28, 1959, and August 9, 1960, and A. Popov in *Sovetskaya Torgovlya*, No. 8/1959, pp. 3 ff.

[2] *Pravda*, August 28, 1959, and October 16, 1959.

been settled for them, they could not be sold to the public and production was being cut down, as all hotels had been supplied.[1] Shortly afterwards, a decree of the Central committee of the party and the Council of Ministers of the USSR (*inter alia*) prohibited the production of old-fashioned dark red and dark orange lampshades.[2] It cannot be said that this is a good instance of flexibility in linking output, retail trade and consumer requirements.

The pages of the trade monthly, *Sovetskaya Torgovlya*, frequently print complaints about the inadequacies and muddle of the distribution system, especially those arising from the separation of production decisions from wholesaling and retailing functions. Since the abolition of the all-union ministry of internal trade, the internal trade division of Gosplan USSR, republican Gosplans, republican ministries of trade, city and *oblast'* trade organs, the consumer-cooperatives and *sovnarkhozy* are all in various ways involved. One critic wrote: 'The most difficult is the linking of trade turnover and the plan of commodity deliveries,' and another, in the same journal, bitterly complained that the assortment of goods delivered by industry do not conform with the requirements and orders of the retailers, and that the arbitration organs systematically uphold the supplier's right to vary the nature of the goods supplied; 'for the past ten years we have been unable to settle the assortment of goods with a single factory in good time.'[3]

The relative failure to adjust production and distribution to the requirements of the consumer has three aspects, or causes, which ought not to be confused in analysing defects or in endeavouring to see ways and means of overcoming them. The first, which has been much emphasized in the last few pages, is the unresponsiveness of the price system to demand, and, on the contrary, the responsiveness of directors to 'success indicators' and plans which cannot of their nature take consumer demand adequately into account. The second aspect concerns the habit of underpricing, the tendency towards tolerating queues rather than raising prices to the extent necessary to eliminate them, with the consequence of a chronic seller's market, with all that this implies in terms of quality of service and, indeed, responsiveness to demand.[4] The third is a question of priorities:

---

[1] *Pravda*, July 5, 1959.   [2] *Pravda*, October 16, 1959.
[3] Y. Sapel'nikov, *Sovetskaya Torgovlya*, No. 6/1960, p. 17, and M. Zykov, ibid., p. 25.
[4] Note the interaction of these two aspects: it is largely because of queues —i.e. of underpricing—that retailers, wholesalers and manufacturers can adopt a take-it-or-leave-it attitude, and concentrate on 'success indicators' without fear of not selling whatever is produced.

during most of the Soviet period, scarce human skills and material resources have been systematically used in heavy industry rather than in consumers' goods industries or in trade; in these non-priority sectors, investments have been relatively low, the quality of managerial personnel relatively inferior. In the case of retail trade in particular, the effect of 'success indicators' is often extremely misleading. Thus labour productivity (in terms of turnover per shop assistant) is higher and distribution costs are doubtless far lower in the USSR than in Great Britain, but this is in large part due to such factors as the far smaller number of shops per thousand customers in the USSR, smaller stocks in relation to sales, much more intensive work of the shop assistants. Indeed, most British shop assistants spend a large part of the day waiting for customers, so in a sense they are 'inefficiently' used, though this is the inevitable consequence of a wider degree of consumer choice and the absence of queues.

But having said all this, it is important for the student of Soviet economics not to overlook a very essential point: whatever may be the inefficiency of the mechanism by which goods are distributed, whatever the inadequacies of the finer adjustments to the citizen's requirements, more goods tend to be produced, retail trade turnover increases by impressive percentages. In certain circumstances, even the appearance of a long queue may represent progress; there is no queue for goods which are not there. The Soviet system does, in normal years, ensure that there will be many more raincoats in three years' time than there are now, even though the styles, sizes, quality and range may all leave much to be desired. More cloth, clothing, shoes, television sets, handbags, and so on, are being produced. In so far as this is so, a steady increase in living standards does occur, and Soviet economists have some reason on their side when they accuse their western *confrères* of being so concerned with optimum distribution and the finer adjustments of output to demand that they overlook the quite essential point of the quantity of goods produced. A million raincoats, though they may not precisely correspond to what the citizen desires and may have to be queued for, are surely better than half that number produced and sold under the most perfect principles of the market and the capitalist price-mechanism.

This argument is certainly not to be ignored. Yet it contains a flaw which modifies its effectiveness considerably. Certainly, *ceteris paribus*, a million raincoats are twice as numerous as half a million raincoats (if one abstracts from the fact that other goods may be more urgently required). However, in terms of use-value, it is not always so. Two raincoats which do not fit are not worth twice as much as one which does. A given number of raincoats in fully assorted sizes and styles, which correspond to consumer requirements, are not 'equal' to the same number of raincoats which are available only in two styles and two sizes, in any but a purely numerical-statistical sense. All this is in the highest degree relevant when comparing Soviet output of consumers' goods with that of a 'capitalist' country. Standardization and a restricted range of choice are not necessarily a bad thing, but they have certain consequences in terms of aggregates of consumer satisfaction, which are none the less real for not being measurable. If a Soviet housewife wishes to buy a certain article and has to make do with another, her annoyance cannot be measured; only the thing she actually buys is statistically recorded. Yet in our conventional measurement of 'welfare', or in our aggregation of the value of goods, it is implicitly assumed that the consumer can choose from a wide range and that these goods are available at established prices. It is a scarcely deniable fact that the Soviet economy falls short in these respects of western standards. Plan-orientated production choices in the USSR are less effective instruments for adapting production to demand than are profit-orientated production choices under 'capitalism', sceptical as one may be about the reality of so-called consumers' sovereignty in the western world. This must have some unmeasured and probably unmeasurable bearing on the relative value of the consumer-goods produced under the two systems.[1] As will be shown subsequently, all this has a bearing also on growth rates.

Meanwhile some alarm is being expressed by Soviet officials about this whole question. A decision to explore ways and means of making production more responsive to demand was taken at the central committee plenum in July, 1960, and an intelligent Soviet economist commented: 'The period is coming to an end when any goods could be produced, with little regard for cost or quality.' He announced, too, a decision which may mark a real qualitative change: 'For 1960 Gosplan has confirmed a list of over 1,000 descriptions of

---

[1] The following somewhat extreme example of 'output' for plan fulfilment instead of for profit might make the general point clearer to some readers. Suppose that a Soviet publisher of popular songs has a plan of 100 songs; a British pop song publisher has no plan, but seeks to maximize profits. The Soviet publisher, other things being equal, would tend to publish more songs (at least 100), because, until he fulfils his plan, he would choose to publish in all cases of doubt. Yet, even on the assumption that an increase in output of pop songs is a good thing (which God forbid!), what meaning would this 'superiority' have in any conceivable terms of worth, value or use? For a vigorous statement of similar arguments, see M. Polanyi, 'Towards a Theory of Conspicuous Production', *Soviet Survey*, October-December, 1960.

various products (producers' goods and consumers' goods) *which may not be produced in excess of the plan.*'[1] This represents good intentions, but serious amendment of structure will surely still be necessary before these intentions can be effectively translated into action.

THE PARTY AND THE CORRECTION OF DISTORTIONS

It may be asked: what have the various controlling, inspecting and checking agencies been doing, to permit numerous deviations from the intentions of the party and government? In particular, we have had occasion to note the vital importance of party officials at republican and *oblast'* levels, their role as supervisors of *sovnarkhozy*, their very considerable influence over factory directors and others in the state's economic network.

There is a vast number of reports in the party press about this supervisory work. It is clear that in many instances the Party units do perform the task which they are meant to perform, notably in preventing disobedience to or direct evasion of plans and instructions, and also in stimulating the adoption of new methods, which might otherwise fall victim to inertia, organizing various forms of 'socialist competition', and much else besides. However, as must have become apparent in the present chapter, the essence of the present problem is not disobedience to orders, but manœuvring designed to show (or sometimes simulate) the fact that orders have been obeyed, i.e. that the plans have been fulfilled. The Party officials are judged, in the economic sphere, by their ability to ensure the fulfilment of various plans within their area of jurisdiction. The secretary of the Party group within the enterprise often finds himself helpless *vis-à-vis* the director even if he wishes to act, because the director of a large enterprise is generally himself an influential Party member. But even the secretary of the Party's town committee (*gorkom*), or the *oblast'* party secretary must inevitably be influenced by their own desire to report to headquarters that various key plans are fulfilled. For them, paraphrasing Dickens, '99·9 per cent—misery; 100·1 per cent—happiness'. It should surprise no one, therefore, to encounter numerous reports concerning the connivance of party officials at various distortions designed to facilitate plan fulfilment within the given plant or area.[2] There is hardly any need to list instances, since hardly a single

---

[1] I. Malyshev, *Pravda*, July 20, 1960. Emphasis mine.

[2] All these lines were being written, a report appeared concerning directorial simulation of plan fulfilment in Leningrad, 'covered' by the party organization, trade union secretary and *sovnarkhoz* officials (*Pravda*, January 27 and 31, 1961). Superior party organs expelled and *dismissed* the director.

one of the 'deviations' discussed in this chapter, or the next, would have occurred if the party supervisors had done their job. Criticism of this tendency among party officials has appeared at intervals in the party press, and there have been examples of party officials ordering local government officers to disobey orders received from the centre in the interests of plan fulfilment in the particular locality,[1] though, as already suggested, such direct disobedience is doubtless exceptional. No amount of appeals to doctrine and to discipline can eliminate it so long as the 'supervisors' are judged by the same criteria as the managers whom they supervise.

THE SPECIAL PROBLEMS OF AGRICULTURE

Soviet agriculture is peculiar in being divided between three very different forms of ownership: state, collective and private (see chapter 2, above), and the organizational and operational problems of each are in many respects different. One species of difficulty relates to the existence of this division. If there are state farms and *kolkhozy* in the same area, there has been in effect no joint planning agency. *Kolkhozy* were controlled by the local party secretary, with the *raion* executive (and, until 1958, the MTS). State farms received their orders down their own state-farm line of subordination, and, though the *raion* party authorities had a formal right to interfere, this right was in fact hardly exercised. Lack of administrative co-ordination was accompanied by all kinds of wasteful duplication of supply agencies, complicated by the fact that *kolkhozy* were entitled to buy many kinds of producers' goods (e.g. building materials) at retail prices through the consumer-co-operatives, while state farms were supplied at much lower wholesale prices through the appropriate *sbyt* agencies.

In June, 1960, these questions received much public attention. Matskevich, the then minister of agriculture, foreshadowed a far-reaching move to achieve some unification between the two categories of enterprises. He proposed the grouping of farms into *raion* unions (*kolkhozy*), or trusts (state-farms); where both categories coexist in the *raion* in almost equal numbers, there is to be a *raion* agricultural union in which both are represented by their chairmen and directors. There is to be further development of inter-kolkhoz —or joint *kolkhoz*-state farm—enterprises for carrying out repairs, manufacturing building materials and so on.[2]

[1] See for example a leader in *Partiinaya Zhizn'*, No. 10/1958, pp. 4-7.
[2] V. Matskevich, *Pravda*, June 15, 1960. Since Matskevich was dismissed soon after, it is not clear whether these policies will be continued.

However, all this would not eliminate one of the principal obstacles in comparing *kolkhoz* and state-farm costs. At present the situation is this: supposing that costs on a given state farm (or on all state farms) and on a *kolkhoz* (or on all *kolkhozy*) for a given product are respectively 100 and 150 roubles per quintal, this provides no basis for judgment about relative efficiency or indeed for any real cost comparison. Obviously, if *kolkhozy* have to pay much higher prices, their costs will be higher even if their efficiency were equal to that of state farms. It is odd that when comparisons are made by Soviet leaders this point generally gets overlooked. Indeed, on occasion, state-farm *costs* are compared with the *prices* at which *kolkhozy* sell to the state.[1]

Yet it is misleading even to compare the selling prices of the two categories of farms, though this is often done.[2] This is because they have to cover not only producers' goods bought at different prices, but also a quite different range of expenditures. A *kolkhoz* must, out of its revenues, pay for practically all its investments (or repay credits which it might receive for investment purposes), insure its buildings, animals and crops, issue produce and/or money to its sick or aged members, pay a sizeable tax on gross revenues, and has in recent years been encouraged to build schools and a variety of rural amenities. A state farm bears few of these burdens; a large part of its investment is budget-financed, any losses are covered by subsidy, its employees receive social-service benefits and qualify for old-age or disability pensions. Obviously, therefore, an equal selling price, *ceteris paribus*, would leave a *kolkhoz* far worse off than a state farm. All this greatly confuses one's assessment of the economic effectiveness of the two types of farm, both on a national and on a local scale.

A state farm, whatever may be its other defects, has a system of cost accounting similar to that of other state enterprises, and there is no undue difficulty in determining what the costs are. It is quite otherwise on a collective farm. The essence of the problem remains that of measuring labour cost, in a system in which the *trudodni* or other payments vary widely. Since the remuneration of peasants on a *kolkhoz* (unlike the wage-paying state farm) is still generally a *residual*, with no fixed rate of pay and extremely wide variations from farm to farm and between area and area, it contains within itself

---

[1] For example, Benediktov, *Kommunist*, No. 18/1956, p. 80.
[2] By Khrushchev and by many other party officials at the plenum of the central committee, December, 1959. However, prices of farm machinery, fuel and fertilizer now appear to be equal as between *kolkhozy* and *sovkhozy*, and these were cut in January, 1961.

such net profit or net loss as the farm has made, and so becomes only of little use as a measure of costs as such (it will be recalled that the categories 'profit' and 'loss' cannot appear in *kolkhoz* accounts, precisely because of the residual nature of peasant remuneration). Output statistics are still almost always 'gross', i.e. inclusive of goods and services bought from outside the *kolkhoz*. For many years, the very existence of 'cost' in *kolkhoz* production was denied by official economists. However, in more recent years both economists and planners have become acutely aware of the need for greater efficiency and for some effective action to reduce costs in general and labour inputs in particular. Therefore they must be measured. How?

Two schools of thought have emerged. One argues that labour costs should be measured on the assumption that the peasants have received the pay rates applicable to state-farm labourers. Then, it is pointed out, one avoids some very confusing results. These could be illustrated by an example. From the table on p. 225, below, it can be calculated that the average pay per *trudoden* in Krasnodar and Kirov were respectively 12·30 and under 5 roubles, approximately.[1] These are averages for large areas. Undoubtedly, a prosperous *kolkhoz* in Krasnodar must pay as much as 20 roubles, an under-average *kolkhoz* in Kirov—say 2·50 roubles, or eight times less. Indeed, similar variations can affect a single *kolkhoz*, or area, as a result of drought. Thus the total value of pay per working day in the *Strana sovetov kolkhoz* in North Kazakhstan was 21·70 roubles in 1956 (when it rained) and 3·70 roubles in 1957 (when it did not).[2] What sense is there in basing a calculation on the untenable proposition that labour cost, per unit of labour actually expended, is eight times greater in one *kolkhoz* than another, or almost six times greater in one year than another? What practical conclusions, other than misleading ones, could be drawn from such a measure of 'cost'? Efficient farms might falsely appear to be high-cost farms, just because they distribute so much more to 'their' peasants.[3] One can also see another advantage in the 'state-farm wage' method: that any actual expenditure of labour has a direct effect on cost calculation. Otherwise, by reason of the 'residual' nature of peasants' pay, one can envisage a situation in which a 30 per cent increase in labour inputs, which was

[1] This includes a valuation of produce distributed as payments in kind. It is by no means clear at what price this valuation was, or should be, made, but this is a complication which we need not pursue here.

[2] G. Lisichkin, *Vop. Ekon.*, No. 7/1960, p. 62.

[3] For this argument, see, for instance, M. Nesmi, *Finansy SSSR*, No. 11/1957, p. 92.

totally unproductive, could lead to a 30 per cent decrease in the value of each *trudoden*, the total amount of peasant income remaining unchanged. In other words, in the *kolkhoz* the marginal cost of labour can appear to be *nil*—unless any additional work performed adds in some way to cost, as it would do if a notional value were assigned to it.

But this view is hotly disputed. It is pointed out that if state-farm wages are in fact not paid to *kolkhoz* peasants, it is quite unreal to measure costs on the assumption that they were paid. If, for instance, in a given area *kolkhoz* daily remuneration is 30 per cent below that of state-farms, then this must affect the real cost and cannot be assumed away. The distortion caused by large variations in pay is admitted, but, so it is argued, the greater efficiency of high-pay farms is such that costs per unit of produce will still generally seem lower there.[1] The protagonists of this view could point to the table on p. 225 as proof of their thesis: costs in Kirov worked out higher than in Krasnodar. The only basis for measurement, they claim, can be whatever is actually paid. The discussion continues, with the consensus of opinion moving towards the second method, i.e. measuring labour cost by the amounts actually paid to the peasants.

Still another method seeks to evade valuation in money altogether, and tries to measure labour time. This has foundered on the lack of reliable information. Assessment in uncorrected hours and minutes can mislead by ignoring quality and skill of work. Assessment in *trudodni* is useless for purposes of inter-farm comparison by reason of a wide divergency in work norms adopted.

The impact of costs on *kolkhozy*, and their effects on remuneration, are intimately linked with prices, and also with the significance to be attached to land rent. These two questions are discussed in chapter 8. At this stage it is sufficient to make the point that the new price structure introduced in 1958, while an improvement on the old, still fails to reflect cost differences, and the relative state purchase prices for different commodities in any particular area would only by accident be rationally related to local shortages or national requirements (except where, as in the case of fruit, prices are free). Therefore it is not in practice possible to base *kolkhoz* plans and programmes on price stimuli, the more so as most *kolkhozy* are also influenced by the free market price, which is generally much higher than either the official buying or retail prices. Kolkhoz chairmen do,

---

[1] For several of the many statements of this side of the argument see I. Laptev and E. Karnaukhova in *Vop. Ekon.*, No. 8/1957, pp. 80, 102, and N. Litvinov *et al.* in *Sots. Sel. Khoz.*, No. 8/1956, pp. 35-42.

of course, seek to manœuvre to maximize farm revenues—net revenues in so far as they are able to identify them[1]—especially if they respond to the pressure of their members who desire higher incomes. Therefore, when delivery plans and administrative pressures permit, the chairmen adjust their behaviour to the available incentives in an effort to increase the value of a *trudoden*—especially as part of the chairman's own salary is paid in *trudodni*. However, systematic behaviour on these lines rapidly leads to trouble with the party and state authorities, and there are many instances of *kolkhoz* chairmen being criticised for behaving too 'commercially'.[2] The tradition persists that money is not a proper success indicator for *kolkhozy*, and that their job is to maximize output per unit of land—though how one measures output of many different products save through the medium of money is not so clear.

Partly as a consequence of the continuing inadequacies of the price system, and partly because of long-ingrained habits, on-the-ground planning is still constantly disrupted by administrative interference. *Kolkhoz* plans have to be geared not only into delivery plans imposed from above (this at least is in line with the rules adopted in 1955-58), but also with whatever current campaign the local party organization happens to be 'pushing'. All kinds of 'plenipotentiaries' (*upolnomochenye*) are despatched by party secretaries to run campaigns on the spot. An abundant critical literature has appeared in recent years concerning stupid forms of party intervention in *kolkhoz* planning and management, intervention motivated by the desire of party officials to report to their headquarters whatever the latter wishes to hear: that the sown area has been increased, even though fallow is desirable for soil conservation purposes; that a high percentage of harvesting was by the currently fashionable two-stage method, even though in the given instance it is unsuitable; that farms have been amalgamated to make bigger *kolkhozy*, even if local conditions are unfavourable for such large units; that milk output has increased, though there is no demand for more milk from this particular *kolkhoz*; that sowing had been ordered to be completed by some early date, though it is agronomically more sensible to delay

---

[1] The qualifying phrase is important. Often, thanks to the nature of *kolkhoz* accounts, it was impossible for chairmen or anyone else to discover whether a given activity was profitable in any sense. For example, see Litvinov, op. cit., pp. 35-42.

[2] For instance, one *kolkhoz* was reprimanded for expanding acreage under sunflower with the object of marketing sunflower seed in cities at a big profit, and another was denounced for marketing produce in remote areas, being called a 'speculator *kolkhoz*' for its pains (1. Korshunov, *Partiinaya zhizn*, No. 17/1956, pp. 28-9).

it; that even seed grain had been delivered to the state, by order of the Party 'plenipotentiary', so as to claim that the plan is fulfilled; that more maize must be sown even if this disrupts the established crop rotation and makes no sense in that locality.[1] The encouragement given by the highest party authorities to regional 'competition' and to ambitious undertakings to double or treble production of, say, meat in some spectacularly short time, ensures the continuance of this highly 'political' agricultural planning. The plenum of the central committee in January, 1961, demonstrated that these bad habits are continuing. It may be thought that farming of all things is not suitable for such treatment. It is an interesting contrast, too, that party officials supervising industries tend to have the same interests as the managers and *sovnarkhoz* members whom they supervise, whereas in agriculture this is seldom the case. The reason must lie in the confused and often internally contradictory nature of success indicators in the *kolkhoz* system, and perhaps in a negative approach to peasants in general.

The last but not the least among the difficulties engendered by the agricultural system concerns distribution. The problems here can readily be deduced from evidence given on the previous pages. Purchase prices are not logically interrelated and change little or not at all in response to shortage or abundance. This, of course, is not peculiar to the USSR, as any student of United States price support legislation must surely know. However, retail prices are similarly inflexible, fail to reflect scarcities and make grossly inadequate allowance for seasonal shortages. To make matters worse, the system of food distribution suffers from some inherent defects. The centre is responsible for covering the needs of some big cities and industrial 'deficit areas' for some basic foodstuffs. However, especially since the decentralization of trade and procurements in 1956-58, supplies to smaller towns and of less 'basic' foods (e.g. vegetables) to the bigger towns depend greatly on the procurement initiatives of local bodies, who draw upon farms in their areas for these supplies. These local requirements are added as necessary to the centre's quotas when particular farms' delivery obligations are being decided. But some areas are much better provided than others, and some *oblast'*

[1] A long bibliography can be assembled concerning these practices, which continue seriously to harm Soviet agriculture. The reader is particularly referred to V. Ovechkin: *Rayonnye budni* (Moscow, 1954), E. Dorosh's 'diary' in *Literaturnaya Moskva*, 2nd issue (Moscow, 1957) and, for more recent information, the speeches of Khrushchev and Polyanski to the central committee plenum (*Pravda*, January 12 and 21, 1961), and P. Prozorov, *Pravda*, January 6, 1961, A. Shevchenko in *Ekonomika sel'skovo khozyaistva*, No. 12/1960, especially p. 22, and many, many others.

and town soviets are more energetic than others in supplying their shops. With centrally-fixed prices often unattractive to the producers, with farm output plans often underfulfilled, and with the trading and procurement agencies having little material interest in showing enterprise, the situation is often extremely patchy. Matters are not helped by the delivery regulations to which *kolkhozy* are subject; for reasons of flexibility, the *kolkhozy* (and in some cases state-farms also) are entitled to substitute certain products for one another in meeting the delivery quotas imposed upon them, but in their choice they cannot be guided by actual requirements because these cannot be transmitted to them by any economic mechanism. One result is that deliveries of milk are generally made in the more readily transportable and less perishable form of butter, and liquid milk is notoriously short at many times of the year in most Soviet cities. Thus in 1958 no less than 65 per cent of all 'milk' delivered to the state in the USSR was in fact butter, over 80 per cent in some republics.[1]

The consequence of erratic and unequal food supplies is a wide disparity in free market prices at different times of the year and in different towns. To some extent the uncontrolled free market can fill gaps, but the existence of the above-mentioned disparities shows that it cannot do so adequately. Peasants and (with some exceptions) *kolkhozy* are not generally in a position to supply remote markets, and communications are often a serious obstacle even to official food distribution, let alone to peasants with a sack of onions and no transport priority. The few who can make the journey glean a big profit from scarcity prices in ill-supplied areas. Thus peasants with two sackloads of citrus fruits find even an air journey from Transcaucasia to Moscow worth while. But there is no self-correcting mechanism, in the absence of a professional trader class and of adequate incentive for official trading initiatives. Indeed, the consumer-co-operative commission traders (p. 49, above) could theoretically market supluses on the peasants' behalf, but they lack inducement to take much trouble to seek out supplies or to transport them over large distances, and they have made little difference to the situation.[2] With the gradual decline of the free market as a source of food, it is in any case essential to reorganize and strengthen the official food distribution machinery and its links with the farms.

---

[1] R. Nazarov, in *Sovetskaya Torgovlya*, No. 6/1960, p. 19.
[2] For criticism of the inadequacies of commission trading, see A. Gavrilov, *Sovetskaya Torgovlya*, No. 8/1957, pp. 13 ff., and also Khrushchev in *Pravda*, January 21, 1961.

There remains the question: why, despite the many reforms of the post-Stalin period, do agriculture and food distribution retain so many elements of irrationality and clumsiness. Part of the explanation is historic: neither *kolkhozy* nor peasants were provided with incentives to produce what was required, and so arose the habit of ordering them about, which persists even when prices and incentives have been much improved. But, while this 'traditional' approach can wither away, another reason may prove more lasting: factors of production in agriculture are capable of producing many different things, can be combined in many different ways, and are subject to unplannable vagaries of weather. It is far more difficult to apply the techniques of central planning to agriculture than to—say—the coal or steel industries, or even textiles. Unplanned variations in output and availabilities are not reflected in prices, and the absence of adequate official inter-regional distribution arrangements (or of a private trading class) ensures spasmodic shortages and seasonal or local food queues. Lastly, as has been noted repeatedly, the social-political aspects of the peasant problem still affect policy, to an extent no longer true in other sectors of the economy.

THE SPECIAL CASE OF FOREIGN TRADE

As was noted above (p. 42), foreign trade is the monopoly of specialized corporations under the aegis of the Ministry of Foreign Trade. Import requirements and exportable surpluses are made known to these corporations by Gosplan and other internal economic agencies—though the corporations and the ministry, by their reports on trade opportunities, also affect the decision-making process.

The first problem that arises concerns calculating the profitability of trade, or calculation of comparative advantage. This is rendered very largely impracticable by the divorce between internal and world prices, as well as between the internal prices of the USSR and those of other countries in the Soviet orbit. The unrealistic official exchange rate was not the primary cause of the difficulty, though it made things worse by introducing an additional confusion into the calculations. Though the rouble was in effect devalued in relation to the dollar in 1961, the essential problem remains. Soviet internal prices still bear a very varied relationship with world prices. For example, Soviet wheat, with an internal wholesale price of some 750 'old' (75 new) roubles per ton, is sold at about £25, giving a sterling-rouble ratio of 1:30 (1:3). However, for many kinds of machinery the ratio would be 1 : 15 (1 : 1·5) or even less; the variety is enormous, even within the same industry. A French delegation compared the prices of Soviet chemicals with those prevailing in France, and they took as basis an exchange rate of 50 old francs=1 old rouble (which would be the equivalent of about 28 (old) roubles to £1, or 10 (old) roubles=$1). Sulphuric acid, at this rate, is three and a half times dearer in the USSR than in France, but caustic soda is one and a half times dearer in France than in the USSR; over thirty examples are cited in this report.[1] These examples are not in the least affected by such factors as turnover tax. They are explicable partly by wide differences in real costs in an economy sheltered for many years from world markets, partly by the consequences of the pricing irrationalities described at length in chapter 4, and partly by genuine differences in the principles of costing; for example, western prices of capital-intensive goods are relatively much more affected by the burden of interest on capital than are the Soviet prices for these goods. Then, in so far as Soviet prices do not reflect relative scarcities, they cannot be a useful guide to trade. For example, a 'cheap' commodity which, in terms of price comparisons, seems eminently exportable may actually be in short supply and need to be imported.

Calculation of comparative advantage therefore runs into most serious obstacles. But in practice these calculations are seldom made at all in the USSR. Trade decisions are very largely quantitative. It is decided that a certain amount is available for sale to this or that 'capitalist' country, or is earmarked under an agreement for China or Czechoslovakia; or the Soviet economy needs a quantity of rubber, copper, chemical machinery, and goods must be exported to pay for them. The quantities concerned are then disposed of, or bought, by the appropriate trade corporation. In deals with capitalist countries, their job is to strike the best bargain they can. In exchanges with Soviet-orbit countries, the general practice is to base payments on world prices. In either event, the trade corporation does not concern itself with the domestic price or domestic costs. It buys or sells as required, and the necessary financial adjustments are then made through the bank and the budget.

Soviet trade deals are very often bilateral in character. This bilateralism is not based on any ideological conviction, but stems from two factors: one is that quantitative exchange, a species of barter, lends itself far more easily to two-way arrangements; the other is that

---

[1] *Revue de l'Institut Français du Petrole*, January, 1960, p. 246. The figures relate to November, 1959. See also very useful article on price relativities in *Economic Bulletin for Europe*, Vol. II, No. 1 (1959), pp. 39 ff.

planning operates far more smoothly if both the prospective imports and the prospective exports are integrated in the plan, and an element of untidiness is introduced when a trading partner earns a surplus which is transferred to some other country which then makes an unexpected demand for goods which the plan has earmarked for other purposes. Of course, none of these difficulties are insuperable, but the fact remains that, even within the bloc, the USSR has very largely stuck to bilateral trade deals, even though formal provisions for multilateral clearing have existed for some years. But the effect, as in all bilateralism, is to confine exchanges to the partner's surpluses, even where these may not be high on the importing country's scale of priorities. Thus, for example, the USSR imports soya beans from China, or dates from Iraq, largely because these happen to be commodities with which the countries concerned can pay for Soviet exports (or repay aid) to them.

It does not require much thought to see that such 'quantitative' trading at world prices unrelated to domestic costs is inconsistent with the application of the principles of comparative advantage. It is evident that the present system can permit sales or purchases to be made which are inherently unprofitable to the Soviet economy. The USSR's allies in Europe, who depend on trade much more than does the USSR itself, have been very conscious of these defects, and various attempts have been made to calculate when, whether, and how far particular trade dealings are worth while. Thus it was discovered that some Hungarian and Polish exports were sold at prices which barely covered the value of the imported raw materials used up in producing the goods concerned. Various ways have been discussed to ensure that choices are made on some objective basis. Thus one such method was as follows: the net earnings of foreign currency (i.e. export value less imports embodied in that commodity) were compared with the cost of production in zloty, and alternative variants were compared to find the most favourable zloty: foreign-currency ratios.[1]

But this is a rather crude attempt, though better than no attempt at all. It does not help appreciably in planning the production of exportable commodities, or, above all, in decisions concerning rational specialization within the Soviet bloc itself, of which there has been so much talk recently under COMECON[2] arrangements.

[1] For more details on this subject, see *Economic Bulletin for Europe*, Vol. II, No. 1 (1959).
[2] Council for Mutual Economic Assistance (sometimes known as CMEA). All European members of the bloc are full participants. China sends an observer.

Should Poland, or the USSR, or Czechoslovakia, specialize on some particular product, which could be produced in each of these countries at x zloty, y roubles and z crowns respectively? Indeed, imagining that only 'socialist' countries exist, at what prices would they exchange various commodities? There seems not to be even the beginnings of a theory to cover so elementary a problem as this. The fact that exchanges take place at present at 'capitalist' market prices is a recognition that criteria must be found outside the 'socialistic' system. Indeed, one eastern official jokingly said—in private—that after the world revolution it would be necessary to preserve one capitalist country: 'otherwise how would we know at what prices to trade?'

This picture of crude barter and economic confusion should not be pressed too far. The USSR still exports timber and imports cocoa. The obvious kinds of international specialization, based on natural conditions or traditional skills, do occur. The USSR does not try to sell its high-price and inefficiently produced clothing in world markets. If it fails to buy cheap and good Italian clothes, it is not because the cheapness and quality are not known, but because of the priorities of the plan. The USSR exports oil to Czechoslovakia because the USSR has oil and Czechoslovakia has not. East German engineering products naturally exchange for Soviet raw materials and fuels. Indeed, the obvious forms of trade are not really 'caused' by market and price relations, but by underlying 'quantitative' realities. But this applies only to the obvious. In the very wide range of goods where a calculation has to be made to determine relative advantage, the Soviet planners are all but helpless, and serious and unnecessary economic loss must result. However, before we in the west adopt a superior attitude in these matters, it is as well to recall that our practice has little in common with our own theories. The discovery that goods can be produced 30 per cent cheaper in some other country is far too often merely a prelude for the imposition of a 35 per cent import duty, or, as in the case of farm products bought by the United Kingdom, of some elaborate combination of quota restrictions, import duties and subsidies to domestic producers. It therefore behoves us to criticize the admittedly very crude Soviet arrangements in the knowledge that we cannot compare them to some pure comparative cost principle actually in operation in western countries.

In another respect, however, Soviet practice is far inferior, and this is a by-product of the monopolizing of trade by specialized corporations. These stand in the way of direct contact between Soviet exporter and customer, the Soviet importer and his supplier, which makes for clumsiness, delays, difficulties over precise specifications, etc., on which it is hardly necessary to enlarge; these have caused much criticism in Czechoslovakia and Hungary, among others,[1] and, one imagines, there must be a good deal of grumbling in the USSR also.

Why has this system survived in this very imperfect form? One suspects that much is to be explained by the development of this structure in a country—the USSR—which is largely self-sufficient and was anxious for most of its history to make itself so. Foreign currency was chronically scarce, and had to be strictly rationed by the centre on the basis of priorities centrally established. The USSR was, in its formative years, isolated politically, and it was a matter of faith that the forces of the world market were something to be guarded against. In any event, as the central plan was the foundation of economic activity, foreign trade had to be fitted into this plan. The planning process itself encourages an autarkic approach, since planners like to take decisions which can be enforced within their area of political-economic responsibility, and show an understandable disinclination to rely on the unforeseeable decisions of others, or on the unplannable vagaries of the world markets. On a less exalted plane of argument, one senses the vested interest of the Ministry of Foreign Trade and its corporations, concerned to channel all trade contacts through their own hands, even where, on general grounds, direct contact between firm and firm was desirable. In more recent years, the expanding levels of trade with countries of the Soviet bloc, and indeed with many other countries too, has placed heavier burdens on the system, so that major reforms of organization, of prices and some development in the still primitive theory of international trade can hardly be very long delayed. It is therefore not surprising to learn that a study of criteria of relative economic effectiveness of production in different countries has been launched by COMECON, which has set up a committee for that purpose.[2]

The practice of trade with non-Soviet countries raises a host of other problems—for instance, discrimination, most-favoured-nation clauses, alleged dumping, the relationship between trade, aid and

[1] For Hungary, see B. Balassa, *The Hungarian Experience of Economic Planning* (Yale University Press, 1959). The Hungarian government now permits a few large enterprises to engage in foreign trade deals directly.
[2] See discussion of these questions by O. Bogomolov, *Vop. Ekon.*, No. 1/1960, p. 17.

politics—which it is not the purpose of this book to pursue.[1] Nor is this the place to argue about the degree to which, so it is alleged, the actual prices at which trade within the Soviet orbit takes place favour the USSR, especially as the evidence is somewhat inconclusive.[2]

[1] For some discussion of these problems, see A. Nove and D. Donnelley, op. cit., especially pp. 21-44.

[2] Interested readers are referred to H. Mendershausen, in the *Review of Economics and Statistics*, May, 1960.

CHAPTER 7

Planning and Investment

COMPLEXITIES

It is perhaps unnecessary again to stress the enormous and growing complexities of planning. Yet these underlie the problems we are considering here. The job must be divided between many offices, some concerned with the common problems of an industry, some with the common problems of an area, others with questions common to many industries and many areas. Production, supply, regional specialization, assessment of consumer demand, current planning, long-term planning, new technique, labour and wages, prices and public finance, all these interrelated and intermingled subjects are necessarily dealt with by different organizations. It is an illusion to suppose that the fact that all these organizations are part of the same 'state' machine makes it any easier for them to march in step. Certainly British experience of nationalized industries should teach us this. We are concerned here not with 'capitalist' characteristics, but with general rules of government and bureaucracy, and with the general tendency of human beings to seek personal gain, moral approbation or promotion, and to take responsibility for the sector or area with which they may be entrusted, rather than to concern themselves with a 'general good' which they can only obscurely apprehend.

An excellent illustration of these problems in their practical aspects can be based on the experience of regional organizations, the *sovnarkhozy*, under the 1957 reform, analysing why certain difficulties have arisen and where these 'fit' into the planning system as a whole. We have seen that the *sovnarkhozy* were set up as part of the effort to break up ministerial-industrial 'empires', which distorted the economy in the interest of ministerial particularism. It is important to note that the driving force behind this particularism was not selfishness or other defects of character of this or that official. The heads of some *glavk* in some industrial ministry set up their own supply arrangements and made their own components because of their anxiety to fulfil tight plan schedules. The reform of 1957 sought

195

to replace ministerial boundary lines with regional boundaries, though, as we shall see, the industrial sector divisions had to a great extent to be preserved or restored in practice.

SOVNARKHOZY AND 'REGIONALISM'

In assessing the importance and indeed the essence of 'regionalism', it is necessary to study the nature of *sovnarkhoz* decisions when they have the power to decide. Much of what they actually do consists in the transmission of, or obedience to, instructions received from above, and in these respects they are cogs in the administrative machine. But the *sovnarkhozy*, as was indicated above (pp. 69-73), do have functions—drafting plans, organizing their fulfilment, supervising contracts and deliveries, and many other matters great and small—which are not covered by precise instructions and where they must use their own initiative. What, then, guides them when there are no orders from above to settle exactly what they should do?

Sovnarkhozy are interested in fulfilling plans for their areas—gross output, cost reduction, adoption of new techniques, labour productivity, and so on. Plans and resource allocation therefore tend to be geared to these purposes, or to the greater glory of the region (i.e. expansion, the attraction of investment resources from the central funds). These aims may fit into the requirements of the economy as a whole, but this would be something of a coincidence. An average *sovnarkhoz* would possess within its boundaries roughly 1 per cent of the industrial productive potential of the USSR. The small workshops, using locally procured materials for local needs, are generally under the *oblast'* or city soviet, or the co-operatives, and do not concern the *sovnarkhozy*. The factories controlled by any *sovnarkhoz* draw their supplies from dozens, or even hundreds, of factories or mines located outside the given region, and supply products to numerous factories or wholesalers similarly located. The major inter-regional deliveries are decided by Gosplan, at republican or all-union level, and these deliveries, once incorporated into the plan, have to be made by *sovnarkhozy* on pain of disciplinary measures or even prosecution before the courts. They must be given priority over deliveries within the region. These disciplinary and legal measures date from 1958,[1] and are sure signs that the *economic* mechanism was not working properly. Indeed, the press in 1957 was full of complaints about 'regionalism' (or 'localism'—*mestnichestvo*),

[1] Decree of praesidium of Supreme Soviet, April 25, 1958.

showing itself in priority being given to the needs of the region instead of to outside customers. The following is a typical quotation:

'There are instances when officials bother only about enterprises subordinate to them, and do not think of the difficulties which their irregularities cause for enterprises in other regions. It is necessary to speak about this frankly, so that these defects do not grow worse . . . *We have met clear instances of tendencies towards autarky.* The Dzerzhinski factory of the Dnepropetrovsk region supplies rolled wire to the Rezhitsa nail-making works. In July the Dzerzhinski factory underfulfilled its plan by 15 per cent but sent to Rezhitsa only 300 tons of rolled wire instead of 1,020 tons. When this outrageous fact was investigated, the managers of the Dzerzhinski factory declared that they had orders from the Dnepropetrovsk *sovnarkhoz* to give priority to enterprises in their own region and to supply them in full.' [Emphasis in the original.][1]

An assemblage of similar examples would fill many closely-printed pages. They show that 'regionalism' is a built-in deviation, which requires to be repressed by invoking non-economic weapons. The weapons themselves are sometimes irrational. For, given that some material is unexpectedly short, it is no more logical to give priority to customers situated outside the given area, so that the entire burden of shortage falls on users within the region, than to do the opposite.[2] However, the 'regionalist' deviation was not cured by the 1958 decree, as the same complaints reappear again and again in 1960.[3]

There are many other instances. Allocation certificates often do not specify the precise type or quality to be supplied and this becomes a matter for negotiation. *Sovnarkhozy*, like the enterprises, are then guided by their success indicators, rather than the requirements of the customer. Then a wide range of consumers' goods which, after 1957, are not subject to central allocation, and *sovnarkhozy* can and do issue orders to curtail their production if local needs are met, since they can have no idea about the needs of outside users and have no incentive or interest to supply them. This explains the numerous complaints about *sovnarkhozy* which 'on various excuses stop production of much-needed cultural-domestic

[1] *Pravda*, September 2, 1957.
[2] This point was made in *Promyshlenno-ekonomicheskaya gazeta*, September 19, 1958.
[3] For instance, article by V. Kurotchenko in *Ekonomicheskaya gazeta*, June 8, 1960.

consumer durables'.[1] What matters it to (say) the Tula *sovnarkhoz*
that its hammers or tin-openers are in urgent demand in Orel and
Voronezh? If any plan is more easily fulfilled by the use of the productive capacity for some other purpose, then it is used for some
other purpose. In fact, it proved necessary to *forbid* the *sovnarkhozy*
to cut production of consumer goods without special permission
from superior authority, in the decree published on August 9, 1960.

In putting forward development plans, the *sovnarkhozy* are
equally unable to take into account the impact of their plans on the
economy as a whole. In this respect they are sometimes in a less
favourable position than the former ministries which were at least
able, within their own sector, to think and calculate on a national
scale. For example, while economists have published articles seeking
to prove that the lignite in the Tula area was high-cost and inefficient, the chairman of the Tula *sovnarkhoz* attacked this view, and
urged the adoption of a plan which envisaged a large increase in
production of this lignite.[2] This is an aspect of the autarkic tendencies, or 'empire-building', familiar among the former ministries, but
now transferred to a territorial rather than industrial-sector basis.

It is not suggested that these defects are such as to eliminate all
the advantages of having regional planning and administrative
bodies. Clearly, they have made possible some significant improvements, but the built-in tendency towards 'regionalism' has necessitated the preservation or reinforcement of strict centralization. The
sovnarkhozy's right to redistribute resources between different industrial sectors has in fact been severely limited, in order to prevent
any initiative which is inconsistent with centralized resource allocation. This has led, for example, to complaints from the Karaganda
sovnarkhoz that it was forbidden to shift funds from coal to building
materials, and from non-ferrous metals to coal, although this was
needed to fulfil plans.[3] By a decision in 1959, *sovnarkhozy* are
strictly forbidden to issue allocated materials to their enterprises
without a *naryad* from above.[4]

This in turn has led to complaints about 'excessive centralization'
of the supply and disposals system, which in fact predetermines

---

[1] Decision of Central Committee of the Communist Party, *Pravda*, July 17,
1960, *Pravda*, September 6, 1958, and also many other sources.
[2] *Pravda*, August 17, 1957, V. Somov, *Vop. Ekon.*, No. 12/1957, pp. 29-33;
Z. Chukhanov, *Vop. Ekon.*, No. 9/1958, pp. 42-4.
[3] *Promyshlenno-ekonomicheskaya gazeta*, March 30, 1958.
[4] I. Baranov and F. Liberman, *Planovoe Khozyaistvo*, No. 9/1959, pp. 39-
40. See also N. Podgorny (*Pravda*, January 12, 1961) concerning disposal of
some of the products of local (i.e. non-*sovnarkhoz*) industry by the republics.

much of the enterprises' activities over the heads of 'their' *sovnarkhozy*. It also involves a good deal of duplication. Thus in the Rostov *sovnarkhoz* alone apart from 27 *snabsbyt* offices organized under various departments of the *sovnarkhoz* itself, there are '13 supply offices subordinated to the *snabsbyty* of the VSNKh RSFSR (i.e. to the republican-level supply and disposals organs) and 32 supply-and-disposals offices and centres of various ministries and organizations of the USSR and RSFSR. Altogether there are in this region 72 *snabsbyt* offices and centres with an establishment of over 7,000 persons. Many of these organizations duplicate each other.'[1]

One other aspect of the *sovnarkhoz* system is worth stressing. This is the small size of the region, explicable only by administrative convenience (adaptation in most cases to existing *oblast'* boundaries) rather than any attempt to relate the regions to any economic area. Two consequences follow from this. One is the very large number of unnecessary boundary difficulties, as when a brickworks in one *sovnarkhoz* obtained its clay from two kilometres away but in another *sovnarkhoz,* from which it was cut off by the new administrative border, so that it found itself compelled to draw its materials thereafter a distance of 180 kilometres.[2] The other is the lack of any planning or administrative organ on the spot responsible for examining the requirements of natural economic areas divided between several *sovnarkhozy* (and several *obkom* party secretaries): for instance the Urals, the Donbas, East Siberia, and so on. Hence some weighty criticism has been directed by some Soviet scholars at the excessive and illogical number of *sovnarkhozy*.[3] Some effort was in fact made to improvise *sovnarkhoz* regional consultations and conferences. In 1958-59 these took place in East Siberia, the Urals, and Baltic states and the Transcaucasian republics, but these were essays in voluntary co-ordination, and created no inter-regional body to carry on the work.[4] One practical difficulty which is also connected with the small size of the regions is that specialized manufacture of certain components, forgings, castings, spare parts and so on, is more economic when supplying a larger area. As a critic put it 'it is impossible to regard as sound the proposals of some *sovnarkhozy* to adapt specialized production only to the needs of their own enterprises, limiting their links with other regions'.[5] After repeated criti-

---

[1] N. Gal'perin, *Vop. Ekon.*, No. 10/1960, p. 68.

[2] N. Gal'perin, *Vop. Ekon.*, No. 7/1958, p. 47.

[3] Notably by Academician Gerasimov and three eminent colleagues in *Promyshlenno-ekonomicheskaya gazeta*, September 14, 1958, and also by Academician Nemchinov in the same journal, October 19, 1958.

[4] Until May, 1961 (see p. 96, above).   [5] V. Kurotchenko, op. cit.

cism on these lines, a decision of the central committee in July, 1960, called for the creation of such specialized factories in the major geographic-economic regions; but this, unavoidably, was made a central (or large-republican) responsibility.[1] We shall see that Gosplan had to create its own large-regional divisions.

The consequence of a regional structure of this character must be, and was, a reconcentration of effective decision-making (above the level of minor details) at the centre. But, since the ministerial form of centralization was abolished in the reform of 1957, this meant a recreation of central planning and administration on a new basis. This process, which is far from completed, led to the proliferation of central agencies which were referred to in chapter 2, with consequences about to be analysed.

But one generalized conclusion may be legitimately drawn from the experience of *sovnarkhozy*: it is that if production and sales decisions are based not on directly economic criteria (e.g. profitability) but on plans and instructions, no *territorial* authority can be expected to make production decisions which are rational in terms of the needs of some larger area.

PLANNING OF MATERIAL ALLOCATION

The first and most obvious problem of post-1957 central planning is the multiplicity of interconnected and overlapping organs which deal with a variety of overlapping and interconnected decisions, and the question of material allocations is mixed up in most of them. Long-term planning and general questions of optimum resource allocation are, since 1960, the task of the Economic-science council (*Gosekonomsovet*), which must have internal divisions, regional, industrial and functional, though just what they are has not yet been published. Gosplan's current planning functions compel division into industrial sectors, its inter-republican supply and disposal division (*snabsbyt*) is in turn divided into sub-departments concerned with particular materials, machines and so on. In addition, Gosplan possesses regional divisions.[2] All the above are at all-union level, but USSR Gosplan's divisions are duplicated at the RSFSR level and in varying degrees also in other republics.

Let us now suppose that a draft plan emerges from a *sovnarkhoz*, within the RSFSR. From many and repeated complaints, it appears that this plan, and the *sovnarkhoz* officials who bring it to Moscow,

[1] *Pravda*, July 17, 1960.
[2] Sixteen big regions (see F. Kotov, *Plan Khoz.*, No. 10/1960, p. 25), reorganized in 1961 (see p. 96).

are liable to find themselves in a bureaucratic maze. Thus each industrial sector is separately considered by the sector divisions of Gosplan, but also by the appropriate territorial division—for the RSFSR Gosplan has, or had in 1959, seven territorial divisions concerned with groups of *sovnarkhozy*.[1] These various divisions each have their own, often unco-ordinated ideas about the development of the particular thing (product, region) for which they are responsible. As a result, confusion can and does occur, and regions are presented with unrealistic or inconsistent plan targets.[2] From June, 1960, there is yet another body, the republican VSNKh, to complicate matters. But all these difficulties are still not the end of the story, since no republican plan is final and the entire process is repeated when republics submit their plans to the all-union Gosplan and other all-union economic agencies. When these have finished, the republics have again to amend their plans. No wonder a vigorous critic complained of 'parallelism' between the all-union and the republican planning organs, and, above all, of the unnatural separation of 'the planning of production and of material supplies'. He also spoke of a 'contradiction' between the territorial and functional division of responsibility.[3] Indeed, it appears that many, if not all, *sovnarkhozy* find it necessary to maintain representatives in Moscow, presumably a kind of super-*tolkachi*.

Of all these problems, the most intractable is the allocation of supplies. Literally millions of allocation certificates (*naryady*) are issued by different supply offices, in Moscow and in the republics. Each represents, in essence, a portion of the output plan of the enterprise which must deliver the allocated product. Yet not only are there many supply departments at different levels which raise difficulties of effective co-ordination (for example, where several products must be allocated to one factory or industry), but the supply departments are, since 1957, separated organizationally from the planning of production. Therefore there are numerous complaints about supply breakdowns, about plans for production which are inconsistent with plans for supplying the necessary materials and components. The interested student can readily convince himself of the serious nature of this problem by consulting any set of relevant

---

[1] These were apparently first set up in 1958, according to A. Shmarev, *Sovetskoe gosudarstvo i pravo*, No. 1/1959, p. 54.

[2] Criticisms of the RSFSR Gosplan in these respects appeared in particular in articles by B. Naimanov in *Pravda*, February 6, 1958, E. Frolov in *Kommunist*, No. 2/1958, and also in *Promyshlenno-ekonomicheskaya gazeta*, September 19, 1958.

[3] I. Kulyov, *Kommunist*, No. 9/1959, p. 24.

specialized publications. For instance, one reads of a building site in Kuibyshev held up through failure to deliver machinery, which in turn is held up by failures to deliver components to the machinery manufacturers in Saratov, which failure is then traced up the line until it is discovered that the Cherepovets steelworks had been expected to deliver steel from a workshop which had not yet been completed; or a Leningrad factory cannot complete textile machines because its plan has not been geared in to the output plan of a factory making one of the necessary components. This kind of failure of co-ordination between 'the sector departments of the Gosplans of the USSR and the RSFSR and the machinery manufacturers . . . arises rather frequently'. And so on, and so forth.[1] The satirical *Krododil* frequently publishes sarcastic comments. Thus a cartoon illustrates the statement of a Moscow party official to the effect that 'to receive ball-bearings from the first Moscow state ball-bearings factory, the neighbouring Likhachev automobile factory's requests for an allocation make a long journey, through fourteen republican and all-union *snabsbyty* and planning organs'.[2]

Uncertainties in supply cause *tolkachi* ('pushers') to flourish. The Dnepropetrovsk *sovnarkhoz* calculated that their metals and chemical factories were visited by 4,000 *tolkachi* in 1959, while 3,000 more descended on machinery factories and 1,000 besieged the *snab* and *sbyt* departments of the *sovnarkhoz* itself. Total: 8,000. All this is, of course, due to the failure of material supply arrangements to cover the production programme, or to fear of this.[3]

Part of the difficulty arises from delays in confirming output and delivery plans. For even if they are confirmed before the end of the previous year, this is only the signal for the detailed sub-allocations, decisions about which enterprise should supply whom, and negotiation of inter-enterprise delivery contracts, which can and do give rise to disputes. This can cause disarray.

Perhaps the best comment came from the economist Liberman. Writing, significantly, in the Party's leading fortnightly, he listed some outstanding examples of muddle over supplies. He pointed out that the system is both far too clumsy and too complex, making such muddles inevitable. So long as supplies are so organized, the

[1] *Promyshlenno-ekonomicheskaya gazeta*, May 13, 1960, and *Ekonomicheskaya gazeta*, June 9 and 10, 1960. Examples can be found in a large proportion of issues of these journals.
[2] *Krokodil*, July 30, 1960.
[3] B. Zolotov, *Promyshlenno-ekonomicheskaya gazeta*, May 15, 1960. This article is an excellent analysis of the causes of this situation.

complexities 'would overwhelm any apparatus of gosplans or supply-disposal organs (*snabsbyty*)'.[1]

Large numbers of *ad hoc* decisions are required to cope with disequilibria discovered after the plans have been approved, and this probably accounts for the continued practice of altering many enterprises' plans several times long after they were current; sometimes, wrote Liberman, this turns overfulfilment of the annual plan into underfulfilment at the last minute, which encourages the concealment of productive capacity and material reserves by directors.[2] As an example of how these alterations come about, a critic in the Party's fortnightly wrote that in 1958 the council of ministers of the RSFSR had to issue 140 statutory orders (*rasporyazheniya*) to secure additional supplies for the Moscow city *sovnarkhoz* alone, because plans were not geared in with supplies. Possibly as a result, many *sovnarkhozy* received 'additional planned tasks' during 1958, but without the necessary materials being provided.[3] Worse still, the organs of the Kazakh republican Gosplan were compelled to change their allocations of rolled steel 538 times, during the year 1959, because of various supply difficulties.[4]

Faced with these headaches, the supply departments at the centre reacted in various ways. One, *Soyuzglavmetall* (metals allocation), attempted strict centralization. Disregarding the republics' nominal powers, it 'undertook centralized distribution of orders for metals' to metal-producing enterprises. This means that after submitting its claim for metal, which goes up the hierarchy all the way up to the USSR Gosplan and down again, and having received its right to an allocation, the used enterprise resubmits its application, which then travels the following route:

'Sector division of *sovnarkhoz*—supply department of *sovnarkhoz* —*snabsbyt* of republic—*Soyuzglavmetall*. In the republican *snabsbyty* the specifications are aggregated by types, qualities and magnitudes, and these are also submitted to *Soyuzglavmetall*.' Commenting on the clumsiness of the system, the authors of these criticisms continue as follows: 'At the present time, *Soyuzglavmetall* and the republican *sbyty* employ several times more persons than worked in the former *glavmetalosbyt*' (i.e. in the metals disposals division before the abolition of the ministries in 1957). 'Every three months there arrive in Moscow the representatives of all metallurgical fac-

[1] *Kommunist*, No. 1/1959, p. 89.　　　　　　　　[2] Ibid., p. 90.
[3] I. Kalinin, *Kommunist*, No. 18/1958, pp. 43-4.
[4] V. Saveliev and S. Ilyin, *Promyshlenno-ekonomicheskaya gazeta*, February 28, 1960.

tories and of nearly all *sovnarkhozy*. Hundreds of men fill the corridors of the (supply) department, invade the hotels.'[1]

Other supply departments are said to conform more closely to the formal arrangements laid down by the regulations, i.e. concern themselves primarily with inter-republican deliveries, leaving a wider range of functions to the republican supply organs. However, judging from the many criticisms of the performance of the RSFSR Gosplan, this does not work very well in the larger republics.

In the smaller republics things cannot be much better, and indeed the chairman of the *sovnarkhoz* of Azerbaidjan suggested winding up republican supply organs and returning these functions to the all-union Gosplan.[2] The Leningrad party secretary, Spiridonov, made two other relevant criticisms. He referred to the Leningrad ship-yards, which assemble parts made in many factories in many parts of the USSR, and deplored the absence of an organization at the centre responsible for ensuring the placing and processing of orders as well as prompt delivery (this job was, of course, performed by the former industrial ministries in respect of 'their' enterprises). Similar criticisms have been made by others.[3] His other point relates to the status of large factories which make a number of products, which, since the reform of 1957, find themselves responsible to several authorities in respect of different products. Thus the Kirov (former Putilov) works in Leningrad is 'subordinated . . . to the depart-ment of heavy machine-building of the USSR Gosplan' in respect of its output of heavy machinery, whereas the metal made by this same factory he describes as 'an orphan' because no one at the centre con-trols it. He urged, consequently, that some organ at the centre should deal with multi-product enterprises.[4]

The observant reader should be rubbing his eyes at this point. How, he should ask, can the Kirov works in Leningrad be 'subor-dinated' to the USSR Gosplan? What about the *sovnarkhoz*, and, for that matter, the RSFSR? The answer, of great importance for the *de facto* running of the economy, seems to be this: important enter-prises, important building projects, anything which seems of all-union importance, are in fact subordinated to central organs, regard-less of formal hierarchical lines, though one imagines this can cause confusion, not least in the much-criticized sector of material sup-plies. Still more lines, or crossed wires, lead through party organs to and from the industrial department of the central committee, which

[1] *Pravda*, July 11, 1960
[2] S. Orudzhev, *Sovetskoe gosudarstvo i pravo*, No. 1/1959, pp. 33-4.
[3] *Pravda*, June 23, 1960.   [4] Ibid.

is perfectly capable of altering plans if this is considered desirable.

Of course, this does not exhaust the range of possible complications. If innovation is involved, then, as we have seen, several other bodies enter the picture (the scientific-technical committee, the committee on automation and machine-building, and so on).[1] If, as is very common, the planning decisions concern investment and new construction, then still more co-ordination is necessary. The decision to invest may concern *Gosekonomsovet* and functional as well as sector and territorial divisions of Gosplan. The provision of the necessary building materials are part of the materials allocation functions of Gosplan, and someone else must take decisions about the production and delivery of machinery to be installed in the newly-built factory. It is easy to see that things can get out of step. Here again, a list of priority construction projects is given centralized attention and support, in an effort to avoid breakdowns where the job is judged to be exceptionally important. However 'to this day we have not eliminated inconsistencies between the basic sectors of our plan: production, material supplies, investment and the bringing into operation of new capacity', said the chairman of the Latvian *sovnarkhoz*.[2]

Who co-ordinates the co-ordinators? The reform of 1957 replaced centralized industrial structures with a system notionally territorial, but in fact based on a multiplicity of central agencies, working through territorial units, but unable to delegate any effective power over resource allocation. These agencies can scarcely do anything which does not impinge on other organizations. The task of keeping them in harmony is of such a nature that new organizations are set up to co-ordinate and to be co-ordinated. (Hence the new organs set up in 1960, described in chapter 2, above.)

This whole section of the book is entitled 'problems', and therefore selects for analysis points of weakness or difficulty. Therefore the above assemblage of criticism must not be misunderstood. The economy works, most factories function most of the time. The punctual arrival of materials is not news and would not be reported in the press. As in all countries, most enterprises are doing this year much what they did last year, and draw their supplies from what for them has become the customary source. There exists an informal network of personal links and contacts, which plays an essential role in overcoming a variety of obstacles. None the less, the prob-

[1] New co-ordinating machinery was set up in 1961 (see p. 74, and *Pravda* April 12, 1961).
[2] To the central committee plenum. *Pravda*, July 14, 1960.

lems discussed are real, not only because they have attracted and are attracting the critical attention of many Soviet planners, administrators and economists, but also because they are built in to the system. One has only to consider realistically each of the points discussed to see that it is not a question of human error or stupidity, correctable by appointing other officials or reorganizing the distribution of work between departments.

In the West some similar problems, though on a smaller scale, arise within a giant firm, and certainly our system does not insure against error and stupidity. Needless to say, delays in construction, unpunctual delivery of machines and other failures are no monopoly of the Soviet system. It is also only right to mention that many errors and scandals similar to those which are denounced or criticized in the Soviet press are unknown to the public in the West, because private firms' business is private. But the Western economy has the very substantial advantage that, in normal times, anything within reason (except large and highly specialized equipment) can usually be bought without any trouble. A workshop which indents on its company's headquarters for some needed tools or timber may sometimes curse headquarters for delay, but it is clear to all concerned that the tools or timber are available if needed. There is nothing approaching the confused maze of Soviet material supply organs. The Western system, it may be argued, is more haphazard and potentially more wasteful in deciding what to produce, in so far as each entrepreneur has less knowledge than have the Soviet central planners of the projects already on foot elsewhere in the economy and of the consequent need for the product in question. Far more effort must be spent on salesmanship, i.e. on disposals. If a *tolkach* is wasteful, so is a commercial traveller. The availability of stocks of materials, it could also be said, is often accompanied by a relative underemployment of productive resources, just as the troubles of Soviet material supply are a by-product of planning designed to use all resources to the full. But, be all this as it may, planning of the Soviet type does run into the difficulties described in these pages, and, at the risk of appearing to overemphasize the negative features of the economy, it is right to say so.

PLANNING BY 'BALANCES'

On p. 81, above, a brief account was given of the planning based on material balances. This is a matter distinct from the actual job of current allocation of materials, though, of course, if done badly it would cause acute difficulties in the course of such allocations. The balances are needed primarily for development, for calculating the consequences of decisions on growth, and they are thus intimately connected with investment decisions. Whatever criticisms can and should be made of the system devised in the USSR, it is right to emphasize that they were pioneers in this very important field.

Until extremely recently, the 'balances' method was still somewhat crudely applied. For major raw materials and some other products widely used in industry, future requirements were calculated on the basis of technical coefficients, so as to enable the planners to foresee the material requirements inherent in their forward planning. But the inter-relationships were not adequately considered. No systematic working out of inter-sector relationships had in fact been undertaken. As has been pointed out by Soviet critics, while the methods used endeavoured to take direct material requirements into account, there was no adequate means of calculating indirect requirements. To use one example given by the Soviet source, the production of a ton of aluminium requires 18,950 kwh. of electricity; the various raw materials used in the production of aluminium also use electric energy, bringing the total to 20,042 kwh. But to this must be added the electricity used by other branches of industry supplying the aluminium industry, for instance, chemicals. When these are allowed for, the amount needed per ton of aluminium rises by a further 20 per cent, bringing the total to roughly 24,000 kwh.[1] It is surprising to learn that these calculations, confined experimentally to twenty-four products, were *begun* within the last two years, using statistics for 1957[2] (of course, the plans for the chemical industry would include its own direct utilization of electricity, but this arises at a separate planning stage). The reasons for this shortcoming were in large part the same as those which inhibited a proper study of inter-sector relationships: statistical returns from enterprises and economic organs were incomplete, followed administrative rather than economic lines of demarcation, often grouped several products or several materials together. For instance, a factory making two different products does not, in its material utilization or allocation figures, distinguish which materials were used for which product. Consequently, when in 1959 the research institute of Gosplan desired to create a true inter-sector input-output picture, information

[1] L. Berri, A. Efimov, *Plan. Khoz.*, No. 5/1960, pp. 34-5. Presumably, though the authors do not say so, part of the extra utilization consists of investment requirements, direct and indirect, of the electricity industry itself.
[2] Ibid., p. 36.

was lacking even in respect of direct material requirements, let alone the more complex indirect utilization data. Full data will therefore elaborate questionnaires, which will be based on a sample survey covering 20 per cent of industrial enterprises, and which 'is being' conducted by the Central Statistical Office. In the end, it is intended to cover 180 important products in newly-worked out and comprehensive 'chess-board' input-output balances, reflecting full utilization of each product, with the help of electronic computers.[1]

Of course, in Western countries we have been largely ignorant of inter-sector material relationships, but this had little practical significance for the functioning of the economy. In the USSR, however, when planning has been based on 'material balances', the slapdash nature of the calculations hitherto used does come as a surprise. How, one may ask, did the economy function at all? The answer seems to be in three parts: inspired improvization often enabled rough calculations to be somewhere near correct; the many grievous errors were 'cushioned' by the existence of non-priority sectors which took the brunt of shortage; and, thirdly, some centrally-held stocks could be used in *ad hoc* rescue operations. Often enough there really was confusion, and the strains and stresses of material supply, already described, were presumably part of the everyday cost of doing things in this way. One wonders, too, whether the systematic failure to take *indirect* material requirements into account was not an important cause of the chronic shortage of many kinds of material.

With the help of mathematics and electronic computors, we may suppose that a more sophisticated version of material balances will be created within a short period. No doubt this will aid the process of planning, and make possible the avoidance of many errors. However, the limitations of the present programme must also be stressed. Thus a list of 180 products is very far from being all-inclusive. More important still is the fact that most of these balances are in physical terms, not in money values. Yet a full analysis of inter-sector relationships, and above all any attempt to compare alternative patterns of material utilization, are scarcely possible without the use of money. The organizational-financial relationships are such as to make it impracticable to provide monetary balances parallel to the material ones, though the desirability of doing so is understood. Monetary balances are in fact being constructed for sixty-five sectors of industry, plus agriculture, building, transport, trade, supply

[1] Ibid., pp. 25, 29, also *Vest. Stat.*, No. 7/1960, pp. 47-8, and M. Eidel'man in ibid., No. 1/1960.

and other branches which, in the Soviet definition, contribute to material production.[1] These will, naturally, be based on existing prices, and will reflect the irrationalities of these prices, and will fail to reflect relative scarcities in so far as prices do not do so. This severely limits the use of these balances as a criterion for planners. No wonder Nemchinov has called for 'a theory of planning prices', and the creation of a truly all-inclusive 'economic budget of Soviet society'.[2] Kantorovich, Novozhilov and others who are pressing for the adoption of linear programming techniques in Soviet planning are also greatly concerned with finding a suitable price-base for making possible rational choice between alternative plan variants. But much more about prices in chapter 8, below.

INVESTMENT CRITERIA

This is a problem closely linked with that of planning by material balances, since the latter point the need to invest in this or that sector. Under the rough-and-ready system in operation so far, a decision to expand (for whatever reason) the aluminium industry was one of the factors determining investments in, and the location of, electricity generating stations, or of a railway line to take the bauxite to the aluminium plant. Let us first take the simplest aspect of the matter: the power station could be thermal or hydro; the railway line could be steam or electric. In each case, higher initial investments are more or less compensated by lower operating costs. Which variant should be chosen, and why? In this form, the question does not affect the rationality of the basic investment decisions as such, but only the means to achieve a given end.

The history of the discussions on investment criteria has been more thoroughly discussed by Western scholars than any other simple aspect of Soviet economics,[3] and so the details of the debates can be passed over fairly briefly here. The need for a criterion for the planners is self-evident; if theory is unable to provide one, a rule-of-thumb approach has to be devised. But several institutional and theoretical obstacles have to be surmounted.

Firstly, there is virtually no capital charge, except amortization, the latter being generally too small to affect calculations significantly. This gives a spurious attractiveness to the capital-intensive

[1] See L. Berri and A. Efimov, op. cit., p. 28, and, on p. 30, a table giving the pattern of an 'inter-sector balance in monetary terms'.
[2] *Vop. Ekon.*, No. 4/1959, pp. 26, 28.
[3] Notably by A. Zauberman, G. Grossman, H. Hunter, M. Dobb, N. Kaplan, H. Chambre (see bibliography).

variant. It is spurious because the loss to the economy in tying up
resources in the capital project is not adequately reflected in the cost
structure, nor is the factor time. It was in fact Khrushchev who in-
sisted on the importance of the time factor, in the context of choice
between hydro-electric and thermal power stations, where this
factor is particularly important.[1] His motive may have been a desire
to achieve maximum results in his lifetime, but motives hardly
matter; in any case, 'time-preference' is everywhere related, *inter
alia*, to the fact that none of us live for ever. It remains true that
capital charges—whether viewed as related to the time factor, relative scarcity of capital, or both—are of quite minor significance in
the USSR. This confuses not only the central planners, but also the
lower-level economic agencies and the enterprises for whom capital
assets appear to be a free gift from above, which naturally leads
them to apply for more than they can hope to get, and gives them
no incentive to attempt, at that level, to decide rationally which and
how much capital assets they require. Since some at least of the central decisions are influenced by applications from below, all this in
no way helps in finding the best use for investment resources. One
aspect of the time factor must also be mentioned: the large number
of unfinished building projects are evidently due partly to overbid-
ding for investment resources, resulting in breakdowns in building
material supplies[2] and partly to the lack of any penalty for delay.
To put the matter crudely, if building operations are suspended for
two years, the extra cost is limited to keeping a night-watchman
plus perhaps deterioration of the half-completed building. Thus
there is a chronic tendency to scatter resources on too many projects (*raspylenie sredstv*), leading to delays in completion, and
hardly a single budget speech by the Minister of Finance fails to
draw attention to this as a serious, but apparently incurable, disease.

The second institutional-practical obstacle is the price system.
Prices of materials, or of the end-products, often bear no rational
relationship to one another, to their relative scarcity, or to their
utility from the standpoint of the user. Consequently the relative
profitability of this or that project could be quite misleading a guide
to action, and some projects may be simply excluded by an absolute
shortage of one or more products which are required to carry it out.
All this is, perhaps, too obvious to require further comment.

[1] In his speech at Kuibyshev, *Pravda*, August 11, 1958.
[2] For the importance of this factor in causing overstrain in 1956, see I.
Kulyov, *O dal'neishem sovershenstvovanii planirovniya i rukovodstva narod-
nym khozyaistvom* ('Znanie', Moscow, 1957), pp. 7-10.

If one also takes into account transport and labour shortages in some areas, and the complications of administrative and territorial demarcation lines, the practical difficulties in the way of finding objective criteria of judgment appear to be formidable. But to them must be added a theoretical-ideological obstacle: any objective criterion which would affect the *direction* of investment was resisted and resented, on two interlinked grounds. Firstly, many of the suggested criteria involved some measurement of a return on capital, which is a concept close to a rate of interest on capital, which was regarded as ideologically offensive. Secondly, the idea of adopting economic criteria for determining the direction of investment was itself suspect, save within the very narrowest range of choice. This view was strongly held by Stalin. He assumed that consumers' goods industries were obviously more profitable, that investment in these industries would provide a higher return than in most branches of heavy industry. The recognition of an objective economic criterion might suggest the shifting of resources into non-priority sectors. In any event, Stalin held the view that these matters are for planner-politicians not economists.[1]

The principle that a given result (given by the plan) should be achieved with due economy of capital, by choosing the variant which 'pays for itself' most quickly, was accepted in principle without much argument at various conferences called to discuss the subject after Stalin's death. This is the so-called period of recoupment (*srok okupaemosti*). If project A requires more capital than project B but will save on current costs, or if the new project will reduce costs compared with existing practice, in such a way that the gain can wipe out the extra investment required over a given period of years, say, ten, then the given investment pays for itself in ten years. If, other things being equal, another variant pays for itself in eight years, then it should be preferred.

Various attempts were made to formulate this concept in forms which could be applied in all the relevant planning offices. The most recent is the *Tipovaya metodika ekonomicheskoi effektivnosti kapital'nykh vlozhenii i novoi tekhniki*, published by the Academy of Sciences in 1960. The formula for the recoupment (or 'pay-off') period may be given as

$$\frac{I_1 - I_2}{C_2 - C_1} = T$$

where I stands for the sums invested, C for the costs of production,

[1] Stalin, op. cit., pp. 22-4, 72. See also chapter 11.

in the two variants which are being compared, and T is Time, i.e. the period of recoupment.

The reciprocal of the above,

$$\frac{C_2 - C_1}{I_1 - I_2} = \frac{1}{T}$$

would represent the coefficient of efficiency of investment. In a choice of investment within any given sector, to the current cost of production involved in adopting this particular variant there should (so it is argued by the majority) be added a kind of imputed cost of capital, a *de facto* interest rate, representing the 'normative' rate of investment efficiency, a 'normative' recoupment period. Allowance must be made, in the recommended method of calculation, for complementary investment needs at least in the 'proximate' branches. The immobilization of capital assets during construction is also to be allowed for in this disguised interest rate. The recommendations do not insist on a single 'normative' rate for the economy as a whole, and in fact envisage the use of different rates in different sectors of industry and of the economy. However, the existence of a rate for the economy as a whole is recognized, it is referred to as a 'general' rate, and, at least by implication, it could be used in inter-branch and inter-sector calculations, where substitutable goods are involved. This is not clearly spelled out, which may be a sign of a compromise, since, as we shall see, this is a controversial question.[1] The existing rate of return in the given sector is to be used as a yardstick: the new project should not be less efficient, should not have a longer recoupment period, unless no possible alternative can be found. But in addition to these value indicators various other calculations are recommended, of a more general character: physical output per man, required inputs of materials and fuel, technical progress, and so on. While, bearing in mind the vagaries of Soviet costs and prices, resort to these non-monetary criteria is understandable, the effect may be to point to conflicting choices. The emphasis on other criteria—other, that is, than the return on capital—is greatest when new techniques are under discussion. Here there is much emphasis, as a rule, on comparison with foreign technologies, or on somewhat ill-defined increases in labour productivity. None the less, agreement on the importance of the recoupment period (efficiency of investment) is now generally accepted. However, it is accompanied by vigorous argument on many unsettled questions.

[1] A very uneasy compromise, according to I. Malyshev, *Plan. Khoz.*, No. 1/1961, p.48.

The first of these has already been hinted at. It is increasingly realized that the search for criteria cannot in practice confine itself to any one branch, or closely inter-related branches, of the economy; it is not just a question of hydro *versus* thermal electricity, or two different projects for a steelworks. There are many permutations and combinations of energy, metals, chemicals, and so on, all inter-dependent. It is not enough, wrote Efimov and Krasovski, to 'compare variants of the same project'. What is needed is 'a more effective structure of capital investments which would correspond to the basic conception of the plan'.[1]

However, this immediately leads to a second difficulty. The actual 'periods of recoupment' in different sectors of the economy differ extremely widely; this was and is the consequence of basing invest-ment decisions on plans for future production devised separately for separate products. The result has been that the recoupment period is in general much longer in heavy than in light industry; it is, ac-cording to Khachaturov, four to five years in light industry, ten years in transportation, sixteen to seventeen years in electric power.[2] Is this a sign of a misdirection of resources, or an inevitable consequence of Soviet-style 'priority' planning? On this there is still a sharp clash of views. Vaag argued that 'the normative recoupment period must be the same throughout the economy'; the deliberate introduction of the priority of heavy industry into the process of calculation must lead, in his view, to wasteful resource allocation.[3] Khachaturov dis-agreed.[4] Strumilin also argued that the priority of heavy industry must be firmly maintained.[5] Yet how can one make the inter-sector comparisons envisaged by Efimov and others of the more intelligent planners without a valid inter-sector criterion? Vaag, of course, did not deny that some decisions must be made (and not only in Russia) for reasons other than estimated return on capital, but urges that planners must consider real costs, 'not those which we create in our imagination'.[6] The same thought was expressed by Zasyad'ko, later to become the head of the Economic-science council: 'Of course, the criterion of return on capital must not be obeyed blindly, it must be modified by political and strategic considerations, but always in

[1] *Plan. Khoz.*, No. 8/1959, pp. 66-7. Emphasis mine.
[2] *Vop. Ekon.*, No. 9/1958, p. 121. Other examples were given by Vaag in *Zakon Stoimosti* (Kronrod), p. 424.
[3] *Vop. Ekon.*, No. 9/1958, p. 130.
[4] Ibid., p. 121, and also *Vop. Ekon.*, No. 1/1961, pp. 72-5.
[5] Ibid., p. 123. But he simultaneously supported a single 'norm of effective-ness' (*Vop. Ekon.*, No. 8/1959, p. 89).
[6] *Zakon Stoimosti* (Kronrod), p. 423.

the knowledge of the cost, the loss, arising from the decision.'[1]

A further point of both theoretical and practical significance arises. What precisely is the nature of the criterion we are discussing? In the discussions, Malyshev advanced the view that 'the economic content of the return on capital is profit', and consequently that 'profit norms should be the same throughout the economy', echoing the ideas of Vaag.[2] Both naturally argued in favour of calculating profits in relation to capital, instead of to costs, and both pointed out the necessity of a rational price system if any calculations are to be soundly based. But any criteria based on a price-system which fails to reflect *use*-value are liable to lead to confusing results. Thus, in the same discussion, the economist Shuster gave the following example. Suppose there are several possible machines which could be produced. Investment in their production would then be decided, according to the accepted criteria, by the return on capital (or profits) resulting from the adoption of this or that variant. By such criteria, machine A may be preferred to machine B. Yet the ultimate user of the machine, the enterprise which acquires it, is also investing, and from its point of view machine B may be much more productive and therefore preferable.[3]

A somewhat different question was raised particularly strongly by Nemchinov: this relates to the need to include capital charges in costs in reality, and not merely in notional calculations of planners. Under the existing system, apart from a very small amortization charge, which averages a mere $3\frac{1}{2}$ per cent of costs of production, the amount of basic capital of an enterprise does not show in its cost-accounting. Nemchinov argued that this is all wrong. It is not enough to talk of a ten-year recoupment period as if it must remain in the minds of planners. It must, in his view, have an accounting reality. A ten-year period should therefore imply an annual payment by each enterprise into the state budget of 10 per cent of the value of its capital assets. The resultant revenue would enable the state to reduce the burden of turnover tax, and costs and prices would more effectively stimulate economy of capital and of time. 'Investments should return to the revenues of society.'[4] The same argument, though without so clear a conclusion, was made by Z. Atlas: 'Enterprises have no incentive to reduce their capital funds.'

[1] *Pravda*, February 3, 1959.
[2] *Vop. Ekon.*, No. 9/1958, p. 135. Also see Z. Atlas, *Vop. Ekon.*, No. 10/1960, p. 71.
[3] *Vop. Ekon.*, No. 9/1958, p. 126.
[4] *Vop. Ekon.*, No. 9/1958, p. 137; and also, at greater length, in *Kommunist*, No. 1/1958, p. 81.

In respect of unused equipment, 'enterprises by present rules do not even pay amortization'. The position in the case of working capital is even worse . . . The enterprise is (financially) indifferent whether it holds stocks to the value of one or of ten million roubles.[1]

A capital charge (whether applied to basic capital only or to basic and working capital) has both a macro- and a micro-economic effect, and reminds one that the distinction between these categories is often blurred in practice. Thus central investment decisions are influenced in various ways by projects put forward from below, and these, as well as the utilization of capital assets on the spot, must inevitably be influenced by micro-economic stimuli; a capital charge would affect enterprise behaviour by affecting their accounts. However, the inclusion of capital charges in costs—which is a form of interest rate—is also relevant to investment criteria calculations at the centre (see also chapter 8, below).

The entire debate has been taken on a higher level by becoming linked with a discussion of optimum planning and the utilization of mathematical techniques, which will be discussed separately, as its implications are so wide. Novozhilov argued, indeed, that the whole question of investment criteria is merely a special case of the general question of the proper valuation and utilization of scarce resources of all kinds throughout the economy.[2] Kantorovich, too, would treat this as an integral part of attaching values to scarce resources, as part of the application of linear programming methods to the Soviet economy, and both he and Novozhilov agree with Nemchinov that capital assets should be charged for; indeed, Kantorovich favours a capital charge ('efficiency norm'—*norma effektivnosti*—for investment) higher than Western interest rates, because of the enormous capital requirements of the Soviet expansion programme.[3] The eminent academician Kolmogorov also argued in favour of seeing the *norma effektivnosti* as a species of charge for time, basing it on the idea that, since in a progressing economy 'labour value will decline with time, the shifting of the expenditure of labour to an earlier period will permit . . . an increase in total production'. Having found a theoretically respectable foundation for Kantorovich's ideas, he continued as follows: 'We must not be upset by the formal analogy [of the *norma effektivnosti*] with the capitalist "in-

---

[1] *Zakon Stoimosti* (Tsagolov), p. 279. But see strong attack on these views by Y. Kronrod, *Vop. Ekon.*, No. 10/1960, pp. 88-94.

[2] See his contribution to the symposium (edited by V. Nemchinov) *Primenenie matematiki v ekonomicheskikh issledovaniyakh* (Moscow, 1959), p. 129.

[3] *Ekonomicheskii rashchyot nailuchshevo ispol'zovaniya resursov* (Moscow, 1949), p. 220.

terest on capital." [1] Meanwhile Nemchinov has applied to this problem the concept of differential rent, as well as of a standard capital charge. This will be discussed in detail in chapter 11.

The discussion continues. As will be shown in subsequent chapters, it is intimately linked with a more general reconsideration of both structure and theory. It is being increasingly realized that a greater attention to rational resource allocation is indispensable, and nowhere more so than in the field of capital investments. However, a balanced view of Soviet performance in investment planning requires at least some consideration for two relevant factors. One concerns the peculiar 'rationality' of moving out of a stage of underdevelopment, when general strategic considerations may logically take precedence over the 'micro-rationality' to which many Western economists pay almost exclusive attention. This point will be taken up again in chapter 12, and implies that it is at least possible that rapid development in the Soviet context (and perhaps also in some other developing countries) was necessarily inconsistent with the utilization of 'normal' investment criteria. Such an interpretation by no means excludes the view that the Soviet economy has moved into a more mature stage in which some of the 'traditional' criteria come into their own.

The second point to bear in mind is that Western practice too suffers from major weaknesses in this field. Of course, perfect competition should theoretically lead to an efficient disposal of resources, including investment resources. But, in the world as it is, this picture would be as unrealistic as would be a faultless all-foreseeing Gosplan. We must remember that major investment projects, involving the construction of a new factory, take several years to complete, and necessarily involve an element of guesswork as to demand and prices at a future date. Especially with chronic inflation and instability of relative prices, typical of the postwar years, few economists in the West would assert that would-be investors are able to exercise foresight under reasonable conditions. Nor does the role of interest rates, which also have fluctuated alarmingly from time to time, accord with rational economic principles of the textbooks. In these conditions, if misdirection of resources is to be avoided, investment decisions must in fact be often based on a forward estimate of demand in quantitative terms, the profits being assumed. This applies particularly to the many sectors affected by monopolies or quasi-monopolies. But it is certainly arguable that it is precisely in a planned economy that it is easier to foresee future demand, at

[1] *Vop. Ekon.*, No. 8/1960, p. 114.

least for basic industrial products. The central planners can forecast the requirements for, say, steel, sulphuric acid and hydraulic presses in 1965, because they have before them the plans for the output of industries using these commodities, and can take investment decisions accordingly. It is true that they may make mistakes, but the boards of directors of the relevant British undertakings are also capable of error, and in addition cannot have so much knowledge of future utilization, or of the development plans of competing enterprises. Investment decisions everywhere involve a mixture of calculation and 'hunch', are in part 'arbitrary' administrative decisions. It is surely arguable that the likelihood of error, and 'macro-error' at that, is somewhat greater in Western economies, even while they are noticeably superior in making adjustments to changing demand. Large investment errors become visible in the West when, as in periods of recession, capital assets are idle or underused, but major losses may also result from failure to take decisions, a failure which could be due precisely to the element of uncertainty. To take some British examples, insufficient investments in the steel and machine-tool industries may well be causing losses to the economy, which we would find it hard to measure, but which cannot be assumed not to exist unless one equates actual investment decisions with an imaginary optimum. As for the public sector in Western countries, perhaps the less said the better. One need only mention the sad history of the development plans of British railways, controversies on fuel policy, and the confused relationship between public and private investments. It would also be a very bold Western economist who could express satisfaction with the assessment of social costs involved in investment choices. Of course, many of these problems, including that of bringing social costs into the calculation, are unsettled in the USSR also. It is indeed not argued that Soviet practice, with its many errors and omissions, produces 'superior' results in the taking of investment decisions. The object of these final paragraphs is merely to emphasize that investment rationality, in any sense of the word, may in practice be just as elusive in London as in the planning offices of Moscow.

CHAPTER 8

The Pricing of Factors of Production

Prices in an economy of the Soviet type have several interconnected roles to play.

Firstly, as Grossman pointed out, 'pricing and accounting have the major purpose of exercising control over and evaluation of enterprise management'.[1] This was certainly Stalin's view, and Bachurin was reflecting it when he wrote, in 1954: 'prices of producers' goods . . . serve primarily for "control by the rouble" over production and resource utilization, for developing and strengthening *khozraschyot*, the stimulation of reduction in costs.'[2] The doctrine at this period was loyal to Stalin's view that the 'law of value' does not apply to goods transferred between enterprises within the state sector (see chapter 11, below). If one assumes the capital stock, inputs and the output plan as given, which Stalin certainly would do in this context, prices then are important only in so far as they enable a superior to identify inefficiency and reward efficiency in carrying out the plan without undue waste. For such a purpose, the average costs incurred in producing the goods in question in all Soviet enterprises is an adequate basis. Obvious differences in equipment or other objective conditions can be allowed for in the cost plan for the particular enterprise, but a price related to average cost does provide the supervisory authorities with some basis for judgment. If costs are too high, it is a signal that something is awry, that work or management is on a low level.

However, since one finds that the assumption that the enterprise is told exactly what to produce is only partially correct, and that inputs are influenced in varying degrees by enterprises' own applications, therefore there is a second important role of prices: as a guide to enterprise decisions at the micro level. If, other things being

---

[1] 'Industrial prices in the USSR', *American Economic Review*, May, 1959, p. 57. This article provides a thorough and stimulating discussion of these questions.
[2] *Vop. Ekon.*, No. 3/1954, p. 35.

equal, price A is higher than price B, and the directors are able to choose, then they would emphasize A as producers, and B as purchasers of inputs. For these purposes, where, by definition, the central plan does not give precise instructions, prices would need to reflect relative scarcities and the requirements of the users.

Thirdly, prices guide the planners at all levels, and the authors of investment projects, in their choices as to how to devise means to further the economic policies of the government. Is it worth expanding plastics? Should aluminium be substituted for other metals? Is it worth building a pipeline to Chelyabinsk to replace locally-mined brown coal? Is it rational to supply forgings and castings to Chelyabinsk from Sverdlovsk? To what kind of textiles should new investments be devoted? Clearly, prices unrelated to costs could cause incorrect decisions to be made, while prices unrelated to scarcities would encourage planners to overindent for commodities in short supply.

Fourthly, there is the comparatively new question of devising prices adapted to mathematical techniques, notably linear programming, which bring up a number of matters of principle, of which much more will have to be said.

Fifthly, through prices the state obtains revenue, and in the case of agricultural produce the state also affects the distribution of income between town and country, and these considerations also affect action.

Finally, retail prices are used to distribute consumers' goods, to allow the citizen to choose which of the available goods he wishes to buy.

These various objectives can contradict one another in many different ways. Thus for 'control' purposes it is convenient to have stable prices. It would confuse the task of measuring success or failure if, half-way through the year, material A were suddenly increased in price by 15 per cent, especially if this material is administratively allocated to user enterprises, so that they cannot choose whether to use it or material B. Hence the general policy of keeping prices steady for long periods. However, this is plainly inconsistent with using prices as a 'micro' guide to scarcities or to demand. Similarly, from the 'control' standpoint the price of the output does not greatly matter; if it is below costs, a subsidy is paid, and here the matter ends. However, the planners could be confused if in their calculations they take coal to be 'worth' 150 roubles a ton when its costs are 200 roubles.

The essence of the problem, as seen by Soviet planners, has been changing, with the growing necessity of devolving more functions to territorial bodies and with the interest shown in linear programming techniques. For these have at least one thing in common: prices become an essential element in 'feeding' back the relative scarcities and demand. To this task the Soviet price system is ill-adapted.

THE SEARCH FOR AN 'OBJECTIVE' BASIS FOR PRICES

Since 1955, Soviet economic literature has been full of debates on prices. Virtually all the participants agree that the existing system is far too illogical, as has indeed already been documented at some length in chapter 4. But they are much less clear about what is to replace it, and it is probable that this lack of clarity is connected with different ideas about the role which prices should play in the economy. Thus Turetski, while favouring the elimination of various anomalies, advocates for heavy industry 'a single price for all products of the same use value'.[1] Since the identical or interchangeable use-values—e.g. in the fuel industry—are associated with different costs, he is against relating prices to average costs or to 'values' based on cost. But at the same time he admits 'in certain cases . . . to the necessity of price differences in the interests of economizing certain scarce materials'.[2] For example, coking coal, being scarce, should be particularly dear for this reason. However, to him these are exceptions. The idea that all things are in some degree scarce seems hardly to have penetrated this professor's imagination. It looks as if he seeks a consistent and stable basis on which to judge enterprise performance, modified by a variety of considerations: acute scarcity, the need to encourage technical progress, social policies and so on. At the same time, Turetski does oppose subsidies, and considers that the normal profit margin in all branches should be such as to cover the normal requirements of enterprises for investment and increases in working capital, and should therefore be greater than the commonly-accepted norm of 3-5 per cent. In so far as prices in many branches of heavy industry provide an inadequate profit margin, these prices are too low. However, Turetski strongly opposes any mechanical linking of price with cost (or 'value'). To derive a consistent price theory from his ideas is a task beyond my powers. In the West, the absence of theory or criteria would make little difference, but in the USSR, with prices fixed by

[1] Turetski, op. cit., p. 103.
[2] Ibid., p. 105. For a vigorous analysis of his ideas, see review of this book by M. Dobb, *Soviet Studies*, July, 1960, and Turetski's reply in ibid., April, 1961.

deliberate action, their absence cannot but have undesirable consequences.

But if there is to be a more adequate criterion for determining prices, what is this criterion to be? On this a vigorous debate has been raging. This is intimately linked with the more theoretical problem of the role of 'value' and the 'law of value' in the Soviet economy, which is discussed in chapter 11.

Essentially, the difficulty is this. Marxian theory was concerned with identifying the elements which determined value and price in a capitalist market economy, and accounting for such phenomena as exploitation and surplus value. Whether Marx was in fact successful in doing these things is a question we need not here pursue. The problem before Soviet economists in a search for an objective basis for prices is to find a means of using this theory in a situation in which a free market does not exist. A number of them responded to this challenge by asserting that prices of commodities should (as a rule) equal their 'values' in the Marxist sense. Various theories have been developed as to how values should be calculated, these being essentially concerned with deciding what should be added to prime cost (*sebestoimost'*). Most of this school believe that pricing in accordance with 'values' implies that all products should bear equally the burden of accumulation and unproductive state expenditures, which are financed primarily out of profits and turnover tax, though they put forward rival formulae about how this sum, the 'surplus product', should be shared out. Details of these ideas will be given in chapter 11, where the 'law of value' is discussed at some length.

These economists generally agree that some deviation from their recommended price bases should be permitted, in usually ill-defined exceptional circumstances. A favourite example is that vodka should be dear and children's shoes cheap. But, in principle, they argue, their respective formulae should determine prices.

These formulae presuppose that the basis for price-determination should be the same for all goods. The authors criticize the present system not only for its internal inconsistencies, but also for disproportionately burdening consumers' goods with more than their share of the 'surplus product', through turnover tax. At present, part of the 'surplus product' of the steel and coal industries, for instance, is 'realized' through the prices of various consumers' goods. This appears on the surface not to matter, since it is a mere revenue-raising convenience, and all payments are between state enterprises anyway. But, argue Malyshev, Kondrashev, Strumilin, Atlas and many other economists, this is an utterly false way of looking at things. This basis of pricing twists out of shape many essential cost comparisons, misleads planners in their assessment of the real magnitude of this or that portion of the national income. For example, consumption is exaggerated in relation to accumulation, industry (to which the bulk of turnover tax is 'credited') in relation to agriculture, some regions in relation to others. Labour is paid in wages which must reflect the high consumers' goods prices, and which are therefore high compared with prices of machinery, the latter being exempted from turnover tax. Consequently even economically inadequate machinery looks profitable to use, since its cost appears low in relation to wages saved. If these critics' advice were taken, the effect would be an increase in prices of producers' goods, and of revenues derived by the state from heavy industry in the form of profits, turnover tax and/or a charge for the use of capital assets. There would be a reduction in such revenues from the consumer goods sector, but, if personal incomes are unchanged, this would be due not to a cut in retail prices but to an increase in costs caused by higher prices of materials and machines. Prices, they argue, would then reflect real social costs.

These proposals are vigorously opposed, notably by Turetski and by Maisenberg.[1] They do not deny that prices ought to have some relation to objective criteria, but regard much greater flexibility as necessary if prices are to be made to serve political objectives and other planning purposes. One of these is the encouragement of technical progress and growth, which, they maintain, demands low prices for the basic materials and machinery. Another is the usefulness of keeping enterprises up to the mark by cutting prices and not allowing 'comfortable' profit margins. Retail prices, they maintain, are different in principle, and there is no reason why wholesale prices of heavy industry should be brought into conceptual line with them.

It is a weakness of the 'law-of-value' price-reform proposals that prices are seen statically, as a reflection of costs, of average costs of production in the given branch, plus some amount determined by rival formulae. Though these proposals may appear more systematic, more worthy of economists, than the 'political' empiricism of Turetski and Maisenberg, the latter seem justified in accusing the authors of all these formulae of ignoring reality. They overlook the fact that Marx's theory of value, whatever its defects may be, was at

---

[1] See Turetski's book, op. cit., and the thoughtful contribution by L. Maisenberg to the volume *Zakon Stoimosti* (Kronrod), pp. 405 ff.

least concerned with a competitive capitalist economy in which market forces operated and tended towards certain kinds of equilibrium. (The dynamics of any economy involve, of course, *departures* from these equilibrium positions.) In the USSR, as elsewhere, if prices were to play the role of influencing decision making, whether by planners or at enterprise level, these static formulae become useless. *At best* they would make the price system neutral in decisions concerning relative scarcities and utility. Turetski and Maisenberg do see that prices should be influencing decision making. Their own weakness lies in their inability to suggest any systematic guide for price determination.

Such a systematic guide is advocated by Novozhilov and Kantorovich. Prices would be based, to use Kantorovich's phrase, on 'objectively determined valuations'. They would be efficiency prices, consequences of an econometric exercise in optimization; given certain aims, the prices would be those which enable these aims to be most effectively attained. This approach involves the application to the USSR of the linear programming techniques in the development of which Kantorovich played a pioneering role.[1] There would be a species of market, if only within the computer. Relative scarcities and opportunity costs would then enter the picture, as would a rental charge for land and mineral workings. Clearly, this would mean a complete change in planning methods, as well as in prices. The arguments about prices and values cited in the present chapter would be swept away as irrelevant. The Novozhilov-Kantorovich approach has provoked strong opposition from the more orthodox economists. The arguments around these concepts, as well as the efforts of Nemchinov to bridge the gap,[2] take us far into the realm in which price policy and the theory of value dwell uneasily together, and detailed discussion of them must be postponed until chapter 11.

It is hardly necessary to stress the vital importance of the price problem, since, as we have seen, prices affect the behaviour of planners and enterprises, and 'wrong' pricing can lead to misallocation of resources and act as a barrier to possible forms of decentralization. Yet most serious theoretical and practical difficulties arise as one endeavours to devise a price system which can meet all the

---

[1] See L. Kantorovich, op. cit., which also contains a reprint of his pioneering work written as long ago as 1939, and ignored by official economics until very recently. Kantorovich also contributes to V. Nemchinov (ed.), *Primeneniye matematiki v ekonomicheskikh issledovaniyakh* (Moscow, 1959), but the main feature of this volume is the appearance of a long contribution by V. Novozhilov.

[2] *Vop. Ekon.*, No. 12/1960, pp. 85-105.

varied requirements which, in the Soviet setting, they are expected to meet. Furthermore, the debate has been almost wholly concentrated upon the question of the basis upon which stable prices are to be fixed by state organs, and no one has yet seriously tackled the aspect of prices most familiar to those who study the market economy, that of inducing a continuous series of adjustments to an ever-changing situation, adjustments which of their very nature do not lend themselves to centralized decision making. Neither a price system statically derived from prime-cost-plus-surplus-product, nor a series of 'objectively determined valuations' à la Kantorovich, provide a basis for the micro-economic role of the price mechanism. Perhaps Nemchinov is aware of this question, because he has confined himself to advocating a species of 'skeleton of basic prices' for some key products, while emphasizing the role of supply and demand and urging the study of demand elasticities, so that detailed prices could be adjusted to the prevailing conditions. He also suggested an original way of using the price mechanism for linking the demand pattern and producers' behaviour without threatening price stability; this could be done by varying the right of the enterprise to retain profits (i.e. the rules governing the size of the enterprise fund) in accordance to the relative scarcity (or abundance), of the given product.

The debate is in full swing, and is rendered urgent by a decision of the Party and government to proceed to a revision of the wholesale and retail price systems in 1961-62.

AGRICULTURAL PRICES AND LAND RENT

In discussing certain irrationalities in Soviet agriculture, notably the very large income differentials, the interlinked problems of prices and rent naturally arose. The problems are connected, because, in the absence of payments by *kolkhozy* of land rent as such, the price system is called upon to 'correct' differences in land fertility and location. Under the 1958 reform, prices are considerably lower in areas of relative natural advantages, than in less favoured regions. For example, wheat prices paid to farms are much lower in the North Caucasus than in the centre or north of Russia. Under the system as it existed before the 1958 price reforms two other means existed for extracting a form of differential rent (under another name) from the better-situated farms: by varying the scale of payments in kind for the services of the MTS, and by varying the quota of compulsory deliveries at low prices. True, this was not done effec-

tively, but these weapons were to hand for doing it. However, both
the MTS and the multiple price system were abolished in 1958, and
consequently the one important means available to the authorities
to 'correct' for natural advantage is by varying the state purchase
price between areas.

The prices are said to be zonally differentiated to take costs into
account, but in practice the very large differences in costs (however

Groups	KRASNODAR			KIROV		
	I	II	III	1	II	III
GRAIN						
No. of kolkhozy in group	8	18	13	14	14	16
Harvest (quintals per hectare)	28·7	28·0	26·2	6·4	7·1	5·8
Costs (per quintal of grain (roubles)	14·06	17·95	21·70	44·56	58·27	87·54
Trudoden, money value of, (roubles)	12·17	12·25	11·56	4·14	5·04	5·23
Labour input per quintal (trudodni)	0·70	0·87	1·18	4·40	4·27	5·38
Average selling price per quintal	59·42	56·66	44·50	71·14	70·86	80·51
MILK						
No. of kolkhozy in group	15	14	10	16	16	17
Yield per cow litres)	2,480	2,280	2,190	1,700	1,800	1,700
Costs, per quintal	103·34	134·64	170·62	83·65	134·25	185·06
Labour input per quintal (trudodni)	6·06	6·47	8·05	7·38	8·80	11·66
Average selling price	105·65	103·52	115·48	109·93	103·22	104·46

calculated) and revenues of *kolkhozy* in different areas are quite inadequately covered by the zonal price-differentiation. Interesting
examples have appeared, *inter alia*, in a thoughtful and well-
documented article by S. Nedelin.[1] He compares statistics for the
fertile Krasnodar *krai* with the Kirov (Vyatka) *oblast'* of north
Russia, and his calculations are worth reproducing in full for grain
and milk. The grouping of *kolkhozy* within the regions (in roman
figures) is based on costs, these being calculated taking into ac-

[1] *Finansy SSSR*, No. 6/1960, pp. 40-50.

count the actual value of payment of *trudodni* in cash and kind, other expenditures being valued at prices paid, or at estimated cost where own produce or own labour was used. All figures relate to 1958, which, according to the author, was a good weather year in both areas. (See table on previous page.)

Note that costs of production of grain were three and a half times higher in Kirov than in Krasnodar, despite the fact that labour was paid two and a half times less per *trudoden* on average. Milk costs look similar, but only by reason of the relatively great underpayment of peasants in Kirov.

The situation has actually been made worse by the 1958 reform. Before this date, part of the 'differential rent' was extracted by differential payments for MTS services (see page 54, above). Thus, Nedelin states that for every hectare of ploughing the *kolkhozy* of Krasnodar paid the MTS 150 kilograms of grain, whereas the less fertile north and centre paid 30-35 kilograms 'despite higher MTS costs'. The cost to the state of one hectare of ploughing (excluding investments) was 19·38 roubles in the favourable conditions of Krasnodar. After the abolition of the MTS, writes Nedelin, the *kolkhozy* of Krasnodar can sell 150 kilograms of grain to the state at the new official zonal price for 97·50 roubles. They therefore score a substantial relative gain as a result of the reform.

Another table is reproduced by Nedelin, as follows (all figures in roubles per quintal, and here 'costs' are assumed to include adequate remuneration for the peasants):

GRAIN (1958)

Zones	Costs	Average purchase price	Price required to cover costs & accumulation	Surplus or deficit
Caucasus	22·00	59·00	30·14	+28·86
Non-black earth Centre	88·00	74·00	120·56	−45·44

It is easy to say that the above tables show that (for instance) Kirov *oblast'* should specialize on dairy produce and not grow grain. To some extent this was recognized, since, under the reforms of 1958, the central authorities did not normally ask for grain deliveries from so high-cost an area. However, the total requirements of the USSR being what they are, state organs must rely on grain from these high-cost areas, and did indeed resume purchases in

1961. The farms of the non-black earth centre (i.e. such *oblasti* as Moscow, Tula, Kaluga, Vladimir) grow a great deal of grain, and the fact remains that zonal variations in prices are still quite inadequate. The inadequacy means that the peasants, who absorb the 'surplus' or 'deficit' in the above table, are much better off in one area than another. The magnitude of cost differences is partially explicable by natural conditions; mechanized extensive farming, to which *kolkhozy* have hitherto been most suited (or least unsuited) is most efficient in fertile steppelands (e.g. Krasnodar), and has been least successful in coping with the small fields and poorer soils of the centre, north and west, to which the available machinery is ill-adapted and where intensive methods (including much fertilizer) are needed to produce adequate yields. These areas also happen to have inherited a high labour density. Of course, costs per unit would in any case be lower in fertile Krasnodar, but the above factors increase the difference, especially in the absence of land rent.

The problem of rent has indeed come into the forefront of the discussion. In an interesting article, a Soviet economist shows conclusively that the pay of *kolkhoz* peasants depends decisively, and unfairly, on soil quality and location of the land. In order to put this right, he proposes a system of taxation (he cannot call it rent, this would be ideologically incorrect) differentiated by land quality, which involves *valuing* land. This is obviously essential, he argues, since regional differentiation (e.g. as in price zoning) quite fails to take into account the wide differences in fertility and other advantages within quite small areas. He proposes the adoption of a system similar to that already in use in East Germany, where land is valued in accordance with the net income which might be derived from it by good husbandry, on a points system. If the existing *kolkhoz* tax system were related to these 'points', then the better-situated *kolkhozy* would pay much more tax, which would even out the unfairness of the present system. He appears also to argue for the adoption of a similar valuation system for state-farm land, though without making it clear whether they should pay tax on the same basis.[1] As against this, Strumilin argues strongly against any use, even disguised, of the concept land rent. Logically its use should presuppose, in his view, prices which would cover costs on the worst (i.e. marginal) land, so far as *kolkhozy* are concerned, although prices in the state sectors, including the state-farm sector, are based and should (in his view) be based, on average cost. This, he asserts, would be nonsense. He therefore advocates a redistribution of net

[1] G. Lisichkin, *Vop. Ekon.*, No. 7/1960, pp. 61-8.

income within the *kolkhoz* system, on a regional, republican and even all-union basis.[1] The argument remains unsettled.

The whole problem of land rent was vigorously debated, and one such debate was published in full.[2] Tsagolov argued that, since producers on marginal land must live, prices must be fixed accordingly, and that a rental charge to offset natural advantages ('differential rent I') would be quite legitimate, although additional income due to investment, hard work and efficiency ('differential rent II') should belong to the farm. A complicated discussion ensued, with some protagonists even arguing that, while the 'value' of agricultural produce is based on marginal land, this does not exclude the payment by the state of a price related to *average* costs, to *kolkhozy* and *sovkhozy* alike. The issue is quite unsettled at the moment of writing. Another view is, of course, inherent in the Novozhilov-Kantorovich approach: land, like other scarce factors of production, would have to be given the valuation which reflected its relative scarcity in relation to the 'programme' regardless of who cultivates it, and a rental charge made accordingly.

The same issue has arisen in some other sectors. For example, a big 'differential rent' should be charged on timber-cutting in the relatively tree-less areas, to encourage lumbering in the remoter forest areas, and, on similar logical grounds, prices of minerals should also include a 'differential rent' charge, or so some economists argue.[3] Others would reject the relevance of rent in these cases, and justify it in agriculture only by reason of the existence of *kolkhozy*.[4] The Nemchinov approach, like that of Novozhilov, clearly envisages the widespread use of the differential rent concept throughout the economy.

CAPITAL CHARGES: AMORTIZATION; INTEREST

The debate has also raged in respect of capital charges. Mixed up in it was the old argument that low prices for capital equipment encourage mechanization and growth, and that this is a 'superiority' of the Soviet over the Western system. Against this, Vaag remarked: 'From the standpoint of *economic calculation*, the boundaries of (rational) utilization of machinery *coincide*. The superiority of socialism over capitalism in no way consists of our ability to

[1] A systematic statement of his case is in *Vop. Ekon.*, No. 7/1960, pp. 81 ff.
[2] N. Tsagolov (ed.), *Zemel'naya renta v sotsialisticheskom sel'skom khozyaistve* (Moscow, 1959).
[3] For example, A. Kulikov, *Vop. Ekon.*, No. 9/1957, p. 80.
[4] A. Pashkov, in Tsagolov (ed.), op. cit., p. 256.

overspend capital investments without considering the economic effectiveness of their utilization.'[1] This view runs counter to the belief that in the USSR it is often profitable to use machinery where in capitalist countries such use would appear irrational, and the Vaag view may be regarded as unorthodox. However, many others advocate a charge for capital, i.e. not only adequate prices for equipment but also a payment by enterprises for the use of capital assets, as a means of encouraging economy in its use, without necessarily drawing such far-reaching conclusions. Clearly, so long as investment decisions are affected in any way by applications from below, the fact that investment appears to cost nothing to the recipients is a constant incitement to over-application, and there is failure to stimulate economy in use at the 'micro' level, even though planners may take a notional rate of return in capital into account when they take investment decisions.

The 'period of recoupment', discussed in chapter 7, is in essence, a measure of the return on invested capital, to which the term 'rate of interest' could be applied were it not for the ideological objections to its use in the Soviet economy. The increasing number of economists who desire to include a capital charge in costs have a number of different approaches. Some favour a charge essentially as a means of encouraging economy, to make capital no longer appear to be free to the recipient enterprises. It is for this reason that interest is charged on short-term credits, a fact which shows that the ideologists' objection to the use of an interest rate in the Soviet economy can be overcome by reference to precedent. On the same grounds, it is frequently argued that the larger part of enterprises' investment needs should be met by long-term (interest-bearing) bank credits, rather than by non-returnable grants. But such suggestions fail to provide any objective basis for the actual interest rate to be charged, just as there seems no rational explanation as to why 2 per cent is a reasonable rate to charge on short-term credits. Alternative approaches would base the charge on something objective: for instance, on the 'normative' rate of return on capital used in investment decisions, on the scale of the economy as a whole or of the given sector, or the relative scarcity of capital (in common with other assets) as this emerges from a linear programming calculation. All these ideas are intimately connected with investment criteria (chapter 7, pp. 209-17), price policy (this chapter, pp. 218-28), and the theory of value (chapter 11, pp. 271-86), and are discussed at

[1] *Vop. Ekon.*, No. 1/1960, p. 99.. His emphasis. For a contrary view, see A. Tolkachov, *Plan. Khoz.*, No. 12/1960.

these points of the book. It should be clear, however, that the present position is anything but satisfactory on either practical or theoretical grounds—which does not prevent some able Soviet economists from attacking even the apparently harmless notion that the return on its capital should be regarded as an essential measure of the profitability of an enterprise.[1]

Another aspect of capital charges concerns the relevance, and desirable magnitude, of the amortization (depreciation) fund. There was general agreement that this fund is too small in relation to production costs to encourage economy. Indeed, it has been too small in the purely technical term that real depreciation has been more rapid than the financial provision for it. For example, one critic cited figures to show the 'loss' in basic capital arising from inadequate depreciation allowances: for example, the total sums set aside for the amortization fund, plus the scrap value, covered only 62·3 per cent of the used-up capital assets in the food industry, the latter being valued at their original costs, and in some industries the 'losses' were even larger,[2] yet in many instances the original cost was below replacement cost. A revaluation of all capital assets was carried out in 1959; on this basis new amortization (depreciation) rates are being worked out in 1960. This does not satisfy some critics. One view is that amortization rates should in effect act as a capital charge, and be related to the investment requirements of the economy as a whole; the amortization charge would then be constant throughout the economy regardless of the actual depreciation of any given capital assets in this or that sector.[3] Another, more widespread, points to a major weakness in the use of amortization funds: too much is spent on capital repairs, when it would appear to be more rational to scrap the equipment and start anew. Often, according to these critics, repairs actually cost more than replacement would have cost.[4] On the fact of it, this is absurd, but it can have two explanations. One is simply that the replacement, though 'cheap', is not available, being in short supply—a situation which must frequently arise where prices do not reflect relative scarcities. The other is of a more bureaucratic character: it will be

[1] See, for example, the views of Y. Kronrod in *Vop. Ekon.*, No. 10/1960, pp. 83 ff.

[2] P. Bunich, in *Plan. Khoz.*, No. 5/1957, p. 51.

[3] Y. Kvasha, *Amortizatsia i sroki sluzhby osnovnykh fondov* (Moscow, 1959).

[4] For example, see A. Vladzievski and M. Yakobson, *Kommunist*, No. 9/1959, pp. 35 ff., and review of letters received on the subject in *Kommunist*, No. 12/1960, pp. 124-6.

recalled that the amortization fund is divided in two parts, that only the part earmarked for capital repairs remains in the hands of the enterprise, and this part must be used for capital repairs only. Consequently, even if a replacement were available at a relatively cheaper price, the enterprise may be unable to use for the purpose the funds which it has available, as these are limited to repairing old equipment. A change in these inflexible arrangements seems probable, involving a more explicit recognition of obsolescence, i.e. the fact that repairable but out-of-date machinery should be scrapped. This might also be reflected in higher amortization rates, which would follow from the presumption of a shorter working life of machinery.

WAGES: A 'DE FACTO' LABOUR MARKET

On the face of it, wages, like prices of materials and equipment, are determined by the state. In practice, it is hardly so, despite the fact that wage schedules are indeed laid down centrally. The reason is essentially that labour is human and mobile, in a sense in which inanimate factors of production are not. This apparently obvious fact requires stressing because many students of the USSR are victims of what I have called the 'totalitarian myth' and suppose that all Soviet citizens obey all the rules all the time. If they did, then many serious problems of wage determination would not arise. Yet they do arise, and did so even when the law barred change of occupation without permission.

We have seen in chapter 4 that wage and salary scales are centrally determined, and cannot normally be varied by any enterprise or local authority. However, wage scales, in all countries, are not by any means the same thing as actual wage payments. This is as true in Birmingham as it is in Kharkov, and for the same reason: because workers are frequently on piece rates, or receive various bonuses, overtime and other extra payments. In the USSR, these payments are regulated centrally: thus overtime is normally paid at time-and-a-half; piece rates are either 'straight' (proportionate to output), or 'progressive' (extra payments per piece over the norm). But the essential point is that the majority of workers in the USSR are on piece-rate payments of some kind, and inevitably the determining factor becomes the fixing of the piece rates, rather than the basic wage as such. True, in a formal sense the basic wage should be equal to the number of 'pieces' normally produced in the given period multiplied by the rate per piece. But despite a long catalogue of decrees and orders demanding an upward revision of norms (time-and-motion study—'scientific' norm-fixing—was supposed to be applied), norms averaged well below the output of the average worker, and overfulfilment of norms grew steadily in the postwar years. Thus in 1950 the average industrial worker overfulfilled his norm by 39 per cent, by the end of 1956 by 55 per cent. In some industries the overfulfilment was much greater than this; thus at the end of 1956 it was 96 per cent in the electro-technical industry, 92 per cent in heavy machinery, 81 per cent in the automobile industry.[1] In others it was less, of course. Note that none of these figures imply that either the output or the labour productivity plans were overfulfilled, since these were and are based not on norms but on actual performance in the preceding year or years.

All this had several consequences. One, as has already been pointed out, was a tendency for money wages to rise faster than planned. Another was to muddle inter-industry wage relativities. Some gained much more than others, in a quite unplanned way. Within a given industry, the effect of efforts to prevent wage increases was often unjust and irrational. For example, orders to increase norms were sometimes applied uniformly to all workers, with the result that, while those who were working with improved equipment found that they would still comfortably overfulfil their new norms, those engaged in hard physical labour were unable to reach the new standards, which led to hardship in the building industry, where many operations were not mechanized.[2] In some enterprises, to avoid such unfairness, orders to increase norms were obeyed, but the increases were then cancelled by so-called 'corrective coefficients', which brought wages back to customary levels.[3]

However, the situation was by no means merely one of confusion. In part, what was happening could be explained by the forces of the market, which corrected obsolete and unsuitable wage scales. The market elements were present because good workers (often *any* workers) were scarce, because labour could drift away despite any legal restrictions, and because, though limited by restrictions on its total wages fund, the management has some room for manœuvre. Let us now examine how things worked in practice.

Suppose an enterprise needed men in two occupations, rated respectively at 750 roubles and 500 roubles a month, and both were

[1] E. Kapustin, *Plan. Khoz.*, No. 7/1957, pp. 29-30.
[2] For details of this, and of changes designed to remove the anomaly, see *Stroitel'naya gazeta*, September 21, 1955.
[3] See, for instance, N. Bulganin, *Pravda*, July 17, 1955.

paid by piecework. Suppose further that the lower-paid job was difficult to fill. To attract workers into it, the management, unable to
increase the basic rate, offered an 'easy' norm, easier, in terms of
effort than other norms in that same enterprise. The real earnings of
the 500-rouble worker could then be higher than those whose basic
rates were 750 roubles; this example shows how the management, by
juggling with norms, can make correctives to the official wage relativities by reference to its own labour-market situation.[1] To some
extent, inter-industry and inter-area relativities were similarly
affected by market pressures, operating gradually over long periods
of time.

Another means of altering the rules while pretending to obey
them is artificial upgrading. Unskilled or semi-skilled labour was
extensively graded as skilled. This was particularly common among
time-workers, who were unable to benefit from 'easy' piece-rates.
Very few workers of any kind were to be found in the unskilled
grades of Soviet industry. Still another method was to 'invent'
bonuses, even, so it is alleged, for politeness and coming to work
sober.The motives were by no means illegitimate: the regulations, if
obeyed, would have involved impossibly low and irrational wage
scales, and so, as Bulganin correctly explained, the rates were
'adapted' to ensure the payment of whatever was regarded as the
proper wage.[2]

However, these substantial 'spontaneous' increases in money
wages could not benefit those on fixed pay, doing work which could
hardly qualify for real or simulated bonuses (though in some instances even they were given extras). Among them were white-collar
office staffs, civil servants, teachers, railway staffs, cleaners and the
like. They were left far behind. There were also a multitude of other
anomalies. These were tackled in instalments in the wage reforms of
1957-61, carried out under the aegis of the State Committee on
Labour and Wages. The reform was simultaneously concerned with
the reduction of hours of work, and with the implementation of a
minimum wages law which raised the very low pay of auxiliary and
unskilled labourers. New schedules were promulgated in various
industries. Basic rates were raised substantially, and so were work
norms; this was done in such a way as to correct excessive differentiation between occupations and skills, and brought earnings much

---

[1] The example given is not imaginary, but is based on actual figures obtained by the author in a factory in the Urals.
[2] Bulganin, op. cit., gave a useful account of many of these 'irregularities'.
See also E. Manevich, *Vop. Ekon.*, No. 1/1959, pp. 37-46.

closer to the (new) basic wages, and norms much closer to the amount of work actually done. Average wages were little affected, showing their usual tendency to rise slowly.

Undoubtedly, these reforms have eliminated some of the confusion which crept into the Soviet wage system. However, the problem remains: how is one to enforce centrally-determined wage scales, which cannot possibly reflect an ever-changing pattern of labour-market relations. It seems abundantly clear, from past experience, that even without free trade-union bargaining the market elements enter powerfully into the process of wage determination in practice. It remains the case that directors will manœuvre to obtain the necessary labour, the extent of their deviations from rules depending on the circumstances of the case: how far the rules are realistic, how far labour in general, or of a particular category, is in short supply, and so on. In some instances, rules which favour some types of workers lead to difficulties: for instance, juveniles (under 18) are entitled to longer holidays, shorter hours, study leave; consequently managers prefer to avoid employing juveniles. In others, managers must overpay, on some pretext or other, to get labour at all. The same is now occurring in those *kolkhozy* which have gone over to fixed money payments. A job which is to be done by five peasants may be 'rated' at 500 roubles by the *kolkhoz* management, but the men may declare that they want 600 or 700 roubles instead; what then? Such cases actually exist.

Wages will therefore remain a sector of the economy in which planning is only very partially effective, either in terms of allocation (direction) or in terms of price (wages). Indeed, save in the unrealistic situation of all-round labour direction backed by military discipline, wages must be influenced by the labour market, though the authorities do exercise some influence on supply by training schemes, organized recruitment or migration, direction of students on completion of their courses, and so on. Either this will be in defiance of the formal regulations, or it will be found necessary to amend the regulations (usually *ex post factum*) to take the market realities into account. Of course this generalization applies more to some categories of labour than to others. In the USSR, as also in many Western countries, it is relatively easier to control salaries of white-collar staffs, and consequently their relative position tends to decline in comparison with industrial workers. It is an interesting and worth-while exercise to compare the social consequences of this in East and West. In both, the office staffs have lost ground, and, in both, the status of the foreman has been adversely affected by the fact that he often earns less than do skilled men working under him.[1] The many similarities of development of wages structures, in countries with such different systems of wage determination, suggest common influences.

Quite recently, a new problem, familiar in the West, has emerged in the USSR: that of unemployment, virtually unknown in the towns since 1930. It is never discussed under that name, since unemployment as such does not exist in Soviet statistics. It arises in several ways. One is an aspect of the location of new industries; these are seldom built in or near big cities in European Russia, but young people reach working age in these cities and have inadequate avenues of employment there. This raises the problem of so-called *trudoustroistvo*, or placing at work, rendered difficult by the virtual absence of labour exchanges (or of course of any private-enterprise employment agencies) and by the fact that employment in new projects in the east is often blocked by shortage of housing and also sometimes hindered by unwillingness to go. A second category is explicable by overproduction of some commodity, in an area where alternative occupations are few.[2] Another, familiar in some Western countries, is the difficulty of finding work for women in districts where heavy industry employs largely men; this arises increasingly because women are being freed from unsuitable work, e.g. in coal mining, for instance in the Kuzbas. Finally, there are the consequences of automation, referred to several times as a social problem of surplus labour in the given area.[3] It is hardly necessary to add that, as in most countries where there is a numerous peasantry, seasonal unemployment has long been a problem in agriculture. Indeed, with *kolkhozy* there was (to some extent still is) a considerable labour surplus, which helps to explain the wasteful methods of labour utilization typical of *kolkhozy*. One way in which seasonal slack is being taken up is by the development of inter-*kolkhoz* industrial activities, referred to in chapter 1.

Needless to say, the West has no claim to having any magic formula for the solution of the problems of labour relations and wage relativities. But neither has the existence of wide central powers over wages in the USSR eliminated the difficulties inherent in trying to deal with millions of human beings at their work.

[1] Oil is mentioned in this context by Panfyorov, in his semi-fictional tale, 'Vo imya molodovo' (*Oktyabr*, No. 7/1960).
[2] On this type of anomaly, see N. Maslova, *Vop. Ekon.*, No. 12/1960, p. 51.
[3] See Panfyorov, op. cit., and also A. Khavin, *Novyi Mir.*, July, 1960.

CHAPTER 9

Trends Towards Reform

REFORM IS IN THE AIR

This book is in imminent danger of being out of date, in its description of structure, by reason of constant efforts to overcome problems by reforms and amendments of existing arrangements. Some of these changes are being actively discussed, others have been tried out in smaller countries of the Soviet bloc. In any case, it is of evident interest to see how far, within the basic pattern of Soviet-style economies, various reforms can overcome the difficulties which we have been analysing in earlier chapters. While there can be no sound basis for prophesying the course of future reforms, at least it should be possible to indicate likely trends; the observant student should have been able to identify some major causes of such reforms. When they come, their precise shape will doubtless be affected, as were the *sovnarkhoz* reforms of 1957, by political factors and personal ambition. But it would be misleading to regard these factors as determinants, just as it would be misleading to ignore them altogether. No doubt when, in 1932, VSNKh was abolished, it could have been viewed as a blow against the then head of VSNKh, Ordzhonikidze. Indeed, perhaps it was. However, on a long-term view we would hardly regard this as the fundamental explanation, and would be right to emphasize the less personal elements in the chain of causation.

WHAT IS TO BE DONE?

In the USSR, a variety of proposals have been put forward. Some are of quite moderate character, requiring little change of system. Thus it is generally agreed that price illogicalities should be eliminated as far as possible. Some economists have urged amendments in the success indicator system: to measure output in net and not gross terms,[1] or to plan sales and not output, to establish targets for several years ahead, to reduce the number of detailed indicators, to devise a composite indicator of efficiency. Numerous examples of

---

[1] This has been recommended for most industrial goods by a national conference reported in *Plan. Khoz.*, No. 5/1961.

proposals on these lines have appeared in recent years. To take just one instance, Liberman urged that each enterprise should have a 'long-term economic perspective' on which it could rely, for five to seven years ahead, in terms of which its efficiency should be measured; such objective criteria of efficiency should be, in his view, output relatively to basic and working capital, labour productivity and profitability.[1] Only in this way would enterprises be able to consider long-term development, be guarded against ever-changing plan indicators and the distortions which arise from striving to fulfil them.

Many economists have urged that an increasing role be granted to commercial relations and the profit motive. Gatovski, the influential editor of *Voprosy Ekonomiki*, repeatedly made this point, speaking of an increasing role of 'price, costs, profits, etc.', at the expense of 'purely administrative methods of control from above'.[2] He argued that 'mechanical allocation of output' should, through 'the development and perfection of trading methods' be based increasingly on 'commercial agreements directly negotiated between enterprises'. This will ensure 'the influence of the demands of the purchasers on the production programmes of the suppliers'.[3] Many others have argued on similar lines. In particular, they have concentrated their attention on the clumsy and bureaucratic system of material allocation. Nemchinov has argued for 'the gradual conversion of material allocations into state trade', with enterprises buying their supplies as required from wholesalers.[4]

They have been less clear about the practical steps to be taken. The bulk of the critics accept the present basis of planning, including the centralization of major decisions on material allocation. Their proposals would involve a much wider range of 'microdecisions' at enterprise level, a big extension of commercial purchasing of materials and components which are not acutely scarce, a substantial reduction in detailed allocation. Assuming less rigid, less 'tight' planning, there is indeed no reason why materials should not be freely obtainable at regional dumps maintained either by republican disposals departments or by *sovnarkhozy*. For example, the economist Razumov urged that ordinary supply and disposal problems be handled between producing and user enterprises, and that this would 'make superfluous the annual allocation of a significant portion of industrial production. The disposal of most

---

[1] *Kommunist*, No. 1/1959, pp. 90-1   [2] Ibid., p. 71.
[3] *Voprosy stroitel'stva kommunizma v SSSR* (Moscow, 1959), p. 146.
[4] *Vop. Ekon.*, No. 12/1960, p. 99.

products intended for other factories will be determined by direct links between them. Supply and disposals organizations will distribute only that part of industrial production intended for capital construction and replacement of basic funds, for external and internal trade, for the creation of state reserves, etc.' The author argues that, by eliminating the time-wasting procedure of bureaucratic allocation, and making possible direct and long-term agreements about quantities and specifications, greater efficiency can be achieved.[1] Evidence quoted at some length in Chapter 7, above, certainly supports this view. The case for such a reform is so strong that a substantial move in this direction, with some exceptions for particularly scarce commodities, seems highly probable. It has already been made in the case of supplies to agricultural enterprises.

Similarly, we must expect a move in the direction of a closer economic link between consumer demand and the production of consumers' goods. A probable line of approach was indicated in a *Pravda* editorial: 'The plans of enterprises engaged in production of consumers' goods will be confirmed on the basis of orders by trading organizations and contracts made with them. Trading organs are forbidden to accept goods if the assortment, quality, pattern, do not conform to the orders placed . . .'[2] If plans were in fact based on contracts, it would mean that factories would not be tempted to produce goods which trading organs do not require, merely in order to 'fit' into plan fulfilment indicators, as is the case frequently at present. If selling became more difficult, if prices were such as to eliminate queues and therefore also the chronic seller's-market situation, no doubt the requirements of the consumers would have a greater influence on what is produced. In this connection it is apparently intended to create adequate stocks of goods at the wholesale level, from which retail stores can buy what their customers require; the wholesalers would pass on the appropriate orders, and changes in the demand pattern, to the manufacturers. All concerned are urged 'systematically to study consumer demand and changes in market trends (*konyunktura rynka*)'.[3]

The logic of all this demands that a growing importance be attached to profits, or, as many Soviet economists put it, a greater role for 'value' categories and *khozraschyot*. The fact that this calls for a major revision of the price system is understood, and revisions for both retail and wholesale prices are announced for 1961-62. How-

[1] *Vop. Ekon.*, No. 10/1960, pp. 18-20.   [2] *Pravda*, October 23, 1960.
[3] Leader in *Sovetskaya Torgovlya*, No. 9/1960, p. 6.

ever, there remain major disagreements about a proper basis for prices, both practical (see chapter 8) and theoretical (chapter 11), and it remains problematical whether the solution chosen will be a satisfactory guide for enterprise decisions. Yet this is a key aspect of any reform. Experience shows that some devolution of decision-making is a vital prerequisite for greater efficiency in general and that devolution to *regional* authorities carries with it serious dangers of 'localistic' irrationalities. Inter-enterprise ties typically cross regional borders, and it is at enterprise level that more rational micro-decisions must be expected to develop. The logic of events seems to point to prices which reflect relative scarcities and fluctuate with consumer demand, but there is as yet little sign that such a view of the price mechanism will actually be adopted by the planners, since it is too suggestive of the so-called anarchy of the free market. Apart from this semi-ideological objection, there is the more practical fear of giving enterprises a material interest in increasing prices, since many are in a semi-monopoly position and could use this position to affect adversely the interests of consumers and of the state. The solution actually adopted will almost certainly place upon state organs the duty of price-determination; it will be for them to decide the size and location of the carrot placed before the donkey, but it will be their duty so to 'arrange' the carrot as to persuade the donkey to pull in the desirable direction. Of course, this would be preferable to the present situation, when the material incentives at micro level often encourage the donkey to pull in the wrong direction. But all this is much easier said than done. Perhaps the Czech reforms, which will be described later in the present chapter, suggest the shape of things to come.

Greater reliance on enterprise initiative presupposes that a larger part of investments in enlarging or re-equipping existing enterprises will be financed by the enterprises themselves, either from profits or through long term (interest bearing) bank credits, and that they will have greater freedom to decide whether or how much to invest to meet the requirements of their customers. There is no reason why, in this respect, too, the Czech model should not be followed.

In this general context, there may well be a reduction in the already modest powers of *sovnarkhozy,* over the actual operation of enterprises. Another possible variant might be the grouping of similar enterprises within a region into a much strengthened sector department, perhaps analogous to a 'trust' or *kombinat*, in the interests of sharing out orders or materials, with the *sovnarkhoz* as a local planning agency and co-ordinator, perhaps linked more directly—

as some *oblast'* officials urge—with the *oblast'* soviet. Of course, there could be a contrary tendency, if the political authorities regarded local self sufficiency as a desirable aim, for example, for strategic reasons. These, and shortage of transport facilities, may well explain the emphasis given to regional and local economic bodies in China.

In agriculture, the granting of greater powers to reformed *kolkhozy* and *sovkhozy*, a reduction in the still very prevalent arbitrary interferences from *oblast'* party and other officials, is much overdue. Gradually, party control over everyday farming activities should come to be no more severe than is the case in industry. Indeed, it is already so in *sovkhozy*. The long standing tradition of treating *kolkhozy* so very differently in this respect will surely wither away, as the management of the enlarged *kolkhozy* becomes both politically reliable and well qualified, and as the internal organization of the *kolkhozy* comes to resemble *sovkhozy* more closely.[1] The shift towards regular 'wage' payments to *kolkhoz* peasants must surely proceed at an accelerating pace. A revision of prices, accompanied by some form of more or less disguised payment of land rent, should increase the role of economic forces as determinants of farming decisions, though state procurements for essential purposes will doubtless continue to be compulsory. Any move towards a more flexible structure must depend, however, on improvements in production, since otherwise the party and state organs are all too likely to continue their present practice of interfering, to ensure that their needs are met.

All the above are reforms which would leave the foundations of the system more or less intact, but which, by injecting greater elements of flexibility and by encouraging the right kind of local initiative, would make the system work better. In a somewhat different category are the ideas of Kantorovich and Novozhilov. It is true that, in advocating the application of linear programming, these two economists are not challenging the existence of a centralized planning system. On the contrary, it can be argued, and in fact is argued by them, that only a system of the Soviet type, in which the ends to be served by the economy can be defined by the supreme political authority, provides the opportunity to apply modern econometric techniques on a nation-wide scale. Indeed, the electronic computer could be regarded as an alternative to an otherwise unavoidable de-

---

[1] It is true that the central committee plenum of January, 1961, and Khrushchev's personal habit of interfering in farming via the party secretaries, are evidence of a contrary trend. However, many voices are raised for more autonomy for farms, even in *Pravda* (for instance, P. Prozorov, January 6, 1961.

centralization, as a unique means of preserving centralized planning. It is also claimed, and Novozhilov in particular makes this point, that the pattern which underlies the linear programming approach is consistent with the granting of a wide degree of autonomy to local bodies and enterprises.

However, while econometric techniques will certainly be used increasingly in Soviet planning, the more far-reaching reforms advocated by the Novozhilov-Kantorovich school are not so likely to be accepted. The controversies around their concepts of value and prices, and the related ones of Nemchinov, will be discussed in chapter 11.

THE PARTY'S ATTITUDES

It is necessary to mention one significant obstacle to major reforms which enlarge the area of economic 'automatism' and restrict the range of decisions of administrative and party organs. This is the self interest of the many party officials and administrators whose present functions consist precisely in replacing the automatic functioning of economic forces. It is true that any conceivable reform of the Soviet economy would leave much to be settled by the central political authorities. For example, general questions of investment policy, the setting up of new enterprises, the provision of investment funds for new or rapidly growing industries, long term development plans, the drafting and amendment of the legal framework within which economic bodies operate, would certainly belong to the centre, and would keep the political leadership fully employed. But the party and state machines at lower levels, especially in the localities, would lose many of their present functions. They are not likely to approve of such reforms, and ideologists reflecting their viewpoints will surely argue that economic forces must be subordinated to deliberate political decision, and that such subordination is an integral part of the transition 'from the realm of necessity to the realm of freedom'. Party tradition would be on their side. Some would hold that this would decide the issue, that party self-interest must overwhelm all other considerations, including those of economic rationality. This, however, is not necessarily the case, because the party has other objectives than control. It is seeking to transform the USSR into world's leading economic power. To achieve this aim it requires a more rational use of scarce resources, greater efficiency in planning and in production. It will doubtless seek to reconcile the achievement of greater efficiency with the pursuit of its narrow self-interest as a ruling group in society. But even this last phrase requires qualification, because 'the party' is not in fact the monolithic body which it claims to be. Within it, precisely because of its mono-poly of political power, there are divergent interests, and this ap-plies even to the narrow group of professional party functionaries: we have already seen that the enlargment of economic 'automatism' does not unduly threaten the power position of the central leader-ship, while adversely affecting *obkom* secretaries.

For all these reasons, the attitude of the party towards ideas of reform is ambivalent; certain proposals may be rejected on ideo-logical-political grounds, but others may have (albeit reluctantly) to be accepted if such acceptance is seen as the necessary price to be paid for a more efficacious pursuit of the aim of 'overtaking America'.

THE CZECH AND POLISH MODELS

Until after the death of Stalin, most countries in the Soviet bloc copied the Soviet organizational scheme down to the smallest detail. Since the special reasons which, for better or for worse, gave rise to the Soviet system of planning were unlikely to apply in all other countries, this gave rise to grievous and probably quite unnecessary errors and irrationalities. So it was hardly surprising to find that several of these countries began to experiment with new ideas once they were free to do so. It is worth studying these experiments not only because of their intrinsic interest, but because they may well serve as a guide to possible future changes in the USSR.

The Czech[1] reform took effect in 1958. It is impossible to describe in full here the many complex changes introduced at that date, and the outline provided below is necessarily incomplete and, through the omission of exceptions and qualifications, not altogether ac-curate.

Firstly, Czech enterprises were reorganized. Where possible, small units were organizationally amalgamated into single enterprises pro-ducing a given commodity. Where, as, for instance, in the textile in-dustry, there were many productive units, separate enterprises con-tinued to exist, and were grouped together into a species of trust responsible for the given product. These trusts are, essentially, unions of enterprises, run by the managements of the enterprises, and are not ministerial administrative bodies, such as were the *glavki* both in the USSR (before 1957) and in Czechslovakia. These trusts have the task of co-ordinating the plans, investments and supply arrangements of the constituent enterprises.

[1] For Czech read Czechoslovak throughout.

The current operations of enterprises and trusts should in principle be based on orders received from their customers, with whom they are free to establish long-term contractual relationships. The annual plans submitted to higher authority consist of agreements to deliver stated quantities, based on negotiations between the producing enterprise and its customers. The assortment and quality of goods thus depend on these negotiations. The allocation of products by *snab* and *sbyt* organs is abolished, save where a given material is particularly scarce. The plans which emerge from this process are submitted to the separate industrial ministries, which still exist (though the sector *glavki* within them are abolished), and to Gosplan. Their task is to ensure consistency with available material resources and with the long term development plan. Part of the demand for various products itself arises from this long term plan, since it is the basis of major investment decisions, involving the setting up of new enterprises or affecting the total balance of the economy. Ministries also carry reserve stocks, to provide for contingencies.

Gosplan drafts a long term (five and ten-year) plan which is concerned with the general lines of development, and with key targets for key industries. In conjunction with the ministries, it drafts the rules within which the enterprises function, 'slanting' the incentives so as to encourage the expansion of production where the long term plan envisages such expansion. However, it is not generally the task of the planning organs or ministries to decide output targets from above. Instead, enterprises are given a long term basis for their work. Far from discouraging directors (as did the former Czech system and does the Russian) from honestly stating their production possibilities, the incentive system gives preferential treatment to those who bid high, rather as does the scoring in contract bridge. Overfulfilment of output plans carries with it no particular advantage. Each enterprise has a long term (five year) set of incentive rules within which to work, differentiated according to its economic situation and the importance attached to the growth of the given sector of the economy. It knows in advance the proportion of its profits it can retain, the rules being so framed that the gain to the enterprise depends primarily on the increase in profits over the preceding period (not, be it noted, on planned or overplan profits). It is for the enterprise to decide, within broad limits, how to use its retained profits. It is encouraged to expand production, or to retool, to meet the requirements of its actual or potential customers. It is free to devote the money to increasing working capital or for investment, or to carry it over for use in subsequent years, as appears best in the circumstances. It may seek credits, long or short term, from the bank if its investment needs cannot be covered immediately out of profits. A substantial portion of the investment programme in fact now arises through the initiative of enterprises (and trusts), and the activities of a large part of the building and machinery industries consist of fulfilling these investment demands, by free contract. Subject to availabilities (e.g. of building materials or imported equipment), the enterprises do not require permission from above for taking decisions on investment within their sphere. The state budget is used to finance investments involving the creation of new enterprises under the long term plan, and to aid in the financing of development in sectors which is regards as essential. However, a very substantial portion of investment in Czechoslovakia is decentralized.

The enterprises are encouraged to achieve their results without taking on additional labour. Wages are related to labour productivity; a given increase in labour productivity over the previous year is followed by an increase in wages by a percentage. This percentage, which is always less than the increase in productivity, is differentiated between industries and is publicized in advance in the form of a table, so that all concerned are aware of the gain which would follow from any increase in labour productivity. The rules remain constant for at least five years. Here again, the basis of rewards is an increase over past performance, not the overfulfilment of a plan determined by higher authority. There is also a premium fund, based on a number of indicators adapted to the special problems and requirements of the given economic sector, but most particularly relating to increases in profits, with additional advantages to those enterprises which adopted ambitious profits plans, as distinct from those who overfulfilled a modest plan. Rewards are also given for the achievement of plans with the least increase in capital investments, so as to encourage economy in these. The premium fund is a source of bonuses for managerial personnel and of other incentive bonuses, payments of which are made according to rules which (to prevent abuses) must be confirmed by state authorities.

The Czech system is intended to create a direct connection between the financial position of the enterprise and its ability to fulfil the requirements of its customers. It eliminates the interest, which Soviet enterprises still have, in modest output and profit plans, it encourages high bids and long term aims on the part of enterprises by relating rewards to increases over the previous period, according to rules fixed for several years ahead. It gives much greater freedom to enterprises in the disposal of their financial resources. It goes far towards eliminating the incentive to produce goods no one wants, merely to fulfil output plans decided by higher authority. However, there is a potential weak spot in the system: prices are still determined by the state, and, in order to make the long term incentive system work, wholesale prices are in principle unchanged for five years at a time. This means that, even if all prices were rationally fixed in the first place, within a year or two there would be unequal changes in the demand pattern and in costs, making the production of some commodities irrationally more profitable than others which may be in greater demand.[1] The Czech economists are well aware of this problem. They expect to solve it partly through the strengthening of the role of the customer (i.e. the purchasing industrial or trading enterprise) on the assortment of production. Thus, even if armchairs become more profitable to produce than sofas, the furniture industry will be unable to dispose of armchairs beyond the requirements of the furniture shops, and only sales count towards plan fulfilment. There are also some other means of pressure, some economic, some quasi-political, by which erring enterprises which seek to use their monopoly position illegitimately can be brought to heel. Perhaps the problem is unlikely to be intolerable so long as acute shortages do not exist, but it remains a potential source of trouble. Indeed, when certain materials do run short, allocation schemes have on occasion to be reimposed, to enforce priorities. One can also envisage difficulties in reconciling the state's long term plans with the operational and investment activities of enterprises, and reconciling both with the foreign trade decisions which play so large a role in the economy of Czechoslovakia. Many complaints of *ad hoc* central intervention in the working of this system have appeared, suggesting that it is by no means as 'free' in reality as it appears to be on paper.

None the less, the Czech reform is a most interesting example of new thinking and reform of structure. Of course, in a relatively small country, the regional problems which figure so largely in the Soviet Union are much less acute; there are no *sovnarkhozy* to complicate matters. None the less, there are features in the Czech pattern which may well be adopted in the USSR at a not to distant date.[2]

---

[1] *Retail* prices, however, can be altered more frequently, by reference to supply and demand considerations, by varying turnover tax.

[2] A useful source on the Czech reforms, in their draft stage, is *Problemy nove soústavy planovani a finančovani československo prumyslu* (Praha, 1957), translated into Russian (fortunately for this author, who knows no Czech) in Moscow, 1959.

Polish discussions on economic reform are much better known in the West. This is due in large part to the eminence of the Polish economists concerned, many of whom—for example, Lange, Kalecki, Lipinski—have international reputations. The discussions have also been much more wide ranging in their implications than any others in the East, reflecting the freer intellectual atmosphere of Poland since 1956. Some, like Kurowski, have been advocating a virtually free market. Others, notably Professor Brus, while supporting the determination of prices by the state, have urged that these be marginal prices. While not going so far as this, a majority of the Polish Economic Council advocated, in 1957, relating Polish prices of basic materials to world market prices, and an industrial price structure which would reflect not average costs of the given industry but those of 'the class of high cost firms'. The same proposals involve the levying of an interest charge of fixed and working capital. Enterprises would then function autonomously, basing their output and supply plans primarily upon contracts with one another, as in Czechoslovakia. Reports have appeared in Poland of 'experimental enterprises', which are trying out the new ideas, but so far, despite much discussion, the reforms have gone less far than in Czechoslovakia. The reason seems to be that the state of Polish economy is much more strained, and consequently the government has felt unable to relax its controls over the allocation of materials and over the output programmes of enterprises.[1]

In Poland too the divisions (*glavki*) of the industrial ministries have been abolished, and enterprises in the same branch have been grouped together into a unit (*Kolegium dyrektorow*) which is expected simultaneously to represent the enterprises *vis-à-vis* the state and the state *vis-à-vis* the enterprises. It is consulted about price-fixing, and has some powers to redistribute investment and other funds within the industry.

During the events of 1956, Poland instituted 'Workers' councils', in an effort to give the workers the feeling that the enterprise is 'theirs'. Workers' councils as such exist only in Poland, among the countries of the Soviet bloc, but in practice their powers are now small, and they do not seem to be of any greater significance in the administration of industry than have the 'permanent production councils' in the USSR.

[1] My colleague, Dr Zauberman, holds that there is a law ('Zauberman's Law') that 'the state of the economy varies in inverse proportion to the eminence of the economists'. This law would seem to have its application to these two countries! For a valuable account of Polish developments, see J. M. Montias in *Value and Plan* (Grossman, ed.) (Berkeley, 1960).

Finally, Poland (and also Hungary) has gone perhaps further than any other eastern country in devising means of adapting mathematical techniques to the tasks of planning the economy. Input-output calculations, a variety of matrix techniques, the search for optimal programming conditions, these have been developed to fairly sophisticated levels, but, largely because of the difficulties facing Poland, actual changes in structure and planning techniques have not been as great as might be deduced from the scale of the discussions and of experimental work. Polish experience and expertise have a significant influence, in this field, on developments in the USSR.

Among other countries of the bloc, Hungary has moved a long distance along the 'Czech' road, but there is not the space to discuss here the quite considerable Hungarian post-1956 reforms. In east Germany a form of *sovnarkhoz* system was adopted, but this seems explicable not by geographic-organizational needs, but rather by the habit of Ulbricht and his colleagues to copy whatever the Russians do.

YUGOSLAVIA

The fascinating experiments in a 'socialist market economy' which have been conducted in Yugoslavia, especially after 1951, require a prolonged specialized study.[1] Here it will only be possible briefly to indicate the respects in which this method of running the economy differs from the Soviet and Czech models.

Firstly, Yugoslav state enterprises are much more independent. With few exceptions, they have no output plan, other than the one they themselves adopt. This is based on commercial considerations, i.e. the demands of the customers. The enterprises compete with one another, to an extent which is impossible in Czechoslovakia, let alone the USSR. This applies to wholesaling and retailing, as well as manufacturing enterprises. The overriding economic motive is profit.

Secondly, prices are much freer. In theory, they ought to be wholly free, so that a real market should operate. In practice, fears of inflation and a desire to peg the cost of living leads to the imposition of price maxima for many products. But this still leaves room for a good deal of price competition.

Thirdly, the bulk of the investment funds of enterprises are borrowed from the bank, which judges the various projects partly by reference to their profitability and partly in relation to state eco-

---

[1] For a useful description of the system, see *Economic Bulletin for Europe* (Geneva), vol. 10, No. 3 (1958), pp. 43 ff.

nomic policies and long-term plans. At one period, it was thought possible to 'auction' investment capital to the highest bidder (among enterprises), but this is no longer done. The state influences the pace of development by directing a large part of its revenues to accumulation, and the direction of development by issuing instructions to the bank about whom to give preference among the claimants for investment funds. A capital charge is made, and investment credits bear interest.

Fourthly, enterprises have financial and organizational links with the local authorities ('communes'), and also, though to a lesser extent, with the republic (Serbia, Croatia, etc.) in which they are situated. The local 'commune' nominates the directors of enterprises (though in Yugoslavia, as in the USSR, the Party plays a vital role in this process, as in many others).

Fifthly, the directors' powers are exercised with elected workers' councils, which, at least formally, are much more powerful within an enterprise than are similar bodies in Poland or the USSR. The state enterprise is supposed to be administered by its workers, and wage levels depend, within limits, on the profitability of the given enterprise. However, to avoid various distortions (e.g. the exploitation by the enterprises of a monopoly position, or excessive inequalities between workers in different factories) the state closely controls the ways in which enterprise revenues can be disposed of, itself taking the largest share of the net product, discouraging 'overpayment' of wages by various fiscal measures. This has had the unfortunate effect of greatly diminishing the interest of the workers in the financial success of 'their' enterprise.

Finally, the bulk of Yugoslav peasants are owners of their land. Collectives, tried out in the 'Stalinist' period, have been almost wholly disbanded. The peasants are free to decide what to grow, there are no compulsory delivery quotas of any kind. They may sell what they wish in the free market. However, all state enterprises (including shops) must buy through peasant co-operatives, at prices which are decided by the state, and this means that any peasants who cannot take their produce to a large city, or whose produce is of a kind of which state enterprises are the only major buyers (e.g. grapes, wheat), are virtually compelled to sell through co-operatives. However, since the peasants are free to decide what they grow, the state's powers in fixing prices are necessarily limited.

Soviet theoreticians attack the Yugoslav system, as the very incarnation of 'revisionism'. Certainly the role of the market mechanism, and the idea that enterprises are run by the workers who work in them, are contrary to current Soviet doctrine, but one suspects that heat is generated more by the political disagreements than by economic heresies as such; the more so as neither the market nor the workers' councils are as free in the real Yugoslavia as they are in the 'Yugoslav model'. But then, as we have had many occasions to note, in few countries does the actual economy correspond to the imagination of the model-builders.

PART III: CONCEPTS AND IDEAS

CHAPTER 10

Some Basic Concepts of Soviet Economics

It is now time to discuss concepts, theories. The fact that this is being done last is not intended to imply any opinion concerning the primacy of matter over mind, of material as against spiritual. It is simply that the concepts and ideas which Soviet economists use are hardly comprehensible unless the institutional framework and practical problems are discussed first. It is true, of course, that basic ideology of Marxism-Leninism exerts a powerful influence on structure and on policy decisions. However, a discussion on the philosophical basis of Soviet communism falls well outside the scope of the present work.

NATIONAL INCOME

The Soviet concept of national income is in line with the classical tradition, in distinguishing between 'productive' and 'unproductive' activities, only the former being considered as generating a real product. As in Adam Smith, civil servants, soldiers, teachers, doctors, 'opera singers and opera dancers', etc., are deemed to be unproductive. The national income therefore consists of the total value of the material product. In the USSR, this value is deemed to equal the sum of the final selling prices of material goods, net of all double counting and of amortization (depreciation) of fixed assets. Since final selling prices of many goods contain turnover tax, this means that such taxes are included in the national income, which becomes the equivalent of a species of 'net national material product at market prices'. (This definition is inexact, because there is only a very restricted sense in which prices reflect market relations, but the essential point is that factor costs are not used as a basis.)

251

The adoption of a dividing line between 'productive' and 'unproductive' involves some awkward demarcational problems. In the Soviet Union, though not in all other eastern countries, passenger transport and personal postal services are excluded from the national income, though several economists have protested that this is an illogical procedure, and some have urged that not only passenger transport but also 'commercial services' (e.g. baths, laundries) should be included in the national income, but so far in vain.[1] The present concept involves, among other things, the idea that a railway signalman is productive when he lets a freight train past his signalbox, but unproductive when he performs an identical action on the approach of a passenger train. Similarly, a typist at a factory is productive, but the girl in Gosplan who may type the letter in reply is unproductive, because a line has to be drawn between 'administration' and productive enterprises, and the two typists find themselves on opposite sides of the line. However, before adopting a supercilious attitude, Western economists would do well to recall some of their own difficulties. Thus there is the old but true story that, in the Western concept, a man diminishes the national income by marrying his cook. Our definitions have also been challenged, by Western economists among them by Simon Kuznets and J. L. Nicholson.[2] If anyone considers that our own concept is simple to apply in practice, let him study the ways by which British statisticians estimate the net product of banking and insurance. The Soviet definition has, in fact, one quite impressive argument in its favour: that international (and to some extent also inter-temporal) comparisons of aggregates of material goods, however imperfect they may be, have a sounder basis than any aggregates of services. The latter are generally deemed in the West to equal the reward of the service provider—e.g. the value of a teacher or a soldier is equal to his pay. But suppose, as is the case, a US soldier's or teacher's pay is many times higher than that of a Russian soldier or teacher? One might well ask: what conceivable bearing have such figures as these on the comparative 'volume' of educational or military services? Whereas, at least notionally, steel can be compared with steel, and tractors with tractors, with no more than the usual index

[1] For a more detailed analysis of this controversy, see A. Nove in *Soviet Studies* (Glasgow), January, 1955, pp. 247-80. For the practice in other eastern countries, see E. F. Jackson, 'Social Accounting in Eastern Europe', *Studies in Income and Wealth*, Series IV (London, 1955). Also V. Sobol' and S. Strumilin in *Vest. Stat.*, No. 4/1957, pp. 79, 85.
[2] See, respectively, *Economic Change* (New York, 1953), pp. 192 ff., and *Studies in Income and Wealth*, Series IV, pp. 145 ff.

number and physical comparability problems (though, alas, these are bad enough). It is important to note that the difference in incomes derived from services are in fact a measure not of the quantity or quality of the services, but of the productivity of the productive sectors. A little thought will show that this is so. Suppose that the material product—or more strictly the consumable material product—per head of population is four times greater in the United States than in Italy. Then, other things being equal, it is quite probable that an Italian hairdresser or civil servant will earn about a quarter of an American hairdresser or civil servant. In this respect, and perhaps others too, the use of the Soviet concept is more practicable and even possibly more logical than the West's. (However, for certain purposes, such as measuring resource allocation within a country, or the standard of living, the inclusion of services is often desirable.)

In the application of the Soviet concept to the national accounts of the USSR, there are several points which could cause confusion in the minds of the unwary. The first is that some services, in themselves unproductive, do in fact form part of the national income, by being rendered to a productive enterprise. The latter's net product is calculated by subtracting from the total value of its output the 'material' expenditure, and also depreciation. But this means that certain services are not subtracted and so remain in the net product. This would apply, for example, to the services of lawyers and engineering consultants, or to journeys by passenger train of employees on behalf of the enterprise, and also to interest payments on credits. Consequently, these and similar services find their way into the national income—but not, as in the West, under heading of legal, technical, banking or transport services, but as part of the net product of the 'productive' branch of the economy to which they have been rendered. This affects the comparability of, for instance, the net product of industry under the Western and Eastern definitions, though, in the West too, the handling of such services by statisticians often lacks logic. The same services rendered to individuals, or to 'unproductive' sectors (for instance, education) would not appear in the national income in the USSR.

A somewhat odd situation arises with trade. It was common for Soviet economists to stress, in respect of the capitalists, the wasteful and unproductive expenditures involved (e.g. advertising, 'speculation', etc.). However, the use of retail prices for national income purposes necessarily involves including the contribution of trade in the Soviet total. Some theorists consider that this is justified because the bulk of expenditures consist of genuine handling costs (e.g. packing, unpacking, sorting). Others are not too happy about this, and consider that not all of Soviet trade should be treated as 'productive'.[1] However, in practice it is so treated.

It may seem unclear to those accustomed to Western concepts how national accounts can be made up on the Soviet basis. Essentially, there is a two-fold process. The first step is to build up the total net product of the 'productive' sectors, being the value of goods produced during the year (plus or minus change in unfinished production). This material net product is divided between sectors of origin as follows, using the actual figures for 1959:

	Per cent of total
Industry	52·7
Agriculture	20·9
Construction	10·2
Transport and Communications	4·8
Others (Trade, Procurements, material supplies, etc.)	11·4
	100·0

Source: *N.Kh. 1959*, p. 78.

In Soviet practice, the national income—or net national product —is built up from the production side, by means of data concerning the activity of productive enterprises in the sectors listed above. It is, of course, equal to the sum of incomes generated in the process of production, i.e. to personal incomes of those engaged in the 'productive' sectors, plus profits and other portions of the net product (notably, under the Soviet definition, turnover tax) which form part of the final selling prices of material goods.

Then comes the second stage; the material product is redistributed. It is transferred, through the budget and by other means, to maintain the 'unproductive' sphere. For example, part of the values created in the footwear industry, which are absorbed by the budget through turnover tax and/or profits levy, is used to finance education, defence or administration, and so, *inter alia,* to pay those engaged in these 'unproductive' pursuits. Education 'generates' no national income (though, of course, part of the education budget is spent on material products, such as desks and books, which figure

[1] 'Buying' and 'selling' are in themselves regarded as unproductive. It is not clear whether free-market trade, which must be deemed to include a large element of 'speculation', is included as such in the national income.

in the net output of industry). But at the second stage, after redistribution, it becomes possible to say meaningfully that education expenditures constitute x per cent of the Soviet national income by use.[1] Western statisticians too use the term 'redistribution', to cover, for instance, social service payments by the state. However, the scale of redistribution is much smaller on the Western definition.

It is noteworthy that the total magnitude arrived at by applying the Soviet definition is not necessarily much smaller than the national income *at factor cost* in its Western concept, provided that the bulk of the 'unproductive' services are financed out of revenues derived from the productive sector. This is far from self-evident, and will be clarified by a simplified example. Suppose that the only appreciable 'services' were defence, education and health, and that these were wholly paid for out of turnover tax levied wholly on industry. Using imaginary figures, one could envisage the following:

Soviet definition		*Western definition*	
Industry	500	Industry (factor cost)	250
(of which, turnover tax)	(250)	Other productive sectors	300
Other productive sectors	300	State services*	250
TOTAL	800	TOTAL	800

* Defence, Education, Health, etc.

That this is not a wholly fantastic picture was shown in a calculation presented to a seminar at the London School of Economics by Professor Grdjić, of Belgrade; he showed that the national income of Yugoslavia comes to almost the same total by the two methods. Of course, if the 'western' calculation were in market prices, the total would be much higher. But it is wrong, in comparing a calculation in terms of factor cost with one in a Soviet definition, simply to add the value of services to the 'Soviet' total.

An interesting point to note is that, by long tradition, the Soviet statisticians include turnover tax in the net product of industry,

[1] For a useful detailed account of procedures, including their application to Western G.N.P. statistics, see M. Kolganov, *Natsional'nyi' dokhod* (Moscow, 1959). The G.N.P. of the United Kingdom was recalculated in detail into Soviet concepts by V. Kudrov, *Mirovaya ekonomika i mezhdunarodnye otnosheniya*, No. 6/1958, pp. 63 ff. See also A. Nove, U.S. national income à la russe, *Economica*, August, 1956, pp. 244 ff.

even if the turnover tax burden falls primarily on the peasant producers of food or materials, or if the actual payment is made by
wholesalers within the system of the ministry of trade. This undoubtedly leads to an overstatement, in terms of any economic reality, of
the contribution of Soviet industry to the national income, and
therefore to a relative understatement of that of other branches of
the economy.

In comparing the structure of the national income expressed in
the two definitions, we should be aware that the relative magnitudes
of personal consumption, investment and state-provided services will
look very different, as may be illustrated with imaginary figures
based on the above table, still assuming that state expenditure is
wholly on defence, education and health. One might then have the
following (figures imaginary):

Soviet definition		Western definition	
Consumption (at market prices)	600	Consumption (net of indirect taxes)	350
Investment	200	State services*	250
		Investment	200
Total	800	Total	800

* I am neglecting here the fact that part of the service expenditures
takes material forms, and is either consumed or invested as such.

Of course, the two totals are in fact usually unequal,[1] in the two
concepts, but this does not affect the fact that the separate appearance of (in this instance) state services in the breakdown sharply
diminishes the share of consumption in the total. This is one of the
reasons for the sharp contrast in the breakdown by use of the Soviet
national income as given in Soviet and in Western publications.[2]
Soviet statisticians commonly accuse their Western *confrères* of
'double counting', since they claim that the consumption of teachers
and soldiers is already included (as indeed it is) under the heading

[1] Particularly when direct taxes play an appreciable role, for then the expenditures of the state on services would not be financed through the prices of
goods. The same would be true if a high proportion of services were not paid
for by the state but, as in the United States, by individuals and corporations.
The figures in the Western 'factor cost' definition would be affected by a
change in the relative importance of direct and indirect taxation.
[2] Another is the relative 'inflation' of Soviet consumption by the inclusion
of turnover tax falling almost wholly on consumers' goods.

of consumption, and that it is misleading for these sums to appear again as representing the 'service' rendered by teaching or soldiering. To the Western statistician, there is no double counting, since he includes the value of the services of the teacher or soldier on both sides of the account—as a product on one side and as an income on the other. This is no place to argue again the pros and cons of the two approaches; the reader must merely be warned of some of the many differences which follow from their use. The question of the availability and reliability of Soviet national income indices is discussed in the Appendix.

A curious change in the Soviet words for 'national income' occurred around 1950. Before that date, the term used was *narodnyi dokhod*, the literal equivalent of the German *Volkseinkommen*. Then, as by a signal, everyone used the words *natsional'nyi dokhod*. Certain quite senior Soviet academics, including Strumilin, have been urging a return to *narodnyi dokhod*. No change of real meaning is involved, and the philosophical significance of the change, though it presumably exists, is certainly not obvious.

GROSS INDUSTRIAL OUTPUT

'Industry' (*promyshlennost'*) in the USSR includes all mining and manufactures, and excludes construction, which is regarded as a separate branch of the economy. It includes also the entire timber industry (except planting and looking after the trees), fisheries and all processing of agricultural products. The slaughter of livestock is regarded as an industrial, not an agricultural pursuit.

Figures on gross industrial output are the sum of the gross outputs of all industrial enterprises, whereas in the West the same designation relates to the output of industry with value-added weights. This affects not only the comparison of aggregate values—the use of the Soviet concept, which includes much double counting, will obviously give a much larger total—but, more important, it affects the index of industrial output.

There are two reasons for this. One is simply that the 'gross' weights used in the Soviet calculation give a disproportionate emphasis to highly fabricated products; in other words, relatively to a net weight calculation, a machine or a pair of shoes are relatively more 'important' in the index than the metal and the leather of which they are made, because the output values of machinery and footwear include the metal and the leather (and much else besides) entering into their manufacture. Clearly, this must have an influence on the index of growth. The second relevant factor is that the 'gross' total so calculated, and the index derived from it, is affected by the degree of vertical integration or disintegration. This follows from the practice of adding together the output of enterprises. If, for instance, the same enterprise makes both the tractor and all its components, then, in this respect, there is no double counting; only the values of the tractors appear in the gross output totals. But if it were decided to make these same components in a specialized enterprise which has a juridically separate existence, then they *and* the completed tractors would be counted, at their gross values, and consequently the total and the index would be increased, without there being any additional output in reality. Of course, the opposite could also happen, with opposite results (but, precisely because of these results, which would affect fulfilment of gross output plans, integration might be deliberately avoided).

The prices used for the purpose of gross industrial output indices are described as 'wholesale prices of the enterprise (i.e. excluding turnover tax).'[1] However, this does not mean that turnover tax is excluded altogether, since only the taxes levied on the products of the enterprise in question are omitted, whereas taxes already paid on materials used by that enterprise are 'in'. The vexed question of price comparison over time is closely related to that of the reliability and credibility of the official growth indices, and will be considered in the Appendix.

In calculating *net* industrial output, e.g. for national income purposes, double counting is eliminated, and with it the influence of turnover tax on weights *within* industry (turnover tax is added to the *total* net product of industry and thereby increases the weight of industry as a whole). No industrial index with net product weights is available for the USSR. However, some other countries have published calculations which enable comparisons to be made. Thus the volume of industrial output in Hungary is available as follows:

	(1949 = 100)		
	1955	*1956*	*1957*
Gross	271	247	276
Net	226	206	232

Source: Hungarian statistical handbook for 1958, (Vol. II, pp. 63–64).

For a critique of Soviet official figures, see Appendix.

[1] *N.Kh. 1959*, p. 831.

GROSS AGRICULTURAL PRODUCTION

Agricultural statistics have a number of peculiarities and complications. Gross output data represent not the total value of output of enterprises, as is the case for industry, but the total value of farm products. There is double counting; fodder grain, for instance, is included as such even though it is consumed by livestock, and this double counting occurs even if the fodder grain in question is consumed by animals on the same *kolkhoz* or *sovkhoz* on which it has been grown. Thus each and every agricultural product is measured in physical terms, valued at the appropriate price and added together. The result is in no sense a measure of the end product of agriculture.

The products of livestock slaughter are, as has been explained, deemed to be industrial. Agriculture produces not meat, therefore, but live-weight animals. However, other livestock products which do not involve slaughter, such as raw wool, milk and so on, are agricultural so long as they remain unprocessed. Gross agricultural output is also deemed to include any increase in the value of work done in connection with the following year's harvest (the equivalent of unfinished production) and work in connection with orchards or tea plantations which take many years to mature.

An important problem in valuing agricultural output concerns the large volume of unsold products, used on the farm or by peasants. Until 1960 the practice was to value the unsold portion of *kolkhoz* and private agriculture at 'average price of realization', i.e. at the average prices which *kolkhozy* and private individuals respectively obtained for their sales to the state and in the market.[1] *Sovkhozy* valued their unsold products at cost. In 1960 new rules were adopted, involving the valuation of *kolkhoz* produce at cost also.[2] The portion that is sold is (and was) valued at the price at which it is sold. Much of the information on details of product use, and also (notably in the private sector) on production, is obtained by sample survey.

An odd feature of agricultural output data down to 1958 was the inclusion in the statistics of the value of work done by the MTS as an additional, independent 'product' of agriculture. This quite gra-

[1] This means that, since private persons sold a larger proportion of their products at the high free-market prices, that their 'average prices' were higher than those of other categories. In fact, they included some elements of Trade.
[2] See useful detailed article by A. Vikhlyaev in *Vest. Stat.*, No. 10/1960, pp. 54 ff. Also on all these questions see A. Nove, 'Some Problems of Soviet Agricultural Statistics', in *Soviet Studies*, January, 1956, pp. 248 ff.

tuitous inflation of the total was attacked by several Soviet statisticians,[1] and disappeared with the disappearance of the MTS.

OTHER SECTORS

These present no especial conceptual problems, though, as in all
countries, there are some difficulties in defining boundary lines. The
gross 'output' of construction is the total value of building and installation work. It includes the value of building materials, excludes
that of the actual installations. Materials, fuel, etc., used up are excluded from any 'net' calculation. Similarly, the contribution of
trade is the total trade margin (gross); these margins less the materials, fuel, etc., used by the trade network (packing costs, lighting,
etc.) equal the net product. Transport and postal services are complicated by the somewhat artificial division between 'productive'
and 'unproductive', mentioned above; some rough estimates are
necessary in allocating common expenditures between these two
categories; but otherwise the same principles hold.

'GROSS SOCIAL PRODUCT'

This concept represents the sum of the *gross* outputs of all the
sectors, double counting and all. It is not to be confused with the
national income. The purpose of such a total as this may appear far
from obvious, but it exists, and a percentage breakdown by sectors
has appeared in a statistical compendium, alongside that of the
national income.[2]

PRODUCERS' GOODS AND CONSUMERS' GOODS

An essential feature of Marx's pattern of analysis is the division
of material production into two main 'departments', or 'sub-divisions' (*podrazdeleniya*), known as I and II. Department I includes
production of all goods which are to be used in the process of production. Department II covers goods for consumption. Both include
industrial and agricultural products. These categories are used in
analyses concerning the basic 'proportions' of the economy, and as
a means of relating these with growth.

[1] For instance, S. Strumilin, *Na putyakh postroeniya kommunizma* (Moscow, 1959), p. 53.
[2] *N.Kh. 1959*, p. 78. (Such a total is implied by the value figures of an input-
output table à la Leontief.)

More familiar, and much argued about, is the division of *industrial* production into group A (producers' goods) and group B (consumers' goods). Group A in its turn is sub-divided into A1 (producers' goods intended for making producers' goods, e.g. steel used in making machinery or machine tools), and A2 (producers' goods used for making consumers' goods, e.g. industrial sewing machines, leather for shoes). Many careless commentators suppose A and B to be identical respectively with 'heavy industry' and 'light industry', but this is not the case. Thus the entire machine building (engineering) industry is classed as 'heavy', but passenger cars and domestic refrigerators made by this industry are classed as B, along with such products of 'light' industry as clothing and shoes, while that part of the textile industry's output which consists of cloth for the clothing industry is included with A. In principle, it is the *use* of any unit of the given product which determines its category, which means that many products are to be found in both groups. For example, cloth sold direct to consumers, rather than to the clothing industry, is in B. Electrical power is A, except when used for domestic purposes, when it is B. In a number of instances, however, when the end use is not precisely known, or one category of use is obviously very much the largest, the product is included in A or B in accordance to its 'predominant end use'.[1]

The share of A in total industrial output has increased steadily. It was 39·5 per cent in 1928, and 71·8 per cent in 1959.[2] It is an essential feature of Soviet economic theory that this has to be so, that producers' goods output (A) must increase faster than consumers' goods output (B), and that, within A, A1 should increase faster than A2. This is said to be a necessary precondition to what is called 'extended reproduction' (*rasshirennoe vosproizvodstvo*). This last term means growth, in the sense of more than reproducing the assets used up in the process of production.

There is much misunderstanding in the West—and in the East—about this allegedly necessary priority (which is strictly concerned with the superior growth of department I as against department II, though the discussion generally seems to concentrate on A and B), and the question deserves closer examination.

The priority of A could be 'justified' in various ways. One of these is not strictly a theoretical argument at all. To a régime whose overriding aim is growth, an emphasis on producers' goods is an aspect

---

[1] For a useful and simple account of the A-B distinction, see Rumyantsev, op. cit., pp. 12-17.
[2] *N.Kh. 1959*, p. 149.

on the vital importance of investment, of the future as against present consumption. This is more than a matter of a propaganda theory; it is simultaneously an instruction to the planners about priorities, so that, in the event of a bottleneck, a shortage of goods wagons on the railways for instance, goods which are A (especially A1) are given preference over B. But there is also a serious economic case to be made, in three parts. One consists of the assertion that, if growth is to occur, A must, as a matter of economic and arithmetical fact, increase faster than B. The second emphasizes not just growth but also technical progress, the growing importance of machines and intermediate goods of all kinds; this argument is reminiscent of Western controversies about increases in the 'period of production', but it must also not be overlooked that A and B, like other Soviet industrial output aggregates, are 'gross' and therefore A grows relatively with any increase in production of intermediate goods in specialized enterprises, even if the goods concerned are ultimately used in the production of consumers' goods. Finally, it could be argued that, as the economy grows more mature, a larger relative amount of capital investment is used for replacement, and that for this reason an increasing share of investment goods (and therefore A) is needed to maintain a constant growth rate.

The A-B (or I-II) relationship is sometimes the subject of propagandist attack by the less well-informed Western critics, who overlook that the immediate result even of decisions to alleviate the lot of the citizen often takes the form of enlarging the output of 'A' goods, such as building materials for houses, water pipes for drainage, equipment for new shops and so on. Nor do such critics spend much effort on analyzing the not unimportant question of whether *in fact* (especially given the Soviet method of computation of industrial output), growth necessarily involves the superior growth of A; nor do they even inquire into the relative rates of increase of A and B in Western industrialized countries. On their part, Soviet economists generally adopt very crude lines of argument, using quotations from Marx and Lenin as 'proof'. This happened when, at the time of Malenkov's fall in 1955, it was considered politically necessary to denounce all theories which did not give due priority to A.[1] The economist A. Katz had put forward the view that a comparatively new trend towards economy of capital (i.e. 'a fall in the ex-

---

[1] See particularly the unsigned editorial in *Vop. Ekon.*, No. 1/1955, pp. 15 ff. On a slightly more sophisticated level, see a book devoted wholly to this subject, A. Pashkov, *Ekonomicheskii zakon preimushchestvennovo rosta proizvodstva sredstv proizvodstva* (Moscow, 1958).

penditure of basic capital per unit of production'), alters the picture; that, as a consequence, consumers' goods output could increase as fast or even faster as that of producers' goods without stopping growth; he was attacked in consequence.[1] The same general line of thought is developed by the otherwise orthodox Polish economist Bronislaw Minc, who also—understandably in the context of Poland—brought in international trade as a modifying factor. However, Soviet economists have attacked his ideas also.[2]

ACCUMULATION FUND AND CONSUMPTION FUND

Another means of dividing the national product is by reference to its use for consumption and for accumulation (investment). Clearly, this is an altogether different line of division to the one discussed above: for instance, an increase in stocks of shirts, which are consumers' goods, is accumulation.

The accumulation fund covers, in practice, very much the same area as a Western capital account: investment in fixed capital, plus increase (minus decrease) in reserves, stocks, etc. The rest of the national income is deemed to consist of the consumption fund, part of which is distributed in the form of personal incomes of 'productively' and 'unproductively' engaged citizens, and part is consumed in institutions of various kinds (e.g. feeding citizens in hospital, or in the army, and also the consumption within institutions of materials—for example, petrol in army vehicles, paper in government departments). It is customary in the USSR to make general statements to the effect that the accumulation fund is about quarter of the national income (in its Soviet definition) and the consumption fund correspondingly three-quarters. The relatively constant relationship of the two funds over a long period of time, during which investment (and the output of producers' goods) has tended to grow faster than consumption, is explicable in terms of changing price relationships: prices of producers' goods have tended to fall relatively to those of consumers' goods.

All this should be simple, but has been needlessly complicated by the assertions of some Soviet economists that the consumption fund is devoted wholly to the 'satisfaction of the personal and cultural requirements of the toilers', and that the remaining quarter of the

---

[1] Katz's ideas were deemed 'anti-Marxist' and were not published. They were summarized in a hostile spirit in *Vop. Ekon.*, No. 1/1955, p. 18.

[2] See B. Minc in *Ekonomista* (Warsaw), No. 5/1956, and in Russian, *Vop. Ekon.*, No. 12/1957, p. 63. The most detailed attempt at refutation is in Pashkov, op. cit., pp. 175-200.

national income covers not only accumulation but also 'other government and social requirements.'[1] If this were so, then the *material* expenditures on defence and administration would be in the accumulation fund, which is clearly nonsense—unless, of course, the consumption of petrol in army lorries and paper in government offices could be deemed to give personal or cultural satisfaction to the toilers. Clarification would present no difficulty if some detailed figures were available, concerning the composition of either of these 'funds'. Unfortunately, this is not so far the case. There is one precedent for treating defence expenditure in a category of its own: thus Voznesenski did so in his book on the war economy,[2] and Strumilin more recently advocated the use of a separate category for defence, which he grimly called 'annihiliation fund' (*fond istrebleniya*).[3] However, official doctrine so far remains wedded to a division into two 'funds' only; it is possible, in this context, that military weapons fall, in peace time, very largely into the accumulation fund by reason of being produced for stock, and increases in stocks may legitimately be considered to be accumulation, an increase in reserves.[4]

Many Western efforts at filling in the statistical gaps have been made, and the interested reader is referred to the bibliography. The shortcomings of various Soviet figures are discussed in the Appendix.

[1] For a full discussion of the many formulations and reformulations of this thought, see A. Nove in *Soviet Studies,* January, 1955, pp. 274-6. See also the wording used, deliberately ambiguous, in *Politicheskaya Ekonomiya*, 3rd revised edition (Moscow, 1959), p. 644, and also useful article by Y. Shnyrlin in *Vest. Stat.*, No. 12/1960, pp. 59-65.

[2] *Voyennaya ekonomika SSSR v period otechestvennoi voiny* (Moscow, 1948), p. 67. He gave, for 1940, the following: accumulation, 19 per cent, consumption, 74 per cent, defence, 7 per cent. Presumably the defence item refers to material expenditure only; soldiers' food, surely, is consumption.

[3] *Vop. Ekon.*, No. 7/1959, p. 128.

[4] In this connection, see A. Nove and A. Zauberman, *Soviet Studies*, October, 1959, pp. 197-8.

CHAPTER 11

Soviet Economics and Economic Laws

Economics has been concerned with exchange relationships, with markets, with the unregulated activities of many men. What, then, is the economics of socialism? One possible answer, for which there is quite considerable warrant in the socialist tradition, is that the 'economics of socialism' is a contradiction in terms, and that the necessary administrative planning functions do not fall under the definition of economics at all. Engels showed himself affected by this kind of reasoning. For him, 'the only value known in economics is the value of commodities. What are commodities? Products made in a society of private producers' . . . which 'enter into social use through exchange'. But from the moment when society enters into possession of the means of production, all these relationships change fundamentally. Social labour is no longer measured in money or value, but 'in its natural, adequate and absolute measure, *time* . . . People will be able to manage things very simply, without the intervention of the famous "value" '.[1] It is clear from the context that Engels was not denying the existence of economic problems under socialism. However, he certainly thought that people would manage without 'commodities', i.e. without goods which acquire exchange values in relationship to one another, to which the analytical apparatus which Marx and he erected would have any significant application. Quantitative decisions by planners, which relate the desires of the citizens to the labour time necessary for satisfying these desires, would be sufficient, and this would be a 'simple' process, once private ownership of the means of production was eliminated. If Engels envisaged a transition period in the course of which value categories remained in being, he managed to conceal the fact.

Following him, Plekhanov made many observations in a similar spirit. One finds the most completely 'liquidationist' attitude to economics in Bukharin's famous *Economics of the transition period*, which appeared as early as 1920. Its title alone showed that he was

[1] *Anti-Dühring* (Marxist-Leninist Library edition, London, 1936), pp. 339, 340.

not contemplating some far-off state of pure communism when he wrote the following:

'Political economy is a science . . . of the unorganized national economy. Only in a society where production has an anarchistic character, do laws of social life appear as "natural", "spontaneous" laws, independent of the will of individuals and groups, laws acting with the blind necessity of the law of gravity. Indeed, as soon as we deal with an organized national economy, all the basic "problems" of political economy, such as price, value, profit, etc., simply disappear. Here the relations between men are no longer expressed as "relations between things", for here the economy is regulated not by the blind forces of the market and competition, but by the consciously carried out *plan* . . . The end of capitalist and commodity society signifies the end of political economy.'[1]

This view presented not only Bukharin's own ideas. As late as 1943, the famous article in *Pod znamenem marksizma,* of which more in a moment, criticized those who, in their lecture courses, alleged that 'since with the liquidation of capitalism the laws peculiar to it have been abolished, then economic laws in the socialist economic system do not and cannot exist'.[2] Incidentally, the Russian language distinguishes more sharply than does English between 'economics' or 'economic' in their strict sense (*ekonomika, ekonomicheski*) and the same words in the more general sense of dealing with material resources, which in Russian can be rendered by *khozyaistvo.*[3] The phrase 'socialist economic system' in the above quotation makes use of this second word, thus avoiding any apparent contradiction.

Illusions about the imminent end of economics were largely shattered by the introduction of NEP in 1921. However, there was now no need even to discuss the awkward problem of the role of economic laws within the state sector, since the survival of money and value relationships could be all too easily attributed to the existence of a large private sector. The outstanding contribution to the economic thought of the period came from E. Preobrazhenski, but he concentrated most of all on the relationship between the private and state sectors, the pace at which the latter could grow at the expense of the former ('primitive socialist accumulation').

For Preobrazhenski too, economic theory as such is related to

[1] *Ekonomika perekhodnovo perioda* (Moscow, 1920). Translation cited from an excellent essay in 'The Origin of the Political Economy of Socialism', by Adam Kaufman, *Soviet Studies,* January, 1953, pp. 273 ff.
[2] *Pod znamenem marksizma,* Nos. 7-8, 1943, p. 65.
[3] Also in German there is *Ökonomie* and *Wirtschaft.*

commodity production, i.e. is conditional upon the existence of private ownership. The 'science of collectively organized production' would replace 'the theory of political economy'.[1]

Such discussions were interrupted by the launching, in 1928, of the first of the five-year plans, which seemed in themselves to be proof of the primacy of governmental decision over real or alleged economic laws. The slogan 'there is no fortress the Bolsneviks cannot take' was widely used, the advice of cautious economists being widely disregarded. While planners and political leaders struggled with the crises and bottlenecks associated with the 'crash programmes' of the period, economics has little to say. No general textbook of economics appeared between 1928 and 1954, and indeed for several years it was found necessary to stop teaching 'political economy' in higher educational institutions.[2] This was a period of Soviet intellectual history when, to put it mildly, it was unhealthy for men to express critical ideas, and economic policy was so intensely 'political' that it was perhaps not surprising that men hesitated before developing theories which could be regarded as, by implication, providing objective criteria against which to judge official policy. Symbolic of the 'liquidationist' trend, coming logically enough during the first five-year plan, which most drastically disregarded 'normal' economic criteria, was the elimination of the word 'statistics' from the name of the Central Statistical Office. In 1931 it was renamed Central Office of National Economic (*narodno-khozyaistvennovo*) accounting, known by its initial Russian letters as TSUNKhU, because 'statistics' was regarded as a word suggestive of the measurement of random, haphazard events, and therefore unsuitable for a planned economy.

In 1941, the name was changed back to Central Statistical Office, and this was a sign of a return to a more realistic approach. There is some evidence to show that the need for a new 'socialist economics' was felt by the authorities, since they too needed objective criteria if expensive errors were to be avoided. The period of 'hurrah planning'[3] was coming to an end. A new textbook was known to

---

[1] *Novaya ekonomika* (Moscow, 1926), p. 19.

[2] The cessation of teaching is referred to in *Pod znamenem marksizma*, Nos. 7-8 (1943, p. 56). The last textbook before 1954 was by I. Lapidus and K. Ostrovityanov, published in 1928. Then came *Politicheskaya ekonomiya, uchebnik* (1st edition, Moscow, 1954). I do not mention books devoted to tearing apart Western 'bourgeois' economics, which were fairly numerous, but irrelevant to the 'economics of socialism', or the very large number of books and articles on this or that actual problem of economic structure or policy.

[3] The term is borrowed from Dr Jasny, who used it to describe the early five-year plans.

have been in draft in 1941. The war interrupted the process, but in the very middle of the war there appeared an unsigned article in a very influential party journal, thought to have been written by Stalin, which was directly concerned with 'the law of value' in the Soviet system.[1] Here, as in other discussions, the law of value must be seen not as a term of abstract analysis, but as expressing the role of exchange relationships and of the entire body of associated economic phenomena (prices, profits, etc.) in society. Or, to put things another way, discussion of the role of the 'law of value' invariably involves the importance of economic laws in general *vis-à-vis* administrative decision based on political considerations.

The author of the article (Stalin?) began by referring to a central committee directive to create a textbook ('short course') of political economy. He vigorously criticized the liquidationists. 'To deny the existence of economic laws under socialism means sliding down to vulgar voluntarism, which consists in the substitution of arbitrariness, accident, chaos, for the orderly (objectively determined, *zakonomernyi*) process of development of production' (p. 65). The author sought economic laws, and found them, or rather their expression, in industrialization, collectivization, planning, distribution of income according to work performed. This was dangerously near to equating economic laws and what the Soviet régime actually does, or has done, of which other instances will be cited. But Stalin, if Stalin this was, was looking for a 'criterion for the correctness of this or that line, this or that policy' (p. 65). Therefore, he was driven to restore the 'law of value' to Soviet economics. By carefully selected quotations from the Marxian classics, he endeavoured to make this appear orthodox. He deduced the survival of the law of value from the fact that labour is not paid an equal sum for each hour of work, that it is paid in money, that purchase and sale occur, that money is used. He treated goods, apparently all goods, produced under these conditions as 'commodities' (*tovary*), which enter into exchange. Therefore, the law of value applies—but, because its operation is restricted, because it cannot affect the distribution of resources within the state sector or the production programme of state enterprises, it applies only to a limited extent, 'in a transformed form' (p. 75). This was not very clear, or satisfactory, but became the basis of subsequent formulations until shortly before Stalin's death.

There the matter rested until 1951. In the interim, Voznesenski had expressed some harmless-sounding theoretical views in his book on the war economy, and was shortly afterwards shot. While he was

[1] *Pod znamenem marksizma*, already cited.

not—as far as is known—shot for his economic theories, a number of economists who had praised him had hastily to apologize, and the entire episode scarcely encouraged the profession to use its intellectual initiative.

In 1951, Stalin himself took a hand in a discussion around a new economics textbook. His contributions to the discussion were published in 1952, under the title of *Economic problems of socialism*. It proved to be his last work.

Although, as we shall see, he had much to say about the law of value, in two respects Stalin reflected the 'liquidationist' tradition. Firstly, he confined the said law virtually to the uncontrolled portions of the economy, and, secondly, he drew a sharp distinction between economic theory and the actual problems of planning. In a violent attack on a certain Yaroshenko, whom, paradoxically enough, he accused of a Bukharinist liquidation of the political economy of socialism, Stalin wrote: 'the problems of rational organization of productive forces, the planning of the national economy, etc., are not the subject of political economy, but the subject of economic policy of the directing (i.e. political) organs'.[1]

Stalin's most interesting contribution was an attack on the formulation concerning the functioning of the 'law of value in transformed form', of which he himself was thought to have been the author and which had been obligatory for all economists. The law of value, and economic laws in general, cannot be 'transformed', he asserted. They exist, independently of the minds of men. The law of value applies to all transactions within the Soviet system in which purchase and sale takes place, i.e. in sales by co-operatives (especially *kolkhozy*) and peasants to the state, by them and by state retailing enterprises to the citizen, and also in foreign trade. In these cases, change of ownership occurs and such goods are 'commodities' in the Marxist sense. If their relative prices are fixed wrong, it affects production; thus (to cite the example he gave) an excessively high price for bread grains in relation to cotton would have discouraged the output of cotton by *kolkhozy*. However, goods circulating within the state sector, i.e. the bulk of producers' goods, are produced and transferred according to plan, without changes of ownership. Such goods are not 'commodities', are not as such subject to the law of value. Of course, they are transferred at a price, money does change hands, and such prices do indeed serve the valuable function of accountancy, efficiency check and so on. In that sense, value categories are relevant to the producers' goods sector. However, the influence of

[1] Stalin, op. cit., p. 72.

the law of value is substantially restricted under the Soviet system.

Stalin explained the need for a reassertion of the validity of economic laws by the danger of overconfidence of young cadres, who, 'overwhelmed by the colossal achievement of the Soviet régime . . . come to imagine that the Soviet régime can "do anything" '.[1] He sought, as in 1943, to provide criteria, to emphasize the objective limitations of policy. He gave special emphasis to the relationship of state economic policy to those uncontrolled or semi-controlled sectors where plans did not determine the behaviour of men, i.e. to the relationships between state organs and, essentially, peasants as producers, and the citizenry as a whole as buyers of consumers' goods. There, evidently, a wrong handling of exchange relationships was liable to lead to positive harm, and here arbitrariness was to be avoided by emphasizing the objective essence of the law of value and the 'commodity' nature of the goods concerned. But he failed to find an objective definition by which actual exchange relationships could be judged, and in his anxiety to assert that state planning decisions (especially about investment), are not guided by considerations of profitability, he had to take the producers' goods sector out of the class of 'commodities', and therefore legitimized a high degree of arbitrariness in price fixing and in investment decisions within the state sector.

THE POST-STALIN REVIVAL OF ECONOMICS

The economics textbook finally appeared after Stalin's death, but with his ideas incorporated in it. Its inadequacy was all too apparent. Even more apparent was the failure of the economics profession to advance new theoretical ideas. In 1955, a clarion call was sounded by the then director of the Institute of Economics, V. Dyachenko. 'Until recently, dogmatism and scholasticism (*nachyotnichestvo*) showed itself quite openly in quotationism. Instead of independent and deep economic research, the authors of many works busied themselves with a selection of, and commentary on, quotations. Facts were selected and presented merely to illustrate and to confirm the assertions contained in the quotations. Matters went so far that the number of quotations was regarded as an indication of the author's erudition. An economist who found a quotation which had not been used many times in the works of other economists considered himself a creative researcher. After serious criticism of dogmatism and scholasticism in the party press, quotationism dim-

[1] Stalin, op. cit., p. 10.

inished, but only on the surface. In many instances matters went no further than the omission of quotation marks, editorial redrafting of the quotations, but in essence things remained unchanged.'[1] He went on: 'The elaboration of key problems of political economy is most backward. For many years not a single solid theoretical work in this field has been published.' And, even more significantly: 'Since the economic discussions of 1951, it has become customary in every work to refer to the objective character of economic laws of socialism, yet not a single work thoroughly examines in what the objective character of this or that law finds expression, how its requirement shows itself, in what respect and how breaches of these requirements can be identified.'[2]

Thereafter a wide ranging discussion developed concerning the nature of economic laws in the USSR, concentrating above all on law of value and 'commodity' production. This discussion is still going on, and in the interests of clarity and brevity only the main propositions of the various protagonists will be set out here.

THE LAW OF VALUE: DOES IT APPLY, AND, IF SO, WHY?

After a growing volume of discussion during 1956, a conference on the law of value was held, and reported early in 1957.[3] This opened the flood gates wide. At this conference, the majority held that Stalin had been wrong in confining the law of value and the designation 'commodity' to consumers' goods and the products of co-operatives, that goods circulating within the state sector were also commodities, and that the law of value had general application throughout the economy. This remains the dominant view. True, minority voices emerged, which repeated Stalin's argument, and, it must be admitted, not without some logic on their side. Those who denied that such goods were 'commodities' generally took for granted the need for objectively determined prices, but held that this need should not rest upon a false identification of these goods with 'commodities' in the Marxian sense. Indeed, one of those who hold this view, Malyshev, has gone further and denied that *any* goods in the USSR are 'commodities', and that the only sense in which the theory of value applies is that there is need to measure and economize social labour, i.e. a sense in which it would continue to apply

[1] *Vop. Ekon.*, No. 10/1955, pp. 3-4. Quotations, of course, were from the holy writ of Marx-Engels-Lenin-Stalin.
[2] Ibid., pp. 6, 8.   [3] *Vop. Ekon.*, No. 2/1957, pp. 71 ff.

even in the fullest and most perfect form of communist society. Yet this same Malyshev is an ardent supporter of pricing based on rational criteria.[1] One scholar even advanced the view that under socialism products have 'value' but yet are not 'commodities'.[2]

However, these are minority views. The majority accept the arguments of Ostrovityanov, Gatovski and Kronrod to the effect that 'commodity' relations do exist in the USSR, that they extend into the state sector, that these relations, and therefore the 'law of value', relate to producers' goods made and used by state enterprises. The main case in favour of this proposition is essentially empirical: that the rational utilization of resources in general, and investment choices in particular, require that all goods be treated as commodities, and that therefore the law of value be deemed to apply to them. While agreeing thus far, some leading economists have come to blows over the 'scholastic' question of why, in theoretical terms, this should be so, and indeed their arguments do seem more convincing on the purely practical than on the Marxist theoretical plane. Ostrovityanov accounts for the survival of value relations primarily by the continued existence of two species of property, i.e. of the non-state sector, which, so to speak, permeates the rest of the economy with the value and commodity categories which it renders necessary. Kronrod, on the other hand, asserts that 'commodity production is inherent in socialist productive relations. It is not brought into them from outside'. In other words, the existence of *kolkhozy* and so on is not the determining factor, but inside the state sector the movement of goods between enterprises is a process of commodity exchange, intimately connected with the necessity to pay the workers unequal sums of money wages.[3]

THE REAL CONTENT OF THE LAW OF VALUE

While the question discussed above could be regarded as an exercise in arid scholasticism, the problem of giving practical content in the Soviet setting to value and value relationships is clearly a matter involving fundamental economic policy. In particular, as we have seen in chapter 8 above, the correctness or otherwise of value concepts is intimately connected with the discovery of objective

---

[1] Examples of such views may be found in the contribution of N. Khessin, in *Zakon Stoimosti* (Tsagolov), pp. 50 ff., and I. Malyshev, *Obshchestvennyi uchet truda i tsena pri sotsializme* (Moscow, 1960).

[2] I. Kozodoev, *Zakon Stoimosti* (Tsagolov), pp. 15 ff.

[3] Both these views are fully argued in *Zakon Stoimosti* (Kronrod), pp. 7-30, pp. 133-67. On the same subject, see K. Ostrovityanov, A. Pashkov, V. Cherkovets, I. Kozodoev, A. Tsagolov, all in *Zakon Stoimosti* (Tsagolov).

criteria tor prices. If the term 'value' is to have any meaning at all, then the value of commodities in relation to one another must represent some real measure of relative cost. The latter must, in turn, find some expression in terms of socially necessary labour power, so as to fit into the framework of Marxian orthodoxy. The Marxian labour theory of value presupposes that labour alone is the source of value, and that value is equal to $c+v+m$ (or s) which stand respectively for constant capital (i.e. goods used up in the process of production), variable capital (reward of labour) and *mehrwert* (surplus value). The term 'surplus value' is usually rendered by Soviet economists as 'surplus product' when it is applied to the USSR, to avoid the implication of exploitation. Stalin urged that 'surplus product' be replaced by some more suitable term,[1] and some economists took to referring to v and m as respectively 'product for self' and 'product for society'. However, the designation used does not alter the problem, which is to identify some objective measurement of real values, real costs, so that these can be used as a guide in price setting and in choosing between alternatives. In applying the Marxian $c+v+m$ formula, most Soviet economists consider it possible to identify $c+v$ as equal to prime costs (*sebestoimost'*), which include materials used up, depreciation of basic capital and rewards of labour. On the scale of the economy as a whole, m can be defined and calculated as that portion of the total value of the material product, i.e. the national income in its Soviet sense (defined in chapter 10), which is not paid out as rewards for labour. However, for each product separately m is not known, because its 'value' is not identifiable as such. As one economist put it, 'so long as we do not know the magnitude of the value of a commodity—and we do not know it—all our discussions about the divergence between prices and values have the character of guesswork'.[2] What, then, can be done to replace guesswork by an objective guide, in the absence of a market mechanism? The practical problem is to find a theory which helps the carrying out of economic policies and serves as a guide to the rational disposal of resources—for purposes determined by the political leadership.

Faced with this challenge, Soviet economists in recent years have proceeded on a number of different lines, but which can be divided into two main categories: theories based on 'cost plus', and those which would derive values from the tasks to be performed, from 'the requirements of society' or of the plan.

---

[1] Stalin, op. cit., pp. 18-19.
[2] A. Pashkov, *Zakon Stoimosti* (Tsagolov). p. 242.

The first category of theories has the task of defining m, i.e. the amount to be added to $c+v$ to arrive at an objective basis. Some economists, notably Strumilin, take the labour theory literally. Since labour is the source of all value, then the total surplus product in the economy should be distributed proportionately to labour cost, in other words to v. Thus suppose c and v were, for a given commodity, each 100 roubles, and that the total value of the surplus product were 80 per cent of the total wages bill in the economy as a whole. Then the value of the product would be $100+100+80=280$.[1] However, another vocal school of thought advocates the share-out of the total surplus product proportionately to fixed and working capital, not to the wages bill. This school, typified by Vaag and Malyshev, find support in Marx's concept of 'price of production' (*Produktionspreis*) which, in volume 3 of *Das Kapital*, modified the pure labour theory by introducing the idea of a constant return to unequal quantities of capital.[2] They claim that only this would ensure efficient use of capital assets, and this connects with their arguments on investment criteria, referred to in chapter 7. Still another group advocate the shareout of m proportionately to cost, i.e. to $c+v$. The latter view could be consistent with a defence of the present practice of confining turnover tax almost wholly to consumers' goods, for, so long as wholesale prices are proportionate to $c+v$, wholesale prices would be proportionate to 'values' and would therefore fulfil an appropriate objective role.[3] On the other hand, the Strumilin and Vaag approaches, much though they differ in other respects, reject the present practice of separate systems and principles of pricing consumers' goods and producers' goods. They argue that 'real' costs, objective values, can and should be derived by relating m to one or more elements within costs and/or to the book valuation of capital assets. This is why they can bear the label 'cost plus', even though they dispute among themselves about just what it is that should be added to cost. The weakness of such theories as a basis for pricing, or indeed for planners' decisions, has already been made clear earlier. These defects have led to consideration being given to the second principal category of ideas.

[1] S. Strumilin, *Vop. Ekon.*, No. 12/1956. The numerical example is mine.
[2] For such views see I. Malyshev, *Vop. Ekon.*, No. 3/1957, L. Vaag in *Zakon Stoimosti* (Tsagolov), pp. 314-16, M. Kolganov in ibid., pp. 314-16. Strictly speaking, Marx's *Produktionspreis* presupposes that all of c, including the capital assets, are used up within the specified period of production, but this is so artificial an assumption that it is rightly ignored by the protagonists.
[3] For this argument, see P. Mstislavski, ibid., pp. 250-4. See also A. Bachurin, *Vop. Ekon.*, No. 2/1957, p. 94, and D. Kondrashev in *Zakon Stoimosti* (Tsagolov), pp. 210 ff., for another variant.

This, in its purest form, is represented by the Novozhilov-Kantorovich school, and a modified version of essentially the same ideas has been put forward by Nemchinov. In the minds of the economists concerned the ideas are not new. Thus Novozhilov and Kantorovich were expressing similar views when Stalin was still very firmly on his throne.[1] However, it was only in 1959 that they came fully into the area of public discussion, and Nemchinov did much to further such discussion.

Novozhilov's ideas depart very far indeed from $c + v + m$. He considers the application of such a formula to value relations in the Soviet setting to be quite misleading. In practice, he argued, Soviet planners have been making some allowance for scarcity as an element which increases real cost, but inconsistently and without any theoretical basis. In their work, the planners are constantly at grips with opportunity cost considerations, and—at least by implication—they value scarce goods by reference to alternatives foregone. The notional allowance for scarcity of capital, now widely accepted as part of the elaboration of investment criteria, should be regarded as a special instance of the general principle of opportunity cost. Theory lags badly behind practice. The effect on value of alternative uses is called by Novozhilov 'feedback costs' (*zatraty obratnoi svyazi*). Planners are handicapped by a theory of value which ignores these realities. 'The problem of measuring inputs (costs) and their results under socialism is not reconcilable with the measurement of inputs (costs) for each separate product by the labour required to produce it.' Indeed, it is only in the pre-capitalist period that, according to Marx, values fluctuate around labour cost. Under capitalism they fluctuate around *Produktionspreis*. Yet, argued Novozhilov, it would be wrong, contrary to the basic laws of dialectics, to assert that capitalism measures real costs less accurately than feudalism. There is no reason why socialism should return to a pre-capitalist form of value calculation, and a mechanical application of *Produktionspreis* formulae will not do either. It would also represent a misunderstanding of what Marx meant in volume 3 of *Capital*. It is wrong to regard the costs incurred in producing any one commodity in isolation as a basis for its value, since production processes of all goods, and the needs they fulfil, are inextricably intermingled. The real measure of the costs of producing any one com-

[1] Kantorovich's first work on a species of linear programming was published in 1939, while Novozhilov proclaimed his present theories in the *Trudy* of the Leningrad Polytechnic Institute, No. 1/1946. However, they were ignored or suppressed for many years.

modity is 'that increment of social expenditures associated with its production'. This must include not only the prime costs of making the means of production, but also opportunity ('feedback') costs, a variable charge reflecting the use of scarce capital, natural and other resources.[1]

Novozhilov would thus bring in relative scarcity and opportunity costs. These he relates to the programme, to the plan. This is why he is so close to Kantorovich's ideas. The latter is much more concerned with linear programming techniques than with constructing an acceptable economic theory, but Kantorovich's 'objectively determined valuations' are for all practical purposes the same concept as Novozhilov's valuations derived from 'feedback costs'. Both are concerned to derive prices of factors of production and of commodities from the programme, from the electronic computer, essentially from and through an optimization calculation in relation to the general requirements of the plan. Both are, in essence, marginal in character, being concerned with the comparative valuation of increments at all stages.

Such a theory would go far towards freeing the Soviet economist from the stultifying effect of a theory which directs his gaze at direct costs, especially labour costs, as the objective basis of values and prices. Novozhilov claimed that his theory would make possible much greater devolution of decision making, since prices would be a more adequate guide to choice between alternatives. Therefore, he pointed to the 'democratic centralist' implications of his ideas. Kantorovich declared repeatedly that very wasteful misallocation of resources would be avoided if his ideas were accepted.

Yet these ideas are still held by only a minority of economists. The majority dispute, and not altogether without reason, not only the theoretical but also the practical implications. Before discussing Nemchinov's attempt to devise an acceptable version of the Novozhilov-Kantorovich ideas, we must examine the nature of their objections.

UTILITY, SCARCITY, MARGINALISM AND LINEAR PROGRAMMING

Soviet economists have long shown a dislike for the concept of

[1] See Novozhilov, op. cit., especially pp. 210-12. For a most useful summary, see A. Zauberman, *Soviet Studies*, July, 1960. It is interesting to note that G. D. H. Cole,, in his introduction to Marx's *Capital* (Everyman's edition, Vol. I, pp. xxviii), made much the same point about the concept of value in the last volume of *Capital* as does Novozhilov.

scarcity.[1] Of course, they are well aware that scarcity is a fact. In their capacity as planners, they are struggling with scarcities and bottlenecks virtually every day. They would argue as follows: yes, we are short of many things, and it is the task of planners to provide what is lacking by expanding production, as and when the priorities of the plan permit. It is true that land, and sometimes certain mineral deposits, are limited and can be treated as scarce in the sense that no decision by planners can overcome the shortage. There could be a case for expressing this sort of scarcity by attaching the appropriate price tags. But other scarcities are correctable by investment decisions, and these decisions should be taken by reference to a material balance analysis. It is wrong to attach scarcity prices to reproducible goods, because, so it is argued, this merely confuses calculations of real cost, which, in the long run, will be determined not by relative scarcities but by the costs at which, when the planners so decide, the scarce commodity could be produced.[2] Since the decision will not be based on the profit motive, there is no point in 'rewarding' anyone with extra income merely by reason of a temporary scarcity. It is true that this involves rationing of scarce materials. (It is also true that, in the case of retail prices for consumers' goods, it is desirable not to ration, to avoid queues, and to fix a price by reference to supply and demand, thereby explaining the variable gap between wholesale and retail prices, i.e. big variations in turnover tax rates.)

This argument is intimately linked with the approach to subjective valuations in general, and also to marginalism. The opposition to a subjective theory of value is deeply embedded in Marxist theory. The source of value must be material, not spiritual, must be based on the conditions of production, not on people's thoughts. It is true that Marxists hold that, to have any value at all, a commodity must have some use, must receive 'social recognition'. But there is no room for greater or lesser degrees of utility in this theory, let alone marginal utility. The orthodox theoreticians do not deny that supply and demand play a role in price formation in a market, and that demand is affected by subjective considerations (though even here they are apt to stress the social nature of individual requirements).

---

[1] See Peter Wiles' stimulating paper, 'Scarcity, Marxism and Gosplan', in *Oxford Economic Papers*, September, 1953, pp. 288 ff.
[2] This would be consistent with G. Myrdal's views (*Economic Theory and Underdeveloped Regions*, Duckworth, London, 1957, p. 89): 'In fact a large part of the economic process . . . has to be directed by changing costs, prices and profit rates through modifying the conditions under which the price system functions.'

However, the conditions of production are regarded as determinants, while supply and demand explain fluctuations, or are the mechanism through which market prices adjust to a situation in which the conditions of production play the decisive role.[1] Marginalism is rejected partly on the formal ground that values are considered to relate to *average* social costs, but also for the more practical reason that prices (except perhaps in agriculture) need not be such as to keep in being the least efficient existing enterprise without subsidies—because in Soviet conditions its costs may be very high indeed.[2] The point is also made, for instance, in the attack on Kantorovich by Gatovski and Sakov, that a decision to increase output of an industrial commodity commonly makes possible the introduction of new mass production techniques and therefore a fall in costs per unit.[3] It should be said in passing that there is some truth under Soviet conditions in the assertion that high cost equipment will not be brought into operation as a result of a decision to produce more, since all available equipment, efficient or no, is already fully utilized. The key point made by the critics, when they are not merely aiming verbal missiles at 'bourgeois vulgar economics', is, to quote Gatovski again, that any proposed valuation based on marginalism and scarcity 'would make of scarcity of resources the economic criterion and guide, which means following a line involving a reduction in growth tempos of our economy, a change in the pattern necessary for such growth, and in particular the superior growth of production of means of production. The superiority in growth tempos engendered by the socialist planned economy would be unrealized. Instead of efforts being made to reduce costs and to adopt the most advanced productive techniques, more backward methods with higher costs would be prescribed, and the losses involved would be disguised by higher prices. All this would adversely affect the sources for increased accumulation. Marginalist schemes are deeply static.'[4]

Kronrod, himself a prominent critic of the existing price system, admitted the limited use of notional 'programming' valuations for specific tasks, but argued: 'To claim to plan the national economy on the basis of such valuations, and therefore to put them in the place of prices, costs, value, etc., this is merely the resurrection in

---

[1] See, for instance, the attack on Novozhilov by A. Katz, *Vop. Ekon.*, No. 11/1960, p. 95. It is also to be recalled that Marshall tended to give primacy to the conditions of production as price determinants in the long run.

[2] Also in the conditions of the British (nationalized) coal industry, where prices are anything but marginal.

[3] *Kommunist*, No. 15/1960, p. 89.

[4] Ibid. See also P. J. D. Wiles' essay on 'Growth versus Choice', *Economic Journal*, June, 1956.

mathematical dress of the old concepts of the subjectivist school, of the old marginalist pretentions. Their utter uselessness has long ago been proved by Marxist-Leninist political economy . . . It is necessary to warn mathematicians and economists of the real danger of becoming too involved in formal patterns, empty abstractions, particularly abstractions of a marginalist kind, even if clad in a complicated system of equations. We need mathematical models which reflect real economic processes, based on strictly scientific Marxist economic teaching.'[1] Similar views were expressed by several other eminent economists. As against this, Academician Kolmogorov argued that 'one should not be afraid that the mathematical apparatus of Marxist theory of the socialist economy will have some formal features in common with, for example, the theory of marginal utility of bourgeois economics. This is explained by the common nature of the mathematical apparatus for solving any variation problems, and . . . in no way affects the specific nature of the questions before us, or the purity of the Marxian approach'.[2]

It must be stressed at once that the problems facing anyone who wishes to devise a theory of value and price for Soviet conditions is an extremely difficult one, and econometrics does not provide any easy solution. It is true that in a sense linear programming techniques can be dynamic, in that the valuations which emerge from the mathematical model can be those which, in theory, should achieve the desired optimum over the time scale required by the planners. Thus these techniques would appear to be free from the reproach of being 'deeply static'. Yet the applicability of linear programming to the economy as a whole is in serious doubt on several grounds. Firstly, there is the question of the imprecision of and unpredictable changes in the parameters. It is hardly possible to define with the necessary clarity the aims of the programme, what it is that should optimized. Many of the essential elements of the plan are in fact dependent on the calculations for which they are to serve as a base. The actual choice made by the planners, especially in the field of investment, alters scarcity relationships in all kinds of unpredictable ways. Then, perhaps even more important, programming techniques cannot take into account external economies, the consequences of indivisibilities. These severely limit the generalized use of 'objectively determined valuations', into which it is hardly possible to bring these considerations. The assumption of fixed technical

---

[1] *Vop. Ekon.*, No. 8/1960, p. 106. This issue contains a fascinating discussion on 'mathematical methods in economics', of which this is a part.
[2] Ibid., p. 114.

co-efficients also limits the 'dynamic' potential of programming, even within one sector, let alone on the scale of the entire economy, since investment decisions and technical progress change the co-efficients. For all these reasons, there is indeed a case for asserting that scarcity prices derived from the programme may mislead planners looking five or ten years ahead. A further difficulty is the immense complexity of the task of applying these techniques in a context wider than a specific industry or a specific problem. No doubt there is much to be said to refute the above objections, but the object of this paragraph is merely to demonstrate that this is not just a question of foolish or ideologically blinded economists refusing to adopt a self-evident solution to their problems.

In this connection, it is of especial interest to examine Polish experiments. Indeed, it is possible that the Polish economy, being smaller and less complex than the Soviet, is being deliberately made a testing ground for econometric techniques. The evidence suggests that linear programming cannot replace the material balances techniques of planning. Programming techniques are as yet incapable of coping with all this. Econometric techniques can be used at two stages. They can help in the process of making rough and rapid estimates of the implications of alternative plans in the very early stages of the long term planning process. This would have to be followed by a more traditional—albeit more sophisticated—kind of material balance calculation. Then, after these basic data become available, programming techniques can be used as consistency checks as part of an effort to secure optimization. This is not as all-inclusive a use of optimization techniques as was envisaged by Novozhilov and Kantorovich, or indeed by some of the Poles, but on this less ambitious scale the experiments do show that the techniques can play a valuable part in planning.[1]

It is with all these criticisms and difficulties in mind that one should judge Nemchinov's attempt to reconcile the various schools of thought and bring in to Soviet economics the essentials of Novozhilov's ideas while causing the minimum ideological offence. He rightly stressed the vital and necessary connection, lost sight of by the scholastic protagonists of labour value theory, between value and the satisfaction of wants. He does this, understandably enough, in Marxian language. 'The socially necessary expenditures of labour

[1] For Polish experiences, see J. Pajestka et al., *Gospodarska Planowa*, No. 5/1960, pp. 12 ff., K. Porwit, *Ekonomista*, No. 5/1960, pp. 981 ff., and also J. M. Montias, *American Economic Review*, December, 1959, and his note in the *Bulletin of the Association for the Study of Soviet-type Economies*, November, 1960.

must be determined by reference not only to the expenditure of labour but also to its results. Only those expenditures are socially necessary which correspond to the requirement of society in given objective conditions of production.' The mere quantity of labour is not enough, one must determine 'how far (this) corresponds to socially necessary labour expenditure . . . Every enterprise must know the social valuation of all the objects of labour and tools of labour (materials and equipment) in units of socially necessary labour time'. But these valuations must be made on the scale of the national economy. These valuations must reflect the 'optimal plan balance, corresponding to the [political] directives and within the available resources (the amount available for capital investment, productive capacity, scarce resources)'. Nemchinov advocates the concept of a 'transformed form of value',[1] corresponding to real costs from the standpoint of the national economy (narodnokhozyaistvennye izderzhki), arrived at by adding to the prime cost $(c + v)$ an amount composed of a standard capital charge plus a differential rent. The latter is to be derived from mathematical (for instance, vector matrix) analysis, i.e. from the programme. This would take into account the relative availability and relative advantages of land, minerals, factories, by reference to the intended results, to the basic lines of the plan. The plan, or programme, would be based on an elaboration of material balances, and this reflects the Polish experiments and removes many of the objections of the critics. The implications of this differential rent, especially for factories (entitled 'buildings rent', but including, of course, the equipment), may not be visible at first sight, but reflection will show that they involve something close to marginalism in disguise—a better disguise, let it be said, than Novozhilov's. There is no suggestion that particular commodities' value has any relationship to marginal cost. Yet his model would in fact relate his 'values in transformed form' to average cost plus a variable margin which looks very much like Marshallian quasi rent. By determining in advance a variable differential rent, a variable profit norm, for different industries and for different enterprises in the same industry, Nemchinov's values are such as to permit an approach to a marginal basis for price. Enterprises producing at well above average cost would perhaps pay no differential rent, but prices based on this concept of value should enable them to cover prime costs and pay the standard capital charge. At the same time, by relating values to the plan programme, i.e. to need, he ties them to

[1] Note the resurrection of the formula used in 1943 and attacked by Stalin in 1951.

the satisfaction of requirements, detaching them from a proportion-ate relationship to actual production cost, a relationship which was a major weakness both of the Strumilin and the *Produktionspreis* approaches. He does all these things without challenging theoretical orthodoxy: he does not ascribe the value of the product itself to relative scarcities, but insists instead that the surplus product be divided proportionately to 'the conditions of the application of labour', i.e. the conditions of production in relation to means and needs, which can lead to similar practical conclusions. Value so de-fined should then be a basis for prices, in the sense that they should fluctuate around this basis, but with departures up and down in the light of circumstances (temporary scarcities, the urgent need to stim-ulate output of a particular commodity, and so on). 'The essential feature of prices is precisely the fact that they depart from value and fluctuate around it . . .' He advocates flexibility, though prices should be fixed by state organs.[1]

Nemchinov's theories, if accepted, would do much to correct some major weaknesses in the hitherto orthodox theory, which virtually ignores the connection between values and degrees of satisfaction of needs. If two goods, both of some use, are unequally valued by the user, then, although they may cost the same to produce, their value is surely unequal. The user may prefer one good to another for 'objective' reasons, as when it is better for some definable physi-cal reason (as, for instance, if a lathe or drill is more effective in operation), or the preference may be subjective, as when most women prefer one dress material to another. In either case, it could be argued in terms consistent with Marxism that the more desired product receives a higher degree of social recognition, in which case it could surely be held that a given amount of labour devoted to the production of a more needed product is 'socially more necessary' than the same amount used to produce something less useful. While such formulations as these are not in the Marxian economic tradi-tion, they will surely have to be adopted, explicitly or implicitly, and we have seen that Nemchinov, as well as Novozhilov and Kan-torovich, have moved in this direction, though by devious paths.[2]

[1] *Vop. Ekon.*, No. 12/1960, pp. 87, 89, 96, 100.
[2] Nemchinov (ibid., p. 90) praised V. Dmitriev, a pre-revolutionary Russian mathematical economist, as a pioneer in the calculation of total real cost. Dmitriev's book is not available here, but it is interesting to find a reference to it in *Archiv für Sozialwissenschaft*, 1907, p. 34, where L. von Bortkiewicz refers to his work, and gives as its sub-title: 'An attempt at a synthesis be-tween the labour theory of value and the marginal utility theory.' Nemchinov, of course, did not refer to the sub-title. (I owe thanks to Dr A. Zauberman for discovering the reference.)

Nor can one be satisfied with the still orthodox treatment of the problem of scarcity. While it is true that, viewed dynamically, the scarcity of today may be a misleading guide, none the less the concept needs to be taken more seriously by Soviet economists. Whatever the basis of long-term investment planning may be, many of the existing scarcities tend to be durable, and to some extent forecastable precisely because the long-term investment programme is known. If 'values', and therefore prices, express relative scarcities, then there could be less rationing (i.e. administrative material allocation), fewer *tolkachi*, much more 'self policing'; these points are rightly stressed by Joan Robinson. But the Soviet theorists are curiously reluctant to see scarcities as relative scarcities. As we have seen, even the cautious Turetski is willing to concede that coking coal is short (*defitsitnyi*) and he draws price policy conclusions from the fact. Yet these conclusions do not extend to systematizing a value and price theory around the fact of *relative* scarcity, even though he is himself aware that a higher price for coking coal will reduce applications for such coal from users who could burn an alternative form of fuel. Novozhilov very aptly reminded his readers that relative scarcity must exist even under full communism; for instance, the most efficient kinds of modern machinery must be relatively scarce at any given moment of time, unless it be assumed that technical progress ceases.[1] He at least is aware of the need to replace the orthodox view of scarcity and utility by something closer to economic reality. We have seen that this is also true of the more cautious ideas of Nemchinov, who links it with his advocacy of ending the 'rationing' of material supplies by administrative allocation. The orthodox theoreticians often fight shy of attaching price tags to capital or land, and the grounds that this would somehow involve a recognition of the 'three factors of production' theory and the denial of the uniqueness of labour as a creator of value.[2] This is a view hardly likely to prevail for long, in the face of the breaches already made in these alleged principles (e.g. capital efficiency norms, interest charges on short-term credits). No doubt it will be found necessary—indeed Novozhilov does so repeatedly—to reassert the belief that labour is the source of all values, and that the materialist conception requires the subordination of subjective valuations to some objective principles connected with the conditions of production. This was quite effectively done by Nemchinov in his com-

[1] Novozhilov, op. cit., p. 164.
[2] See in particular Katz's attack on Novozhilov, already cited, for examples of such an attitude.

ments on Novozhilov and Kantorovich; he labels the 'differential costs' involved in Novozhilov's concept of opportunity cost as 'differential labour cost', without in any way altering the reality of the concept. He emphasizes that capital equipment for which a charge is made is the product of 'past embodied labour'. He denies that Kantorovich's objective valuations, derived from linear programming, have the economic significance claimed for them by their author. However, Nemchinov favours the use of Kantorovich's methods all the same, 'as a means of solving problems of rational resource allocation',[1] though at a later or lower stage in the process of planning. It is much too early to forecast the fate of his proposals.

SOME OTHER ECONOMIC 'LAWS'

From time to time, one encounters assertions that certain propositions constitute economic laws, though the word 'law' would appear to require inverted commas if the propositions in question are to have logical meaning. For example, there is said to be a basic *law of socialism*, defined by Stalin and frequently repeated since: 'the provision of maximum satisfaction of the constantly growing material and cultural needs of all society by means of a constant increase and perfection of socialist production on the basis of the highest technique'. Stalin also defined capitalism, though in somewhat less flattering terms (maximum profits, pauperization, exploitation, robbery, war, etc.).[2] This is partly just propagandist generalization, but also, so far as socialism in concerned, involves a politically convenient but analytically disastrous assumption that whatever decisions are taken by the Soviet government at any given time (for instance, about the satisfaction of the people's wants) necessarily conform to the above-named law, represent the objectively determined maximum at that stage of development.

The same is true of the often reasserted '*law of planned (proportionate) development of the economy*', which always appears in just this form, with the word 'proportionate' in brackets. As far as can be judged, this is little more than a statement to the effect that the economy is planned and that the planners, by reason of the social ownership of the means of production, can determine the correct 'proportions', e.g. between investment and consumption, industry and agriculture, and so forth. Occasionally, it is pointed out that it

[1] See his postcript to his symposium, pp. 476-8, and also his article in *Vop. Ekon.*, No. 12/1960, pp. 85 ff.
[2] Op. cit., pp. 38, 40.

does not follow that the correct proportions are in fact observed, only that it is possible, and indeed necessary, for the proper functioning of the economy, that they should be. Stalin himself made this point.[1] In this case, it is a 'law' in a quite special sense, and a different word should be used. From time to time one comes across this 'law' in the course of arguments against excessive reliance on 'automatic' economic forces; in this guise, it amounts to emphasizing the primacy of conscious political control of the 'proportions' (i.e. primarily over investment). Unfortunately, it is seldom made clear by what objective criteria one is to judge whether the planners at any given moment are in breach of the 'law', save in those instances in which there are plain errors; for example, if the investment plan fails to provide the metal and energy required for the growth targets of the plan itself, clearly the 'proportions' are wrong. Similarly, the neglect of agriculture over many years could be regarded as leading to a breach of this 'law'. However, until the alleged disproportion is identified as such by the political leadership, it has hardly been possible to invoke the 'law' as a criterion.

Also involved is the doctrine concerning the priority of department I (or A goods) over department II (or B goods), discussed in chapter 10. This raises another species of question: how much priority is correct? What is *in fact* the limit on investment, on the rate of growth to be planned for? If accumulation is around 25 per cent of the national income, why not 40 per cent, or 15 per cent? Which is the 'legal' proportion? To this there is, as far as can be judged, one more or less orthodox answer, though it is seldom given in this form. Briefly, it is 'the principle of ensuring the *maximum possible* rate of technical progress, which determine the most rapid growth of social labour productivity, of the volume of social production'.[2] The object is the maximum possible growth rate. But what is at any given moment possible depends on a number of factors, some 'physical' (thus the labour force must be fed and clothed, which provides an essential floor to the consumption fund), some of a more intangible kind (thus, in normal times, incentives involve some more or less steady improvement in living standards). This may not sound like an economic law, but it may in fact be a fair definition of economic policy underlying the so-called planned (proportionate) development of the USSR. Unless it has meaning in this

[1] Ibid., p. 8.
[2] Katz, op. cit., p. 103. Emphasis mine. For a mathematical exploration of this problem of a maximum, see B. Ward in *Value and Plan* (ed. Grossman, University of California, 1960).

sense, the 'law' in question is merely an assertion that Soviet planners take the right decisions most of the time, and that they are not (or should not be) guilty of major inconsistencies.

There is also a *law of the necessary conformity of productive forces and productive relations*. This may seem scholastic jargon, but in fact, when originally formulated by Stalin in 1938, it fulfilled an important political economic purpose. According to Marx, history progresses through contradictions, and one of the principal motive forces in historical change is precisely the fact that productive forces get out of line with productive relations; as, for example, when the potentialities of the machine age were held back by a feudal organization of society. In such cases, there was liable to be a strong tendency towards a revolutionary situation, in which the disequilibrium was corrected by violence. Stalin was concerned to exempt the USSR from this awkward species of contradiction. Hence the law of 'necessary conformity'. True, things do go wrong, there are difficulties, but, if these take the form of contradictions at all, these are 'non-antagonistic', do not lead to conflict, can be put right by appropriate party and government decision. Indeed, this 'law' in fact asserts that they *must* always be put right, since any suggestion that in any given instance it has not been done would be to allege that the law which cannot be broken has been broken. Therefore, this is yet another example of identifying state action (any state action) with objective necessity, politically very convenient but analytically useless, or meaningless. Some Soviet economists have been criticizing the theory, by emphasizing the role which 'contradictions' do in fact play in Soviet economic life.[1]

SOVIET ECONOMICS—AND OUR OWN

After a prolonged period of intellectual stagnation, Soviet economics has come to life, and, especially since 1956, has been the scene of genuine argument. This has also been the case in several other Communist countries, above all in Poland. These arguments are an integral part of the search for a new balance between central orders and local initiative, between political 'campaigning' and an orderly utilization of economic forces; they are stimulated by the conscious search for a more effective utilization of scarce resources in a more

[1] For instance, see Y. Kronrod, in *Voprosy stroitel'stva kommunizma v SSSR* (Moscow, 1959). This 'law' is very well explained in the invaluable article by Kaufman, op. cit. Stalin's 1938 formulation appears in *Problems of Leninism* (1945 English edition), p. 586.

mature and complex economy. In other words, the economists' debates are part of the general trend towards necessary reform in the economic field, and, because the party leadership's own economic aims render reforms and new thinking necessary, it is very improbable that the process will be stopped. Interesting though the debates have been, many of the ideas expressed have been rather obviously wide of the mark, and it is possible that some western economists would regard the confusions of their Soviet *confrères* with superior amusement. Yet such amusement should be tempered with a greater consciousness of the inadequacies of much western economic analysis of the dynamics of change, and with the thought that the problem of underdeveloped countries raise many of the questions with which Soviet economists have been wrestling.[1] If development is undertaken by deliberate government action, in a way which either modifies or ignores the pressures of the market, the guide lines provided by market relations are disrupted. They need to be replaced—by what? If valuations are not provided by a market, can they be usefully derived from a pseudo market within an electronic computer? Are marginalism and the concept of factor cost only meaningful where there is a continuous process of adjustment to market pressures, where, so to speak, water can find its own level? Is a price theory derived from equilibrium analysis relevant to a state of affairs in which the scales are deliberately weighted? Have western economists in fact any sort of agreed approach to the economic problems of development? Can we really be satisfied with the (usually unconscious) philosophical assumptions underlying welfare economics? In the face of all these question marks, it is as well to approach the errors and omissions of Soviet economists without any undue superiority complex.

[1] More of this in the next chapter.

CHAPTER 12

Assessment

THE SOVIET ECONOMY AND THE ECONOMICS OF DEVELOPMENT

The Soviet economic system was developed in order to serve certain purposes, notably the rapid industrialization of the Soviet Union. Despite a justifiable degree of scepticism concerning exaggerated official claims—of which more will be said in the Appendix—the achievements of the system are indeed impressive. Despite great difficulties, big errors, much suffering and cruelty, and a destructive war, the USSR today is second only to the United States and is publicly challenging America to an economic race, claiming that American *per capita* production figures can be reached by 1970. Once again, a certain scepticism about the actual figures should not detract from our appreciation of the magnitude of the achievement. Yet the economy seems to be suffering from a number of major inefficiencies, it has been allocating resources irrationally; or such, at least, would be the conclusions legitimately drawn from the data presented in many of the preceding chapters. It may be asked: is there not an inconsistency here? If the USSR has indeed succeeded in overcoming many serious obstacles to growth, has built up its economic might so rapidly, then perhaps its policies and its economic structure were not, after all, so very irrational? Surely the system did possess features which contributed to rapid growth in the Soviet setting? Perhaps the weaknesses and distortions analysed in earlier chapters are the obverse side of methods of industrialization which have, or had, a rationality of their own? Did we not, perhaps, adopt implicitly standards of judgment too 'western', too narrowly economic, to form a sound basis for assessing the performance of the Soviet system? These are serious questions, and the criticism which they contain does have a certain validity. Unless we appreciate this, we shall be in imminent danger of falling into the error of regarding essential features of the Soviet economic system merely as aberrations, or as the projection into the economic field of power-seeking megalomania of particular leaders. A particularly useful corrective

288

is to examine those features of the system which arose as a response to problems of development as such. This task is facilitated by the growing literature on development, produced by western economists who have studied how to overcome obstacles to industrialization in underdeveloped countries outside the Soviet bloc.

As a lead in to this analysis, let us take the Soviet habit of 'campaignology' in the economic field, with which so much waste and so many excesses are associated. The repeated appearance of campaigns are, to use the legal phrase, evidence of system. The Soviet method of industrialization was a series of leaps forward, of which successive five-year plans were a formal expression, and within them there was a concentration of publicity and resources on some particular sectors, with a neglect of other important matters, which led to bottlenecks which led to new campaigns, each of which tended to be 'overdone' in its practical application. There was wasteful discontinuity, the methods were highly political, economic calculation in its usual sense took a back seat. Why?

One reason, certainly, related to the political structure. Below the topmost leadership of the Communist party, the activities of officials and directors are more or less circumscribed within basic policy directives from the top of the pyramid. Any major change in investment policy, or even in technical method, generally requires a decision of the top leadership. But the men concerned are very busy, and often fail to take the necessary decision unless the need is extremely pressing, or fail to halt a campaign already current unless and until its harmfulness is abundantly obvious. By then another campaign may be necessary to set things right. This is in part due to the weakness of 'countervailing forces' in the USSR: in the West such forces would prevent excesses, and, by taking gradual initiatives in a decentralized way, render the campaign approach unnecessary in normal times. It should be added that the Communist party in the Soviet Union, in so far as it replaces spontaneously operating economic forces, organizes its own activities around campaigns, a point to which we shall return in a moment. Students of Soviet economic history know of a great many examples of belated decisions which, once finally taken at the centre, become campaigns; two recent examples are the drastic shift towards non-solid fuels and the decision to treble in seven years the size of the chemical industry. Soviet agricultural history is full of party-imposed 'panaceas', always taken too far and replaced by other campaigns.

But it is certainly not enough to seek explanations of 'campaignology' solely in the logic of political centralization. There are other reasons, which may indeed help to explain the high degree of centralization. One such reason has already been referred to in chapter 5, when a long quotation from Oscar Lange included the reference to a war economy as a parallel to the Soviet method of industrialization. Since Oscar Lange is a high official of a Communist state, some readers may well regard this as apologetics rather than evidence, and so it is worth citing an American scholar, who does not appear to have studied the Soviet Union or, in all probability, to have seen Lange's formulations. He wrote: 'One field of experience may provide some guidance: the planning of "total war". For a short time the present writer was engaged in wartime planning, and he has been struck since by the *nature* of the problem confronting economic planners during the war and in underdeveloped countries . . . The process required the breaking of a succession of critical bottlenecks . . . In short, "total war", like planning development of poor and stagnant economies, involves marked and discontinuous structural changes, and resource allocation without reference to the market.'[1]

Myrdal, in his already cited book, emphasized the complexity of the task of development, the importance of politico-social factors, the frequent need to mobilize people around slogans devized by politicians if the forces of inertia and traditionalism are to be overcome. Equally relevant to our theme is the so-called 'unbalanced growth' school, of which Hirschmann and Perroux may be cited as two outstanding representatives.[2] All the above-named economists are essentially concerned with development *strategy*. Given a decision to develop, the correct strategy is not to seek 'optimization' in its narrowly economic sense, or to attempt the impossible task of a balanced advance on all fronts; rather is it necessary to choose methods which will facilitate the breaking out of the 'interlocking vicious circles' which obstruct the movement forward. One should seek to set up creative tensions, seek out the kind of disequilibria which will act as stimuli for further change. The traditional economic criteria must be replaced by new ones, related to this concept of strategy. Some sectors should be given priority because, in Perroux's phrase, they 'exercent un exceptionnel pouvoir déstabilisant'.[3] Hirschmann argues that 'in these basic types of investment decisions, it is, therefore, not sufficient to supplement, qualify and otherwise

[1] B. Higgins, *Economic Development* (New York, Norton and Co., 1959), p. 453.
[2] *The Strategy of Economic Development* (Yale, 1958), and *La Coexistence Pacifique* (Paris, 1958).
[3] Op. cit., p. 478.

refine the usual investment criteria. We must evolve entirely new aids to thought and action in the largely uncharted territory of efficient sequences and optimal development strategies'.[1]

It is instructive to note that the approach and priorities of the 'unbalanced growth' school have a number of things in common with those actually adopted by Soviet planners. Thus they tend to emphasize not only the need for the conscious organization of development, but also for five or ten-year plans, and being ambitious: 'a gradualist approach is almost certain to be self defeating'.[2] Hirschmann and Perroux stress the need for capital-intensive, modern methods in key sectors, despite the relatively great scarcity of capital and the fact that other sectors or auxiliary processess within the modernized sector remain 'hand operated', a situation typical of much of the Soviet economy to this day, and treated by some critics as self-evident proof of irrationality. The shortage of decision makers is, for Hirschmann, an argument for choosing those variants which 'set up incentives and pressures that make for . . . induced investment decisions',[3] i.e. which compel other decisions to be made. By these strategic criteria, heavy industry should be given priority: 'this means intermediate or "basic" industries whose products are distributed as inputs through many industrial sectors besides going directly to final demand. It is clear that such industries should be given preference over "last" [i.e. consumers'] industries, if they are at all economically feasible'.[4] If such policies were to be applied, certain traditional concepts of western economics must undergo modification. As Higgins puts it: '. . . Nor are the required adjustments strictly marginal. In such countries growth itself must be managed, and "sectoral planning" is necessary. The various rates at which heavy industry, light industry, agricultural improvement, transport and communications, housing and the like are to be pushed becomes a matter of conscious policy. Planning of this kind involves a calculus, involving a cost benefit comparison, but it is no longer a purely marginal calculus'.[5]

It is no part of the present book to argue whether the above-expressed views are sound. The point is that they are not derived from Soviet experience, yet—surely not a coincidence—they advocate an approach which does have some features familiar to the student of the Soviet economy. Efficiency and rationality, it appears, take on a new dimension in the context of development strategy, even in non-Marxist and non-communist eyes.

[1] Op. cit., p. 79.   [2] Higgins, op. cit., p. 454.   [3] Op. cit., p. 151.
[4] Ibid., p. 118.   [5] Op. cit., p. 451.

There is a fairly obvious objection to the application of this ana-lysis to the Soviet Union. It may be argued that the 'unbalanced growth' economists are concerned with stimulating spontaneous acts, whereas in a totally planned society such as the USSR it can all be done by deliberate action of the party and government. From this it might be thought to follow that balanced growth is possible—per-haps even only possible—in a Soviet type economy. Indeed, one of the protagonists of 'unbalanced growth', P. Streeten, has gone so far as to equate the 'law of planned (proportionate) development of the economy', so dear to Soviet theoreticians, with balanced growth.[1]

This last view, surely, is based upon a misunderstanding of this so-called 'law', or else upon an indentification of the plan with inter-sector balance, even when the plan provides for extremely unbal-anced growth between sectors. But, quite apart from this, the entire *rationale* of the Soviet 'campaign' approach to economic planning rests upon the inherent limitations of central control, or, more pre-cisely, upon the need to stimulate not only the executants but also the controllers. Again, it is necessary to challenge the 'totalitarian myth' of the monolithic perfectly obedient society, in which every-one can be told precisely what to do, as if in the Soviet Union too there is no problem of overcoming interia, even among the party officials themselves. Campaigns are, among other things, a means of goading the goaders, of mobilizing the controllers, of providing suc-cess indicators for officials at all levels. The deviations engendered by campaigns are the analogue to the distortions caused by success indicators at the 'micro' level and analysed in chapter 5, above. Of course, the importance of the controlling mechanism as a growth stimulator is all the greater where, as in the Soviet system, there is no built-in growth-inducing force, where the intervention of author-ity, and the targets set by authority, must act as a substitute for the automatic functioning of the profit motive.[2] Hence the vital role of campaigns as controller mobilizers. Hence the value of bottlenecks as stimulators to effort. Of course, it would be misleading to assert that Soviet planners deliberately create bottlenecks. But they adopt growth tempos which cause acute shortages and strains, while de-nouncing those who wish to adapt the growth tempos to the bottle-necks (as they say, *ravnyatsa na uzkie mesta*). Strain and campaigns go together.

[1] 'Unbalanced growth', *Oxford Economic Papers*, June, 1959, p. 169.
[2] On all this, see a stimulating discussion by G. Grossman, 'Soviet growth: routine, inertia and pressure', *American Economic Review*, May, 1960.

Therefore, the campaign method seems to have a logic. It also carries with it a big risk of waste, of gigantomania, of all kinds of bureaucratic deformations. Obviously, the logic of 'campaigns' as a method in no way argues in favour of any particular campaign, which may indeed be utterly wrong headed, explicable by crude miscalculation, Stalin's megalomania and other irrational factors. It is also true that this whole approach must involve certain inherent weaknesses and gives rise to the many problems discussed in Part II of the present book. None the less, we must see that the adoption of such planning techniques were not due to the mere whim of an all-powerful dictator or to the self interest of the *apparatchiki*, though such things did play their role, and indeed still play a role, in Soviet economic development.

This line of thought should lead the critical reader to look again at the concept of rationality. Already in chapter 5 we noted two meanings: optimum resource allocation as such (i.e. without assuming any goals other than the efficient functioning of the economy), and the economically most rational means of achieving given ends. It is clear enough that these two concepts can contradict one another: arrangements which facilitate optimum allocation may be inconsistent with the pursuit of postulated ends. To take a non-Soviet example, the Irish government subsidises economic activities in Gaelic-speaking areas, to preserve a way of life which it regards as good. Given the purpose, this is not an uneconomic use of resources. However, as one thinks over the logic of 'development strategy', it becomes clear that there are other and more sophisticated 'levels' of rationality in the context of growth. For development involves actions which are political and social and have a logic of their own. In so far as such actions serve the cause of development, they must be held to fulfil economic purposes, yet these same actions *as such* may well inflict economic loss, and if one were merely seeking the *economically* most rational means of achieving given ends, they could well be utterly illogical and pointless. To take another non-Soviet example, borrowed from Myrdal, it could well be that the spirit of nationalism was an essential unifying factor, an essential motive force for development, in some countries; this may give rise in certain circumstances to the political necessity of taking measures against foreign firms, measures which, in themselves, actually harm development.[1] Irrationalities at one level may appear logical on another. In examining some rather obvious inefficiencies of the Soviet system, we should never completely lose sight of the aims pursued,

[1] Op. cit., p. 73.

and of the obstacles which had to be overcome. There are social-political 'external economies'.

However, the claim that one is pursuing certain aims does not exempt the 'pursuers' from criticism at any level of their activities. The fact that obstacles had to be overcome does not mean that they were in fact overcome intelligently. In any case, one's realization that certain aims were pursued in no way implies that the aims were 'good', or worth the sacrifices which were imposed on a people which was given little choice about either ends or means. Value judgments about aims and means would take us far outside the scope of the present work, and the point is only made lest it be thought that the line of argument adopted in this chapter is an essay in apologetics. A more immediately relevant line of criticism concerns the fact that, in the Soviet Union, some obstacles were tackled with such crude brutality that the damage so done itself came to constitute an obstacle; the forced collectivization of the peasantry is an obvious example. Then the fantastically over-ambitious nature of the first five-year plan, and of some sector plans at more recent dates, led to waste on such a scale that a similar rate of growth could well have been achieved at far less economic and human cost if they hastened more slowly. Vast miscalculations occurred, resources were wasted on a prodigious scale on enormous 'prestige' projects (canals, 'transformation of nature', etc.) using much forced labour.[1] In no sense whatever should one argue that the errors and coercion which actually occurred were somehow 'necessary', let alone justified *ex post* by growth rate statistics or victory in war. Nor is it legitimate to claim that no other way existed for Russia to industrialize. Yet, without subscribing to the misleading doctrine that whatever is real is rational, that whatever happened had to happen, it remains true that what did happen had a certain logic, that it was connected with the problems of rapid development in post revolutionary Russia, that many of the problems encountered are common to underdeveloped countries in general, and that our picture of the relative efficacy of the Soviet economic system must take these things into account. This requires a view of rationality rather wider than that adopted by many western economists who examine the Soviet scene. It may be added that this broader view could with advantage be adopted by some western political scientists, who see the Soviet political structure (including its economic aspects) almost solely as the manifestation of power hunger on the part of totalitarian oligarchs. There is surely much more to it than that.

[1] On all this, see N. Jasny in *Soviet Studies*, April and July, 1961.

But it is time to return to the questions posed in chapter 5, when we spoke of the changing nature of problems. Even if it were accepted that the Soviet system did cope with some success—and at heavy cost—with the task of building a great modern industrial state, it may be legitimately argued that it is incapable of coping effectively with running a modern industrial state once it has been built. The evidence in Part II of this book points that way. So, indeed, does the nature and direction of the economists' arguments with which we were concerned in chapter 11. Perhaps the (genuinely) totalitarian elements of the Stalin system did, on balance, facilitate the rapid building up of basic industries; by imposing priorities, enforcing a high rate of accumulation, destroying the power of social groups to press for the satisfaction of their requirements (which would have modified the priorities), the régime facilitated growth. The institutional, political, psychological arrangements were geared to these purposes, and sacrificed 'efficiency' to them, or rather, measured efficiency in terms of growth. But Stalin is dead, his system is being modified. Do arguments derived from 'development strategy' any longer apply?

CAN THE SYSTEM COPE WITH A MATURE ECONOMY?

The Soviet Union is at present in a stage at which it could be described as the least developed industrial country, or the most developed underdeveloped country. If such an assertion seems paradoxical in the light of the statistics of her industrial output, there is none the less an important sense in which it is true. Soviet development has been extremely uneven, large sectors of the economy are primitive, living conditions (housing especially) poor. Living standards have increased comparatively modestly from their 1928 levels, a fact which contrasts strikingly with the very great rise in industrial production. Part of the explanation, in all probability, lies in the large volume of misdirected industrial production, associated with the major irrationalities in resource allocation which were typical of the Stalin period; these raised the capital output ratio well above the possible, and greatly increased the output of 'unnecessary' intermediate products, which go to swell the industrial output index without providing a commensurate increase in the output of final products. In any event, growth was exceedingly unbalanced. Now Khrushchev, while endeavouring to maintain growth tempos in a race to overtake America in economic might, is simultaneously trying to bring forward the sectors of the economy which were left behind in Stalin's 'leaps forward'. This is certainly not a baseless 'interpretation', since Khrushchev himself announces that these are indeed his policies,[1] and there is ample evidence that action is being taken. There is a growing realization that the 'campaign' method does harm, and the decision, taken in January, 1961, to plan continuously five years ahead is an example of the gradual spread of a more balanced approach to planning (even though the agricultural decisions taken in the same month show that old 'campaigning' habits die hard).

Here we encounter a major 'contradiction'. The entire system of economic administration and party control is closely geared in with the old methods, was designed for development campaigns, leaps forward, is associated with straining after targets, success indicators and the like. It is altogether too easy to attribute the continuation of these methods, and of the centralization which goes with them, solely to the vested interest of the party machine. No doubt this vested interest is an important factor. However, it is also true that piecemeal reforms often prove self defeating. As we have had repeated occasion to observe in chapter 7, partial measures to give greater powers of decision to men on the spot frequently lead to even greater irrationalities and compel a return to centralization, because, in the absence of genuine market relations, only the centre is in a position to determine what is needed.

Yet the centre also lacks the necessary information about what is needed, or is unable to translate its requirements into precise and enforceable orders. We have seen how the planning organs are tending to be overwhelmed by the growing complexities of the task of linking a multitude of interconnected production and supply decisions. With the transition to a more mature economy, the nature of rationality has, so to speak, changed its meaning. The economic discussions, the ideas of men like Nemchinov, Novozhilov, Kantorovich, the fact that their views are published and discussed, shows the existence of an influential school of thought which regards major structural changes as necessary. Their opponents, men like Katz or Gatovski, use against them arguments which, in essence, are based on the view that the 'development strategy' stage is far from over, and that the old methods can be reformed without being discarded. The habits and self interest of the party machine may well incline them to support the 'conservatives' on this question, and they may respond with new slogans about new campaigns, which would simul-

[1] *Pravda*, January 21, 1961.

taneously justify their leadership and the retention of the campaign techniques which go with it. Indeed, Khrushchev's slogan about overtaking America can be interpreted in this light. Yet the pursuit of this very aim adds to the 'contradiction', since it requires much greater attention to efficient resource allocation (the more so because of the steps being taken to develop the hitherto backward sectors of the economy). Change there must be.

THE EFFICACY OF THE SYSTEM IN COMPETITION WITH THE WEST

Until recently, comparisons between the western and the Soviet economies were, as a rule, thoroughly misleading. This was not due principally to statistical problems; these were and are, admittedly, very awkward, but the real point is a different one. Efficacy, if the word is to have any meaning at all, must relate to the ability of the given system or measures to cope with the situation which is actually confronted at the given time and place. How, therefore, can one compare the functioning of an already developed economy, like that of the United States or Great Britain, with the methods used to industrialize, with a development strategy? It is like comparing chalk and cheese. However, with the emergence of the Soviet Union as an industrial power, and bearing in mind the insistence of its leaders that they intend to overtake the west in economic might, the possibility of meaningful comparison of systems increases. At least, it is possible to say something on the subject which is not meaningless.

None the less, before doing so it is necessary to utter a word of warning. The relative performance of the two systems in this or that sector must be judged by reference not to some abstract optimum, but to what is or would have been possible. This point can be illustrated by taking as an example the very great superiority of the United States in labour productivity in agriculture. Let us suppose, for the sake of argument, that this is five times greater than in the Soviet Union.[1] What conclusions can we draw from this? Surely, before saying anything worth while, we must take into account at least the following. Soviet soil is, on average, less naturally fertile; the

[1] Soviet sources claim a $3:1$ ratio (for instance, Y. Yoffe, *Plan. Khoz.*, No. 3/1960, pp. 50 ff.), but they seem to add rather too generously to the published American labour force. Western estimates, on the other hand, have tended greatly to overstate the Soviet farm labour force.

climate is very much less favourable, the risk of drought and frost damage much greater; there is a much greater density of rural population in relation to the area of cultivateable land, and it was scarcely possible to shift peasants into non-agricultural employment faster than was in fact done. One might also take the human situation into account: the Russian peasant is not an American farmer, and a large proportion of the Soviet farm labour force consists of women. All this in no way affects the many criticisms we can and should make of the conduct of Soviet agriculture; we are indeed also entitled to note that productivity of both labour and land has risen more slowly than in many western countries during the past thirty years, and might, therefore, conclude that there is nothing about *kolkhozy* and *sovkhozy* especially conducive to the growth of agricultural output; many would, with some reason, regard this last sentence as altogether too polite. Yet the fact remains that, even if Soviet farm policies were ideal, productivity would certainly be considerably lower in the Soviet Union than in the United States. Relative efficiency is a tricky concept.[1]

In any event, no one disputes the fact that Soviet productivity throughout the economy is well below American levels, and that the Soviet economy is much less well equipped. According to Soviet claims, the leeway can be made up by 1970. In the absence of adequate information about the relative magnitude of the two economies, some scepticism may be permitted concerning the Soviet estimates of their present relative position; for example, Soviet industrial production in 1960 may well not have been as much as 60 per cent of the American. However, as Khrushchev himself pointed out in a speech in which he named this figure, this would affect only the question of when—not whether—the USSR overtakes America.[2] The Soviet Union, so it is argued, grows and will grow much the faster, and in a matter of time it is an arithmetical certainty that she must overtake, unless nuclear weapons interrupt the inevitable march of history.

Is this so? Granted that the Stalin system was a means of rapid industrialization, is the Soviet system at its present stage able to keep up the pace? What are its elements of relative strength?

It can maintain a high rate of investment, a rate which will remain independent of business fluctuations and the uncertain prefer-

[1] For an excellent survey of factors affecting industrial productivity comparisons, see W. Galenson, *Labour Productivity in Soviet and American Industry* (Columbia University Press, 1955).
[2] *Pravda*, January 25, 1961.

ences of individuals. While a larger proportion of these investments are apparently being devoted to the formerly neglected sectors (agriculture, housing, textiles, retail trade, etc.), a high degree of priority is still, and will continue to be, attached to the growth inducing sectors of heavy industry. The movement forward is hardly likely to be interrupted by the crises or recessions which adversely affect the growth of western economies from time to time.[1]

The Soviet effort can glean advantage from the immense educational 'investments' of the past years. Much greater attention is paid to science, indeed to knowledge as such, not only by the authorities but also among the people, since the USSR has largely escaped the large scale 'commercialization of the moron' with its encouragement of mental laziness and ignorance. Although the Soviet educational system has its serious shortcomings too, they are least apparent in the scientific and technical field. The concentration of so many of the best brains in pure science must bring nearer the day when Russians will emerge as important innovators. Though hitherto they have tended to copy western methods, outside of a narrow and predominantly military field, there is no reason why, in the future, they should astonish us only with Sputniks.

The development of new ideas on industrial technique is extending the possibilities of automation in industry, and the Soviet economic system may be especially well adapted to automation. This is because it can assure long runs of standardized products, planned well in advance, with few risks of unexpected changes, of uncontrollable competition or opposition from trade unions. Soviet scientists should be able to produce the necessary equipment, in view of their achievements in the related and more complex field of astronautics.

It must also be stressed that the system is in general well adapted to a rapid growth in the output of basic products—minerals, steel, cement, fuel and so on. As was already metioned in chapter 6, the defects associated with the success indicator system affect such products very little, since they are more or less homogenous and so relatively easy to plan. Large scale investment in expansion of these basic industries is facilitated by the existence of a long term plan which makes possible a reasonable forecast of need for many years ahead, and by centralization of investment finance. The weaknesses which relate to adaption to consumer demand and the finer adjustments of diversification hardly matter in these sectors.

[1] However, see J. Olivera's theory of cyclical growth under collectivism, *Kyklos*, 1960, pp. 229 ff.

A further very important 'advantage' in the growth race is backwardness itself, and this in two ways. In the first place, the existence of inefficiencies in resource utilization, of misemployed or underemployed labour in agriculture and so on, provides reserves in the move forward, which are not available in countries in which these reserves have already been drawn upon. In this sense, evidence of past or present inefficiencies is evidence of additional growth potential, unless it can be shown that the system is inherently incapable of curing the inefficiencies. A second 'advantage' of backwardness is the stimulus to growth which it provides, by the high degree of unsatisfied and urgent demands for more material goods. The Soviet Union is short of so very many things. The United States, by contrast, has reached saturation point in many sectors of its economy. Any major increase in its output of agricultural products, motor cars, washing machines, would be more likely to give rise to embarrassment rather than satisfaction; it is hard enough to sell what is produced already. Whereas in the Soviet Union there is need for expansion, and plenty of room for cost reductions through the introduction of modern techniques; for instance, many consumer durables are still made very largely as by-products of heavy engineering, in the so called *tsekhi shirpotryoba* (consumers' goods workshops) described in chapter 1.

To this list of factors which, on balance, favour the Soviet Union some would add an alleged superiority in foreign trade. Dr Balogh, for instance, is apt to warn us of the likelihood of very intense Soviet competition on world markets, while less serious writers make our flesh creep with stories of massive trade offensives. It is impossible to discuss in detail here the reasons for viewing such alarms with scepticism, but there are certainly grounds for such scepticism. Despite a sizeable increase from the very low levels of the Korean war period, Soviet trade with the entire non-communist world in 1959 was still quite small, half or less of that of a country such as the Netherlands.[1] Except where the partner's trade with the west was disrupted by political quarrels (such as Cuba in 1960, for instance, or Egypt in 1956), Soviet share in trade has generally been very modest. The somewhat clumsy and bureaucratized system of foreign trade corporations is not conducive to efficient trading practices. While it is true that the monopoly of foreign trade has been used, and will doubtless continue to be used, to secure certain political

[1] Soviet trade volume is generally compared with 1950 or 1937, when it was much below normal. Its growth looks far less impressive if based on comparisons with 1913, or even 1930.

advantages to the Soviet Union, the idea that the USSR is or shortly will be in a position to 'flood the world's markets' seems quite baseless; this presupposes very large exportable surpluses, over and above the internal needs of the Soviet Union itself and of its allies. Of these, China alone must continue to lay claims on a large proportion of Soviet exports of capital goods. There is no sign of a plan for such vast surpluses. Oil is, for the time being, a significant exception, but even oil is only embarrassing to the west because, thanks largely to the west's own import restrictions, it is sent to only a few countries, instead of being 'diluted' within the vastly larger world market. It is quite unrealistic to deduce the emergence of large exportable surpluses from statistics of projected increases in output. Obviously, it all depends on domestic utilization. For example, Soviet steel production has indeed risen spectacularly, but very little is exported, and indeed there are continued restrictions on its use in Russia, for instance, in construction.

Other analysts, for instance, Isaac Deutscher, imagine that there is strength in the economic unity of the Soviet bloc, and in the specialization and joint planning which it makes possible.[1] The reader of the present book, who must have noted the grave difficulties in the way of proper co-ordination even of *sovnarkhozy* within the USSR itself, will surely approach such ideas with due caution. Undeniably, some form of planning and trade co-ordination exists, through COMECON. However, its limitations are all too easy to document. It has yet to be demonstrated that it is any easier for two Soviet countries than for two 'capitalist' countries to co-ordinate their economies through trade. In any event, these arrangements extend only very partially to China. While it is true that long term trade agreements are made and are geared in with long term plans, it would be going too far on the evidence to ascribe any trade superiority to the Soviet system.

It is unnecessary to analyse here the internal weak spots of the Soviet system, which must be set against the elements of strength listed above, since they have been dealt with at considerable length in Part II of this book. It is enough to recall some of the more important ones. There is, firstly, the tendency of planning organs to be overwhelmed by the complexity of their tasks, especially in the linking of production and supply decisions, while unable, in the absence of market and price criteria, to devolve decision making powers to local and enterprise levels. Secondly, agriculture is still inefficiently planned and wastefully administered. Thirdly, there is a marked

[1] *The Great Contest* (Oxford, 1960).

failure to link demand and production; the position of the consumer and the citizen *vis-à-vis* those who minister (or should minister) to his wants is deeply unsatisfactory, and very far below normal western standards. There are the complex and interrelated questions of price reform, investment criteria, innovation, success indicators, discussed in chapters 6 and 7. One of the unknowns in assessing the prospects of the Soviet Union 'overtaking' the United States is precisely that we cannot tell whether, and how, the necessary adjustments will be made. These are the difficulties of adjusting the system to deal with problems of a developed, as distinct from an underdeveloped, economy, and they raise most serious questions of economic, doctrinal and political kinds. It is by no means clear whether these adjustments can be made without thereby slowing down growth rates, and indeed generating political and social changes which could have vast consequences.

There are a number of other factors which may tend to slow down growth. There is the difficulty encountered in expanding agricultural production, a difficulty only partially explicable by institutional weaknesses. With almost all potentially arable land in use, further advance requires very considerable intensification, much more fertilizer, irrigation, new roads, and many other things which cost much effort but which are now likely to yield diminishing returns. The location of certain important mineral and fuel reserves is causing a shift of industry towards the east, yet there are few towns there, few people, very few railways or roads. There must be heavy expenditures on social overhead capital. Yet part of the explanation for the very rapid expansion of earlier years lies in the fact that it was possible to utilize very much more intensively already existing railways and urbanized areas, and readily accessible natural resources. This led, of course, to great strain on railways and to acute overcrowding in the cities, but it did make possible the concentration of resources on industrial growth. The capital output ratio will probably increase. Finally, we earlier mentioned that backwardness itself acts as a growth stimulus. This stimulus must grow weaker as growth proceeds, not only in some vague psychological sense but in reality. Gradually the spectre of overproduction will raise its head—for a few products, as we have seen earlier, it has already raised it. But this will mean the end of a period in which what is produced can be lightheartedly 'adjusted' to the task of quantitative growth. The 'right goods' are needed, consumer requirements and quality cannot be ignored. There must be greater diverisification. Yet it is far simpler to increase output if one is producing a few standardized

articles at full capacity.[1] While not a major problem yet, because
the economy does still suffer from so many scarcities, all this can
surely lead to increasing difficulties as the Soviet Union gets nearer
to American levels. (It may be worth remarking in passing that,
while Soviet consumers' goods production must move towards
greater diversity, there is a tendency towards standardization, or concentration on a very few models, in western countries. Perhaps one
day we will meet in the middle . . .).

Of course, in any full assessment of the relative pace of development of the Soviet and western worlds, it would be essential to take
into account the economic policies and possible difficulties of
western countries. It appears from his speeches that Khrushchev
expects the west to be increasingly and adversely affected by 'antag-
onistic contradictions', not least those arising from its relationship
with former colonial territories and underdeveloped countries generally. While it is right to recall that, in recent years, such 'capitalist'
countries as West Germany, Japan, Italy, have matched Soviet industrial growth rates, and that the western system has shown a
marked superiority in resource allocation as distinct from aggregate
growth, there are plainly no grounds for complacency about the
west's relative position. On the other hand, one sometimes encounters among western observers a spirit of pessimism, which may
be based on an acute consciousness of elements of weakness and
instability in the western economy, combined with an inability to
see how formidable are the problems faced by Soviet planners as
they search for a way of adapting their system to the requirements
of the mid-twentieth century. 'Contradictions' are no western
monopoly.

A MODEL FOR UNDERDEVELOPED COUNTRIES?

One of the more important ways in which Soviet ideas exercise
an influence on people in the uncommitted world is through the
quite widespread belief that the USSR—and perhaps China also[2]—
demonstrates how it is possible rapidly to transform a peasant
country into a great industrial power. In the earlier part of this
chapter, we have seen that certain western economists who study
problems of development outside the Soviet bloc recommend
policies which are in some respects similar to those pursued in the

[1] This point is vigorously stressed by P. J. D. Wiles, in his 'Growth versus
Choice', already cited.
[2] A study of the Chinese economy, while certainly desirable, is well outside
the scope of the present book and of its author's knowledge.

USSR. It is also to some extent true that the obstacles which were so ruthlessly tackled under Stalin's rule exist in many underdeveloped countries. The Soviet Communist party smashed through the 'interlocking vicious circles', to use Hirschmann's phrase again. They forced the peasants and other private interests to conform to the priorities and financial requirements of the plans for rapid industrialization. They imposed an industrializing ideology. Through a one-party state, through party organization, through the suppression of any persons or groups holding contrary opinions, they were able to mobilize the people to carry the process through despite heavy cost and much suffering. All this is another way of saying that the totalitarian aspects of Soviet rule, which we in the west find most distasteful, may actually be a source of attraction to some statesmen and intellectuals in underveloped countries, who find, for reasons analysed as some length elsewhere,[1] that they are unable to break out of the vicious circles, unable to mobilise their apathetic and sometimes obstructionist peasants, unable to overcome a variety of vested interests, unable to cope with the inflationary and balance-of-payments crisis which seems inevitably to accompany attempts at development. The practical consequences of the path advocated by Myrdal, Hirschmann and others of their way of thinking may, whether they wish it or not, lead far along the road of political despotism and ideological enthusiasm, because this path can be effectively followed only by a government which can take charge of much of the economy and pursues the aim of development with a fervour not usually associated with democracy or tolerance. It is interesting to note that Bauer, who opposes this whole approach, is aware of this and uses it as an argument against state-sponsored industrialization.[2]

Yet there are a number of features of the Soviet model which should serve as a warning rather than as an example. It must be recalled that, when the first five-year plan was launched in 1928, the Soviet Union already possessed some industry, considerable technical, scientific and statistical cadres, a fairly extensive railway system, and, perhaps most important, food surplus. This provided a basis and a margin which most overpopulated Asian countries do not possess. The disasters of compulsory collectivization led to a sharp drop in farm output in the USSR; there was in fact wide-

[1] See Myrdal and Hirschmann, works cited. See also A. Nove, 'The Soviet model and underdeveloped Countries', in *International Affairs*, January, 1961.
[2] See especially P. Bauer, *United States Aid and Indian Economic Development* (Washington, 1959).

spread famine in 1933. To follow the Soviet model of collectivization, to launch a struggle with the property-owning peasantry, might
have fatal results in Asia, for people and regime alike. True, the
Chinese experience seems to have been rather different, and it is also
true that some government-induced change in archaic systems of
farming may well be indispensable. But it is surely right to say that,
while the peasant problem is indeed a major factor in the interlocking vicious circles,[1] the Soviet way of solving it should not be a
model for anyone. The Soviet-style industrializing ideology in fact
tends to strengthen those elements which have contempt for
peasants and are all too ready to neglect agriculture. Then the Soviet
authorities largely destroyed handicrafts, the private small-work-
shop industry. This greatly contributed to the drastic fall in living
standards in the first years of the 'thirties, and represents a loss in
material and human terms which should surely be avoided. The
same is true of the liquidation of the private trader, as part of the
war on the 'speculator', when the state was incapable (indeed is still
in certain respects incapable in the USSR) of effectively replacing
him. Last but not least, the too complete rejection of conventional
economic rationality criteria, the reliance on the campaign approach, untrammelled by free expression of opinion by those
adversely affected, led to waste on a scale which underdeveloped
countries should surely do all in their power to avoid. Such slogans
as 'there is no fortress the Bolsheviks cannot take', and the many
similar slogans directed in China against the so-called 'rightists',
open the door far too wide to policies which are irrational in terms
of any criterion.

Part of the 'magic' of the Soviet example also lies in the acceptance of official Soviet growth-rate statistics, which, were they really
correct, would indeed be evidence of magic. It is the reluctance of
western economists to believe that miracles happen in economics,
even under a Stalin, which have led them rightly to question these
indices. Of course, rapid industrialization of the USSR is a fact. But,
properly deflated, the figures compare reasonably with those of
Japan, and reminds us that there was also a Japanese road, neither
western nor communist. But we cannot do more here than to mention it, in a book devoted to the Soviet Union.

Finally, it seems important to realise that, although the Soviet
methods were crude and in important respects irrational, few will
hearken to such warnings if those who utter them do not show
awareness of the very serious problems which underdeveloped coun-

[1] On this whole question, see in particular A. Erlich, op. cit.

tries face on their road to modernization. The western path, a reliance on the free market, is often irrelevant, often leads nowhere. As one American economist put it, 'laisser-faire will not do the job, and totalitarian physical planning is unlikely to do the job well'.[1] Even if it were certain to do the job badly, men would still turn to it if other methods are ineffective. Hence the serious need for imaginative study both of problems of development in various countries and of the positive and negative features of the Soviet system at various stages of the industrializing process.

[1] B. Higgins, op. cit., p. 456.

APPENDIX

A Note on the Availability and Reliability
of Soviet Statistics

Availability

A few years ago, it would have been easiest to make a quite short list of the few figures which were available. The fact that the contrary procedure is now the most convenient one is a measure of the 'liberalization' achieved since the death of Stalin, or rather since 1956, when the systematic publication of economic statistics gradually began again after a long interval. However, there are still some conspicuous gaps, of which the following are the most important.

(*a*) Output figures for some *industrial products* are missing, among them non-ferrous metals, ships, aircraft, many chemicals, some machines, as well as military weapons.

(*b*) While more is now appearing about the breakdown of the *labour force*, including agriculture and the military services,[1] numbers in particular industries are not given in any detail.

(*c*) Very little has been published on earnings, either of wage-earners or of peasants. Such information as we have still has to be reconstructed from scattered and ill-defined statements. By contrast, Poland, Hungary and Czechoslovakia publish detailed wage statistics.

(*d*) Neither *national income* nor *gross industrial output* statistics are available except in the form of aggregate indices or of totals which are not broken down into their constituent parts, save occasionally into rough percentages.

However, let us give credit where credit is due. Gone indeed is the day when one had to search for statistics in leaders' speeches and make do with percentages of an unknown base. The statistical compendia on the economy as a whole, on agriculture, on various republics and localities, on transport, and so forth, together with the reports on the 1959 census, do give us a sizeable stock of statistics to work on, despite the remaining gaps. One difficulty is that many of the figures given are ill-defined; there is an unfortunate lack of

---

[1] Until it was decided to publish the numbers in the armed forces (1960), the number of peasants and the age and sex distribution of the population were unpublished, no doubt to prevent calculation by residual.

explanatory notes; though minor attempts are being made to remedy this, we badly need longer explanations, and a new edition of a handbook on economic statistics is much overdue.[1] The lack of clarity about definitions, and especially changes in definitions, is a constant danger; it affects budget data, and also a number of the output figures and indices.

Credibility: physical output figures

(a) *Industry*. Whatever the vagueness of definitions, the first question to ask is: are the figures true, or are they invented? Very few persons now believe that they are invented. The evidence against such a view is very strong. Despite captured documents,[2] despite the presence in the West of various Soviet officials who had defected, no evidence exists that the central Soviet statisticians invent figures to order, to produce propaganda effect. By this is meant that no one issues orders to print a figure of 400 knowing that the correct one is 350. Further support for this view comes from the fact that, when certain figures were discreditable, they were on occasion simply suppressed; many years later, they were published and showed that there was a fall in production in the 'suppressed' year. If it were possible simply to invent, then such behaviour would be pointless. Of course, we must note that selective suppression is a means of distorting a statistical table, but it is not invention. Not to tell the whole truth is not the same as telling a lie. Therefore we can legitimately conclude that when, for example, the Soviet authorities announce that 60 million tons of steel or 300 million pairs of shoes have been produced in a given year, this accords with the records of the Central statistical office in Moscow.[3] However, there are several qualifications to be made. One of these relates, not for the last time, to ambiguities of definition. Footwear sometimes includes only leather footwear, sometimes all footwear, the definition of leather footwear can and does alter, handicraft production can be omitted from the base-year without this being stated. Furthermore, most commodities for which statistics are published are not homogenuous, are in reality many different kinds of goods aggregated under a single head for statistical convenience. The methodology of aggregation is often unspecified. Of course, this is often true of similar statistics in all countries. But the point is that rewards for growth are so important in Soviet industry that the definitional

[1] There used to be such an explanatory handbook, entitled *Slovar-spravochnik po sotsia'lno-ekonomicheskoi statistike*, but this was last published in 1948.

[2] Especially the *1941 Plan*, published in America by the American Council of Learned Societies, after it had been taken from the Germans.

[3] This is also the broad conclusion of G. Grossman in his searching examination of *Soviet Statistics of Physical Output of Industrial Commodities* (Princeton, 1960).

changes, and the adjustment to definitions at local level, can aim deliberately at whatever result looks best from the standpoint of statistical publicity. This point is also relevant to the reliability of aggregate indices, and we shall return to it.

The figures may correctly reflect the data available in Moscow, yet this data could be wrong by reason of statistical 'padding' by the reporting agencies, especially the enterprises. They are interested in claiming plan fulfilment, and this could lead them to exaggerate. Scattered reports of measures against directors who indulge in such practices confirm that such dangers exist, but measures are taken to minimise them. The close link between production and disposals (*sbyt*) puts a limit on the amount of likely cheating: to report non-existent production which one would be called upon to deliver is asking for trouble. There are also some temptations to conceal output, in order to keep extra stocks in hand or to cover up pilfering or some semi-legal deal. Defective goods, on the other hand, seem frequently to be foisted on customers in the guise of standard products, the quality inspectors being overruled. On balance, one should expect some exaggeration in reporting, and no doubt the possibilities of getting away with it vary in different sectors and at different periods. Unless it can be shown that the *extent* of exaggeration changes, the rate of growth remains unaffected, for obvious reasons; this is the 'law of equal cheating', which the author of these lines 'invented' in 1956.[1] There seems no evidence one way or the other, in industry at least, to suggest that the rate of growth since (say) 1937 or 1950 has been affected by falsification from below.[2] However, it is manoeuvring within the system of success indicators—without actually cheating—which seems much the most serious source of distortion. Reference back to the large number of plan-fulfilment 'dodges' listed in chapter 6 will provide a host of examples of how the wily director can distort the truth without actually breaking the regulations.

Clearly then, care is needed in interpreting the various figures, exaggeration is possible. But an excess of scepticism can lead to unfortunate results. Thus a certain American commentator noticed that cotton and wool cloth output figures were below the previous year in physical terms while the official statistical report claimed an increase, and jumped to the conclusion that this was evidence of cheating. It was not; there had been a shift of statistical reporting from linear metres to square metres, the object of which was in fact to stop cheating by those who sought to fulfil plans by making cloth narrower. This illustrates the danger of using the 'cheating' hypothesis. Far better is it to assume that the figures represent some aspect of reality, and proceed, on that assumption, to

---

[1] In *Lloyds Bank Review*, April, 1956, p. 3.
[2] This is also the conclusion of Grossman, op. cit., p. 133.

examine with care the coverage and definition of the figures cited.

(b) *Agriculture*. For many years, until 1953, crop data were published in terms of 'biological yield', for reasons which cannot be gone into here.[1] It is very much to the credit of N. Jasny to have been the first to have documented and calculated with great ingenuity and surprising accuracy the extent of the consequent exaggeration.[2] This was due partly to the nature of the 'biological' statistics, which purported to represent the on-the-root crop, and were therefore gross of the considerable harvest losses, and partly to the tendency of the inspectors to exaggerate the on-the-root crop estimates, since certain delivery obligations of *kolkhozy* (payments to the MTS) were dependent upon them. In 1952, the grain harvest was said to have been 130 million tons. This has been officially revised downwards to 92 million tons, an exaggeration greater than many of the fiercest western critics thought possible.

Biological yield figures were dropped in 1953, and for several years no physical output data were published at all. Then they reappeared, and are now available in abundance, for every major farm product, down even to non-cow milk and non-sheep wool. However, there are several reasons for supposing that the 'law of equal cheating' may fail to operate in agriculture. Firstly, the large volume of unsold products makes it harder to keep track of reality. Secondly, a series of agricultural campaigns (grain, maize, meat, milk, and so on) have placed great pressures upon local officialdom, and we have Khrushchev's own word for it, at the January, 1961, plenum of the central committee, that it drove them into various kinds of simulation and exaggerated reporting (including the purchase of butter in the shops and its re-delivery to the state as new produce). Thirdly, the much better prices now paid for produce probably led to a discouragement of various forms of evasion by which production remained unreported.[3] Finally, the very large proportion of meat and milk originating in the private sector is very inadequately counted, through a sample survey, and seems to be unreliable and possibly overstated. For all these reasons, there are grounds for supposing that both the absolute level of and the rate of increase in the output of some farm products are overstated, though we cannot tell by how much.

It is also noteworthy that the definition of meat includes offal, lard, rabbits, poultry, and so is wider than that usually adopted in the West. Maize figures include the grain equivalent of ensilaged cobs since 1955. American analysts have claimed that milk sucked by

[1] See A. Nove, 'Some Problems in Agricultural Statistics', *Soviet Studies*, January, 1956.
[2] See his *Socialized Agriculture in the USSR*, and other works.
[3] An interesting parallel may be found in Great Britain, where an increase in the official buying price for eggs shortly after the war led to a spectacular rise in the *reported* number of eggs laid.

calves is included in the Soviet milk statistics, but this has been denied.[1]

Indices: are they credible?

According to the official statistics, gross industrial output rose almost twenty-one times between 1928 and 1955. The highest western estimate, by F. Seton, allows for a twelve-fold rise. The lowest, by W. Nutter, supports a much lower figure, a five-and-a-half-fold increase. There are some others in between.[2] There is not the space here to comment in detail on the many western attempts to reconstruct an index of industrial production, based on Soviet physical output series. The point is that all are unanimous in completely rejecting the official index, even while at odds with each other about the 'correct' figure. My own view tends to favour the Seton index, because the much lower figures of Nutter and some other analysts seem to me inconsistent with what is known and accepted about Soviet fuel utilization and freight transportation. However, this still leaves the official index way up above the realms of possibility.

It is not that this index is deliberately 'cooked'. But all indices are conventional aggregations, necessarily lacking in accuracy. So much depends on price weights and on the treatment of new products, especially where, as in the machinery sector, these are extremely numerous. Anyone who wishes to make any such calculations should take an awful warning from A. Gerschenkron's calculations, in which he showed that, from 1899 to 1939, American production of machinery increased more than fifteen-fold with 1899 price weights, but less than doubled with 1939 price weights, and he emphasized the enormous difficulties due to changes in type and design. What is 'truth' when such divergences are possible?[3] This is why the care and refinements of some attempts to aggregate all available physical output data for the USSR seem to me to lead to such uncertain results, which would remain uncertain even if there were none of the sizeable statistical gaps in the output series.

The official series suffers from the following defects:

(a) Until 1950, the weights used were those of 1926-27. Apart from giving 'preindustrialization' weights to the fastest growing sectors of industry, the introduction of new products gave an opportunity (for directors) to manœuvre so as to adopt for them high '1926-27' prices. Despite occasional efforts to check this practice, the big rise in costs in the 'thirties meant that the prices at which new products were introduced into the index were higher than they would have cost in 1926-27. There was then a tendency to concentrate on

[1] See *Comparisons of the United States and Soviet Economies* (Washington, 1959), p. 236, and V. Starovski, *Vop. Ekon.*, No. 4/1960, p. 105.
[2] See bibliography for references.
[3] *A Dollar index of Soviet machinery output* (Rand Corporation, Santa Monica, 1951).

the production of items bearing high '1926-27' prices, even at the cost of underfulfilling plans for the less highly valued items, because plan fulfilment was measured in 1926-27 prices. All this led to a creeping inflation of the index, made easier by the fact that it was genuinely difficult to determine what is a new product and what it would have cost to produce in 1926-27.[1]

(b) It is a 'gross' index, in the sense described in chapter 10. Therefore, it is affected by vertical disintegration.

(c) While since 1950 the index is no longer based on 1926-27 prices (it was calculated first in 1952 and then in 1955 prices), the growth rates prior to 1950 were simply chained on to the new index, and were not recalculated; or, if they were, the results have not been published. Much remains unclear about how the index is compiled. For instance, suppose that machinery output is expressed in 1955 prices, the problem of valuing new models remains, and, since in all countries such valuations are somewhat artificial, this makes possible the systematic selection of the highest of a range of possible figures, which can lead to distortion. It is only right to add that all analysts agree that the post 1950 indices are markedly less unreliable than those for earlier years. However, whatever the price base and whatever the regulations, the directors and local officials tend so to choose between possible alternatives as to be able to report a large increase in output. Because of the unavoidable imprecision of the regulations and of the definitions, the index can be affected by such choices in ways which are unlikely to arise in the West (where there is also a degree of imprecision and of arbitrary comparison), because increases in production as such are not vital 'success indicators' in a western firm.

With so much room for more or less legitimate manœuvre, Soviet statisticians can select the base and the weights which help them to show very large increases, and omit to publish calculations which reflect less credit on the system. For instance, base-year weights give a larger increase in output than end-year weights, so, in discussing industrial production indices, one Soviet statistician went so far as to proclaim that end-year weights were contrary to science, a remarkable doctrine indeed.[2] Yet, when Soviet statisticians calculate a cost of living index, they are careful to use end year weights,[3] which minimize the increase in prices and so represent real wages in a more favourable light.

National income

The official index is at all times to be treated with a degree of sus-

---

[1] See A. Nove, '1926/7 and all that', *Soviet Studies*, October, 1957, pp. 117-30. Soviet journals have denied these exaggerations, but contemporary evidence, cited in the above-named article, is against them.

[2] D. Savinski, *Vest. Stat.*, No. 10/1958, p. 39.

[3] A. Gozulov, *Ekonomicheskaya statistika* (Moscow, 1953), p. 359.

picion. The official claim to a seventeen-fold increase in the period 1913-55, for instance, is utterly incredible. Thus it seems very widely agreed, by Soviet economists among others,[1] that the national income of the Russian empire in 1913 was approximately a fifth of that of the United States. If the official claim were even remotely correct, the Soviet national income would now be well ahead of that of the United States, which, even allowing for the familiar vagaries of index numbers, just is not acceptable. Then it is decidedly odd that the national income can increase by seventeen-fold when one of its principal components, agriculture, showed a rise (in gross output) of only 70 per cent. The computational methods are not properly explained. There seems to have been a substantial overstatement of the growth of the net product of trade and construction, at least during the period of '1926-27' prices.[2] But even in more recent years strange things happen to national income data. Thus the increase in 1958 was originally reported as 9 per cent (over the previous year), but then was revised to 11 per cent with not a word of explanation.[3] One can but show reserve in using officials claims, and seek explanations where possible to clear up doubtful points.

Some other items

Housing data (in square metres) may be given in *living* space (excluding kitchens, corridors, etc,) or in *total* space (*obshchaya ploshchyad'*). The former is roughly two-thirds of the latter, and the unwary are sometimes confused between them.

Real wage and other such figures are sometimes given by reference to the year 1940, or to some early post-war year. It should be noted that these were not good years for the consumer, and that a fairer picture of progress achieved requires a calculation based on some better year, say 1937 or 1928. This is never done by the official statisticians. It is important to distinguish data on real wages, which, allowing for the chosen base year, check well against other figures, from vague and barely credible claims about 'real income per head'; these include estimates of the value of social services and such indirect 'income' as the length of vacations with pay, and the methods used are never explained.

Conclusion

Despite some justifiable scepticism about certain Soviet data, it should be clearly stated that the published physical output series and many other figures must be taken seriously, that they generally represent an expression (though sometimes an ambiguous or dis-

---

[1] Y. Kronrod in *Sovetskaya sotsialisticheskaya ekonomika, 1917-57* (Moscow, 1957), p. 168.
[2] See A. Nove, '1926/7 and all that', already cited.
[3] See *Pravda*, January 16, 1959, and *N.Kh. 1959*, p. 308.

torted expression) of reality. Much greater doubt attaches to some of the index number series, which are in some instances just not credible. Yet these comments are by no means intended to deny that the Soviet system has achieved rapid growth. Undoubtedly it has, though not at the tremendous pace which the official indices allege. Its achievements have, indeed, been such that it is surely about time that some of the wilder claims were quietly buried.

A SHORT BIBLIOGRAPHY

NOTE.—Copious references to Soviet books and periodicals have been made in the text and will not be repeated here, save for those cases where titles of books and periodicals have been given in footnotes in abbreviated form.

Space is not available for a full bibliography and the very large number of relevant books and articles in Western languages. The list given below represents a selection of books, together with a few references to particularly useful articles. Many other articles are referred to in footnotes in the text.

(A) *Books and periodicals abbreviated in text:*

Direktivy KPSS: Direktivy KPSS i sovetskovo pravitel'stva po khozyaistvennym voprosam, 4 vols., Moscow, 1958.

Zakon Stoimosti (Tsagolov): *Zakon stoimosti i evo rol' v narodnom khozyaistve SSSR* (ed. Tsagolov), Moscow, 1959.

Zakon Stoimosti (Kronrod): *Zakon stoimosti i evo ispol'zovanie v narodnom khozyaistve SSSR* (ed. Kronrod), Moscow, 1959.

N.Kh. 1956: Narodnoe khozyaistvo SSSR v 1956 godu (statistical compendium), Moscow, 1957.

N.Kh. 1958: Narodnoe khozyaistvo SSSR v 1958 godu (statistical compendium), Moscow, 1959.

N.Kh. 1959: Narodnoe khozyaistvo SSSR v 1959 godu (statistical compendium), Moscow, 1960.

Sel. Khoz 1960: Sel'skoe khozyaistvo SSSR (statistical compendium), Moscow, 1960.

Plan Khoz.: Planovoe khozyaistvo. Organ of Gosplan.

Vop. Ekon.: Voprosy ekonomiki. Organ of Institute of Economics.

Vest Stat.: Vestnik statistiki. Organ of Central Statistical Office.

Sots. Sel. Khoz.: Sotsialisticheskoe sel'skoe khozyaistvo.

(B) *Some works in Western languages:*

ECONOMIC HISTORY OF THE PERIOD

A. Baykov: *The Development of the Soviet Economic System* (Cambridge and New York, 1947).

E. H. Carr: *A History of Soviet Russia: Socialism in One Country,* vol. 1 (London and New York, 1958).

M. Dobb: *Soviet Economic Development Since 1917* (London, 1948).

A. Erlich: *The Soviet Industrialization Debate* (Cambridge, Mass., 1960).

H. Schwartz: *Russia's Soviet Economy* (New York, 1950).

GENERAL DESCRIPTION OF THE ECONOMY

B. Balassa: *The Hungarian Experience in Economic Planning* (New Haven, 1959).

E. Boettcher: *Die Sowjetische Wirtschaftpolitik am Scheidewege* (Tübingen, 1959).

R. Campbell: *Soviet Economic Power* (Cambridge, Mass., and Boston, 1960).

PROBLEMS OF GROWTH AND ITS MEASUREMENT

A. Becker: 'Comparisons of US and USSR National Output: Some Rules of the Game,' *World Politics*, October, 1960.

A. Bergson (ed.): *Soviet Economic Growth* (Evanston, 1953).

G. Grossman: 'Soviet Growth—Routine, Inertia and Pressure,' *American Economic Review*, May, 1960.

D. Hodgman: *Soviet Industrial Production, 1928-51* (Cambridge, Mass., 1954).

N. Jasny: *The Soviet Economy during the Plan Era* (Stanford, 1951).

Joint economic committee of the US Congress: *Comparisons of the U.S. and Soviet Economies* (3 vols., Washington, 1959).

N. Kaplan and R. Moorsteen: 'An Index of Soviet Industrial Output,' *American Economic Review*, June, 1960.

A. Nove: *Soviet Economic Strategy* (N.P.A., Washington, 1959).

W. Nutter: 'Some Observations on Soviet Industrial Growth,' *American Economic Review*, May, 1957.

F. Seton: *Soviet Industrial Expansion,* Manchester Statistical Society paper, 1957.

F. Seton: 'Soviet Progress in Western Perspective,' *Soviet Studies*, October, 1960.

D. Shimkin and F. Leedy: 'Soviet Industrial Growth,' *Automobile Industries*, January 1, 1958.

THE STATE ENTERPRISE AND MANAGEMENT

J. Berliner: *Factory and Manager in the USSR* (Cambridge, Mass., 1957).

D. Granick: *Management of the Industrial Firm in the USSR* (New York, 1954).

D. Granick: *The Red Executive* (Garden City, New York, 1960).

J. Kornai: *Overcentralization in Economic Administration* (London and New York, 1959).

NATURAL RESOURCES

D. Shimkin: *Minerals, a Key to Soviet Power* (Cambridge, Mass., 1953).

AGRICULTURE AND COLLECTIVE FARMING

N. Jasny: *The Socialized Agriculture of the USSR* (Stanford, 1949).
O. Schiller: *Das Agrarsystem der Sowjetunion* (Tübingen, 1960).
H. Wronski: *Le Troudoden* (Paris, 1957).

THE COMMUNIST PARTY ORGANIZATION

M. Fainsod: *Smolensk under Soviet Rule* (Cambridge, Mass., 1958).
L. B. Schapiro: *The Communist Party of the Soviet Union* (New York and London, 1960).

NATIONAL INCOME

A. Bergson: *Soviet National Income and Product in 1937* (New York, 1953).
A. Bergson and H. Heymann: *Soviet National Income and Product, 1940-48* (New York, 1954).
J. Y. Calvez: *Revenu National en URSS* (Paris, 1956).
'An Estimate of the National Accounts of the Soviet Union,' *Economic Bulletin for Europe,* vol. 9, no. 1 (May, 1957).
M. C. Kaser: 'Estimating the Soviet National Income,' *Economic Journal,* March, 1957.
A. Nove: 'Soviet National Income Statistics,' *Soviet Studies,* January, 1955.

LABOUR AND WAGES

Emily C. Brown: 'The Local Union in Soviet Industry,' *Industrial and Labour Relations Review,* January, 1960.
Emily C. Brown: 'Labour Relations in Soviet Factories,' *Industrial and Labour Relations Review,* January, 1958.
Janet Chapman: 'Real Wages in the Soviet Union, 1928-52,' *Review of Economics and Statistics,* May, 1954.
W. Galenson: *Labour Productivity in Soviet and American Industry* (New York, 1955).
W. Hofmann: *Der Arbeitsverfassung der Sowjetunion* (Berlin, 1956).
S. Schwarz: *Labour in the Soviet Union* (New York and London, 1953).

BUDGET AND PUBLIC FINANCE

R. W. Davies: *The Development of the Soviet Budgetary System* (Cambridge, 1958).
F. D. Holzman: *Soviet Taxation* (Cambridge, Mass., 1955).

ECONOMIC THEORY AND MARXISM

H. Chambre: *Le Marxisme en Union Soviétique* (Paris, 1955).
T. J. Hoff: *Economic Calculation in the Socialist Society* (London, 1949).
O. Lange: *On the Economic Theory of Socialism* (The Hague, 1938).
Joan Robinson: *An Essay on Marxian Economics* (London, 1942).
J. Schumpeter: *Capitalism, Socialism and Democracy* (London, 1943).

VALUE, PRICE, ECONOMIC RATIONALITY

M. Dobb: 'Soviet Price Policy,' *Soviet Studies,* July, 1960.
D. Granick: 'An Organizational Model of Soviet Industrial Planning,' *Journal of Political Economy,* April, 1959.
G. Grossman: 'Industrial Prices in the USSR,' *American Economic Review,* May, 1959.
G. Grossman (ed.): *Value and Plan* (Berkeley, 1960).
N. Jasny: *The Soviet Price System* (Stanford, 1951).
A. Nove: 'The Politics of Economic Rationality,' *Social Research,* summer, 1958.
P. J. D. Wiles: 'Scarcity, Marxism and Gosplan,' *Oxford Economic Papers,* September, 1953.
A. Zauberman: 'Economic Thought in the Soviet Union,' *Review of Economic Studies,* vol. xvi, no. 39, 1948/49.
A. Zauberman: 'New Winds in Soviet Planning,' *Soviet Studies,* July, 1960.

INVESTMENT CRITERIA

H. Chambre (ed.): 'Le Developpement du Bassin du Kouznetsk,' *Cahiers de l' ISEA,* Paris, no. 100 (April, 1960).
H. Chambre: 'A propos des Critères du Choix des Investissements,' *Cahiers de l' ISEA,* Paris, no. 104 (August, 1960).
M. Dobb: 'The Problems of Choice between Alternative Investment Projects,' *Soviet Studies,* January, 1951.
G. Grossman: 'Scarce Capital and Soviet Doctrine,' *Quarterly Journal of Economics,*
F. Holzman: 'The Soviet Ural-Kuznetsk Combine,' *Quarterly Journal of Economics,* August, 1957.
N. Kaplan: 'Investment Alternatives in Soviet Economic Theory,' *Journal of Political Economy,* April, 1952.
A. Zauberman: 'A Note on the Soviet Capital Controversy,' *Quarterly Journal of Economics,* August, 1955.

PLANNING METHODS

H. Chambre: *L'Aménagement du Territoire en URSS* (Paris, The Hague, 1959).

M. C. Kaser: 'The Reorganization of Soviet Industry,' in *Value and Plan*, cited above.

H. Levine: 'The Centralized Planning of Supply . . .,' in *Comparisons of the U.S. and Soviet Economies*, cited above.

'Les Methodes Actuelles Soviétiques de Planification,' *Cahiers de l' ISEA*, Paris, no. 7 (August, 1959).

J. M. Montias: 'Planning with Material Balances in Soviet-type Economies,' *American Economic Review*, December, 1959.

TRANSPORT AND OTHER SECTOR STUDIES

G. Gardner Clark: *The Economics of Soviet Steel* (Cambridge, Mass., 1956).

A. Gerschenkron (with A. Erlich): *A Dollar Index of Soviet Machinery Output, 1927/8-37* (Santa Monica, 1951).

H. Hunter: *Soviet Transportation Policy* (Cambridge, Mass., 1957).

EDUCATION AND SOCIAL SERVICES.

A. G. Korol: *Soviet Education for Science and Technology* (New York, 1957).

N. de Witt: *Soviet Professional Manpower* (Washington, 1955).

Discussion articles, 'Towards a Communist Welfare State?' *Problems of Communism*, nos. 1 and 3, 1960.

STATISTICS

C. Clark: *A Critique of Russian Statistics* (London, 1939).

G. Grossman: *Soviet Statistics of Physical Output of Industrial Commodities* (Princeton, 1960).

N. Jasny: *The Soviet 1956 Statistical Handbook: a Commentary* (East Lansing, 1957).

N. Jasny: 'Some Thoughts on Soviet Statistics,' *International Affairs*, January, 1959.

Symposium on 'Reliability and Usability of Soviet Statistics,' *The American Statistician*, 1953.

'Accounting prices' 130
Accumulation fund 263–4
  policy 295
Administration, expenditure on 50, 52, 106
'Advances' to peasants 123
Agricultural tax 57, 102, 108
Agriculture, labour force 297, 300
  machinery, supply of 90, 174
  planning 47, 67, 87–90, 182–9, 295, 301
  prices, see Prices, agricultural
  procurements, see Procurements
  production, definition and valuation of 259, see also Gross Agricultural production
  statistics, reliability of 310
  ministry of 88–9, 182
  relative priority of 150
Allocation, certificates 37, 84
  of materials, see Material supplies
Allocations to national economy (budget) 104–5, 106, 108
Amortization 34, 108, 111, 214
'Anti-Party group' 68
Arbitrariness, in economic life 17
Arbitration 93–4
Artel' 60
Artisans, co-operative, see Co-operatives, producers'
  individual 60, 102, 305
Assortment of products, problems of 20, 155, 182
ASSR (Autonomous Socialist Soviet Republics) 25
Audit 92
Autarky, in international trade 193
  regional, see 'Regionalism'
Average cost principle 129

Bachelor tax 102
Balances, see Material balances
Banks, see Gosbank, Savings Banks, Investment Banks, Stroibank

Bilateralism 190–1
Biological yield 310
Bonuses, for directors 31, 160–1, 163
  in collective farms 122, 124
  staff 117
Bottlenecks 80, 81, 147, 148, 292
Bread, tax on 99, 137
Brigade, in a collective-farm 46
Budget, expenditures 104–8
  republican rights 79, 107
  revenues 53, 98–104 (see also under headings of various taxes)
  state 83, 86, 97–108
Building, see construction
Buildings tax 102
Bureaucracy 68, 91, 142
By-products, utilization of 69

'Calendar' planning 161
'Campaigns' in economy 146, 150, 289
Capital assets of enterprises 30, 36
Capital charges 209, 214, 273, 281
Capital fund, collective-farms 51, 110, 124
Capital repairs 111
Central Committee (of Party) 67, 81, 142, 187
Central Statistical Office 66, 75, 267
Centralized investments 108
Centralization of decision-making 16, 63, 64, 69, 72, 79, 95, 128, 142, 145, 147, 152, 198, 204, 295
Centrosoyuz 41
Chairman, of collective-farm 47, 95, 96, 123
Chemical industry 69, 75, 81, 150, 289
Chief Departments, see Glavki
Chief engineer 116
China 305
Circulating capital, see Working capital
Coal industry 132
Coercion, role of 145
Collective agreements 125

Collective farms, internal organization of 45–57, 87, 95, 182–9
  history of 45
  relations with MTS 20, 46, 54–5, 182
  revenues and expenditures 48–53, 124, 138, 183, 185
  statistics on 29, 47, 48, 50, 123
  statute 46–7
  taxes on 50–1, 98, 101 (see also Agricultural planning; Prices, agricultural; Trudodni; Chairmen, Labour, collective farms)
Collectivization of agriculture 29, 304
Combines, see Kombinaty
COMECON 191, 193, 301
'Command economy' 143
Commission sales, of farm produce 49, 58, 138, 188
Commodity, definition of 118, 269
Communist Party, economic role of 17, 31, 47, 65, 81, 94–6, 119, 125, 127, 140, 142, 181–2, 186, 296
  organization of 24–6
  policies of 22, 82, 94, 187
  relations with Government 94–6
Comparative advantage 190
Compensatory payments, from budget 100, 107, 141
Compulsory deliveries, of farm produce 49, 136–7
Conformity of productive forces and productive relations, law of 286
Construction, control over methods of 109, 113
  organizations 39, 65, 87
  ministries of 64, 65, 79
  State Committee of 65, 75, 87, 109
  valuation of 260
Consumer demand 91, 147, 164, 171, 181
Consumers' goods 65, 103, 134–6, 175, 179, 197, 300
Contingency reserve (in budget) 105
Contracts 37, 71
Contradictions, role of 286, 297, 303
'Control by the rouble' 112
Control, Committee (Ministry) of Soviet (State) 92
Co-operatives, consumers' 30, 41–2, 49, 58, 91, 138, 182, 188
Co-operatives, producers' 28, 43–5

Co-operatives, tax on 43, 98, 108
Cost—estimates in construction 86, 109, 133
  of production (agriculture) 182–5, (industry) 34, 117, 129, 140, 147, 176, 213
  reductions 32, 161–2, 169
Costs, 'real' 273, 274, 281
Council of Labour and Defence 62, 65
Council of Ministers, functions 24, 65, 72, 115
Council of People's Commissars, see Council of Ministers
Counterpart sales 138, 140
Countervailing forces, lack of 289
Courts, role of in labour disputes 126, 127
Credits 36, 37, 51, 110, 111–13, 168, 175
Credits, foreign 102
Cultural fund, in collective farms 50, 52
Customs duties 102
Czechoslovakia, planning system in 157, 166, 242–7

Decentralization, financial 79
Decentralization of planning, see under Planning, Sovnarkhozy and Communist Party
Decentralized investments 22
Defence expenditures 106–7, 149, 264
Demand, see Consumer demand
'Democratic centralism' 142
Department I and Department II 285
Depreciation, see Amortization
Differential rent, see Rent
Differentials, see Wage differentials and Trudodni
Director's fund, see Enterprise fund
Directors, functions and powers of 31, 38, 39, 96, 129, 163, 181
Direct taxes 101–2
Discipline, in collective farms 53, 58
Discipline, workers 118, 126
Disposals, see Material supplies, and Wholesale trade
Disputes, see Labour disputes
'Dual subordination' 93

Econometrics, use of 208, 215–16
Economic Council 65, 115
Economic laws, in USSR 15, 18, 265, 284
Economic rationality, see Rationality
Economic Science Council, see Gosekonomsovet
Education 106, 299
Efficiency of investment, coefficients of 212, 215
Enterprise fund 33, 165–6, 170
Enterprises, characteristics of, State 27–42, 142 (see also under Industrial, Agricultural, Construction, etc., enterprises)
Entertainment tax 102
Establishments commission 93
Exaggeration, in output reporting 311
Exchange rates 189
Export organizations 42
Exports, planning of 82
'Extended reproduction' 261

Factory schools 118
'Feedback' costs 275
Finance, Ministry of 86, 92, 111, 116
Finance, public, see Budget
Food prices, see Prices, retail
Forced labour 149, 294
Foreign trade 42, 76, 102, 105, 189–94, 300
Free market 29, 49, 58, 124, 134, 139, 188
'Functional' organization 61, 63, 64, 72
'Funded' materials, see Material supplies
FZU, see Factory schools

Glavki 62, 64, 83, 195
Gorkom 26, 181
Gosarbitrazh, see Arbitration
Gosbank 75, 91, 111–14, 168
Gosekonomkommissia 67, 78
Gosekonomsovet 75, 76, 77–8, 86, 129, 200, 205
Gosplan 37, 62, 65, 75–8, 79, 82, 84, 85, 86, 89, 90, 94, 113, 128, 135, 178
Grading, of peasants 122
  of workers 116
Grain, prices of 99, 137–8
Gross agricultural output 259

Gross industrial output, as plan 'indicator' 155, 158, 159
  statistics of 257, 308
Gross social product 260
Ground rent (as budgetary revenue) 102
Growth, emphasis on 16, 32, 179, 262, 278
  factors affecting 292, 299

Heavy industry 261
Hoarding, of materials 38
Housing 20, 34, 105, 147, 150
Hungary, planning system in 157

Ideology, role of 304
Illegal economic activities 28, 38, 60
Incentives, see Wage systems, Bonuses, Enterprise fund, Success indicators
Income tax 101–3
Indicators, see Success indicators
Indirect taxes, see Turnover tax
Indivisible fund, see Capital fund
Industrial production, definition of 257 (see also Gross industrial production)
  by collective-farms 48, 56
Industrialization, in USSR 16, 22, 53, 65, 145–7, 150, 216, 289
Inflation 114–15, 116, 131–2
Innovation 70, 162, 167–171
Input-output 81, 208 (see also Material balances)
Insolvency of enterprise 112, 130
Inspection, agencies of 12, 92–3
Insurance 50, 51, 102, see also Social insurance
Integration, vertical and horizontal 68
Interest 101, 110, 112, 215–16, see also Recoupment period
Inter-Kolkhoz enterprises 56, 182
Investment, Banks 113–14
  criteria 209–17
  financing of 34, 36, 71, 105, 108–111, 132, 168
  planning 22, 66, 79, 80, 82, 86, 108–111, 209–10, 213, 285
  unplanned 108–9
  collective farms 51, 110, 183

KGB, *see* Police
Khozraschyot in agriculture 53, 54, 182–5
in state enterprises 32, 132, 165–6
Kind, payments in (to peasants) 123
Kolkhozy, see Collective farms
Kombinaty 64
Kontraktatsia 49, 56
Krai 25

Labour and Wages, State Committee on 75, 116
'Labour-days', *see Trudodni*
Labour, direction of 118–19
discipline 119, 126
disputes, procedures for settling 126
market 118, 119–21, 147
on collective farms 52–3, 147–8, 183–4
people's commissariat of 115
productivity, how measured 161
productivity in agriculture 297
supply 147–8, 151
Laws, economic, *see* Economic laws (*and under each of the laws*)
'Law of equal cheating' 309
Light industry 132, 261
Linear programming 215, 216, 276
Livestock, ownership of 29
Loan service 106
Loans, mass-subscription 98, 101, 102, 126
Local authorities, economic role of 71–2, 177
Local industry 37, 71, 72
'Localism', *see* 'Regionalism'
Losses (of enterprises), *see* Subsidies, and Insolvency

Machine Tractor Stations (MTS), organization and finance 20, 46, 54–5, 98, 105, 140
status and pay of personnel 122
valuation of 'product' of 265
Managers, *see* Directors
Marginalism 276, 291
Market, *see* Free market
Market forces, in Soviet economy 15, 279
Material balances 66, 80, 150, 206–9, 280
Material supplies, problems of 37, 65, 76, 77, 78, 82, 90, 175, 182, 198–9, 200
organization of 37, 40, 66, 70, 78, 82–5, 90, 182, 198–206
Mechanization 148
Mestnichestvo, see 'Regionalism'
MGB, *see* Police
Multiple prices 133–4, 137, 176
MVD, *see* Police

Naryad, see Allocation certificate
National income 251, 312
Natural resources 302
New Economic Policy (NEP) 27, 136
New products 71, 128
New technique, *see* Technical progress
Nomenklatura 95–6
Non-commodity operations, tax on 98, 101
Norms, labour 117, 122
material utilization 37

'Objectively determined valuations' 279
Obkom 26, 47, 94–5, 181
Oblast, economic role of 25, 69, 71, 91, 93, 187, 240
Obsolescence 151–2
Orgnabor 119
ORS 42
Overfulfilment of plans 162, 181
Over-quota purchases, of farm products 49, 137

Party, *see* Communist Party
Peasant private plot, *see* Private sector
Pensions 106
Piecework 115–16, 126
Plan fulfilment, inducements for, *see* Success indicators
Plan of enterprise 34, 156–7, 169, 201
'Planned (proportionate) development of the economy', law of 284, 292
Planning, organisation of (at centre) 61–78, 142, 200, 201, (in republics) 78–9
system, nature of 145–50 (*see also* planning agencies by name, Material balances, Agricultural planning, Investment planning)
Poland, planning system in 157, 246–7, 280

Police 92, 107
Politbureau 26
Political structure 24–6
Politics, role of in economic decisions 17–18, 66, 68, 145–7, 157
Praesidium, of Communist Party 26 of Supreme Soviet 24
Price mechanism, role of 147, 178, 185, 277
Prices, agricultural 48, 56, 124, 128, 136–41, 185, 187
how determined 128–42
in foreign trade 192
of 1926/7 133, 311
of production, see Production price
of producers' goods 109, 128, 134, 220–2
principles underlying 129, 131, 132, 165, 173, 178, 273
retail 79, 100, 103, 134–6, 140, 147, 178
State Committee on 129, 135
Priorities 81, 146, 150, 179, 213, 261, 285, 291
Private Sector, collective-farm peasants 27, 29, 53, 57–60, 182, 188
craftsmen 27, 60, 102
plots of workers and employees 59–60
Procurements, of farm products by state 48, 88, 188
Producers' goods 103–4
Production price (*Produktionspreis*), in Marx 274
Productivity, see Labour, productivity
Profits, deduction from, to budget 31, 98, 100, 101
of state enterprises, role of 32, 34, 35, 129, 132, 165, 214
Progressive piecework 117
Project-making 75, 86
Prokuror 92
Purges, effects of 149
'Pusher', *see Tolkach*

Queues 134
Quotas, of deliveries, see Compulsory deliveries

Raikom 26, 47, 94–5, 182
Railways 42, 80
Raion 25, 94, 182

Rationality 148–50, 216, 289, 292
Rationing 147, 283
Recoupment period (in investment) 211–14
Regional Economic Councils, *see Sovnarkhozy*
Regionalism' 82, 165, 196, 200
Regionalization 96, 199–201
Rent (land) 46, 185
Repair Technical Station (RTS) 55]
Republican ministries 25
Republics, powers of 25, 64, 69, 71, 72, 78, 79, 90, 94–6, 107, 135, 200
Research 106, 167
Reserves 82, 264
Retail prices, see Prices
Retail trade 29, 40–2, 90–2, 134–6, 174–81, 187–9
Risk-taking 169
'Rural addition' (to prices) 136
Russian Republic (RSFSR) 78, 199

Salaries, see Wages
Savings Bank 101
Scarcity, role of 132, 134, 139, 210, 215, 276, 282
Science, expenditures on 106
Secret police, see Police
Self-criticism 20
Sellers' market, consequences of 176, 178
Service enterprises 42
Services, exclusion from national income 252
Shoe repairs 60
Shturmovshchina, see 'Storming'
Simulation, of plan fulfilment 181, 309, 310
Smety, see Cost-estimates, construction
Snabsbyt, see Material supplies
Social-cultural expenditures 106
Social insurance 50, 102, 106, 125
Social services 128
'Socialist competition' 127, 181
Socially-necessary labour 280
Sovkhoz, see State farms
Sovnarkhozy 63, 67, 72, 74, 75, 77, 78, 81, 82, 84, 91, 95, 108, 113, 129, 130, 142, 156, 158, 165, 170, 175, 196–200

Sown area, by category of producer 29
Soyuzglavtorg 90
Spare parts 158
Specialisation 68, 199
Standard of living 295
State Bank, *see* Gosbank
State Economic Commission, *see* Gosekonomkommissia
State enterprises, *see* Enterprises, state
State farms 40, 140–1, 183, 227
State Planning Commission (Committee), *see* Gosplan
State reserves, *see* Reserves
Statistics, reliability and shortcomings of 29, 307–14
sources of 19
STO, see Council of Labour and Defence
Stockpiling 100, 105
Stocks, excessive holdings of 175
'Storming' 160–1
Strategy (of development) 290
Strikes 21
Stroibank 114
Subsidies 105, 130, 140, 141, 183, 277
Success indicators 31, 155–67, 167–9, 170, 173, 178, 181, 292
Supply and demand, role of 132, 135, 176
Supreme Council of the National Economy, *see VSNKh*
Supreme Soviet 24, 83
Surplus product 273
Surplus value (*see* surplus product)

Tariff-qualification manual 116
Taxes, *see* Agricultural tax, Collective-farm tax, Income tax, Turnover tax, etc.
Technical progress 70, 167, 169, 279, 299, *see also* Innovation
Timber-cutting levy 102
Time-preference 210, 215
Tolkach 38, 85, 201, 202
Torg, see Retail trade
Totalitarianism 18
Tractormen, pay of 122
Trade, *see* Foreign trade, Retail trade, Wholesale trade

Trade, Ministry of 90, 175
Trade Unions 115, 125–7
Transport enterprises 42
problems 68, 188
Trudodni 50, 52–3, 121–5, 183–6
Trusts 63
Turnover tax 98–100, 103–4, 132, 133, 134, 138, 140, 176

Unbalanced growth 291
Underdeveloped countries 288, 303
Unemployment 148
Unfinished production 159
Union-republican Ministries 25, 64, 72
United States, comparisons with 297
Use-value 164, 173, 214
Utility 276

Valued-added, as a plan indicator 159
Value, theory of, law of 215, 267
Vesenkha, see VSNKh
Vodka, tax on 100, 104, 134
'Voluntarism' in economic policy 268, 308
VSNKh 62, 63, 71, 78

Wages, anomalies 116
differentials 115, 120–1
systems 116–18
fund 117–18, 120
how determined 115–19, 120–1, 125
policy 115, 120
statistics of 19, 118, 119–21, 307
War economy 22, 146–7, 149, 161, 290
Wholesale prices 128–34, 274
Wholesale trade 90, 91, 133
Workdays, *see Trudodni*
Workers and employees, numbers of 120
Working capital 36, 37, 105, 112, 215

Yugoslav model, 247–9

Zayavka, see Material supplies
Zoning, of prices 136
of wages 115

INDEX OF NAMES

Aboltin, V. 160
Abramov, D. 48
Allakhverdyan, D. 100, 109
Antonov, N. 158
Antonov, O. 163, 169, 173
Atlas, M. 112
Atlas, Z. 214, 221
Azarkh, S. 99

Bachurin, A. 132, 166, 218, 274
Balassa, B. 193
Balogh, T. 300
Baranov, I. 198
Bauer, P. 304
Benediktov, I. 183
Berliner, J. 164
Berri, L. 207, 209
Bocharov, I. 94
Boettcher, E. 151
Bogomolov, O. 193
Bor, M. 100
Brus, W. 246
Bubnovski, N. 94
Bukharin, N. 265, 266
Bulganin, N. 68, 232, 233
Bunich, P. 230

Chambre, H. 209
Chapman, J. 121
Cherkovets, V. 272
Chukhanov, Z. 198
Cole, G. D. H. 276

Denisov, A. 94
Deutscher, I. 301
Devons, E. 161
Dmitriev, V. 282
Dobb, M. 209, 220
Donnelly, D. 43, 194
Dorosh, E. 187
Dvornikov, I. 126
Dyachenko, V. 270

Efimov, A. 70, 78, 207, 209, 213
Eidel'man, M. 208

Engels, F. 265, 271
Erlich, A. 46, 305
Evtikhiev, I. 91

Fainsod, M. 95
Figurnov, S. 118, 120
Fomin, A. 79, 85
Frolov, E. 201

Galenson, W. 298
Gal'perin, N. 199
Ganshtak, V. 169
Gatovski, L. 237, 272, 278, 296
Gavrilov, A. 188
Gerasimov, I. 199
Gerschenkron, A. 311
Gozulov, A. 312
Granick, D. 148, 164
Grdjic, G. 255
Groman, V. 66
Gromova, G. 41
Grossman, G. 209, 218, 292, 308, 309

Higgins, B. 290, 291, 306
Hirschmann, A. 290, 291, 304
Hunter, H. 149, 209

Ilyin, S. 54, 203

Jackson, E. 252
Jasny, N. 29, 45, 50, 121, 131, 267, 294, 310

Kaganovich, L. 68
Kalecki, M. 246
Kalinin, I. 203
Kantorovich, L. 209, 215, 223, 224, 228, 240, 241, 275, 276, 278, 280, 282, 284, 296
Kaplan, N. 209
Kapustin, E. 232
Karagedov, R. 166
Karnaukhova, E. 122, 185
Katz, A. 262, 263, 278, 283, 285, 296
Kaufman, A. 266, 286

Khachaturov, T. 213
Khavin, A. 149, 235
Khessin, N. 272
Khrushchev, N. 47, 56, 59, 67, 89, 183, 187, 188, 210, 240, 296, 297, 298, 303, 310
Kirillov, I. 112
Kirzhner, D. 118
Kisman, N. 102
Koldomasov, Y. 84
Kolganov, M. 255, 274
Kolmogorov, A. 215, 279
Kolychev, L. 54
Kondrashev, D. 159, 221, 274
Kondratieff, N. (Kondratiev) 66
Kontorovich, V. 157, 158, 159
Kornai, J. 157, 163, 164
Korshunov, I. 186
Kostousov, A. 75, 171
Kosygin, A. 78
Kotov, F. 200
Kozodoev, I. 272
Krasovski, V. 213
Kronrod, Y. 213, 215, 222, 230, 272, 278, 286, 313
Kudrov, V. 255
Kulikov, A. 228
Kulyov, I. 175, 201, 210
Kuparadze, G. 123
Kurotchenko, V. 197, 199
Kurowski, S. 246
Kuzmin, I. 94
Kuznets, S. 252
Kvasha, Y. 230

Laird, R. D. 148
Lange, O. 22, 145, 151, 246, 290
Lapidus, I. 267
Laptev, I. 185
Laptev, V. 77, 79
Lebedev, N. 169
Lenin, V. 262, 271
Leontief, W. 81, 159, 260
Levine, H. 83
Lewis, W. A. 148
Liberman, E. 237
Liberman, F. 198, 203
Lipinski, E. 246
Lisichkin, G. 184, 227
Litvinov, N. 185, 186
Lokshin, R. 175

Lomatovski, E. 41
Lopovok, G. 93
Lyashko, M. 71
Lyubimov, N. 158

Maevski, I. 79, 85
Maisenberg, L. 222, 223
Malenkov, G. 68, 134, 262
Malyshev, I. 181, 212, 214, 221, 271, 272, 274
Manevich, E. 166, 233
Markov, V. 162, 168, 170
Marshall, A. 278
Maryakhin, G. 102
Marx, K. 222, 265, 271, 272, 275, 276, 286
Maslova, N. 235
Matskevich, V. 182
Mendershausen, H. 194
Mikhailov, M. 162
Minc, B. 263
Moiseyev, M. 137
Molotov, V. 68
Montias, J. M. 246, 280
Mstislavski, P. 274
Myrdal, G. 277, 290, 293, 304

Naimanov, B. 82, 201
Nazarov, R. 188
Nedelin, S. 40, 225, 226
Nemchinov, V. 132, 199, 209, 214, 215, 223, 224, 228, 237, 241, 275, 276, 280, 281, 282, 283, 284, 296
Nesmi, M. 184
Nicholson, J. 252
Nikolaeva, G. 156
Nikol'ski, V. 117
Nikitinski, V. 126
Novikov, I. 78, 139
Novozhilov, V. 132, 209, 215, 223, 228, 240, 241, 275, 276, 278, 280, 281, 282, 283, 284, 296
Nutter, W. 311

Okhapkin, K. 123
Olivera, J. 299
Ordzhonikidze, S. 236
Orudzhev, S. 204
Osad'ko, M. 124
Ostrovityanov, K. 55, 267, 272
Ovechkin, V. 187

Pajestka, J. 280
Panfyorov, F. 95, 235
Pashkov, A. 228, 262, 263, 272, 273
Perikov, E. 43, 44
Perroux, F. 290, 291
Pervukhin, M. 67, 68
Petrov, A. 158
Petukhov, K. 76, 170
Plekhanov, G. 265
Plotnikov, K. 36, 110, 112, 120
Podgorny, N. 85, 198
Polanyi, M. 180
Polyanski, D. 187
Popov, A. 177
Popov, V. 120
Porwit, K. 280
Preobrazhenski, E. 266
Prokopowicz, S. 121
Prozorov, P. 187, 240

Razumov, N. 85, 237
Robinson, J. 283
Rovinski, N. 107
Rozhin, V. 125
Rumyantsev, A. 35, 116, 129, 161, 261

Saburov, M. 67
Sakov, M. 278
Sanina, A. 55
Sapel'nikov, Y. 90, 178
Saveliev, V. 203
Savinski, D. 312
Semyonov, V. 140
Serebryanyi, G. 141
Seton, F. 311
Shevchenko, A. 187
Shmarev, A. 201
Shniper, R. 175
Shnyrlin, Y. 264
Shuster, A. 214
Sidorov, M. 156
Skvortsov, L. 79
Slavnyi, I. 102
Smith, Adam 251
Sobol, V. 252
Somov, V. 198
Spiridonov, I. 171, 204

Stalin, J. 17, 19, 55, 64, 79, 82, 211, 218, 242, 268, 269, 270, 271, 273, 275, 281, 284, 285, 286, 293, 295, 296, 298, 304, 305
Starovski, V. 311
Streeten, P. 292
Strumilin, S. 18, 151, 213, 221, 227, 252, 257, 260, 264, 274, 282
Studenikin, S. 75, 89
Suchkov, A. 137

Terentiev, M. 138
Teryaeva, A. 124
Tolkachov, A. 229
Tsagolov, N. 215, 228, 272, 273, 274
Turetski, Sh. 99, 100, 129, 130, 134, 136, 137, 138, 220, 222, 223, 283

Ulbricht, W. 247
Uryupin, F. 100

Vaag, L. 213, 214, 228, 229, 274
Vainshenker, D. 169
Venzher, V. 55
Vikhlyaev, A. 259
Vladzievski, A. 230
Vlasov, V. 75, 89, 92
Volin, A. 129
Voznesenski, N. 66, 68, 264, 268

Ward, B. 285
Wiles, P. 277, 278, 303
Wronski, H. 122

Yakobson, M. 230
Yaroshenko, L. 269
Yezhov, A. 66
Yoffe, Y. 297

Zaslavskaya, T. 124
Zasyad'ko, A. 77, 78, 213
Zauberman, A. 209, 246, 264, 276, 282
Zaurov, M. 159
Zolotov, B. 202
Zverev, A. 33, 35, 87, 105, 107, 110, 132
Zvorykin, A. 118
Zykov, M. 178